Bartolomeo Scala, 1430-1497, Chancellor of Florence

THE HUMANIST AS BUREAUCRAT

Engraving taken from a fresco on the ceiling of the Uffizi, Florence.

Bartolomeo Scala

❧ 1430-1497 ❧

Chancellor of Florence

The Humanist as Bureaucrat

Alison Brown

Princeton University Press
Princeton, New Jersey

Copyright © 1979 by Princeton University Press
Published by Princeton University Press, Princeton, New Jersey
In the United Kingdom: Princeton University Press, Guildford, Surrey
All Rights Reserved
Library of Congress Cataloging in Publication Data will be
found on the last printed page of this book
Publication of this book has been aided by a grant from
The Andrew W. Mellon Foundation
This book has been composed in Linotype Janson
Designed by Bruce Campbell
Clothbound editions of Princeton University Press books
are printed on acid-free paper, and binding materials are
chosen for strength and durability.
Printed in the United States of America by Princeton
University Press, Princeton, New Jersey

Contents

[v]

Preface

Bartolomeo Scala, chancellor of Florence from *1465* until his death in *1497*, was the son of a provincial tenant miller. From secretary to Pierfrancesco de' Medici, he rose steadily to the Gonfalonierate of Justice and permanent membership of the Council of Seventy in Florence. He survived the fall of the Medici and died in office after serving for an almost unrivaled period of thirty-two years.

His is the classic new man's story and he has suffered for it. Francesco Guicciardini soon after his death described him as a man of mediocre talent who owed his success entirely to the favor of Lorenzo de' Medici and achieved the Gonfalonierate of Justice "to the great anger and indignation of all men of good birth."[1] Angelo Poliziano ridiculed his literary achievement during his lifetime. Despite a eulogistic biography by D. M. Manni in 1768 and a few articles in the Miscellanea di Colle di Val d'Elsa, his press has on the whole been consistently unfavorable.[2]

Although his career was frankly opportunistic, it does him less than justice to overlook his importance as a reformer and apologist of the modern centralized state. The Medici certainly promoted his rapid social advance and provide a major theme of his life. Like Savonarola's party later, however, the Mediceans attracted enthusiastic reformers and modernizers as well as opportunists, and Scala was one of them; a careerist who was also a severe and rigidly consistent moralist and reformer; an ardent Medicean who yet survived the fall of their regime; a lawyer as well as a politician, whose fastidious legalism and pragmatism

[1] *Storie fiorentine*, p. 79: "con grandissimo scoppio e sdegno di tutti gli uomini da bene."

[2] Manni's biography, the articles of del Lungo, Dini, Gentile and Marzini, and the sketch of G. B. Benvenuti are listed in the bibliography below. There are also brief bibliographies of Scala in Kristeller, *Supplementum*, 1:128, and Rochon, *La Jeunesse*, pp. 255-256. He is dismissed by Garin, "I cancellieri umanisti della repubblica fiorentina," pp. 26-27, and assessed more favorably by Kristeller, "An Unknown Correspondence," pp. 335-337, where he is described as "still a neglected figure." On Francesco Guicciardini and Poliziano, cf. ch. 8 below.

combined to provide the first justification of Medicean paternalism in the secular state.

I have attempted as far as possible to reconstruct Scala's life as it developed (treating separately, however, his work as chancellor, his social life and his writings). Eminences grises are difficult to document, but the amount of first-hand material that survives is considerable, consisting of Scala's tax returns, letters, an early account book, a literary notebook, published and unpublished writings, notarial copies of his transactions, chancery documents for his period of office illustrating his reforms, copies of his official letters and orations, and reports of ambassadors with whom he dealt, not to mention published primary and secondary material including the recent invaluable study of the institutions and development of the Medicean regime.[3] More will inevitably be discovered, but it should not substantially alter this account of Scala's life as it emerges from existing material.

Of the many friends who have assisted in the birth of this book I feel gratitude overwhelmingly to two: Sir Ernst Gombrich, who could properly be called its father, and Professor Paul Oscar Kristeller, its midwife. It was Ernst Gombrich who originally fired and sustained my interest in the Renaissance by his teaching at the Warburg Institute and to whom, therefore, I feel that particular sense of gratitude owed to an inspiring and formative teacher; more than this, however, it was he who also introduced me long ago to Bartolomeo Scala as a subject for research. I owe its successful conclusion to the unstinting support of Paul Kristeller, whose scrupulous reading and constructive criticism of an earlier and longer draft have also contributed greatly to the present book and saved it from many more errors than it would otherwise contain.

Throughout this long period of gestation I have received help in many different forms from innumerable friends and colleagues whose generosity in giving and sharing information I have attempted always to acknowledge in footnotes. Other help is difficult to acknowledge adequately. I owe a particular debt, I think, to Professor Nicolai Rubinstein, not only because his work on Medicean government has provided an essential basis for this study, but also because I have been privileged to work closely with him over a number of years, which has enriched my work

[3] Rubinstein, *The Government of Florence under the Medici (1434-1494).*

in many ways. Professor Carlo Dionisotti and Professor J. B. Trapp have both given me generous help and advice in preparing the manuscript and transcriptions. William and Dale Kent have contributed perceptive comments and suggestions, as well as the stimulus of their inimitable friendship. Italian archivists and librarians have been as kind and helpful as it is possible to be, and I would like to express my particular thanks to the staff of the State Archives in Florence, who have been unfailingly generous and tolerant at times of crisis, to Dr. Gino Corti in Florence, to the staff of the National Library, the Laurentian and Riccardian Libraries in Florence, the State Archives in Milan, Lucca and Siena, The Biblioteca Estense in Modena, the Vatican Library and Archives, and the British Library in London. I am indebted to the British Academy and the Italian Government for grants toward the cost of travel in Italy.

My debt to my family is immense. Julian Brown has helped me on an embarrassingly wide range of fronts, both academic and domestic, and it is largely thanks to him and with his help that I have been able to attempt translations of Scala's more abstruse Latin writings, particularly his Apologues. *Although I have been able to spend all too brief periods of time in Italy, I am grateful to him and to my mother for enabling me to work there at all, even more to Charlotte and Rachel for their tolerance and for their help in valiantly pursuing Scala's traces in southern Tuscany on broiling afternoons as children, and for their interest and companionship now. I owe to Mary and Felton Gibbons the hospitality of their house on several occasions and to Ruth Rubinstein the engraving of Scala reproduced as the frontispiece.*

The biography was originally intended to have an appendix of illustrative documents to include all Scala's letters and unpublished writings, and for this reason I have quoted more extensively from his letters than I perhaps should otherwise have done. In order to avoid overburdening the footnotes with material that will now be published separately, I have not given the text of these long extracts unless essential.

December 1977   ALISON BROWN

Abbreviations

AS:	Archivio di Stato
ASF:	Archivio di Stato, Florence
	Acq. Doni: Acquisti e Doni
	Capt. P. G.: Capitani della Parte Guelfa
	Cento Delib.: Consiglio del Cento, Deliberazioni
	Comp. relig. soppr.: Compagnie religiose soppresse
	Cons. Prat.: Consulte e pratiche
	Conv. Soppr.: Conventi soppressi
	Dieci Delib.: Dieci di Balìa, Deliberazioni
	Leg. Comm.: Elezioni e lettere ad oratori dei Signori
	MAP: Mediceo avanti il Principato
	Minut.: Minutari delle lettere missive (Prima Cancelleria)
	Misc. Repubb.: Miscellanea repubblicana
	Missive: lettere missive originali (Prima Cancelleria)
	Otto Delib.: Otto di Pratica, Deliberazioni
	Provv.: Provvisioni
	Risp. verb. orat.: Risposte verbali degli oratori dei Signori
	SS. Delib.: Signori, Collegi, Deliberazioni ordinaria autorità
	SS. Delib. sp. aut.: Signori, Collegi, Deliberazioni speciale autorità
	SS. Dieci, Otto: Signori, Dieci, Otto, Legazioni e Commissarie, Missive, Responsive
	Strozz.: Carte Strozziane
ASI:	*Archivio storico italiano*
ASLomb:	*Archivio storico lombardo*
ASMi SPE:	Archivio di Stato, Milan, Sforzesco Potenze Estere
ASV:	Archivio secreto vaticano, Rome
	Intr. Exit.: Introitus et exitus
	Reg. Vat.: Registri Vaticani
ATL:	Anziani del Tempo della Libertà (Lucca, AS)
BNF:	Biblioteca Nazionale, Florence
GSLI:	*Giornale storico della letteratura italiana*

Laur.:   Biblioteca Laurenziana, Florence
Marucell.:   Biblioteca Marucelliana, Florence
Misc. Stor.
  Vald.:   *Miscellanea storica della Valdelsa*
Modena MS: Modena Bibl. Estense, MS Campori 235 ४ P. 2.5.
OLD: *Oxford Latin Dictionary*
P.G.:   *Patrologie grecque*
P.L.:   *Patrologie latine*
Riccard.:   Biblioteca Riccardiana, Florence
RIS: *Rerum italicarum scriptores*
Vat. Lat.:   Biblioteca Vaticana, Rome, Fondo latino

The names of the following frequently referred-to Florentine institutions have not been italicized:

Accoppiatori: electoral officers, often with important discretionary powers

Balìa: special council with full powers for limited periods

Catasto: tax, first introduced in 1427

Cento: Council of One Hundred

Decima: tax, first introduced in 1495-1498

Dieci di Balìa: magistracy of Ten, elected with full powers in times of war

Mercanzia: merchants' tribunal

Monte: public-funded debt

Notary of the Riformagioni: notary responsible for drawing up and presenting legislation

Notary of the Tratte: notary in charge of the registers of names of those drawn for office

Otto di Guardia: police magistracy of the Eight of Ward

Otto di Pratica: magistracy of Eight on foreign policy

Podestà: chief judicial officer, chosen from outside the Florentine state

Signoria: principal government magistracy with important legislative as well as administrative functions, consisting of eight priors and their leader, the Gonfalonier of Justice, who represented the state for his period of office

PART ONE

Career

CHAPTER I

Childhood and Education

I came to the republic naked, disadvantaged, of the lowest parentage, full of confidence but absolutely penniless, without reputation, patrons or kinsmen. *Scala to Angelo Poliziano, 1494*[1]

Like other self-made men Bartolomeo Scala could afford to boast of early hardship in his comfortable old age, but the evidence suggests he did not exaggerate. He was born just outside the small town of Colle di Val d'Elsa in south-western Tuscany on 17 May 1430,[2] the son of a tenant miller. His father, called simply Giovanni di Francesco, held the mill at Onci according to the *mezzadria* system (receiving a half share of its profits in return for his labor), and we know from his tax return of 1429 that his declared possessions were minimal, his credits more than outweighed by his debts.[3]

Bartolomeo's place of birth contributed as little to his future success as his parentage. Colle was provincial.[4] It had been an independent commune from the twelfth century un-

[1] Poliziano, *Opera*, pp. 393-394: "Veni nudus omnium rerum bonarum, egenus ad rempublicam, vilissimis ortus parentibus, multa cum fide, nullis omnino divitiis, aut titulis, nullis clientelis, nullis cognationibus."

[2] ASF *Tratte* 61 (p. 132, "Veduti et seduti Gonfalonieri di Giustizia," 1 April 1480, the reference to which I owe to Prof. Nicolai Rubinstein). This confirms the date given by Manni (*Vita*, p. 5), which appeared to have been refuted by the tax return of Bartolomeo's father dated 7 March 1429, where "Bartolomeo" is described as an 8-month-old baby (ed. Dini, "Bartolommeo Scala," pp. 60-62). However, this child evidently died before the birth of his brother, who in accordance with contemporary practice was given his name and subsequently the nickname "Vopiscus," not in this case as the younger twin, but as the younger brother, to survive, cf. Pliny, *Nat. Hist.*, 7.10.47, quoted by Zeno, *Dissertazioni Vossiane*, 2:254; Manni, *Vita*, p. 4 (the use of this nickname is confined mainly to the 1450s, in letters and poems to Scala by Donato Acciaiuoli, Francesco Filelfo, Cristoforo Landino, and in the titles of Scala's own *Life of Vitaliano Borromeo*, *On Whether a Wise Man Should Marry*, "Elegia" in praise of Pius II, and the eclogue "Eritus").

[3] Ed. Dini, "Bartolommeo Scala."

[4] On Colle, Biadi, *Storia*; Repetti, *Dizionario*, 1:749-759; Targioni Tozzetti, *Relazioni*, 7:401-459.

til the middle of the fourteenth century, when it accepted Florentine overlordship in return for military protection.[5] Like an early Roman *municipium*, which owed allegiance to Rome without Roman citizenship, Colle received in return for its loyalty no citizenship rights in Florence: anyone wishing to emigrate to the metropolis had to pay taxes there for twenty years before being allowed to invest in the Florentine dowry bank and thirty years before exercising elective offices in the city.[6] Although the economic crisis of the mid-fourteenth century had in practice led to a less rigid interpretation of the statutes, theoretically they should have made Bartolomeo's achievement impossible.[7]

In one respect, though, he was fortunate. Like other Tuscan communes, Colle enjoyed an early tradition of learning which survived into the fifteenth century and must have helped to launch him on his successful career.[8] Its statutes had granted

[5] *Capitoli*, ed. A. Guasti, 1:253-257, cf. *Cronica di Giovanni Villani*, ed. F. Dragomanni, Florence, 1845, bk. 10, ch. 173, bk. 11, chs. 46, 81; *Cronica di Matteo Villani*, ed. Dragomanni, Florence, 1846, bk. 1, ch. 43. Colle belonged to the Florentine *distretto* and not the *contado* (*Statuta*, "Friburgi," 3:601; *Capitoli*, ed. Guasti, p. 257).

[6] "Submissio et acceptatio et capitula terre Collis," 24 August 1481, ASF SS. *Delib. sp. aut.* 35, fol. 113v (the thirty-year restriction was for offices "tam per viam extractionis quam electionis"). In addition, citizens of subject towns had to pay the *estimo* to Florence, Molho, *Florentine Public Finances*, pp. 23-45. On Roman citizenship and the early *civitas sine suffragio*, A. N. Sherwin White, *The Roman Citizenship*, Oxford, 1939, esp. pp. 37-45. The question of Florentine citizenship has not been fully discussed, but see J. Kirshner, "Paolo di Castro on *Cives ex Privilegio*," *Renaissance Essays in Honor of H. Baron*, ed. A. Molho and J. A. Tedeschi, Florence, 1971, pp. 229-264 (esp. the bibliography on p. 230, n. 3) and " 'Ars imitatur naturam': a Consilium of Baldus on Naturalization in Florence," *Viator* 5 (1974):289-331.

[7] M. Becker, "An Essay on the 'Novi Cives' and Florentine Politics, 1343-1382," *Medieval Studies* 24 (1962):35-82, esp. 40, 82. According to the 1415 *Statuta* ("Friburgi," 2:754-755), taxes had to be paid for only twenty years "in offitiis notariatus" while for other offices they had to be paid for thirty years (by members of the major guilds) and twenty-five years (minor).

[8] O. Bacci, "Maestri di grammatica in Valdelsa nel sec. XIV," *Misc. Stor. Vald.* 3 (1895):88-95; on Mino da Colle, one of the earliest teachers of grammar in Tuscany, G. Zaccagnini, *ibid.* 39 (1931):3-16; H. Wieruszowski, *Politics and Culture in Medieval Spain and Italy*, Rome, 1971, pp. 347-377.

special privileges to teachers and students and, although loss of sovereignty may have reduced its civic ambition "to be adorned with learned men,"[9] there is evidence throughout the fifteenth century of well-known grammarians still visiting the town.[10] Colle never possessed a school for higher studies, however, and for more than elementary education it was necessary to study "in Siena or . . . some other place removed from the said town of Colle where a studium is held."[11] Siena was some twelve miles from Colle, Florence twice as far away. For the ambitious, the attraction of Florence with its intellectual pre-eminence and expanding administration must have been over-riding, and it was there that Bartolomeo and subsequently two of his five brothers went to make their fortunes.[12]

Bartolomeo never returned to live in Colle but his ties with it remained strong. He held the ambiguous status among his compatriots of one more honored than loved for success achieved outside his place of birth, profiting from his status in Florence to win privileges in Colle[13] and at the same time

[9] Biadi, *Storia*, p. 31 (quoting rubric 31 in bk. 2 of the Statutes: "Cupientibus nobis hanc Rempublicam nostram doctis viris decorari"); cf. Targioni Tozzetti, *Relazioni*, 7:450.

[10] At the beginning, Maestro Onofrio di Angelo of San Gimignano (C. Mazzi, "Cartieri, tipografie e maestri di grammatica in Valdelsa," *Misc. Stor. Vald.* 4 (1896):186-187; Bandini, *Catalogus codicum latinorum*, 2, cols. 232-233, 565); in 1448, Battista of Volterra (M. Morici, "Maestri Valdelsani in Pistoia dal sec. XIV al XVI," *Misc. Stor. Vald.* 9 (1901):41); in 1457 and 1478 Luca of San Gimignano, Marsilio Ficino's teacher (della Torre, *Storia*, pp. 489-493); in the early 1470s Benedetto Colucci of Pistoia (*ibid.*, pp. 706-709; A. Chiti, "A proposito dell' insegnamento di B. C. a Colle," *Misc. Stor. Vald.* 9 (1901):198-200). On 1 July 1483 Lorenzo de' Medici commended ser Piero da Barga to the priors of Colle as "maestro di schuola," *Protocolli del carteggio*, ed. del Piazzo, p. 250. In the early 1470s a printing press was established in the town; Biadi, *Storia*, pp. 44-45; Repetti, *Dizionario*, 1:759; della Torre, *Storia*, p. 705.

[11] ASF *Notarile* G 109 (Gentile di Pela Pasci, 1466-1469), fol. 66r: the will of a citizen of Colle, bequeathing money for the further education of his son, "ad studendum ad civitatem Senarum vel ad alia loca remota a dicta terra Collis ubi studium teneatur."

[12] On Scala's brothers, see ch. 9 below.

[13] On 10 November 1466 Scala and his male heirs were granted immunity from taxes on their persons and property in the district of Colle up to the value of 1,000 gold florins, and, "in signum maioris gratitudinis et amoris"

exerting political influence there, to the chagrin of the na-
tives.[14] At other times he acted in Florence as spokesman for
Colle in matters concerning their mutual interest, and he must
have been influential in suggesting that the unusual privilege
of full Florentine citizenship be offered to his compatriots to
stiffen their resolve in the Pazzi war in 1479.[15] He bought
houses and land in the town after he was appointed chancellor
of Florence, and he was qualified for political office there.[16]
Never an emotional man, he confessed to the Florentine war
magistracy in October 1479 that his heart "shattered into a
thousand pieces" when he witnessed the assault of Colle, and
at the end of his life again paid tribute to its courage at that
time.[17] Whatever his feelings for the place of his birth, how-

they were awarded the arms and insignia of Colle: Siena, AS, MS *Comune
di Colle*, Delib. 162, fol. 170r-v; cf. 163, fols. 118v-119r (26 August 1471),
appointing the Podestà's judge to establish the extent of his tax exemption,
which was in dispute.

[14] See, for example, ser Gentile di Pela Pasci's letter [to Scala], ed. F. Dini,
Misc. Stor. Vald. 9 (1901):211-212: "quando voi vorreste notare gli uomini
che sono et parlano in favore degli adversari vostri, arete a notare i tre
quarti e più degli uomini di questa terra." Ser Gentile's letter lacks an addressee or date, but although it is almost certainly addressed to Scala, it does
not appear to refer to a high-handed attempt of Scala's to acquire the mill in
which he was born, as Dini suggests (pp. 209-210), but to a boundary dispute between Colle and Siena, which Scala admitted to the chancellor of
Siena, Agostino Dati, "me . . . ad nauseam fastidivit," Dati, *Opera*, fol. 137v.

[15] See ch. 4, nn. 47 and 48 below; and on the offer of citizenship, Biadi,
Storia, pp. 129-130; Targioni Tozzetti, *Relazioni*, 7:455-456; cf. ASF *Dieci
Missive* 10, fol. 101r-v.

[16] ASF *Conv. Soppr.* 95, 212 (Ricordi di Bernardo di Stoldo Rinieri), fol.
131 left (3 August 1462); *Notarile* G 109 (1466-1469), fols. 83v-84v (27 September 1467), 116v-118v (27 March 1468), 127r (30 May 1468); *Notarile*
G 109 (Gentile di Pela Pasci, 1470-1474), fols. 83v-84v (19 October 1471),
104v-105v (13 July 1472), 131r-132r (10 May 1473). On Scala's Monte
Vasone estate, see ch. 9 below. In 1474 Bartolomeo headed the list of citizens eligible for the Gonfalonierate of Justice in Colle, the only citizen in
his *terzerio* entitled to be represented in the first three electoral bags with
two tickets, ASF *Tratte* 15 (unfoliated): "Registrum reforme terre Collis
1474. Giugno." In the 1480s he was drawn several times as Gonfalonier of
Justice and rejected as "absens," Siena, AS, *Comune di Colle*, 165, fols. 53v,
199v; 166, fol. 217v.

[17] Scala to the Dieci di Balìa, 16 October 1479: ASF *Dieci Responsive* 25,
fol. 332: "andò a me l'animo in mille parti"; *Apologia contra vituperatores
civitatis Florentiae* (= *Defense*), Florence, 1496, fol. a5r.

ever, after he moved to Florence his first loyalties always lay with the city of his adoption, by which he was granted honors and full rights of citizenship.

His achievement in overcoming the disadvantages of his provincial birth and poverty was not unique. The appointment of Coluccio Salutati, a notary from Buggiano, as first chancellor in 1375 established the precedent for a series of such appointments in the following century: of Leonardo Bruni, Carlo Marsuppini and Benedetto Accolti from Arezzo, of Poggio Bracciolini from Terranuova nearby.[18] But in some respects Scala's achievement was greater than theirs, for he started with more disadvantages and achieved higher honors. We shall follow the steps of his slow but sure-footed ascent.

By the time Scala reached Florence, the golden period was over.[19] The papal court had left the city, and so had the Greek delegates to the Council of Florence.[20] Many of the first generation of scholars who had brought it fame by their teaching and by their discovery and translations of ancient manuscripts had died; others had left with the papal court.[21] The economic and political climate had changed, too, and for almost the whole decade from 1444 to 1454 public teaching was reduced and the university itself was intermittently closed.[22]

[18] Becker, "An Essay on the 'Novi Cives,'" p. 82. On Salutati's early career, R. Witt, "C. S., Chancellor and Citizen of Lucca, 1370-1372," *Traditio* 25 (1969):191-216. On the families of Bruni, Marsuppini, Accolti and Poggio Bracciolini, Martines, *Social World*, pp. 166-167, 127-129, 343-344, 123.

[19] In general, Voigt, *Die Wiederbelebung*; V. Rossi, *Il Quattrocento*, rev. edn Milan, 1956; Cammelli, *I dotti bizantini*; della Torre, *Storia*; Sabbadini, *Le scoperte*.

[20] della Torre, *Storia*, pp. 239-285; Cammelli, *I dotti bizantini*, 2:50-51; Holmes, *Florentine Enlightenment*, pp. 244-245, 260-262.

[21] Niccolò Niccoli died in 1437, Ambrogio Traversari in 1439, Leonardo Bruni in 1444; Poggio Bracciolini and George of Trebizond went to Rome with the papal court in 1443.

[22] Gherardi, *Statuti*, pp. 259-262, 489. Appointments in the Studio in 1442-1445 and lists of back payments made in 1451 are listed in ASF *Monte* 2364, fols. 100r-101v; 2190, fol. 30r-v; 2275, fol. 35r-v; 1121, fol. 25r-v; and 1652, fols. 462v-463r (the references to which I owe to the kindness of Prof. Anthony Molho). In addition to the back payments made in May-December 1451, payments were made on 29 February 1452 to some sixteen teachers, presumably the first third of their annual salary, ASF *Monte* 1652, fol. 463r.

It was during the latter part of this decade that Scala was a student in Florence. He recalls: "there was a great shortage of books and teachers . . . everyone tried to achieve what he could by his own exertions."[23] A fellow student of Scala's, Jacopo Ammannati, later a cardinal, also remembered the hardship of their student years together when they lived "close to each other" and "were both very badly off."[24] So again Scala's account of his early poverty is corroborated by other evidence. According to Ammannati, a self-made man like himself, they both achieved success and prosperity "by hard work and God's favor," studying the same subjects with "almost the same teachers."[25]

What were these studies and who were Scala's teachers? Ammannati was taught poetry and oratory by Leonardo Bruni and Carlo Marsuppini before leaving Florence by the beginning of 1449 as secretary to Cardinal Capranica.[26] So Scala,

---

The appointment of St. Antoninus as archbishop of Florence in January 1446 was another blow to the new learning, della Torre, *Storia*, pp. 252 ff; Masai, *Pléthon*, p. 342, and n. 1.

[23] In a letter to Poliziano, *Opera*, p. 147: "et librorum et praeceptorum . . . penuria permagna fuit, suo quisque Marte quid possent vires experiebatur."

[24] In a letter to Scala, *Epistolae et commentarii*, fol. 227r, 5 March 1472: "Vicini habitavimus . . . Paupertatem etiam gravem pertulimus." Cf. his account of his early friendship with Scala reported by Alessandro Braccesi in a letter to Scala of 10 November 1470: "diu hominem . . . novimus et amicus est nobis," ed. Kristeller, "An Unknown Correspondence," p. 352 (cf. 337).

[25] *Epistolae et commentarii*, fol. 227r: "Iisdem litteris ac prope praeceptoribus operam dedimus . . . denique aspirante Deo nostrae industriae ambo ad honores et vitae commoda emersimus."

[26] Jacopo Gherardi, *Jacobi Amanati . . . brevis vita* in *RIS* 23, pt. 3 (1904):3; G. Calamari, *Il confidente di Pio II, Cardinale Iacopo Ammannati*, Rome-Milan, 1932, 1:26; *Dizionario biografico*, 2, *s.v.*; della Torre, *Storia*, pp. 329-331. The first letter Ammannati wrote to Donato Acciaiuoli after leaving Florence is dated 8 January 1449 (BNF MS Magl. VIII, 1390, fols. 103v-104v), and according to M. Catalano he worked for Capranica from 1448, ten years before his death, *Commentarius de vita et scriptis Dominici Capranicae Cardinalis Firmani*, Fermo, 1793, p. 133. This antedates Gherardi, according to whom Ammannati went to Rome, "ad finem iubilei sedente Nicolao V. pont. max.," in 1450 (*Brevis vita*, p. 3), which is usually cited as the *terminus ad quem* for Scala's arrival in Florence (e.g. Manni, *Vita*, pp. 5-6; Dini, "Bartolommeo Scala," p. 62, n. 2).

too, must have studied these liberal arts subjects, and if his teachers were "almost the same" as Ammannati's, Marsuppini must have been one of them, for Bruni died in 1444 when Scala was only fourteen years old.[27]

In addition to poetry and oratory, Scala also studied law in Florence. It was an obvious subject for a boy with a career to make, since it opened the way to offices in the papal and state chanceries, as well as in the law courts and universities. As he is described as a *iurisperitus* in 1454, he must have studied law as his principal subject in the university since at least 1449, perhaps combining it with other subjects as Francesco Filelfo had done as a student at Padua: law *diebus ordinariis* and *diebus extraordinariis* oratory in the morning and philosophy in the afternoon.[28] Despite the economic troubles of the university at this time, surviving accounts show that when it reopened briefly in 1451 there were more lawyers on the roll than other teachers.[29] Of these, Benedetto Accolti was prob-

[27] According to the oration "habitam initio lectionis mee in gymnasio florentino in adulescentia mea," Ammannati himself taught oratory and poetry in the Studio and may have taught Scala (*Epistolae et commentarii*, fols. 330v-331r). However, his name does not appear in the Monte records, where Antonio Pacini of Todi, tutor to Piero and Giovanni de' Medici, is recorded as teacher of "arte oratoria et poesia" and "rettoricha" in 1444 and 1445, receiving payments for teaching in 1446 and 1451, ASF *Monte* 2190, fol. 30r; 2275, fol. 35r; 1121, fol. 25v; and 1652, fol. 462v. On Marsuppini's Chair in 1451, see n. 35 below.

[28] C. de Rosmini, *Vita di F. Filelfo*, 1:6, n. 1. Scala is described as *iurisperitus* by Francesco Filelfo in letters to Donato Acciaiuoli and Andrea Alamanni, 4 [?] August 1454, *Epistolae*, fol. 86v, 87r. On the length of his studies cf. Martines, *Lawyers*, p. 31.

[29] ASF *Monte* 1652, fols. 462v-463r, lists some thirty-four teachers (without subjects) to whom money was owed in 1451, of whom at least fourteen are lawyers; the remainder include six to nine doctors of medicine, two theologians (who may also have lectured on philosophy and Dante), one teacher of Greek, one of rhetoric, two grammarians, one astrologer, one notary and two friars. In August 1451 the Studio had been awarded 740 florins for civil and canon law out of a total budget of 1,700 florins, 350 of which went to Carlo Marsuppini for poetry and oratory, Gherardi, *Statuti*, p. 261. On the scope and resources of the Florentine Studio, in addition to Gherardi, see G. Brucker, "Florence and its University, 1348-1434," in *Action and Conviction in Early Modern Europe: Essays in Memory of E. H. Harbison*, ed. T. K. Rabb and J. E. Seigel, Princeton, N.J., 1969, pp.

ably the most preeminent, but there were also Domenico Martelli, Otto Niccolini and Girolamo Machiavelli, who were all leading and active citizens in Florence.[30] Although he is not listed as a lawyer in the university accounts, Carlo Marsuppini was "the most learned of all the men I have ever known in civil law," according to one law student.[31] He evidently combined theory with practice, on the one hand as a humanist restoring legal texts to their original condition unadulterated by the work of later glossators, "just as Petrarch first recalled the Latin language, which had long been in decline and unknown to us, to the light of day"[32]; on the other, with unrivaled skill "solving the riddles of Roman law and loosing the bonds of criminals fettered on unproven charges."[33]

220-236; H. Rashdall, *The Universities of Europe in the Middle Ages*, ed. F. M. Powicke and A. B. Emden, Oxford, 1936, 2:47-51, 59-62.

[30] On Accolti, *Dizionario biografico*, 1, *s.v.*; Martines, *Lawyers*, pp. 502-503; the doctoral thesis of Robert Black (London University, 1974). In 1451 he received two back-payments of £169 15s 0d and £128 before receiving £186 13s 4d "per parte di lettura" on 29 February 1452, probably representing an annual salary of 140 florins, ASF *Monte* 1652, fol. 462v (cf. Gherardi, *Statuti*, p. 462) and 463r. Martelli received two back-payments of £58 6s 8d and £44 before receiving the same payment of £186 13s 4d as Accolti on 29 February 1452, as did Niccolini (preceded by two back-payments of £72 18s 4d and £55) and Machiavelli (back-payments of £53 8s 8d and £40), ASF *Monte*, 1652, fols. 462v-463r. On their political activities, Rubinstein, *Government*, pp. 94, 97, 98, 103 (Machiavelli), 25-27, 99, 132, 134, etc. (Niccolini), 93, 95, 172, 175, 183, etc. (Martelli). Machiavelli and Martelli were members of the commission appointed to review the laws in 1445, when Cosimo de' Medici was Gonfalonier of Justice, Cambi, in *Delizie*, 20:250.

[31] Giovanni Fortiguerra, in his doctoral oration delivered in Arezzo, ed. L. Chiappelli, "Carlo Marsuppini e Giovanni Fortiguerra, precursori di scuola umanistica di diritto romano," *Archivio giuridico* 38 (1887):405: "iuris civilis omnium quos ego unquam noverim doctissimus fuit." The oration is dated "intorno al 1460" by Maffei, *Gli inizi*, p. 44.

[32] Ed. Chiappelli, "Carlo Marsuppini," pp. 405-406, etc.: "Nam Franciscus Petrarcha. . . . Latinam linguam, quae longo tempore lapsa et incognita nostris fuerat, primus in lucem revocavit."

[33] "Nemo quidem melius Romani aenigmata iuris / solvit et ambiguis vincula caeca reis," Landino, *Carmina omnia*, p. 110, "Eulogium in Carolum Arretinum" (Landino was also a pupil of Marsuppini's). *Caecus* probably here has the meaning "unsubstantiated" and "unproven," *OLD*, 3b.

We do not know if Marsuppini taught law to Scala, although it is possible to see traces of his influence in Scala's later dialogue *On Laws and Legal Judgments*.[34] His influence on Scala in the field of poetry and oratory is, however, indisputable, reflected immediately in a practice "Oration on justice," which Scala wrote less than three months after Marsuppini was appointed to the Chair of Poetry and Oratory in 1451, and subsequently in a series of other writings.[35] Scala later played an identical role to Marsuppini's as liaison between the Medici and the Florentine chancery, in which as a lawyer and humanist he was able to offer the same combination of intellectual and practical talents. For these reasons it is difficult not to see Marsuppini as the most formative influence on Scala during his university years in Florence.[36]

In August 1454, with Marsuppini dead and the university closed, Scala went to complete his education at the feet of Francesco Filelfo in Milan. He lived in the household of Count Filippo Borromeo, possibly acting as tutor to his sons,[37] and al-

[34] For example, in Scala's horror of medieval postglossators and his admiration for the brevity and elegance of Justinian's *Institutes*, *De legibus et iudiciis dialogus*, esp. pp. 261-262, 279; cf. ch. 11 below. On contemporary interest in law reform stimulated in Florence by the acquisition of an ancient MS of the *Digest* in 1406 from Pisa, Maffei, *Gli inizi*, pp. 84-94.

[35] In August 1451 the Commune authorized a salary of fl. 350 for the teaching of rhetoric and poetry (Gherardi, *Statuti*, p. 261), and on 29 February 1452 Marsuppini was paid £466 13s 4d as the first third of this salary, ASF *Monte*, 1652, fol. 463r. The influence of Marsuppini and his successor Cristoforo Landino on Scala's writings is discussed in ch. 10 below. On Marsuppini, G. Zippel, *Carlo Marsuppini d'Arezzo, notizie biographiche*, Trento, 1897; Vespasiano da Bisticci, *Vite*, 2:234-237; Martines, *Social World*, pp. 127-131; and on his writings, Voigt, *Wiederbelebung*, 2:194-195.

[36] Cf. ch. 2 below.

[37] *Vita Vitaliani Borrhomaei*, p. 6: "apud Philippum Filium [Vitaliani] essem annum iam fere"; cf. the report of the Milanese ambassador in Florence in 1469 that Scala "allevòssi a Millano in caxa del C[onte] Filippo Bonromeo" (ch. 3, n. 20 below). Unfortunately the Borromeo account books for the period 1454-1455 were destroyed in the last war, as Count Vitaliano Borromeo kindly ascertained for me, but from the notice of them published by G. Biscaro in 1914 ("Note di storia dell' arte," pp. 88-89) it emerges that payments of 7 florins a month were made in 1445 and 1451 to "Maestro Fermo da Caravaggio maestro di schuola in casa" and in 1464 to

though he stayed only a year before returning to Florence, it was a formative year for him in several respects. It was the only occasion on which he lived outside the Florentine state and it opened him to ideas and a way of life very different from those offered by Florence: in place of the civic patriotism and respectful antiquarianism of its humanists, the stimulating but irresponsible Filelfo; in place of the bourgeois republicanism and old-fashioned communal institutions of Florence, a more socially diversified but administratively centralized state. They left their mark on Scala, as we shall see.

Scala arrived in Milan with letters of commendation to Francesco Filelfo, not from the Medici (who disliked Filelfo), but from members of two much older and more distinguished Florentine families, Donato Acciaiuoli and Andrea Alamanni.[38] They both formed part of the young intellectual pressure group in Florence at that time, the self-named "chorus of the Florentine academy" who were clamoring to have the univer-

---

"Maestro Giovanni da Monte," suggesting that this position could have been held by Scala in 1454-1455. On the Borromei, see n. 50 below.

[38] Filelfo to A. Alamanni and D. Acciaiuoli, *Epistolae*, fols. 86v, 87r; cf. della Torre, *Storia*, pp. 370, 372-373. The letters may be misdated 4 August ("pridie nonas augustas") as Donato's commendation (which alone survives) is dated "6 August" in his autograph notebook (see n. 40 below). On the Acciaiuoli, Curzio Ugurgieri della Berardenga, *Gli Acciaioli di Firenze*, Florence, 1962; P. Litta, *Famiglie celebri italiane*, 1, tav. 5 and 6; *Dizionario biografico*, 1, *s.v.*; on Donato, whose maternal grandfather Palla Strozzi and stepfather Felice Brancacci were exiled as anti-Mediceans in 1434, E. Garin, "D. A., cittadino fiorentino," in his *Medievo e rinascimento*, pp. 211-287; della Torre, *Storia*, pp. 322 ff; Vespasiano da Bisticci, *Vite*, 2:256-285; and the bibliography in Martines, *Social World*, pp. 348-349. Jacopo Ammannati refers to Donato as "nobilis et doctus" in a letter of 5 November 1468 (*Epistolae et commentarii*, fol. 168v, cf. Garin, "D.A.," pp. 216-217). A perceptive appraisal by Gentile Becchi is in ASF *MAP* 61, 28 (2 March 1471 to Lorenzo de' Medici): "Bene sapete che la pulcritudine di Donato . . . che piace in chotesta civiltà non regge poi in questi assasinamenti [in Rome]. Se voi mi dicessi che temi tu del nostro Donato, teme sforzamente in dimostrarsi, et uscendo per boschi incogniti non si smarisca. Più honore credo vi farà che quest' altri." On Andrea Alamanni, della Torre, *Storia*, pp. 294, 315-316, 368-371; the bibliography in Martines, *Social World*, pp. 345-346, and n. 39 below.

sity reopened.[39] They must have come to know Scala as students, and their friendship with this miller's son and their respect for his "not inconsiderable talents"[40] are an early tribute to Scala's ability, confirmed a decade later when these same "academicians" supported him as their personal candidate for the chancellorship.[41]

Scala was ambitious as well as able, as we can also see from Donato Acciaiuoli's commendation.[42] His ambition to meet Filelfo was quickly achieved and only a month later he was congratulated by Donato on becoming an intimate friend of so learned a man.[43] Filelfo was a gifted but difficult person: one of the foremost scholars of Greek in Italy and an exciting teacher who had drawn large crowds to his lectures in Florence in the early 1430s, making the city "reverberate" with his vernacular orations on liberty and justice at a time when the Medici and Albizzi parties were fighting to establish control of the city.[44] He was a man of wide-ranging interests, but

[39] The phrase is Donato Acciaiuoli's in a letter to Filelfo, 27 June 1461 (BNF MS Magl. VIII, 1390, fol. 37v); cf. della Torre, *Storia*, pp. 285, 359-365; Cammelli, *I dotti bizantini*, 2:52-53. Donato calls Andrea Alamanni "defensorem et quasi patronum studiorum et nostre achademie principem" (Fossi, *Monumenta ad Alamanni Rinuccini vitam contexendam*, Florence 1791, p. 79, 15 April 1455); cf. Rinuccini, *Lettere e orazioni*, p. 11.

[40] "virtutes suas . . . non mediocres," Donato Acciaiuoli to F. Filelfo, 6 August 1454 (BNF MS Magl. VIII, 1390, fol. 86v; della Torre, *Storia*, p. 372, n. 2).

[41] "achademici del grecho Argiropolo," see ch. 3, n. 5 below.

[42] "doctissimorum virorum observantissimus sit amicitiamque tuam consequi velit, me rogavit ut ad te aliquid scriverem seque tibi plurimum commendarem," letter of 6 August above.

[43] Donato Acciaiuoli to "Bartolomeo Opisco Coll[ensi]," 5 September 1454, BNF MS Magl. VIII, 1390, fol. 88v; cf. della Torre, *Storia*, p. 371, n. 7, and p. 372, n. 3: "Tibi vero plurimum gratulor quod in eius familiaritatem veneris, quem ego tanti facio, ut non solum cum doctissimis viris aetatis nostre comparandum putem, sed etiam inter antiquos illos numerandum." Cf. his letter to Filelfo on the same day (*ibid.*, fol. 88r-v, partly quoted by della Torre, *Storia*, pp. 371-372, n. 8): "Conmendatio autem mea pro Bartolomeo Collensi quantum apud te valuerit non solum tuis litteris, sed etiam suis certior factus sum."

[44] On Filelfo, C. de Rosmini, *Vita di F. Filelfo*; E. Garin in *Storia di Milano*, 7:541-561; G. Benadduci, "Contributo alla bibliografia di F. F.,"

litigious and perhaps superficial, his ambition outrunning his achievements.

Scala was too young to have known Filelfo in Florence, for Filelfo was made to leave when Cosimo de' Medici returned triumphantly in 1434.[45] But some of Filelfo's zestful disrespect for the shibboleths of the Medicean Florentines may have remained to influence Scala in Milan. While there, Scala practiced a genre of historical writing frowned on in Florence, eulogistic biography, and in it he supported Valla's radical opinion that new Latin terms should be adopted for new institutions, only modifying his intention both of writing a eulogistic biography of the Medici and of using new words for new institutions on his return to Florence.[46] Scala also probably acquired his limited knowledge of Greek from Filelfo in Milan, where he borrowed manuscripts from Filelfo's rich library (which he was later accused of not returning) as well

Atti e memorie d. R. deputazione di storia patria per le provincie d. Marche, 5 (1901):459-535, and now the doctoral thesis of Robert Adam, Oxford, 1975. On his orations, G. Zippel, *Il Filelfo a Firenze (1429-1434)*, Rome, 1899, p. 33 and *ibid.*, n. 1; Gherardi, *Statuti*, p. xx, n. 2; Vespasiano da Bisticci, *Vite*, 2:287; and Niccolò Strozzi to Matteo Strozzi, in Bec, *Les Marchands écrivains*, p. 370: "E quasi tutta la terra rimbomba di questa sua oratione volghare." There are copies of his orations on liberty and justice (emphasizing the importance of preserving liberty in a state where men are born free but are everywhere in chains, and in seeing that laws once promulgated are observed) in Laur. MS Redi, 130, fols. 78r-79v, 122v-125v. On the political situation in these years, see now Dale Kent, *The Rise of the Medici: Faction in Florence, 1426-1434*, Oxford, 1978.

[45] Zippel, *Il Filelfo*. Filelfo subsequently wrote a series of attacks on Cosimo ("Commentationum Florentinarum de exilio liber ad Vitalianum Borrhomaeum," BNF MS II, II, 70, partly ed. Garin, *Prosatori latini del quattrocento*, pp. 494-517, etc.; *Satyrae*, Milan, 1476; "Exhortatio" to the Florentines and to Cosimo to recall the exiles in 1440, Laur. MS Strozz. 105, fols. 1r-20r; "Oratio in Cosmum ad Exules," Milan, Bibl. Ambr. MS V, 10 sup.) and he sustained a continuous relationship with the exiled Rinaldo degli Albizzi and Palla Strozzi (e.g. *Epistolae*, fols. 22r, 33v, 36v, 39r, 84v, etc.; *Commissioni di R. degli Albizzi per il Comune di Firenze*, ed. C. Guasti, bk. 3, Florence, 1873, pp. 672-673).

[46] See ch. 10, n. 18 below. The letters patent appointing Scala a ducal counselor and secretary in 1469 affirm that "Mediolani a teneris annis studiis humanitatis operam navavit" (ed. D. Moreni, *Notizie istoriche,* 3:75-76; cf. Benvenuti, *Quadri storici*, p. 81).

as from the son of his patron Filippo Borromeo.[47] Filelfo, too, was a client of the Borromeo family, and his greatest kindness to Scala may have been to introduce Scala to Filippo Borromeo as a tutor for his son Giovanni.[48] Scala in his turn repaid his debt of gratitude both to his patron and to Filelfo in writing a biography of Filippo's father Vitaliano, in which he described Filelfo as "the most learned of the scholars of his day."[49]

Vitaliano Borromeo had been one of the leading feudatories of the Milanese state, a banker and patron as well as a rich landowner, whose fifteenth-century brick palace still survives in central Milan.[50] Decorated inside with Aesop's *Fables* and Petrarch's *Triumphs* by Michelino Besozzo and other artists, it contrasts strikingly with the massive stone edifices built by his Florentine counterparts, and could have provided Scala with the inspiration for the house he later built for himself in Florence, decorated with a frieze of fables of his own inven-

[47] On Filelfo's Greek MSS, H. Omont, "La bibliothèque grecque"; Calderini, "Ricerche." On Scala's limited knowledge of Greek, see ch. 10 below. On his loans from Filelfo, see below (n. 55), and from Giovanni Borromeo, MS Riccard. 834, fol. 173r (Francesco to Nicodemo Tranchedini, 2 February 1464): "Et si Bartholomeum Scalam usquam offendas, sibi dicere memineris, e verbis filii Comitis Philippi Bonromei, me ipsum orare ut sibi libros Ptholomei emendatos quamprimum remittat, cui me etiam commendes obsecro."

[48] G. Biscaro, "Documenti milanesi inediti su F. F.," *ASLomb.*, ser. 4, 19 (1913):215-220. Filelfo wrote orations for the Borromei (*Orationes*, Venice, 1491, fols. 48r-50v, 29v-31r) and dedicated his "Commentationum . . . de exilio liber" to Vitaliano, whom he praised as a "publicum et munificentissimum hospitium quoddam . . . omnium eruditorum, omnium bonorum, religiosorum, nobilium, principum, imperatorum, regum summorumque pontificum" (ed. Garin, *Prosatori latini*, p. 496).

[49] *Vita Vitaliani Borrhomaei*, p. 18: "Franciscus Philippus [Philelphus], doctorum qui per eam tempestatem viverent doctissimus."

[50] On the Borromei, "lords of all the fortresses of Lake Maggiore" (quoted from B. Corio's *History* by D. M. Bueno de Mesquita, "Lodovico Sforza and his Vassals," p. 210), see *Famiglie notabili milanesi*, ed. F. Calvi, bk. 2, Milan, 1881; and on their patronage and their palace, Biscaro, "Note di storia dell' arte," p. 81; M. L. Gengaro, "Aggiunte per la storia della pittura lombarda del sec. XV," *Bollettino d'arte* 39 (1954):296-305, esp. 300-302, fig. 2-8; G. C. Bascapé, *I palazzi della vecchia Milano*, Milan, 1945, pls. 87, 88; *Storia di Milano*, 6:804-807.

tion.[51] Scala never knew Vitaliano personally, although he based his biography on the first-hand evidence of people he met in his house. His patron was Vitaliano's son Filippo who succeeded his father as count of Arona and was, like him, a banker who also played a responsible political and diplomatic role in the state.[52] In everything but their feudal rank and standing the Borromei resembled the Medici family in Florence, and Scala's experience in their household was not wasted when he later worked as a member of the Medici household, not least the courtly servility he must have learnt in Milan. While he was there he also met Duke Francesco Sforza and doubtless also his powerful centralizing secretary Cicco Simonetta, whose influence, too, can be detected in the reforms Scala later introduced into the Florentine chancery.[53]

After Scala returned to Florence in the autumn of 1455, he was apparently without employment but still in close contact with his friends in Milan. In one letter we find him searching for scarlet cloth to match a sample he had been given, possibly acting as an intermediary between the Borromei in Milan and their relations in Florence.[54] In another, to Filelfo's son Xen-

---

[51] See ch. 9 below.

[52] *Vita Vitaliani Borrhomaei*, pp. 6-7, 21. On Filippo, E. Lazzeroni, "Il consiglio secreto," *Atti e memorie del 3° Congresso Storico Lombardo*, Milan, 1939, pp. 119-120, n. 85; Santoro, *Gli uffizi*, p. 6.

[53] See Scala's letter to Bona and Gian Galeazzo Sforza (25 November 1477, ASMi SPE Fir. 293): "Sum iam ab ineunte fere aetate, cum Mediolani diversarer, Francesco Sfortiae . . . carus." He also wrote a poem on Francesco Sforza's mother, see ch. 10, n. 58 below. On Cicco, *I diari di Cicco Simonetta*, ed. A. R. Natale, 1 (Milan, 1962): xiii-xv. On the chancery, *Storia di Milano*, 7:524-526; C. Santoro, *Gli uffizi*, pp. xx-xxi, xxiii-xxv; *Acta in Consilio Secreto . . . Mediolani*, ed. A. R. Natale, 1 (Milan, 1963): xxxi-xxxiii; "Ordines primi et veteres ducalis cancellariae secretae," Milan, Bibl. Trivulziana, MS 1325, fols. 86r-102. On Milan in the fifteenth century, *Storia di Milano*, 7: 520-538, and on feudalism there, Bueno de Mesquita, "Lodovico Sforza and his Vassals."

[54] Modena MS, fol. 6r. The letter lacks a beginning and name of addressee, and is undated. The Florentine branch of the Borromeo family descended from San Miniato: Giovanni Borromeo in Florence was one of eight rich citizens elected as "Officiali de Banco" to raise money in 1467 (ASMi SPE Fir. 273, May 1467); Count Giovanni Borromeo from Milan stayed in his

ophon, he vows "by all the gods and by the sacrosanct and inviolable law of friendship" that he has returned all the books borrowed from his father: the missing volumes of Diodorus Siculus he suspects are "hiding among your father's manuscripts" and he urges Xenophon to get his father to hunt for them and tell him as soon as they are found.[55] To Filelfo himself he writes a letter of great interest, which shows him for the first time in contact with the Medici family and acting as emissary between Filelfo and Giovanni di Cosimo, then, as Scala says, busily engaged in building his villa at Fiesole: "having dined," Scala wrote to Filelfo,

I set out in the afternoon for Fiesole where Giovanni was rusticating, absorbed in his building. My business with him was of some importance, and after we had discussed many matters together, I eventually gave him your greetings, in your own words, and showed him your letter and your poem. He read them very carefully and then spoke most warmly in your praise, saying he had written to you that very day, and urging you, if you thought him worthy of the kindness, to undertake the work of interpreting Petrarch's poems, which in themselves are somewhat obscure. If you did so, he would be completely indebted to you, and you would earn the eternal gratitude of all devoted readers of Petrarch, of whom there are many, particularly in this

house in 1470 on his way to Rome (Lorenzo de' Medici, *Lettere*, 1, no. 66), and the failure of the Pazzi family to inherit his patrimony through marriage was a contributing factor to the Pazzi conspiracy in 1478 (see Poliziano's *Commentarium*, ed. A. Perosa, p. 14, n. 1).

[55] Modena MS, fol. 6v. On Xenophon, who worked in Genoa and Padua before becoming chancellor of Ragusa in 1460, see his father's *Epistolae*, fol. 71r-v, etc.; Calderini, "Ricerche," pp. 232, 235, 290; de Rosmini, *Vita*, 3:107-126. On 11 March 1458 Filelfo wrote to Palla Strozzi to ask if he had any more volumes of Diodorus Siculus to add to the "quinque prima volumina" he already possessed (*Epistolae*, fol. 101r). There are in fact two MSS of Diodorus belonging to Filelfo in the Laurentian Library, MS 70, 18, bearing his arms, and MS 70, 34 (Omont, "La bibliothèque grecque," p. 139, no. 13: "libri IV," and Calderini, "Ricerche, pp. 290-291). On Filelfo's loans, *ibid.*, p. 289.

city. I, too, not only advise and urge you, but beg and be-
seech you, to do so, for I think it would be no small addition to your glory.[56]

Filelfo had begun his *Commentary* on Petrarch's poems at the
behest of Filippo Maria Visconti some years earlier but, although he apparently never got beyond the first one hundred
and five poems, these were in great demand and frequently
printed.[57] Giovanni de' Medici had been asked to bring about
a reconciliation between his father Cosimo and Filelfo in
1447, and Scala was evidently working for the same objective.
Cosimo, however, steadfastly refused to have anything to do
with Filelfo, although his sons and grandson were less unre-
lenting.[58]

While Scala visited Giovanni de' Medici on Filelfo's behalf
in Florence, Filelfo concerned himself with some business affair of Scala's in Milan.[59] On another occasion he wrote to

[56] Modena MS, fol. 6r. On Giovanni de' Medici's villa, Vasari, *Vite*,
2:442-443.

[57] See P. C. Decembrio's *Vita di Filippo Maria Visconti*, *RIS*, 20 (old ser.)
1731, cols. 1013-1014; de Rosmini, *Vita*, 2:14-15; N. Quarta, "I commentatori
quattrocentisti del Petrarca," *Atti d. R. Accademia di Archeologia, Lettere
e Belle Arti*, Naples, 23 (1905):269-324. On the same day that he commended Scala to Filelfo, Donato Acciaiuoli also wrote to ask Filelfo for the
"commentarium quoddam in Triumphos Petrarche olim a te compositum,"
but a month later he wrote to tell Scala not to bother any more, since his
friend wanted "Conmentum in Triumphos Petrarche, non in cantilenas,"
5 September 1454: BNF MS Magl. VIII, 1390, fols. 86r (cf. Garin, *Medievo
e rinascimento*, p. 220, n. 13), 88v (della Torre, *Storia*, p. 372, n. 3). In fact
the printed *Commentary on the Trionfi* attributed to Filelfo is not by him
(Quarta, and de Rosmini, *Vita*, 2:15).

[58] Sforza Secondo Visconti to Giovanni de' Medici (16 December 1447,
ed. Fabroni, *Magni Cosmi . . . vita*, 2:115). On Filelfo's other attempts at
reconciliation with Piero and Giovanni, with gifts of writings and translations, see his *Epistolae*, fols. 41v, 96v-97r, ASF *MAP* 6, 114; 17, 120 (cf. della
Torre, *Storia*, pp. 367, n. 3, and pp. 367-368, n. 4). On Cosimo and Filelfo,
Gutkind, *Cosimo de' Medici*, pp. 116-118. Piero de' Medici agreed to be
godfather to Filelfo's son Federigo and Lorenzo de' Medici to another short-
lived son Celestino (see British Library, Add. MS 21, 520, fol. 7, Filelfo to
Lorenzo de' Medici, 6 May 1474, and ASF *Notarile* M 530, fol. 37v).

[59] The so-called "Vermiam . . . rem" which "magnopere expecto" (Scala

Scala more lightheartedly to accuse him of having abandoned the Muses to serve Aphrodite: "But beware, my dear friend. We know that Love is blind, and I want you not only to appear to be a very clearsighted man, but also to be one. Behave yourself."[60] Yet it proved to be Filelfo, not Scala, who found difficulty in being clearsighted, and in the following May he wrote to ask Donato Acciaiuoli to remind Scala about the spectacles he wanted to be sent from Florence, repeating his request in a letter to Andrea Alamanni in June; for someone, he wrote, turning the phrase he had already used to Scala, who has a reputation among certain people for being wise must also appear to be very clearsighted.[61] In the years that followed, the positions of the two men were reversed, Filelfo the vagrant humanist seeking the favor of Scala, the prosperous chancellor of Florence. On at least one occasion Scala was instrumental in procuring letters of safe-conduct for Filelfo to pass through Florentine territory and to visit Florence.[62] But the two men were prevented from reestablishing their old friendship by Filelfo's death in Florence in 1481, only fifteen

---

to Filelfo, Modena MS, fol. 6v), referred to by Filelfo in letters to Scala of 5 and 23 October 1455 (*Epistolae*, fol. 90v), is possibly connected with the city of Worms (called "Vermis" by Poggio Bracciolini, *Opera*, ed. Fubini, 3(1):81) or with Count Pietro dal Verme, an important vassal of the duke of Milan (cf. Bueno de Mesquita, "Ludovico Sforza and his Vassals," pp. 198-199).

[60] 19 September 1455, ed. E. Legrand, *Centdix lettres grecques de F. Filelfe*, Paris, 1892, p. 78.

[61] *Epistolae*, fol. 94v (31 May 1456); Legrand, *Centdix lettres*, p. 88 (22 June 1456). On the manufacture of concave lenses in Florence and the demand for them in Milan, see now V. Ilardi, "Eyeglasses and Concave Lenses in 15th-Century Florence and Milan: New Documents," *Renaissance Quarterly* 29 (1976):341-360.

[62] *Epistolae*, fol. 208v (29 March 1469); cf. de Rosmini, *Vita*, 2:185-186; and Filelfo to Piero de' Medici, 12 July 1469, ed. G. Benadduci, "Prose e poesie volgari di F. F.," *Atti e memorie d. deputazione di storia patria per le provincie d. Marche* 5 (1901):166. Filelfo spent four days in Florence at the end of October 1469 (de Rosmini, *Vita*, 2:191-193), and on 25 August 1475 he wrote again to ask a favor of Scala: "qua in re tua mihi diligentia opus est, ex incluso chyrographo cognosces" (Milan, Bibl. Trivulziana, MS 873, fol. 499v).

days after he returned to teach again in the university from which he had been banished nearly fifty years earlier.[63]

Scala's future lay in Florence, not Milan, although in 1455 this was not obvious. It was in this year that Giovanni de' Medici became director general of the Medici bank on the death of Giovanni Benci and, although Scala gives no indication of what his important business was with him in Fiesole, it may have concerned some transaction between Milan and Florence, possibly involving the Borromei.[64] At this moment Scala's future was uncertain and his career could have taken one of several directions: he was qualified as a lawyer and could have practiced law, he could have been employed as a tutor or teacher, he could have entered the world of business and commerce. His options lay wide open.

His name first appears in official circles just over a year after his return from Milan. A commission had been appointed to examine the state of the chancery under the elderly Poggio Bracciolini who, after a lifetime spent in the papal court— "which nourished me for fifty years with honor and praise"— was too old for the work of chancellor and spent much of his time in his villa outside the city.[65] The problem was discussed in a series of special meetings of leading citizens, and on 27

[63] de Rosmini, *Vita*, 2:270; cf. Fil. Sacramoro to Gian Galeazzo Sforza, 2 August 1481, ASMi SPE Fir. 303: "El Philelpho passò de questa vita martis di sera al' un' hora di nocte, che fu l'ultimo del passato. Tri dì stete amalato cum uno pocho di febre e soprazonto di fluxo." On Filelfo's later career, de Rosmini, *Vita*, 2:176ff, 226ff, 268-270.

[64] de Roover, *Banco Medici*, p. 104. There is evidence of a friendly relationship between the Borromei and Medici in ASF *MAP* 137, 46 (20 or 22 January 1447), 163, fol. 30 (8 August 1464), and 34, 484 (4 October 1479, Giovanni Borromeo to Lorenzo de' Medici, promising to do for him what was in his power, "per l'antiqua amicitia et amore fraterno quale sempre vi ho portato"). The Medici employed a Giovanni di Lazzaro Borromeo in the Milan branch of their bank (de Roover, pp. 187, 388).

[65] Poggio, *Opera*, 3 (bk. 14, ep. 13): 271: "quae me quinquaginta annos cum honore et laude nutrivit. . . . Ego animi quietem appeto et perquiro, quae in hac mobili civitate nequaquam inveniri potest." On his appointment as chancellor, E. Walser, *Poggius Florentinus, Leben und Werke*, in *Beiträge zur Kulturgeschichte des Mittelalters und der Renaissance*, 14 (Leipzig, 1914): 382; Marzi, *Cancelleria*, pp. 219-224.

December 1456 a commission of four men (Otto Niccolini, Dietisalvi Neroni, Matteo Palmieri and Franco Sacchetti) recommended that Poggio should be reappointed annually, together with a second chancellor, ser Antonio di Mariano Muzi, and four assistants. Since there were no teachers in the university at that time, the commissioners also suggested that two of these assistants should teach there, one in the morning, the other in the afternoon, solving the problems of both chancery and university simultaneously. Four men were shortlisted as suitable to teach in the university: Cristoforo Landino, Antonio del Rosso, Bernardo di ser Francesco Nuti and "Bartolomeo da Colle."[66] We do not know if the report was accepted, although ser Antonio Muzi subsequently acted as second chancellor.[67] Bartolomeo of Colle, as he was still called, was not apparently chosen for this work and by the end of the following year he was employed in a private capacity by Pierfrancesco de' Medici. Finally he had entered the orbit of the Medici, who had had so little to do with his earlier years. It was his own ambition and his student friendships with influential Florentines that launched him on his path to success and not, as Guicciardini thought, the Medici. Once he entered their orbit, however, for reasons of mutual interest he did not leave it.

[66] ASF *Cons. Prat.* 54, fols. 61r-v, 67v-71r, 79v-80v (debates of 27 November and 8 December and "relatio super facto cancell[erie]," 27 December 1456, partly ed. Walser, pp. 404-406).

[67] Marzi, *Cancelleria*, pp. 221, 231, 244.

CHAPTER II

Secretary in the Medici Household

The more those who serve you are honored, the more praise will redound to you. *Scala to Pierfrancesco de' Medici, 1461*[1]

We first find Bartolomeo Scala working for Pierfrancesco de' Medici in August 1457.[2] In September he was too busy even to greet his friend Antonio Guidotti before leaving to visit Pierfrancesco in the Mugello, but as a loyal Medicean himself Guidotti accepted his excuse unhesitatingly: "for you are a faithful hero, and by Hercules you do well to remain faithful to your master."[3] Scala had apparently urged him to report to Pierfrancesco about the recent Ricci conspiracy against the Medici regime in Florence, and now Guidotti wanted Scala to find out if this had been well received and what Pierfrancesco had said.[4] So already Scala is involved in Medicean politics and playing a confidential role among the supporters of the regime.

Pierfrancesco de' Medici was twenty-seven years old at the time, still politically immature. His father Lorenzo had died in 1440, leaving him in the care of his uncle Cosimo until he

---

[1] ASF *MAP* 2, 477, ed. Gentile, "B. S. e i Medici," p. 135, doc. 3: "et a voi quanto e servidori vostri saranno più honorati, tanto più loda ve ne risulterà."

[2] Scala to Sandro Pagagnotti, 6 August 1457, ASF *MAP* 98, 281.

[3] Antonio Guidotti to Scala, 15 September 1457, ASF *MAP* 96, 461, ed. Gentile, "B. S. e i Medici," pp. 133-134, doc. 1: "Abiisti ut scribis in agrum Mugellanum multis insalutato amico occupationibus impeditus. Accipio plane excusationem, fidelis enim es hero et bene hercle facis fidelem te domino servare tuo." On Guidotti's position as a Medici partisan, see especially ASF *MAP* 17, 359 (to Piero de' Medici, 9 February 1464). On his offices, Cambi, *Delizie*, 20:235, 325, 383, 300; Rubinstein, *Government*, pp. 252, 263, 280, 290, 308; ASF *Cons. Prat.* 54, fols. 97v, 156v. According to the *Libro* of Antonio Billi (ed. C. Frey, Berlin, 1892, p. 46), Antonio di Migliorino Guidotti made the model of the Rucellai loggia, Rucellai, *Zibaldone*, p. 144.

[4] Letter of 15 September above. On the Ricci conspiracy, Cambi, *Delizie*, 20:349-350; Rinuccini, *Ricordi storici*, p. lxxxvi; Rubinstein, *Government*, p. 89.

came of age in 1451.[5] Then the Medici estate was divided between Pierfrancesco and his older cousins Piero and Giovanni
and, although Pierfrancesco's sons later suspected Cosimo of
profiting from their father's minority,[6] outwardly their relationship was conducted with scrupulous fairness and friendli-
ness. Yet there were reasons for concern, and even in 1457 it
might have been possible to foresee the rivalry that finally
split the two branches of the family. As Cosimo's sons, Piero
and Giovanni stood to inherit their father's primacy in Florence and they were already initiated into the political life of
the city. Pierfrancesco was not; but in compensation his patrimony as an only son was twice that of Piero's and Giovanni's
and in Florence money had political value. Hitherto Pierfrancesco seemed uninterested in politics, preferring to spend his
days in the wild and beautiful castle of Trebbio in the Mugello which had been allotted to him in 1451, dealing in horses
and descending to Florence as infrequently as possible. Left to
himself, he might have remained aloof. But in May 1456 this
man of "unusual" and "somewhat rustic" charm married
Laudomia, daughter of the prominent Medicean Angelo Acciaiuoli, and Angelo was concerned that Pierfrancesco should
enjoy his share of the family's influence by cultivating Cosimo
and playing a more active part in the state.[7]

Bartolomeo Scala became associated with Pierfrancesco
shortly afterwards, doubtless as a result of this new situation.
Perhaps Angelo Acciaiuoli, as a cousin of Scala's friend Donato Acciaiuoli, was responsible for introducing him to Pierfrancesco's household, or perhaps the Medici themselves chose

[5] On Pierfrancesco, see Pieraccini, *La stirpe*, 1:149-155; on his father, *ibid.*,
pp. 43-47; and on his death in 1440, de Roover, *Banco Medici*, p. 89. I discuss Pierfrancesco more fully in a forthcoming article to be published in
the *Journal of the Warburg and Courtauld Institutes*: 42 (1979).

[6] ASF *MAP* 88, n. 392, fol. 508; on the division of the Medici estate,
MAP 161.

[7] "L'animo gentile et pelegrino," N. Tranchedini to Francesco Sforza,
2 December 1454, ed. Magnani, *Relazioni private*, p. iv; "hai un po' del
salvaticho," Angelo Acciaiuoli to Pierfrancesco, 4 March 1457, ASF *MAP*
2, 442, ed. Pieraccini, *La stirpe*, 1:150.

him. Scala already knew Giovanni de' Medici and he dedicated his *Life of Vitaliano Borromeo* to Piero during or after his visit to Milan.[8] What is certain is that the years Scala spent in his employment coincided with Pierfrancesco's initiation into the Florentine *cursus honorum* as he attained his political majority. Pierfrancesco was appointed a member of the Balìa of 1458 although not yet of statutory age; then one of six ambassadors (with his father-in-law Angelo Acciaiuoli) to congratulate and offer homage to Pius II in the autumn of 1458; a year later a member of the Signoria, although still younger than he should have been for this office; and in September 1460 a member of the all-powerful disciplinary magistracy of the Eight of Ward (Otto di Guardia), which had been given absolute authority (or *balìa*) to deal with political crimes after the discovery of Girolamo Machiavelli's conspiracy against the regime in 1458.[9]

Although Scala acted principally as Pierfrancesco's business secretary, he must also have been involved in his political career, acting as mentor and perhaps also as tutor to the young man. It was in the year when Scala began to work for him that Pierfrancesco asked Carlo de' Medici to procure him

[8] On the date of the presentation copy of the *Life* to Piero de' Medici (Laur. MS 68, 27), Brown and de la Mare, "B. Scala's Dealings," p. 239, n. 10. Although its script (by Paganus Raudensis) and illumination suggest it was completed during Scala's stay in Milan in 1454-1455 (revealing Scala's early hope of patronage from Piero), a later date cannot be ruled out: if written in 1454-1455, one would have expected it to have been dedicated to Scala's patron in Milan, Filippo Borromeo, as Vitaliano's son the most appropriate dedicatee; moreover, its inclusion in Piero de' Medici's so-called 1456 Inventory does not provide an absolute *terminus ad quem* for its presentation to Piero, since the second hand of the inventory (in which it is listed) also lists works written after this date (*ibid.*), so it could possibly have been copied from a Milanese MS of the work after Scala's return to Florence.

[9] Rubinstein, *Government*, pp. 107 (n. 5), 290; C. Guasti, "Due legazioni al sommo pontifice," in his *Scritti storici*, Prato, 1894, pp. 85-90; Cambi, *Delizie*, 20:362, 377; ASF *Otto di Guardia* 2723 bis, fol. 57r, and *Tratte* 81, fol. 5r. The minimum age for both the 1458 Balìa and membership of the Signoria was 30 years. On the Otto di Guardia, Antonelli, "La magistratura," pp. 3-39; and on its special powers in 1458 and 1460, Rubinstein, *Government*, pp. 111-112.

books in Rome.[10] In 1460 Scala delivered lectures on Virgil in Pierfrancesco's house in Florence, which the poet Luigi Pulci wanted to attend,[11] and he completed his treatise *On Whether a Wise Man Should Marry* at Trebbio one Christmas.[12] So Scala may have been intended to stimulate in Pierfrancesco an interest in learning and culture to match that of his urban cousins, although we do not know if these studies were primarily for Pierfrancesco's benefit, or for Scala's, serving as *passatempi* during Pierfrancesco's protracted absences and country pleasures.[13] Significantly, perhaps, Scala dedicated his Trebbio treatise to Piero de' Medici, not Pierfrancesco. For his patron, he wrote a poem he may have considered more suited to his tastes in memory of his champion racer Swallow.[14]

Scala's principal duties were those of secretary and factotum to Pierfrancesco, and his surviving letters provide early evidence of the technique he used in all his subsequent dealings with the family: he was clear, efficient, quick to act and give advice when necessary, yet deferential and unwilling to act without instruction unless he knew what was required of him. Since Pierfrancesco was a partner in the Medici bank, sharing many contracts with his cousins Piero and Giovanni,[15] much

---

[10] Carlo de' Medici to Pierfrancesco, 9 December 1458, ASF *MAP* 137, 86, see Pieraccini, *La stirpe*, 1:151.

[11] Bastardello of Francesco Castellani, ASF *Conv. Soppr.* 90, 134, fol. 19v, quoted by C. Carnesecchi, "Per la biografia di Luigi Pulci," *ASI*, ser. 5, 17 (1896): 378, recording that Pulci borrowed a MS containing Virgil's *Bucolics*, *Georgics*, and the *Aeneid*, "el quale libro mi chiese per andare a udire da messer Bartolomeo da Colle torna in casa di Pierfrancesco de' Medici, e debbemelo restituire salvo," 2 January 1460.

[12] See ch. 10, n. 24.

[13] Scala's letter to Pierfrancesco from Florence on 25 March 1459 (ASF *MAP* 4, 378) suggests perhaps the latter: "Qui di nuovo non ho che scrivervi. Attendesi alla anima più che ad altro."

[14] "Carmina in laudem equi Petrifrancisci de Medicis," see ch. 10 below. Evidence suggests that Pierfrancesco may have dealt in horses, Pieraccini, *La stirpe*, 1:152.

[15] Although de Roover does not discuss Pierfrancesco's role in the Medici bank as such, there are references to his partnerships in *Banco Medici*: 127, 338, 359, 551. Cf. also the *Inventario* to *MAP*, especially vol. 4 (Rome, 1963).

of the work Scala did for him was concerned with the bank. In Pierfrancesco's one surviving letter to Scala, for instance, Scala was told to press on with other urgent business without further instruction, to do everything possible to get Pierfrancesco's debtors to pay up now they had been sentenced and the holidays were over, to tell Pierfrancesco's associate Bernardo Vespucci to find out what his mother wanted to do and then see to it that the business did not have to be discussed again, and finally to authorize a payment that was not for the moment to be put down to his account: "do what I write to you and advise me of' everything."[16]

When Scala knew what Pierfrancesco wanted to be done, he would act without specific instruction.[17] However, in 1459 he forwarded Pierfrancesco a letter from "the Cardinal" (of Rouen, Guillaume d'Éstouteville), who the previous autumn in Rome had promised Pierfrancesco to be his guest on his way to the Congress of Mantua, asking Pierfrancesco to "let me know if you want me to reply and if you would like me to say one thing rather than another—although you have Sandro [Pagagnotti, Pierfrancesco's land agent] there, fit for more important matters than this. I mentioned it, though, be-

[16] Pierfrancesco de' Medici in Trebbio to Scala in Florence, 19 December 1457 (not 1459 as inventoried), ASF *MAP* 98, 525: "Fate quello vi scrivo et di tutto avisate." Both Francesco Buondelmonti and Bartolomeo Gianfigliazzi, mentioned in the letter, are listed as Pierfrancesco's debtors in the 1458 Catasto for sums of fl.56 27s and fl.24 25s respectively, ASF *MAP* 82, no. 182, fol. 594v: "I sopradetti debitori sono più anni passati." In a letter to Pierfrancesco of 13 April 1457 (*MAP* 2, 447), Bernardo Vespucci refers to "quello tristo di Lorenzo di Chresci," the same debtor whom Scala had to pursue as one of the first tasks we know he performed for Pierfrancesco (ASF *MAP* 98, 281, letter of 6 August 1457).

[17] See, for example, his letter to Pierfrancesco of 20 January 1460 (ASF *MAP* 137, 94): "Io, perchè sapevo vostra intentione, di nuovo scripsi per vostra parte una lectera al Podestà e una a ser Michele. . . ." On 16 January 1460 it had been agreed "quod dicta terra Prati de cetero reformari possit absque reformatoribus civibus florentinis," but because of disagreement among the citizens about the new election bags, three Florentines (including Piero de' Medici) were asked to assume authority for a limited period on 10 June 1460, ASF *Prato, Statuti e Riforme*, 657, fols. 478r-479v, cf. *SS. Delib. sp. aut.* 32, fol. 33r.

cause I know your way of writing from past experience."
Pierfrancesco was evidently happy for Scala to reply and returned the letter to him with a note indicating what to say.[18]

Scala's letter to Pierfrancesco of 22 November 1461 is clear
and incisive: informing him of the return to Florence of a certain notary, ser Amanzo, whom on Pierfrancesco's instructions
he had attempted to have taken by the Otto di Guardia, he
reported that the man had got wind of this and had escaped,
setting his friends on to Scala:

> I replied to them all that he was guilty of everything, be-
> cause he had swindled, and that I could not depart from
> your instructions nor forgive a wrong done to you, that it is
> for you to forgive him and for me to follow my instruc-
> tions. This is why I hear he is coming to you about it. I
> wouldn't like to say you shouldn't forgive him, but I do
> urge you very strongly not to trust his promises—of which
> he'll make plenty—unless he gives sufficient security for
> them, for by now we've surely had enough of his fine talk.
> If it's not too much trouble, please write me a line if he
> arrives, to say what you've done with him.[19]

[18] Letters of 21 March 1459 (ASF *MAP* 4, 377: "Se vorrete ch'io risponda,
me n'avisate, et se volete ch'io risponda più una cosa che un'altra, benchè
havete costì Sandro atto a maggior cosa che questa, ma dicevolo perchè
io ho il modo vostro dell'altre volte") and 25 March 1459 (ASF *MAP* 4,
378: "Risponderò come dite"). Pagagnotti is addressed as "factore di Cosmo
[de Med]ici in Cafagiuolo" in a letter from Piero de' Medici, 12 September
1454 (ASF *MAP* 12, 213). He also helped to administer Medici lands in
Prato. Scala's earliest surviving letter as Pierfrancesco's secretary is written
to Pagagnotti (ASF *MAP* 98, 281), and on 15 April 1463 he paid Pagagnotti
fl.2 13s 6d "per some 2 di doghe da botti," ASF *Conv. Soppr.* 95, 212, fol.
131 right. Pagagnotti refers to Scala in a letter to Pierfrancesco of 28 May
1458 (*MAP* 5, 743). Both men, with Giovanni Cavalcanti, were appointed
arbitrators between the two branches of the family on 28 September 1483,
ASF *Notarile* G 620 (Simone Grazzini, 1472-1494), fol. 198r, and Pagagnotti
on subsequent occasions (*ibid.*, fols. 216r, 230r).

[19] ASF *MAP* 137, 107. A ser Amanzo Martini drew up a deed of sale of
land to Scala on behalf of the Cestello in Florence in 1477, see ch. 9, n. 36
below.

On 24 October 1459, Scala was appointed chancellor of the Guelf Party in Florence,[20] and almost at once his letters begin to be filled with items of news concerning his new work: "In the Party we are busy with the scrutiny," he wrote to Pierfrancesco on 20 January 1460. "The Catalonian and Sicilian galleys were retained by the Commune once more, and I think that this year they will stay behind. To our pleasure the Sienese have announced two galleys for Flanders, and it is said that Piero Mannelli is building his hopes on them, but we shall see what happens. Nothing else."[21]

In May he sent Pierfrancesco news from Genoa of the arrival of "your Barbary galleys" in Genoa on 8 May and their departure on the 11th with at least 1,500 ducats' worth of freight and twenty-two merchants from Genoa: "Bongianni and all of them were well, what good news!" This letter contains many other pieces of news that doubtless stemmed from the palace of the Guelf Party, including a report that the Florentine galleys from the Levant were said by someone in Siena to have reached Palermo and were "very rich."[22]

[20] His appointment was confirmed on 20 November 1459, adding fl.3 to his monthly salary of fl.5 on condition he paid a notary as his assistant, ASF *Capt. P. G.* 9 rosso, fol. 55r. On the Guelf Party, U. Dorini, *Notizie storiche sull' Università di Parte Guelfa in Firenze*, Florence, 1902; F. Bonaini, "Della Parte Guelfa in Firenze," *Giornale storico degli archivi toscani* 1 (1857):1-41 (ed. 1335 Statutes); 2 (1858):171-187, 257-289; 3 (1859):77-99, 167-184; G. Salvemini, *La dignità cavalleresca*; and G. A. Brucker, *Florentine Politics and Society, 1343-1378*, Princeton, N.J., 1962, pp. 99-104 and *passim*. Scala's appointment and reforms are discussed in more detail at the beginning of ch. 3 and in ch. 7 below. I discuss the Guelf Party under Scala's chancellorship more fully in an article to be published in *ASI*.

[21] ASF *MAP* 137, 94. The scrutiny Scala refers to was for the offices of *provveditore* and *camarlingo*, ASF *Capt. P. G.* 9 rosso, fols. 56v-57r, 58r-v. Between August 1459 and January 1461 the Guelf Party gradually assumed control of maritime affairs: on the galleys to Catalonia and Sicily, Mallett, *Florentine Galleys*, p. 79.

[22] ASF *MAP* 2, 464 (14 May 1460). "Your Barbary galleys" are presumably the two great galleys that sailed for Barbary in April 1460 with Andrea della Stufa as their captain and Bongianni Gianfigliazzi one of their patrons, Mallett, *Florentine Galleys*, append. A, p. 164; cf. de Roover, *Banco Medici*, pp. 340-341. "The Florentine galleys from the Levant" are possibly the two great galleys that sailed to Constantinople and the Black Sea in August 1459 and returned midsummer 1460, Mallett, *Florentine Galleys*, p. 163. There are

Although Scala continued to correspond with Pierfrancesco after his new appointment, he was no longer expected to live as part of his household in Florence. In the course of 1460 he was asked to buy a house for himself. But despite the fact that he was now earning a communal salary, the cost of renting and furnishing a house involved him in financial difficulties, which he confided to Pierfrancesco; Pierfrancesco suggested he should discuss them with Cosimo, but Scala thought the moment inappropriate:

because when I was with him last night I found him in bed and in considerable pain, still from gout, although they say he hasn't had such a bad night tonight as last night. I did not write earlier because I did not know about it until I had been there. I have not seen him, but I was told by Fallaio last night that Piero, too, had had a bad night and they were afraid he was ill. They almost all agree now that Giovanni's illness is a phlegm, so they've got all three down at once. Perhaps you're better off down there, although I think you're wiser than me in my affairs, not to mention your own. Make me speak of love *Et testis est deus*. So for the moment I doubt if I'll have time to discuss it, and especially such matter, with Cosimo. But whether I do or not, all I care about is that I have done my duty in finding a house as I was told to. For the rest, you all know my position and what I can do without your help. As long as I am in your service, I have nothing to worry about.[23]

---

more references to galleys in Scala's letters to Pierfrancesco of 18 and 22 November 1461, ASF *MAP* 5, 752 (ed. Gentile, "B. S. e i Medici," p. 135, doc. 4) and *MAP* 137, 107.

[23] Letter to Pierfrancesco of 14 May 1460, ASF *MAP* 2, 464; this extract ed. Gentile, "B. S. e i Medici," p. 134, doc. 2. Some of his household purchases at this time are listed in ch. 9 below. During the period 1460-1464 Scala appears to have rented houses from several people, including Carlo della Casa and Agnolo di ser Niccolò Biffoli. According to Sanpaolesi ("La casa," p. 277), Scala "rimase in casa di Cosimo fino a 1460 quando si transferì in una casa di sua proprietà in Via San Gallo"; but this was not the house listed in his 1469 Catasto, which he bought only on 4 September 1467 (the date of its purchase is incomplete in his own tax return, ASF *Catasto* 923

This letter, like other earlier letters, shows Scala fully involved with the affairs of other members of the Medici family.[24] But although he was by now being increasingly pulled
into the orbit of the senior branch of the family, when in need
he still referred first of all to Pierfrancesco—as in April 1461,
when he wanted to matriculate into the Guild of Lawyers and
Notaries: "Both for my office and for the honor, and for many
reasons it is unnecessary to relate to you, I have wanted to be
matriculated as a doctor [of law]. The present proconsul [ser
Paolo di Lorenzo Beniwieni] is a very great friend of mine and
could give me considerable help, especially in arranging the
fees so that I would not have to pay anything if possible, or at
least the very minimum." He had discussed the matter with
Angelo della Stufa, "who I think would willingly do what he
could for the servants of your family" and Stufa seemed well
disposed to discuss it and support him: "However, in order to
make him even keener, I would be glad if you would be kind
enough to write a note and commend me to him. And in case
it was necessary in your absence, he could speak on your behalf to whomever he had to, which I am sure he would do
willingly. This is an honorable matter and I set great store by
it. As for you, the more those who serve you are honored, the
more praise will redound to you. I recommend myself to you.
It seems like a thousand years since I saw you."[25]

Pierfrancesco must have accepted Scala's argument about
the mutual profit they would gain from his entry into the
guild—to which he should already have belonged as chancellor of the Guelf Party—for Scala's name appears among the
list of doctors of the guild from whom payment had been
received under the date of 2 May 1461. Thanks to the good
offices of his "very great friend" the proconsul, a fee of merely

---

(S. Giovanni, Leon d'Oro), fol. 290r, but it is contained in the return of
Rinieri del Pace, ASF *Catasto* 911 (Carro 1469-1470), fol. 482r).

[24] Cf. below, nn. 29-33, 37, 38.

[25] Letter to Pierfrancesco of 5 April 1461, ASF *MAP* 2, 477, cf. Marzi,
Cancelleria, p. 237, n. 3. Ser Paolo Benevieni was appointed Proconsul for 4
months from 1 April 1461, ASF *Giudici e Notai*, 181, fol. Iv, cf. 26, fol. 5v.
On Scala's relationship with Angelo della Stufa, see ch. 3, esp. n. 35 below.

19s 7d was paid to his messenger four days later instead of the
statutory 25 florins.[26] This was perhaps the last favor Pierfrancesco—but not his descendants—performed for Scala. In 1466
Pierfrancesco signed a republican oath against the regime then
headed by his cousin Piero, and his relationship by marriage
to Angelo Acciaiuoli, one of the principal conspirators against
Piero de' Medici later that year, prevented him from holding
office again until after Piero's death in 1469. Scala, by contrast, had firmly committed himself to the party of Pierfrancesco's cousins. However, he remained on friendly terms with
Pierfrancesco and his sons and acted as arbitrator between the
two branches of the family in the 1480s, which helped him to
emerge virtually unscathed from the revolution in 1494.[27]

Although Scala was employed in these early years as Pierfrancesco's secretary, he already knew Giovanni de' Medici, and
in the course of working for Pierfrancesco got to know him
and other members of his family increasingly well. Pierfrancesco, as we have seen, was a partner in the Medici bank with
his cousins and, although by 1457 the two families lived in
separate (but almost adjoining) houses in Via Larga,[28] contact
between them was close. During Pierfrancesco's sojourns in
the country Scala must have come to know his cousins as well,

[26] ASF *Conv. Soppr.* 95, 212, fol. 84 left (6 May 1461): payment of 19s 7d
to "Ghuglielmo di Christofano, donzello al prochonsolo, per la sua matri-
chola." On the conditions and payment for matriculation, see S. Calleri,
*L'Arte dei Giudici e Notai di Firenze nell'età comunale e nel suo statuto
del 1344*, Milan, 1966, pp. 30-31; Martines, *Lawyers*, pp. 28-29, 31, 32. In ASF
Giudici e Notai, 181, fol. 64r, Scala is entered under the heading (fol. 60r):
"In hac parte huius libri describentur omnes et singule presentationes pre-
sentis anni 1461 secundo Maii 1461," for the payment of fl.1 2s (like other
lawyers).

[27] The oath is ed. Pampaloni, "Il giuramento pubblico," pp. 233-238. On
Scala's arbitration, see n. 18 above.

[28] By the time of his 1458 Catasto, Cosimo was living in his newly constructed palace in Via Larga and Pierfrancesco in the house they formerly
shared a door or two away, toward San Marco, ASF *MAP* 82, no. 182, fols.
559r, 571r; cf. I. Hyman, "15th-Century Florentine Studies: the Palazzo
Medici and a Ledger for the Church of San Lorenzo," Ph.D. thesis, New
York, 1968, p. 78.

if not better, than his own absent master, and his letters reflect his growing intimacy with their branch of the family. In March 1459, for instance, Pierfrancesco told Scala "to go to Cosimo and tell him it's not true what he's been told" (that he wanted to enter the joust to be held in honor of Galeazzo Maria Sforza), which Scala promised to do at once and let him know Cosimo's reply.[29] Four days later he informed Pierfrancesco that his wife, Laudomia Acciaiuoli, "and all of us are well, Laudomia still apparently at her father's house"—as she was the following year when Scala wrote to Pierfrancesco.[30] On 20 January 1460 Giovanni di Cosimo told Scala he was going out (to Cafaggiolo) to meet the pope, and the previous day Scala had been with Giovannino to discuss Pierfrancesco's note to the Catasto officials.[31] In May, as we have seen, Pierfrancesco suggested Scala should discuss his financial problems with Cosimo, and in September that year Scala wrote a long letter to Giovanni de' Medici that reveals how intimately he was already involved in Medicean politics.

On 4 September 1460 Scala wrote to describe to Giovanni in Bagno a Morba the recent meeting of the Colleges of the Guelf Party.[32] Ever since he had been appointed its chancellor, Scala had been fully involved in the attempt to reform its organization to make it better adapted to assume the work of the Sea Consuls and the Six of Arezzo. One measure suggested was to elect the superintendent or *provveditore* instead of

[29] Scala to Pierfrancesco, 21 March 1459, ASF *MAP* 4, 377. Cosimo had written to Pierfrancesco on 17 March after hearing his nephew wanted to enter the joust, contrary to what he had previously understood; though not enthusiastic, he promised to do what Pierfrancesco wanted (*MAP* 2, 452). But in the event Pierfrancesco did not enter and gave his horse and armor to Guido da Faenza.

[30] Letters to Pierfrancesco of 25 March 1459 and 14 May 1460, ASF *MAP* 4, 378 and 2, 464.

[31] Letter to Pierfrancesco of 20 January 1460, ASF *MAP* 137, 94.

[32] Forlì, Bibl. Comunale, Autografi Piancastele. I am grateful to Dr. Antonio Rotondò for directing me to this letter many years ago. Pieraccini (*La stirpe*, 1:86) refers to a letter from Scala to Giovanni at Petriolo dated 4 September 1459 in *MAP* 10, 19 bis, which I have been unable to identify. On the baths at Petriolo and Morba, Repetti, *Dizionario*, 1:223-224.

choosing him by lot, for—as Scala reported—"it was essential he should be a picked man and not drawn by lot, in view of the importance of the thing. It was put to the vote several times and met with very little success both in votes and words except for my own. It would perhaps have gone better if you had been there to encourage them." Since the *provveditore* had to be drawn by the 10th of that month, Scala wanted Giovanni to know what had happened—for the same reason that he later wanted Lorenzo de' Medici to know the results of the meetings—"so you can write to tell me if there is anything particular I should do beforehand."[33] The following year, in July, Piero di Niccolò Malegonnelle was elected *provveditore* instead of being drawn by lot. Giovanni de' Medici acted as his guarantor for the fine of 500 florins newly imposed on those who exercised the office with another salaried office at the same time and, when Piero incurred the fine by drawing an extra 3 florins a month for his office as captain of the Six of Arezzo, the Colleges rapidly absolved him, or rather his sponsor Giovanni de' Medici, from paying it.[34] In February 1463 it was decreed that the office of treasurer should be replaced by a bank of merchants and, in order to ensure the right decision was made without pressure being applied, the bank of Giovanni and Pierfrancesco de' Medici was to take over the office temporarily—providing not only "security for money deposits" but "amazing service and help in every daily occur-

---

[33] Letter of 4 September above: "era necessità fusse huomo scelto et non sortito per la inportanza della cosa. Andò a partito alcuna volta; hebbe pochissimo favore et di fave et di parole, se non quante ne feci io. Sarebbe forse ita di miglior voglia se cci fussi suto voi che havessi riscaldato. . . . Ho voluto ne siate avisato acciò che se vi paresse ch'io prima dovessi fare più una cosa che un'altra, me ne scriviate." Cf. his letter to Lorenzo de' Medici of 1 April 1473, p. 74 below. On measures to reform the Party, see ch. 7 below. On the work of the Sea Consuls, Mallett, "The Sea Consuls," pp. 156-169; and on the Six of Arezzo (for whose work the Guelf Party assumed responsibility in August 1460), *Statuta*, "Friburgi," 3:70-73. On Scala's pay rise for this extra work, ch. 7, n. 5 below.

[34] ASF *Capt. P. G.* 9 rosso, fols. 63r (21 July 1461), 65r-v (14-18 January 1462).

rence and eventuality." It was subsequently this bank that paid Scala's salary as chancellor.[35]

Scala also corresponded with Giovanni's elder brother Piero about Guelf Party business. Piero had been confirmed as one of the six supervisors of the rebuilding of the Guelf Party palace in November 1459 when Scala was elected its chancellor, and their first meeting the following January was held in the Medici palace.[36] It was to Piero that Scala wrote in May 1464 (after Giovanni's death the previous year) concerning the dismissal of the chaplain of the Party for not reporting that the canons had left the chapel undecorated. The matter was being kept as secret as possible until Piero had decided what to do, and Scala told him he believed there was no harm in delaying a decision in order "to arrange the thing better."[37] When Piero was too incapacitated to retain this office in November 1465, his place was immediately filled by his son Lorenzo, who was scarcely seventeen years' old and under age. Scala was already in communication with Lorenzo about other matters[38] and by then the Guelf Party was no longer his concern. He had been appointed first chancellor of the republic in April 1465 and in that office he served Piero, and later Lorenzo, with unswerving devotion, as we shall see.

What was Scala's relationship with Cosimo de' Medici, father of Piero and Giovanni and guardian of Pierfrancesco, undisputed head of the family and unofficial ruler of Florence?[39]

[35] *Ibid.*, fol. 68r (8-9 February 1463): "non solo voi potere essere sicuro delle vostre pecunie quivi dipositate, ma anchora in ogni caso et bisogno che intervenisse . . . prestarvi maravigliose comodità et aiuti." Cf. *Conv. Soppr.* 95, 212, fol. 143 right: payment to Scala from Giovanni and Pierfrancesco de' Medici, "dipositari della partte guelfa."

[36] ASF *Capt. P. G.* 9 rosso, fol. 55r-v.

[37] Letter to Piero de' Medici of 31 May 1464, ASF *MAP* 17, 415: "per acconciare la cosa meglio."

[38] See the postscript to his letter to Lorenzo of 31 December 1463, ASF *Strozz.* ser. 1, 136, fol. 55. On Lorenzo's appointment "loco Petri eius patris impediti," ASF *Capt. P. G.* 9 rosso, fol. 75v (28 November 1465).

[39] Apart from work at present being done on Cosimo, there is a judicious summary of his position in the state in Rubinstein, *Government*, pp. 128-135; cf. Brucker, *Renaissance Florence*, New York 1969, pp. 119-125; on his

"That most divine man" Scala called him in 1463; after his death in 1464, "this man to whom I owe everything," "whom I am accustomed to call a human God"; in the 1490s, "Father of our country, who embraced me and received me into the service of his family."[40] Of course Scala flatters and idealizes, like everyone else, but his protestations of devotion suggest a close bond: what exactly had Cosimo done to deserve them? As head of the Medici family, Cosimo must have approved his appointment as Pierfrancesco's secretary, perhaps accepting his friend Angelo Acciaiuoli's commendation or seeing in him an instrument for his own advantage. Scala took him messages from Pierfrancesco, and Pierfrancesco suggested Scala should discuss his troubles with Cosimo in 1460. Possibly as a result of this, Cosimo invested 500 florins in the Monte Commune for Scala. Although it was described by Scala in his tax returns as a gift "for his life and for the lives of his sons and descendants," Cosimo—with more shrewdness than generosity—merely credited him in his tax return with the shares in the Monte and interest on them for Scala's lifetime, after when "both the credit and the interest" were to revert to the Medici.[41] Whatever the imme-

---

banking interests, de Roover, *Banco Medici*, with pertinent comments in Molho, *Florentine Public Finances*, esp. pp. 187-190, 218-219; on his relationship with condottieri, C. C. Bayley, *War and Society in Renaissance Florence*, Toronto, 1961, pp. 120-124, 227; and in general there is useful material in the biographies of Fabroni and Gutkind, and in Pellegrini, *Sulla repubblica fiorentina*.

[40] Letter to Lorenzo de' Medici, 31 December 1463 (ASF *Strozz.* ser. 1, 136, fol. 55: "divinissimi viri avi tui Cosmi"); preface to the *Collectiones Cosmianae* (Laur. MS 54, 10, fol. 4v: "ego vero omnia huic viro debeo"); letter to Agostino Dati (Dati, *Opera*, fol. 138r: "quem ego humanum Deum appellare sum solitus") and letter to Angelo Poliziano (Poliziano, *Opera*, p. 394; "pater patriae nostrae me complexus est, recepitque in familiae obsequia"). Cf. also his poem "In figuram Cosmi," *Carmina illustrium poetarum italorum*, 8: 489, his dialogue *De legibus*, ed. L. Borghi, p. 273, and his apologue "Sapientia," *Apologi centum*, ed. C. Muellner, p. 27. On eulogies of Cosimo in general, see my article, "The Humanist Portrait," esp. pp. 200-204.

[41] ASF *Catasto* 923, fol. 290r: "In sul Monte fl.500 di Monte donò Chosimo de' Medici a messer Bartolomeo sopradetto a vita sua e de' sua figliuoli e discendenti"; and ASF *Catasto* 924, fol. 310r: "Messer Bartolomeo Schala è creditore di fl. 500 di Monte e mentre che vive avere le paghe e dopo la morte sua torna questi a la chasa el credito e lle paghe."

diate purpose of this money, it established Scala unequivocally
as the "servant of the Medici house" he described himself as
in 1461, and when Cosimo died in 1464 Scala was included as
one of the household, with fourteen yards of cloth given to
him to wear for the funeral in San Lorenzo.[42]

No letters survive between the two men, and there is no evidence that Cosimo ever gave any active political direction to
Scala as chancellor of the Guelf Party, leaving this to his sons.
We would be wrong, however, to dismiss their relationship as
no more than a business arrangement. Cosimo probably did influence Scala profoundly, but not until the end of his life and
then as much through his conversation as his money. About
a year before he died Cosimo apparently wanted to pass the
time by getting Scala, "chancellor in the palace,"[43] to read
Aristotle's *Ethics* to him, so he asked Donato Acciaiuoli to
organize his notes of Argyropoulos' lectures on the *Ethics*,
"and as he corrected them, Donato sent the notebooks along
to Cosimo and messer Bartolomeo read them out."[44] Vespasiano da Bisticci's account is substantiated by a writing of
Scala's, the *Dialogue of Consolation*, which he sent to the
young Lorenzo de' Medici after the death of his uncle Giovanni in 1463.[45] It purports to describe an actual conversation
that Scala—worried by Cosimo's health and state of mind—
held with him during one of Scala's many visits after Giovanni's death. Although it is a purely literary piece, its por-

[42] See the Inventory made by Piero de' Medici on his father's death, ASF
MAP 163, fol. 3r, ed. Fabroni, *Magni Cosmi . . . vita*, 2:255.

[43] Vespasiano da Bisticci, *Vite*, 3:74-75, "cancelliere in palagio." The
meaning of the phrase is discussed by Marzi, *Cancelleria*, pp. 238-239, who
suggests it implies Scala· was working in the chancery before his appointment as first chancellor in 1465 (rather than alluding to his subsequent
appointment, for which the normal phrase was "cancelliere *del*" not "*in*
palagio"). It may also refer to his unofficial position within the Medici
household. He is described in Piero's Inventory as "Cancellieri alla Parte
[Guelfa]."

[44] *Vite*, 3:75: "e secondo che Donato emendava, egli mandava i quinterni
a Cosimo e messer Bartolomeo leggeva," cf. della Torre, *Storia*, p. 407, n. 2.

[45] Laur. MS 54, 10, fols. 104r-122v. The *Dialogue* is discussed more fully
in ch. 10 below.

trait of the two men carries conviction and helps to throw light on the basis of their relationship.

In the *Dialogue* Cosimo plays the role of the Christian realist: a man weary with living and awaiting true happiness in the next life yet unwilling to succumb to inertia and depression; Scala the pagan Stoic. The antithesis between their positions is exaggerated, but it is supported by enough contemporary evidence to suggest a basis of truth.[46] Reflecting as it must do some actual discussions between the two men, it also reveals their shared interest in speculative philosophy and practical politics. Nothing unusual in that, perhaps, in an age of philosophizing merchants.[47] But beneath Cosimo's suave exterior lay a shrewd and hard-headed politician, and it is difficult to believe that the conversation of his last years did not contain as much practical as speculative wisdom, which the young Scala was privileged—and surely intended—to hear.

Cosimo's contemporaries emphasized his speculative wisdom, and we are told that he liked nothing better than to philosophize about such topics as whether statutory law was subject to moral philosophy or was itself a part of philosophy, or whether it was better to be the ruler of an army or a republic. He suggested both for discussion when interrupted in *tête-à-*

[46] See, for example, the portrait of Cosimo in Poggio Bracciolini's dialogue *On the Misery of the Human Condition* (*Opera omnia*, 1:86-131, esp. 103), and in Bartolomeo Platina's *De optimo cive* (ed. F. Battaglia, Bologna, 1944, pp. 179-236), or the combination of introspection and practicality in Vespasiano da Bisticci's account of Cosimo's interview with Eugenius IV (*Vite*, 3:45-46, quoted and discussed by Gombrich, "The Early Medici as Patrons of Art," *Norm and Form*, pp. 37-38), and in Ficino's account of Cosimo's sympathy with Xenocrates' description of the misery and imbecility of old age, in his *Liber de morte*, which he immediately belied by the vigor with which he demanded an instant translation of the book before he died (della Torre, *Storia*, pp. 560-561). On his interest in pagan philosophy, see Ambrogio Traversari's dedication to him of his translation of Diogenes Laertius' *Lives* (Venice, 1475), Ficino's preface to him "in primos decem Dialogos [Platonis]," ed. Kristeller, *Supplementum*, 2:103-105, and to Lorenzo "in Plotinum," *Opera omnia*, 2:1537; cf. della Torre, *Storia*, p. 457; also Scala's preface to the *Collectiones Cosmianae*, Laur. MS 54, 10, fol. 3r. On Scala's "paganism" and Stoicism, see ch. 13 below.

[47] On the rationalistic and pragmatic ethos of the merchant ruling class in Florence, see Bec, *Les Marchands écrivains*, esp. pp. 301-330.

têtes with other friends by the philosopher Iohannes Argyropoulos.[48] What we are not told is what he was discussing with Otto Niccolini, a lawyer, teacher and prominent Medicean, or Nicodemo Tranchedini, the pro-Medicean ambassador of the duke of Milan, when Argyropoulos arrived. More of the drift of Cosimo's thought is revealed by the fact that he supported his argument for preferring the rule of republics to armies by quoting from memory various ancient authorities, including Cicero: "especially from the sixth book of the *Republic*, quoting sentences word for word as if he were not reciting them from memory, but reading them from the book itself."[49] By the sixth book of Cicero's *Republic* is meant the well-known *Dream of Scipio*, in which Cicero reproduces Plato's argument in the *Phaedrus* for the immortality of the soul.[50] Preoccupied as he was with his forthcoming death, it would have provided Cosimo with much inspirational reading, especially its offer of "a special place in the heavens" and "an eternal life of happiness" to all those who had "preserved, aided or enlarged their fatherland," as surely Cosimo had done. In this dream Scipio Africanus told his son that the whole state would turn to him in recognition of his political virtues: "The senate, all good citizens, the allies, the Latins, will look to you: you shall be the sole support of the State's security, and in brief, it will be your duty as dictator to restore order in the commonwealth, if only you escape the wicked hands of your kinsmen."[51] Just before he died Cosimo apparently delivered

[48] See Vespasiano da Bisticci, *Vite*, 3:67-68; and Rinuccini's preface to Cosimo of his translation of Plutarch's *Consolation to Apollonius*, *Lettere ed orazioni*, pp. 61-62; cf. della Torre, *Storia*, pp. 398-399.

[49] Rinuccini, *Lettere ed orazioni*, p. 62: "tum praecipue in sexto *De Republica* libro, sententias ita ad verbum referres, ut eas non ex memoria repetere, sed ex ipso libro legere videreris."

[50] Cf. Cicero, *Tusculan Disputations*, 1.22.53: "Ex quo illa ratio nata est Platonis, quae a Socrate est in Phaedro explicata [*Phaedrus*, 245 C] a me autem posita est in sexto libro de re publica." The *Somnium Scipionis* from bk. 6 was the only part of the *De republica* known (apart from fragments in St. Augustine) until the nineteenth century.

[51] *De republica*, 6.12-13 (Loeb trans.); cf. also the fragment 6.1.1. According to A. J. Festugière ("Les thèmes du Songe de Scipion," *Eranos Rudbergianus*, Gotenburg, 1946, pp. 370-388), the Dream was original and

a similar homily to his son Piero, telling him that his justice, piety and care for his *patria* would be rewarded with a life of eternal happiness: "So please God, in whose hands are states and their rulers and princes, who are considered vicars of the gods on earth, that when a little later he will order you to return to a truer and more lasting home, as he is now recalling me . . . you will obey confidently and joyfully."[52]

It is, of course, difficult to isolate the practical from the speculative: Cosimo the calculating merchant and politician must have hoped his achievement as a statesman would secure him more certain immortality than his practices in the world of business and politics, and he would for this reason have been impressed by the argument of the *Phaedrus* and the *Dream of Scipio*, as well as by the writing of the *prisci theologi* propounded by Gemistus Pletho in Florence and later by Ficino. Not all his fellow citizens would have been prepared to view Cosimo, and even less Piero, as one of God's vicars on earth, however, and yet this was clearly the role that Cosimo—and subsequently Scala—assumes for them.

As secretary and confidant to Cosimo and his family, Scala was filling the place left empty by the death of Marsuppini ten years earlier. Marsuppini had once been secretary and tutor to Lorenzo, Cosimo's brother, as Scala later was to his son. He won the Chair of Oratory and Poetry in the university in Florence through the influence of the Medici, and later became pro-Medicean chancellor of the republic.[53] Like Scala, he was given shares in the Monte by the Medici and he, too, was appointed a secretary and secret councillor of the duke of Milan.[54] When he died, the Medici were personally respon-

---

specifically Roman "en attribuant l'immortalité aux âmes des grands politiques qui ont voué toutes leurs forces à la patrie," a view of possibly Stoic derivation also held by Varro (pp. 371-372).

[52] It is described by Scala in a letter to Lorenzo and Giuliano de' Medici after the death of their father in 1469, BNF MS Magl. VIII, 1439, fols. 74v-76r.

[53] On Marsuppini, ch. 1, n. 35 above.

[54] On his Monte shares, ASF *MAP* 161, fol. 12r (inventory of Cosimo and Lorenzo de' Medici's *credita Montis*, submitted by Cosimo on 28 January

sible for having his epitaph written, the Milanese ambassador reporting to Francesco Sforza that on his death "it seems to Cosimo he has been left alone, having lost so great a man."[55] There are many parallels between Marsuppini's career and Scala's, and Cosimo may well have seen in Marsuppini's pupil a fit successor to his former friend and political ally.

Scala was not living in the Medici palace during the last year of Cosimo's life but he was evidently a constant visitor there; he heard his dying speech to Piero, and was included as a member of the Medici household for Cosimo's funeral on 2 August 1464. What began as a business relationship ended as a personal friendship, "for as you know" he later wrote to Cosimo's grandchildren, "he was deeply fond of me and I was devoted to that man and admired him greatly."[56] After his death Scala compiled a volume of writings dedicated to Cosimo or written in his praise, the *Collectiones Cosmianae*. As if it were a *festschrift* collected by a devoted pupil for his master, Scala intended this volume to express his gratitude to the man to whom he "owed everything."[57] He sent the volume to Lorenzo, either soon after Cosimo's death or after Piero's death

1441): "Item unum creditum flor. 640 Montis Communis cantans sub nomine et nominibus dictorum Cosme et Laurentii, quod creditum dixit et asseruit dictus Cosma spectare et pertinere in veritate ad alium, videlicet, ad Carolum domini Gregorii de Aretio." Marsuppini subsequently invested fl.2,000 in the Pisa branch of the Medici bank when the Medici reduced their investment in it by this amount to fl.2,000 (de Roover, *Banco Medici*, p. 397). On his appointment in Milan, Santoro, *Gli uffizi*, p. 4 (on Scala's, *ibid*., p. 11). This was evidently not an *ex officio* privilege enjoyed by all Florentine chancellors.

[55] On his epitaph, Francesco Aretino to Piero de' Medici (19 July 1459), ASF *MAP* 14, 47; Zippel, *Carlo Marsuppini*; and Lazzari, *Ugolino e Michele Verino*, pp. 14-15, n. 3. Boccaccino's letter to Fr. Sforza is ed. Magnani, *Relazioni private*, p. iii: "Ad Cosmo pare esser rimasto solo, havendo perduto tanto huomo."

[56] BNF MS Magl. VIII, 1439, fol. 73r: "me enim, ut vos scitis, vehementer amavit, atque ego virum illum et colui et sum admiratus."

[57] Laur. MS 54, 10, fol. 4v: "aliqua saltem ex parte officio meo, quoniam vero omnia huic viro debeo, satisfecerem." On this volume, to which I was introduced many years ago by Sir Ernst Gombrich, see my article, "The Humanist Portrait," esp. pp. 186-187.

in 1469.[58] It was apparent when Cosimo died that Piero would not long survive his father and that the succession would soon pass to Lorenzo, "the hope of the city," and Scala must have hoped that as well as expressing his gratitude to the Medici, his volume would also serve as a memorial to Cosimo by teaching his example to the young Lorenzo. Scala never wrote the biography he planned to write of Cosimo;[59] but the frequency with which he referred to him throughout his life in innumerable different contexts makes it plain how deeply he was influenced by this austere man, who subsequently came to represent for him Plato's ideal philosopher ruler, as powerful as he was wise.[60]

[58] Sabbadini ("Briciole umanistiche: B. Scala," *GSLI* 50, 2 (1907):59-60) dates it "circa 1470" on account of Scala's prefatory letter describing Lorenzo as the "urbis spei" and referring to his "maximas occupationes," whereas P. G. Ricci ("Una consolatoria inedita del Marsuppini," *Rinascita* 3 (1940):365, n. 1) thinks its "tono complessivo" and absence of all reference to Giuliano suggests a date between 1478-1492. However, Lorenzo is described as "urbis spes" by Landino in a letter dated as early as 1465-1466 (in Bandini, *Specimen*, 1:109, dated by Marzi, *Cancelleria*, pp. 240-241; cf. Naldo Naldi to Lorenzo, 23 January 1464, Fabroni, *Magni Cosmi . . . vita*, 2:237), and it was of course a commonplace in a preface to refer to one's patron's many occupations. The writing and contents of the MS suggest it was prepared soon after Cosimo's death (also the fact that the material was presumably collected while Scala had easy access to the Medici library; and that it excludes the consolation Scala apparently wrote on Cosimo's death, see BNF MS Magl. VIII, 1439, fol. 74v: "in Consolatione, quae de morte Cosmi a nobis edita est"). Since the prefatory letter is written on a detached page, it could have been written and added later.

[59] See the preface to his *Vita Vitaliani Borrhomaei*, p. 7, and the preface to the *Collectiones*, Laur. MS 54, 10, fols. 3r, 4r.

[60] Cf. ch. 11 below.

CHAPTER III

Medicean Chancellor of Florence

They listen to every word he utters and are eager for his advice, which they follow closely. He is body and soul to Piero the Magnificent, and his Magnificence has put him where he is. *Sacramoro Sacramori to Galeazzo Maria Sforza, 1469*[1]

The death of Cosimo de' Medici at the beginning of August 1464 was followed only eight weeks later by the death of the chancellor of Florence, Benedetto Accolti.[2] For the whole of that winter the chancery worked without an official head until finally, in April the following year, 1465, Bartolomeo Scala was appointed first chancellor in his place. It has been suggested that Scala was working in the chancery in an unofficial capacity for this period, but it seems more likely that the appointment of a successor to Accolti was delayed by the political confusion caused by Cosimo's death and the ensuing economic crisis, as well as by the threat of plague, which kept citizens out of Florence during the winter months. This was the excuse given for the delay in deciding how to honor Cosimo after his death, and it may also have caused discussions on the chancery to be adjourned until the spring.[3] Finally, on 24 April 1465, Bartolomeo Scala emerged publicly as the successful candidate.[4]

Scala's supporters had not been idle in the preceding months. Foremost among them was Angelo della Stufa, who wrote to Piero de' Medici on 15 December 1464: "I have just received a note from one of the Signoria, a very close friend of mine, who—knowing how keenly I favor Bartolomeo Scala—informs me that this morning all the 'academicians' of the Greek Argyropoulos and others met to support him for the chancery." If this came about, Angelo continued, "we would be

---

[1] See n. 20 below.

[2] Accolti died on 26 September 1464, Marzi, *Cancelleria*, p. 231.

[3] *Ibid.*, p. 239; "Acta Decemvirorum" from the *Collectiones Cosmianae*, ed. Fabroni, *Magni Cosmi . . . vita*, 2:257. The series of bankruptcies which started in November 1464 and gave "grandissimo travaglio alla nostra città" are described by Rinuccini, *Ricordi storici*, pp. xciv-xcv; on the political situation at this time, Rubinstein, *Government*, pp. 139-140.

[4] Rinuccini, *Ricordi storici*, p. xcvi.

beside ourselves." He could not imagine Scala would face any competition, but he wanted Piero to appreciate the support he had received, so that any competition there was could be removed and Piero could devote the necessary time to his plan, "which is right, both on account of his ability—etc."[5]

This letter is invaluable. In the first place it tells us—what perhaps we might have guessed—that Piero de' Medici was planning to get Scala appointed chancellor several months before April 1465: Scala had been living in the Medici household, had been broken in for the work of chancellor in the Guelf Party and, if one is correct in seeing him as Marsuppini's successor in Cosimo's confidence, was probably intended by Cosimo to become first chancellor one day. Far more important is the information that Scala was independently supported by another group of men, academics, not politicians. These were the men who had already shown their respect for Scala's ability in commending him to Francesco Filelfo in 1454, members of leading Florentine families like the Acciaiuoli and the Alamanni, who were by no means fervent Mediceans. They may have attended Scala's classes on Virgil in 1460 and would certainly have heard about them, and their esteem for Scala was clearly inspired by intellectual rather than political considerations. It goes far to counteract the impression created by the comment of Alamanno Rinuccini (or later that of Francesco Guicciardini, then disillusioned with the Medici regime) that Scala was "unworthy of such an honor."[6]

---

[5] ASF *MAP* 17, 117: "In questo punto ho una poliza da uno de' S[ignori], molto intimo mio, il quale sappiendo quanto sono desideroso del fatto di messer Bartolomeo Schala, m'avisa chome questa mattina sono stati tutti gl' achademici del grecho Argiropolo e altri a ffare operatione per lui per la chancelleria. E bene che mi paressi che in tutto, quando avessi luogho, noi fussimo fuori di noi e che io non potessi credere potessi avere alchuno chonchorso, pure te n'ò voluto avisare, acc[i]ò che tu possa intendere il favore a questo e se à fondamento alchuno, e che quello avessi si lievi via, e che tu metta quel tempo debbi nella impresa tua, la quale è giusta e per la virtù sua, etc. . . ." I owe my knowledge of this important letter, and the transcription, to the generosity of Dott. Gino Corti. Angelo della Stufa's close friend in the Signoria was probably Giovanni di Lorenzo Benci, subsequently Scala's father-in-law, Cambi, *Delizie*, 20:390-391.

[6] *Ricordi storici*, p. xcvi: "benchè non degno di tanto onore."

Not that hostile comment was lacking at the time, but it came from the lively and irreverent pen of Luigi Pulci and other disappointed Medici clients rather than from the *ottimati*. On the very day that Braccio Martelli wrote to tell Lorenzo de' Medici of Scala's appointment,[7] Pulci wrote to congratulate Lorenzo on being prevented by his absence from helping "in his newly confirmed petition him with whom the friend of the Valdarno del Corno wanted to enter the garden of the Borromei by means of the walls, or indeed with whom he prunes the vine-arbors when he cannot reach them by foot with his pruning hook." He plays allusively on the words *scala* (a ladder), and *pennatuzzo* (a pruning hook or quill pen), to refer to Scala's appointment as chief letter writer of the republic. As the son of a miller himself, he resented the success of the "gouty, blundering, ingratiating" Scala: "truly, when times are hard, it's a good thing to be a miller, because by means of flour one can do many things. . . . May flour live for ever, world without end. . . . I will become a miller . . . I shall tread the path from Colle. . . . If I were to go on writing until tomorrow, I could write of nothing but flour and flour again."[8]

No evidence of Scala's appointment survives in official records, but the fact that many years later, on 22 March 1483, he was reappointed for five years from "the 24th of April" that year appears to confirm the date given by Alamanno Rinuccini as the day of his appointment, which would normally run meticulously for so many years from the day it was first made.[9] There is other internal evidence that April

[7] 27 April 1465, ed. I. del Lungo, *Gli amori del Magnifico Lorenzo*, Bologna, 1923, p. 41, and in *Nuova antologia*, ser. 5 (May-June 1913): 13: "Tu arai inteso . . . messer Bartolomeo Scala avere vinto tutto e di già exercitare l'officio." Lorenzo had left Florence on 19 April at the latest to attend the marriage of Ippolita Sforza in Milan, and was at Bologna on 21 April, Rochon, *La Jeunesse*, p. 102, n. 37.

[8] 27 April 1465, *Morgante e lettere*, ed. De Robertis, pp. 935-937, referring to Scala's "scappucciate, gl'inchini, le 'nvenie, i sergeri." On Pulci, Scala and the Medici, see S. S. Nigro, *Pulci e la cultura medicea*, Bari, 1972, esp. p. 10 and bibliography.

[9] ASF *Tratte Deliberazioni Append.* 2, fol. 45r-v. According to the early seventeenth century Priorista of Raffaello Calamari, however, Scala

saw the beginning of a new era in the chancery.[10] And on 10 May 1465 Scala was replaced as chancellor of the Guelf Party by Cristoforo Landino, "as a result of the vacancy at present caused by the recent appointment of messer Bartolomeo Scala, our former chancellor, to the office of First Chancellor of our Signoria."[11] Eighteen months later advantage was taken of the Balìa appointed after the failure of the Pitti conspiracy to confirm Scala in office, although his first appointment had not yet expired: paying tribute to his ability, reliability, wide learning and success so far, and admitting the difficulty of finding someone with the right combination of qualities for the office, the preamble to the decree hoped that by confirming him in office for a long period he would be able to do even better by devoting himself entirely to the service of the republic. Swept

<hr>

was elected on 4 April 1465 (BNF MS II, VI, 86, p. 348), but "24" may be intended. The only other reference to his appointment I have found is in an index in ASF *Carte di Corredo* 45, fol. 1r: "Notarii et Cancellarii servientes aliquando in Palatio incidenter reperti: Cancellarii Dominorum: D. Bartholomeus Scala—1465."

[10] In ASF *Carte di Corredo* 64 (a notebook listing letters written by the Signoria, edited by M. del Piazzo, *Protocollo*), letters dated 19 September 1464 to 9 April 1465 are marked off and numbered separately (fols. 42r-46r, see 44r: "99 lettere usque hic"). A new hand (A. Braccesi? cf. ASF *Leg. Comm.* 16, fol. 60v, subscribed with his name) first appears on 18 March 1465 (fol. 45r), again on 23 March, 3-5, 9 April (fols. 45v-46r) and consistently on and after 18 April (fols. 46r-60r; cf. also ASF *Signoria, Otto, Dieci, Missive,* 4, fols. 23-26, February-April 1465). There is also a hiatus in the series of *Missive* between 15 September 1464 and 20 April 1465 (vols. 44 and 45), an elegant copy later being made of letters written after 20 April (Munich, Staatsbibliothek, Clm 10781, fols. 101-261; cf. Kristeller, *Supplementum,* 1: xxxv-xxxvi; but not, as I previously suggested in "The Humanist Portrait," p. 210, n. 140, in Scala's autograph). Moreover, before leaving Florence Lorenzo de' Medici wrote to Peregrino Agli "sopra la substitutione del nuovo Canciellere et de' due coadiutori," ASF *MAP* 16, 177, ed. F. Flamini, *Peregrino Allio,* Pisa, 1893 (Nozze Cassin-D'Ancona), p. 21. So far evidence of Scala's appointment has not emerged from the records of the Monte, by then responsible for paying the chancellor's salary.

[11] ASF *Capt. P. G.* 9 rosso, fol. 71r: "per essere stato nuovamente assumpto messere Bartolomeo Scala proximo passato Cancelliere per le sue excellentissime virtù al uficio del primo Cancellieri de' nostri Magnifici et Excelsi Signori." Cf. also Scala's letters to N. Tranchedini of 5 October 1464 (about Guelf Party matters) and 29 July 1465 and later ("from the chancery"), Riccard. MS 834, fol. 108v, partly ed. Gentile, "B.S. e i Medici," p. 136, docs. 5-7.

in on the high Medicean tide of reaction, Scala was confirmed in office by the Balìa for the unprecedented period of ten years after the end of his present term of office.[12]

The same method was used to grant Scala citizenship and other privileges in 1471. On 13 September 1471, seizing the opportunity offered by the next extraordinary council or Balìa after that of 1466, Scala was granted full Florentine citizenship and the privilege of reelection by the Cento after discussion by the Signoria alone, who could also decide which communal offices he could hold as chancellor.[13] A month later the Signoria accordingly decided to allow him to exercise drawn internal but not external offices, as well as prestigious embassies for which he might be elected—relieving him only of the tedious administrative jobs that exiled citizens to outlying parts of the Florentine state.[14] Thanks to the citizenship he had been granted, he rapidly became eligible for the highest political offices in the city and, as we shall see, was soon elected a prior and later Gonfalonier of Justice.[15] He was confirmed in office for another five years in 1483 and for another twenty-five years less than a year later, which must have been intended to be confirmation for life.[16] The fall of

---

[12] ASF Balìa 30, fol. 31r-v (decree of 3 October 1466). Scala was probably appointed for 3 years in the first instance as Accolti had been (itself a precedent, ASF Cento Delib. 1, fols. 15r (20 February 1459), 40r (27 February 1461; cf. Marzi, Cancelleria, p. 231). Scala's 10-year appointment was anticipated by the confirmation of Bartolomeo Guidi as notary of the Riformagioni for 10 years by the 1458 Balìa and equaled by that of ser Antonio Adami as notary of the Tratte for 10 years by the 1466 Balìa (Cento Delib. 1, fol. 57r, Marzi, Cancelleria, pp. 235-236). Before the creation of the Cento in 1458 the chancellor was appointed by the Signoria and Colleges for renewable periods of one year.

[13] Ed. C. Bartolini in Scala's Vita Vitaliani Borrhomaei, Rome, 1677, pp. 35-37.

[14] On 15 October 1471, referring to the authority granted to them on 13 September, ASF SS. Delib. sp. aut. 33, fol. 9r (cf. 34, fols. 88v-89r).

[15] In 1473 and 1486, see ch. 4, nn. 21, 112, below.

[16] ASF Tratte Delib. Append. 2, fol. 45r-v (22 March 1483); ASF SS. Delib. sp. aut. 36, fol. 88r (ed. Marzi, Cancelleria, p. 607, 15 January 1484: but according to a note in ASF Provv. 174, fol. 113r, not transcribed by Marzi with the rest of the text on p. 607: "facta fuit dicta confirmatio per dominos et collegia die 3 decembris 1483 pro annis xxv ut in libro de-

the Medici regime led to his dismissal on 28 December 1494, however, but he was recalled three days later to share his office with a co-chancellor, whom he outlived. He died in office on 14 July 1497 after serving as chancellor for thirty-two years, one year longer than his famous predecessor Coluccio Salutati.[17]

The scope of Scala's long office and the notable program of reform he introduced as chancellor are subjects for separate discussion.[18] His work was consistently directed towards creating a modern secretariat, capable of executing the orders of a centralized sovereign state with a new style of documents and organization. As such, it was primarily of administrative, rather than political, importance. Nevertheless there were, of course, political overtones to his work: a modern centralized secretariat could also serve the increasing autocracy of the Medici, and Scala's career was too closely associated with the Medici for him not to have reciprocated their favors. Inevitably, evidence is hard to come by, but it is important to discover what we can about the nature of this reciprocal relationship and Scala's position in Florentine society.

According to the ambassador of the duke of Milan, Sacramoro Sacramori,[19] writing nearly four years after Scala's appointment as chancellor, Scala was a man eminently worth the cost of cultivating, "because he is continually to be found in every government while the members of the Signoria change, as you know, and because he is a man of wisdom, as I have said. Even though he exercises no vote in the consultations and discussions they hold, they nevertheless listen to every

---

liberationum [fol.] 189"); cf. Rinuccini, *Ricordi storici*, p. cxxxvii. Scala was presumably confirmed in office in April 1478, but I have been unable to find any record of this. After the chancery reform of 1487-1488 he was confirmed in office "pro tempore quo durat tale suum officium," 22 January 1488, ASF *SS. Delib. sp. aut.* 36, fol. 138r-v, ed. Marzi, *Cancelleria*, p. 611.

[17] See ch. 5, n. 46 below.   [18] See chs. 6 and 7 below.

[19] On Sacramoro Sacramori (henceforth referred to simply as "Sacramori," to be distinguished from his nephew, Filippo Sacramoro de Menclotiis, "Filippo Sacramoro," subsequently Milanese ambassador in Florence), see L. Cerioni, *Diplomazia Sforzesca*, 1:220-221.

word he utters and are eager for his advice, which they follow closely." He continues: "He is body and soul to Piero the Magnificent and his Magnificence has put him where he is. He was brought up in the house of Count Filippo Borromeo. He wishes to know that he may be numbered among the other servants of your Excellency. A good word I could show him from you would make him all the keener."[20] Sacramori returned to the subject of "that messer Bartolomeo Scala, Chancellor of the Signoria" only five days later, as we shall see. His first description of Scala, however, identifies the two important themes of Scala's life: his institutional importance in Florence as the one stable person in the government, and (vital to the duke of Milan) his political position as a devoted Medicean.

Piero de' Medici was already a sick man when his father died, and later he played even less part in the public life of the city.[21] Exercising influence, as he must have done, from behind the closed doors of the Medici palace (where Scala

[20] Sacramori to G. M. Sforza (7 January 1469), ASMi SPE Fir., 276: "A la quale per stravaganza me occorre significarly che l'ha qui uno gran partexano et servidore: et è homo da bene et da farne gran capitale et vale el pretio: cioè el Cancell[er]o de questa Excelsa Signoria, che per trovarsi continuo in omne regimento et muta de Signori, come sa Quella, et per essere luy savio, come ho ditto, etiam ch'el non habbia a rendere fava in le consultationi et raxonamenti fanno, tamen li guardano molto a la boccha et intendono volontera soi pareri, et molto li seguitano. Col Magnifico Piero l'è anima et corpo, et sua Magnificentia l'ha messo ly; allevòssi a Millano in caxa del C[onte] Filippo Bonromeo. L'è desyderoso de intendere ch'el sia connumerato in el numero de li altri servituri de Vostra Excellenza. Una bona parola che io li possa una volta mostrare de Quella lo farrà tanto più ardente."
[21] See Angelo Acciaiuoli's description of Cosimo and Piero in letters to Francesco Sforza on 12 July 1464, Rubinstein, *Government*, p. 136, n. 3. In consultative meetings in 1469 Piero was referred to as "the absent senator" whose opinion had nevertheless to be canvassed (ASF *Cons. Prat.* 60, fols. 77r, 83v, 25, 29 June and 2 September 1469; cf. *Cons. Prat.* 56, fol. 123r, 5 January 1461, when Piero "ait se ab his qui adsunt veniam petere si quemadmodum et alii consueverunt ipse ad dicendum non adsurrexerit. Notam enim esse omnibus illis egritudinem suam per quam stantem coram illis loqui omnes impediri illum intelligant"). On Piero's offices in Florence, Pieraccini, *La stirpe*, 1:52; Cambi, *Delizie*, 14: 307; 20: 268; Rubinstein, *Government*, pp. 238, 271, 274, 284; in general, Rubinstein, *Government*, pp. 136-173.

was already a familiar figure), Piero would have found Scala an invaluable link with the Palazzo della Signoria, where business was officially conducted. No wonder Sacramori describes him as Piero's "body and soul." Even before Scala was confirmed as chancellor after the Pitti conspiracy, Piero installed him in a rent-free house in Via Larga where he lived for three years: Medicean chancellor for all to see, as Scala himself recognized when he later reminded Piero he had been given the house in exchange for his support.[22]

Scala's two surviving letters to Piero give no idea of his relationship with him at this time.[23] Most of his business would have been discussed without record, but it is safe to assume that Scala would have given him the sort of information about letters, elections and meetings he later confided in Lorenzo de' Medici, in return conveying Piero's wishes to the appropriate officials and seeing that they were acted upon. In a glimpse Nicodemo Tranchedini gives us of Scala in 1468, we find him firmly supporting Piero in an argument about Florence's newly acquired fortresses of Sarzana and Sarzanella. In the face of Galeazzo Maria Sforza's opposition, Piero told Tranchedini that it was not worth wasting breath in discussing the matter, for he had to do what pleased the people in order to retain the favor Cosimo had won from them, "in the light of which he and the others of his family lived."[24] When Tranchedini approached Scala, "and told him all I had said to Piero, urging him to be responsible for advising Piero to do something for appearances' sake, he gave me exactly the same reply, that this was not a matter for discussion, and that if

---

[22] See ch. 9, n. 12 below.

[23] 31 May 1464 and 12 September 1469, ASF *MAP* 17, 415 and 137, 283. In his letter to Lorenzo de' Medici of 31 December 1463 (ASF *Strozz*, ser. 1, 136, fol. 55) he refers to Piero as "patrono et domino meo."

[24] N. Tranchedini to G. M. Sforza (24 July 1468), ASMi SPE Fir. 275: "cum el lume del qual viveva lui e gl' altri de casa sua." Florence acquired the fortresses from Lodovico Fregoso for fl.37,000. On Tranchedini, Milanese ambassador in Florence from 1453 to 1468, Cerioni, *Diplomazia Sforzesca*, pp. 242-243; and the bibliography in E. Lazzeroni, "Il Viaggio di Federigo III in Italia," *Atti e memorie d. 1° Congresso Storico Lombardo*, Milan, 1937, pp. 327-328, n. 174.

Piero did discuss it, he would forfeit all the credit and good will he enjoyed." The following day Piero repeated his opinion "with pungent words" and Tranchedini, admitting he understood the popular sentiment, allowed the matter to drop.[25]

Later that year we again find Piero de' Medici and Scala collaborating, along with Angelo della Stufa, this time in support of Milan. All three men were thought by the Milanese to have played an important part in winning for Milan the aid it asked for, Angelo della Stufa by playing a leading part in a special meeting "as one of us slaves and servants of your Excellency would do," Scala by writing a confidential letter to Sacramori about their final decision, and Piero by engineering this "with considerable dexterity."[26] Ever since Cosimo de' Medici had drawn Florence from its long-standing allegiance to Venice by his close friendship with Francesco Sforza, his regime had been closely associated with Milan and the Sforza, from whom it received military support in return for payments of money.[27] By contrast, the opposition to the Medici

[25] Letter of 24 July: "Di poi parlai cum el Canc[eller]o de la Comunità et dissili tucto quello ch'io havevo dicto cum el Magnifico Piero, strengendolo a doverlo confortare a piglare qualche forma in questo facto, qual mi respuxe quello medesimo, che questa non era cosa da raxonare, et che Piero raxonandone se perderia omni credito e benivolenza che ello havesse, ed è vero ch' io comprendo che questa cosa sia molto a chore a quello populo perchè li pare havere facto un bello acquisto"; letter of 25 July 1469, *ibid.*: "perseverando Piero in proposito," he said, "cum parole pungente che mai ve restituiriano quelle terre."

[26] On the political situation, in general *Storia di Milano*, 7:255-256; Pastor, *Storia dei papi*, 2:396-400; G. Nebbia, "La lega italica del 1455: sue vicende e sua rinnovazione nel 1470": *ASLomb.*, n.s. 4 (1939):124-125. On the *pratica* of 5 August "super tribus rebus quae a Duce Mediolani petuntur" (which Angelo della Stufa "è suso a menare," "e fàllo così volontera et de così perfetto core, come faressimo uno de nuy schiavi e servi de la Ex[cellentia] V[ostra]," N. Tranchedini and S. Sacramori to G. M. Sforza, 4 August 1468, ASMi, SPE Fir. 275), continued on 11 August, ASF *Cons. Prat.* 60, fols. 30r, 30v-31r. On Scala's contribution, see below; on Piero's, who "in specialità ha voluto che questa posta se tiri, et hàllo fatto cum bona destrezza," see the ambassadors' letter of 14 September 1468, ASMi, SPE Fir. 275.

[27] On the Medici/Sforza alignment, Rubinstein, *Government*, pp. 132, 154-155, 164, 176, and Soranzo, "Lorenzo il Magnifico," pp. 48-50. An idea of the basis of their relationship is given by Angelo Acciaiuoli's letter to

party drew its support from the old Venetian *entente*.[28] With
the Venetian ambassador busy canvassing support from citizens of every sort and kind in Florence, the question of how
far Florence should support Milan in its request for help was
bound to divide the principal political factions deeply. Meetings were held in August but no decision was taken until the
middle of September. Then, on the evening of the 13th, Bartolomeo Scala wrote to Sacramori in Latin (his language of
privacy): "the whole affair is concluded according to your
request. But it is very secret. However, you will be summoned tomorrow morning and will then know what has been
decided—and it will greatly please you. Farewell. At home,
the first hour of the evening." Without awaiting his sum-
mons in the morning, Sacramori attached this note to the letter he had already written to Galeazzo Maria Sforza and despatched it, in order not to delay the good news. The following day, as Scala predicted, he and Tranchedini were told that
they were fully supported by Florence, which would send an
ambassador to Venice at Milan's request.[29] Clearly this was a

---

Francesco Sforza referring to criticism of Florentine subsidies to Milan (3
June 1464, Milan, Bibl. Ambros. MS Z 247 sup., fol. 332): "et benchè qui
sia stato usato da alcuno cittadino dire noi non voglamo essere trebutarii
del Duca di Milano, nientedimeno quando alla S[erenità] V[ostra] paressi
che fussi più utile il darvi per 3 anni 50,000 fl. l'anno et che la Ex[cellen]tia
V[ostra] fussi obligata a darci tanti cavalli potrebbe essere che . . .".; cf.
Rubinstein, *Government*, p. 155 and n. 3.

[28] On the Venetian lobby after Cosimo's death, Rubinstein, *Government*,
pp. 154-155. The Florentine exiles were led by the Venetian *condottiere*
Bartolomeo Colleoni "with the tacit backing of Venice" in 1467-1468 (*ibid.*,
p. 173). On 7 August 1468 Tranchedini wrote that the Venetian ambassador
in Florence, Piero Morosini, "continuamente manda et pratica cum molti
citadini et de omne volere et sorte" (ASMi SPE Fir. 275). On an anti-
Venetian oration by Scala which may relate to this period, see ch. 4, n. 57
below.

[29] ASMi SPE Fir. 275: "Tota res conclusa est secundum petitionem tuam.
Sed in secreto magno est. Tu tamen cras mane vocaberis et quid sit deliberatum scies et vehementer placebit. Vale. Domi hora fere prima." The note
measures approx. 6″ x 4″ and has a covering note attached to the *verso*
which reads: "havendo già scripto questa el prenominato, D. Bartholomeo
nostro me ha mandato questa pollice. Pure perchè forsi induxiariano a
domane a sera et tempo vorrà a scrivere, havemo voluto avanzare uno dì

victory for the Milanese faction in Florence, to which Piero
de' Medici, Angelo della Stufa and Scala had all contributed.

It was at the beginning of the following year, on 7 January
1469, that Sacramori commended Scala to Galeazzo Maria
Sforza as worth the cost of cultivating. Five days later he commented that Scala was so devoted to the duke that "he almost
seems to exceed his office": "It seems to me my duty to make
him known to you, for he is as useful a friend as few others
one can have in this city, because he is a fixture as I wrote before. I have tested what he is good for and how much he can
—and does—help. He has many times besought me that, if
his trust and affection are such that he deserves to be numbered among the other servants of your Excellency, I should
merely tell you about him, and that more than that he does
not want. And this I have promised to do, telling him that I
hoped to be able to assure him in reply that I had done so."[30]
Galeazzo Maria must have made some appropriate reply, for
on 24 January Sacramori reported that "that letter and embassy to Jacopo Guicciardini and messer Bartolomeo Scala are
doing good work. Such men set great store by these things,
because they give them reputation among the people."[31]

perchè, como havemo dicto, pensamo che V[ostra] Ex[cellentia] stia in
grande expectatione," ASMi SPE Fir. 275 (13 September 1468). On the
14th, the ambassadors wrote: "determinano volere tutto quello che Vostra
Ex[cellentia] vole senza alchuna contradictione," cf. n. 26 above. On Latin
as Scala's language of privacy, see, e.g. letters of 30 August 1475, 26 August
1476, 27 June 1477, [1]5 December 1479, 12 January 1480, etc., ASF *MAP*
32, 445; 33, 693; 34, 170, 420 and 414.

[30] S. Sacramori to G. M. Sforza (12 January 1469): ASMi SPE Fir. 276:
"Quello d. Bartholomeo Schala Cancellero de questa Exc[els]a S[ignoria] è
tanto de la V[ostra] Ex[cellen]tia che quasi pare exceda el suo offitio.
Parme mio debito farlo intendere a Quella, perchè l'è così utile amicho
quanto pochi se possano havere in questa ciptà, perchè è uno asso fermo,
como scripsi per altra mia. Ho provato quello ch'el vale et quanto el pò
giovare et giova. Hàmme molte volte pregato che se la sua fede et affectione
è tale che la meriti essere connumerata in li altri serviduri de V[ostra]
Ex[cellentia], che io *solum* fazzo relatione de lui a Quella, che altro non
vole. Et così li ho promesso fare, et dittogli che spero per qualche mia
resposta farlo certo haverlo fatto."

[31] To the same, 24 January 1469, *ibid.*: "Quella lettera et ambasciata a
Jacomo Guizzardini et d. Bartholomeo Schala fanno bone operationi. Et

It would surely have flattered Scala to have seen himself classed with Jacopo Guicciardini in this way. In fact there were other no less aristocratic Florentines who did not scruple to sell their services to Milan—Angelo Acciaiuoli, Tommaso Soderini and Jacopo's elder brother Luigi among them.[32] Above all there was Angelo della Stufa who also worked for the duke of Milan.[33] He played an important part in Scala's life and was perhaps more responsible than any one else for engineering Scala's rise to power. He wrote to Piero de' Medici about the appointment of a new chancellor of the Guelf Party in 1459 and, although he does not mention Scala in his letter, as one of the captains of the party at the time he may have been responsible for putting Scala's name forward. He

---

quisti tali se piglono molto cum queste cose, perchè a loro daghono reputatione in questo populo."

[32] A list of regular payments made to Angelo Acciaiuoli, 1453-1460 (c. fl.100 or fl.200 a month depending on whether he was in Milan or not) is in Milan, Bibl. Ambros. MS Z 247 sup., fols. 355-356; cf. *Dispatches . . . of Milanese Ambassadors in France and Burgundy, 1450-1483*, ed. with transl. P. M. Kendall and V. Ilardi, Ohio, 1970, 1: xlii. On Galeazzo Maria Sforza's gift of 500 ducats to Tommaso Soderini in 1471, Soranzo, "Lorenzo il Magnifico," p. 73, n. 70. Sacramori wrote to Cicco Simonetta *à propos* Luigi Guicciardini (14 July 1470, ASMi SPE Fir. 279): "L'è bono el dinaro che megliora el soldo. Vedete che ha fatto fare quello benefitio a d. Loysio." In general, see Sacramori's letter of 11 January 1471 (ASMi SPE Fir. 281; cf. Soranzo, "Lorenzo il Magnifico," p. 72, n. 69: "Possono talvolta simili spese reportare utile grandissimo anchora che li siano cose triste et vituperose a chi riceve. Ma qui pare che non se vergognino troppo: havemo veduto quanto operi simile medicina cum D. Loysio Guizzardini. . . . El cancellero ha havuto de por si bona mano che è pocho piazuto le sue lettere nel Reame. De M. Agnolo de la Stufa non dico niente, ma l'è altro cervello et conditione de quella de costui" (on whom, see following note).

[33] On Angelo della Stufa's family and life, *Delizie*, 15: 318-328, and on his offices, *ibid.* 14: 308; 20: 255, 329, 332, 360, 407; 21: 6; Rubinstein, *Government*, p. 105, n. 2, pp. 240, 284, 300, 302, 310. On his initial diffidence about accepting 200 ducats from Sacramori, Sacramori to G. M. Sforza (27 October 1470, ASMi SPE Fir. 280): "feci resistentia assay a non li vollere et dimostrò più presto despiacere che appiacere de tal dono . . . Io li resposi et strinselo cum tale raxon[amento] che pur el se lassò consegliare." His close relationship with Milan is illustrated by many unpublished letters in the Milanese Archives, also by the story reported in *Angelo Polizianos Tagebuch (1477-1479)*, ed. A. Wesselsky, Jena, 1929, p. 10.

was thought by Scala to be willing to support his guild matriculation in 1461 as a servant of the Medici, and he was responsible for promoting Scala for the chancellorship in 1465. As
Sacramori put it with his usual bluntness, "Messer Bartolomeo
belongs completely to Angelo and is almost in part made by
him."[34] Favors need to be reciprocated, and in February 1469
Scala hinted to Sacramori, "as if off his own bat," that Angelo
della Stufa would like to return from his embassy in Milan
with a knighthood from Galeazzo Maria: "and it will be done
to give him reputation and put him in the front rank, being,
as he is, so dedicated and partial a servant." Despite Scala's
close relationship with Angelo, Sacramori continued: "I am
nevertheless of the opinion that what he said comes from
higher up, because when I jested with Angelo about it—at
long range, so to speak—by saying that it was quite something
to have this honor in this city [Florence], and other such re-
marks, he made no reply but pursed his lips. It could be, however, that I have made a false assumption."[35] Angelo della
Stufa was finally knighted by Galeazzo Maria in August 1470,
but his honor was confirmed by the councils in Florence with
the utmost difficulty—unlike that of his protégé, Scala, whose
knighthood from the pope Scala claimed, with justifiable
pride, was approved with overwhelming popular support.[36]

[34] See n. 35 below. Angelo's letter to Piero de' Medici about the appointment of the Guelf Party chancellor is in ASF *MAP* 17, 273 (16 October
1459).

[35] Sacramori to G. M. Sforza (24 February 1469, ASMi SPE Fir. 276):
"Fazzo pensiero che Agnolo da la Stufa forsi aspiri a questo [insegna de
militia] venendo a la Ex[cellentia] V[ostra], perchè messer Bartholomeo
Schala Canc[eller]o de questa Signoria raxonando como da luy cum mi, el
me tresse questo motto: El se vole che Agnolo nostro, che è tutto duchescho,
se ne torni honorato·de militia de là; et faràssi per el S[igno]re darli reputatione et fare ch'el sia de li primi feritori, essendo lui così sviserato et
parciale servidore como ello è. Et benchè ditto d. Bartholomeo sia tutto
de Agnolo et quasi fatto im parte da luy, pur ho oppinione che tal raxona-
mento venga de più inanci, perchè mottegiando io così da longe al ditto
Agnolo, che l'era assay in questa ciptà havere tale insegna, cum altri motti
aproposito, el non me respose, ma fece la boccha ridirezza. Potria anchora
essere ch'io prosumeria male."

[36] On Scala's knighthood, see ch. 4, n. 108 below. The diploma conferring
Angelo's knighthood is in *Delizie*, 15: 320-322, dated 12 August 1470. It was

Scala's knighthood lay in the future and he was hungry for honors now. One day he had Sacramori shown the privilege he had received from Ferrante, king of Naples, "in gratitude for which," Sacramori reported, "he showed considerable favor to his Majesty's affairs."[37] This must have been the document appointing him a royal councillor and secretary on 17 December 1467, which had been followed in June 1468 by a similar award from the king of France, Louis XI, appointing him a royal councillor.[38] "I pretended not to understand what he was getting at, because I did not want to have to give him a reply," Sacramori confessed. However, he sent a copy of Ferrante's privilege to Cicco Simonetta, suggesting that Ferrante may have been similarly spurred on to make this award by Scala's desire for honor and reputation. Describing him again as "a very decent and reputable person" from whom he sometimes extracted "an interpretation of the daily happenings here," Sacramori suggested that it would not be wasted effort to satisfy him, since it would cost nothing.[39] Accordingly, in

finally approved by all the councils on 5-10 October 1470, having been at first defeated in the Council of the People, ASF *Libri fabarum*, 69, fols. 55r-57v; cf. Salvemini, *La dignità cavalleresca*, p. 147, no. 24. On his difficulties, see Lorenzo de' Medici's letter to him of 5-6 October 1470 (*Lettere*, ed. R. Fubini, 1, no. 67: "si conosce manifestamente questo non essere proceduto per vostri cattivi [porta]menti o defecti, ma più presto per invidia"), D. Acciaiuoli to D. Pandolfini (23 October 1470, BNF MS Magl. VIII, 1390, fol. 55r-v: "equestri dignitate ornatus et, exceptus a civibus, honorificentissime urbem est ingressus"); Sacramori to G. M. Sforza (4 October 1470, ASMi SPE Fir. 280: "non so che s[ci]agura sia la sua, benchè molte cose concorrano a questo. . . . Concorre a questo principalmente la pocha gratia che ha d. Agnolo nel populo. . . . Concorre l'invidia de questi chavalleri . . . fin de torre a un tracto reputatione a d. Agnolo et molto più a Lorenzo, per saperse quanto l'è de sua Magnificentia").

[37] See n. 39 below.

[38] The diplomas are ed. Moreni, *Notizie istoriche*, 3:72-75; cf. Benvenuti, *Quadri storici*, pp. 80-81. Angelo della Stufa was also appointed a secret councillor by Ferrante, *Delizie*, 15:324-326 (24 October 1468).

[39] Sacramori to Cicco Simonetta (13 April 1469, ASMi SPE Fir. 276): "Ho *alias* scripto che uno de quilli de chi per le cose che a la giornata occorreno qui io cavo a le fiade constructo l'è questo d. Bartholomeo Schala cancellero di questa S[igno]ria, homo molto da bene et de bono credito per le raxone scripte al prefato Ill[ustrissi]mo S[ignore] nostro.

the following month, on 7 May 1469, Scala was awarded the
honor he had been angling for by being appointed ducal secretary and secret councillor, like a predecessor in the chancery, Carlo Marsuppini.[40]

Subsequent favors did cost Galeazzo Maria Sforza money.
In the year following Piero de' Medici's death in December
1469, the Milanese lobby underwent a period of decline, but
at the very moment when Florence seemed on the point of
signing a separate treaty of alliance with Ferrante of Naples
it activated itself and secured a Signoria favorable to its interests. On the eve of its election, Scala wrote a short note to
Sacramori from the Palazzo della Signoria: "I cannot leave the
palace where I have been all day. They have taken an excellent decision which will please you, and things will turn out
well and as we wanted. I will tell you tonight if not before.
And should you see Lorenzo first it would please me—not
saying, however, that you have heard anything from me."[41]
The following day a Signoria considered favorable to Lo-

L'è desyderoso de honore et reputatione. El Re, che forsi hebbe le medesime
informationi de luy che hora do io, li mandò uno privilegio del tenore che
la V[ostra] M[agnificentia] vederà per la inclusa copia, el perchè esso como
grato prestava favore assay a le cose de sua M[aes]tà . . . Et uno giorno el
me fece mostrare del ditto privilegio, demostrando per circuitione che
desyderaria essere nel numero de li honorati dal prelibato Ex[cellentissi]mo
S[ignore] n[ostro] del titulo de Secretariato. Io non li ho voluto dare
resposta, mostrando non intendere el fin perchè luy me ha ditto quanto el
me ha ditto. Pur ne ho voluto advixare la M[agnificentia] V[ostra] perchè
parendoli che la spesa non fosse inutile non costando, ella ne possa far
qualche parola."

[40] The decree is dated 7 May 1469 and is edited with the renewal of 1481
by Moreni, *Notizie istoriche*, 3:75-79; cf. Santoro, *Gli uffizi*, pp. 11, 50. In
contrast to Scala's, Marsuppini's appointment was "pro honore tantum et
dignitate."

[41] ASMi SPE Fir. 279. On the same day, 27 June 1470, Sacramori wrote
to Galeazzo Maria Sforza (ASMi SPE Fir. 279): "Racomando a V[ostra]
Ex[cellentia] D. Bartholomeo Schala, Canc[eller]o de questa Signoria, che
li soy deportamenti bony el merita." In the same letter he reported how
Lorenzo de' Medici, in the *pratica* held to discuss the situation, "saltò . . .
non da giovene nè da timido, ma da savio et sviserato de V[ostra] prefata
Celsitudine." In his list of members, he distinguishes those who "remained
alone" from Lorenzo's supporters.

renzo was elected, and on 30 June Galeazzo Maria thanked Lorenzo, Luigi Guicciardini and Bartolomeo Scala for the affection they had shown him, telling Scala: "Sacramoro of Rimini writes and replies to us daily about the affection you bear us and what you do and arrange on our behalf, for which we are indeed indebted to you."[42] On the 13th Scala's note to Sacramori was even more succinct: "Rejoice! Our league was reestablished on the 8th, with the greatest unanimity of the parties. Farewell."[43] Sacramori hastened to send it to Galeazzo Maria "for his greater satisfaction," Milan now being included in the league. Galeazzo Maria responded by asking Sacramori how to reward Scala for his pains, and on 25 July he sent Sacramori a bill of exchange for 200 ducats, suggesting that it would be tactful to present it to Scala as a contribution to the "certain farm or house" he had heard Scala was buying in which he wanted to have "a share" and that he was making this "small present with the intention of doing even better in the future."[44] Scala responded with courtly eloquence: "I am very happy and happier than ever before in my whole life, for I understand from Messer Sacramoro that I am favored by you not only with words but with deeds worthy of a magnanimous prince and most excellent lord. . . . You have

[42] G. M. Sforza to Scala (30 June 1470, ASMi SPE Fir. 279): "Sagramoro da Riminio ogni dì ne scrive et replica de la affectione che ne portate et quello che fate e operate a beneficio de le cose nostre, del che certo ve ne restamo obligati." In his letter to Lorenzo (*ibid.*) he refers to "la prudentia et animosità havete usata in questa deliberatione ultimamente presa per quelli Ex[cellentissimi] Signori" and his prudence, "abbrazando sempre caldamente le cose nostre."

[43] ASMi SPE Fir. 279: "Gaude. La Lega nostra a dì 8 è rifacta con grandissimo consenso delle parti. Vale": with Sacramori's covering letter, "et per più vostra satisfactione vi mando incluso el primo adviso che io ne hebbe, che fo dal nostro d. Bartholomeo Schala."

[44] G. M. Sforza to Sacramori (25 July 1470, ASMi SPE Fir. 279): "Volemo mo[do] che con bono modo tu daghi dicti dinari ad esso M. Bartholomeo et gli dighi che havendo nuy inteso como l'ha comprato certo podere o sia casa, gli volemo anchora nuy havere parte; et che gli facemo questo picolo presente con intentione de fare per l'advenire anchora meglio; et qui usaray quelle parole te parerano conveniente." The "farm" or "house" he refers to was probably a *podere* Scala bought in Scandicci in October 1470 for fl.600, ch. 9, n. 24 below.

a most faithful servant, of little worth but great trust, of little prudence, but great diligence and most fervent to work for the honor, reputation and glory of your Illustrious Lordship."[45] The diplomatic implications of Scala's part in this apparent *volte-face* will be discussed later,[46] but Sacramori later claimed that Scala had had to work so hard for the reward Milan gave him that his letters did not please the Neapolitans at all.[47]

Galeazzo Maria Sforza's gift was an appropriate one for Scala in 1470. At the beginning of 1468 he had married a six-teen-year-old Florentine girl, Maddalena Benci, daughter of a merchant selling wholesale drugs and spices, Giovanni di Lorenzo.[48] She brought with her a dowry of 1,000 florins and nuptial gifts of 200 florins, a good average dowry, but Scala was unable to withdraw money from the Monte and soon found himself in financial difficulties. In August 1469 he re-

[45] On 18 August 1470, ASMi SPE Fir. 279.

[46] See ch. 7 below. The outcome was not necessarily the victory for Milan that Scala tactfully presented it to be, since Milan never ratified the general league and peace treaty which was signed in Rome on 22 December 1470: it was rather a victory for Lorenzo de' Medici and his supporters to have persuaded Otto Niccolini not to desert the old Milanese alliance in favor of Naples and Venice.

[47] See n. 32 above.

[48] BNF MS II, IV, 378, p. 347; MS Magl. 26, 145 (Gabella de' Contratti), p. 123; and Manni, *Vita*, p. 11. On her father (Giovanni di Lorenzo di Giovanni di Taddeo) BNF MS II, IV, 378, pp. 345-349, notes from books belonging to his father Lorenzo and his sons Giovanni, Filippo and Tommaso; Cambi, *Delizie*, 20:391 (for Giovanni's priorate in 1464). Giovanni acted as procurator of the canon law teacher Felino Sandei of Ferrara, Giustiniani, *Alamanno Rinuccini*, p. 252, n. 4; D. Maffei, *Il giovane Machiavelli banchiere con Berto Berti a Roma*, Florence, 1973, p. 82, n. 85. Giovanni and Tommaso Benci were referred to by Ficino as "nostri conphilosophi"; they were the sons of the Lorenzo di Giovanni who wrote a poem of advice to Giovanni on how to get on in a warehouse or bank, Kristeller, *Supplementum*, 2:169, 1: cxxxi-ii, and *Studies*, pp. 170, 223; della Torre, *Storia*, p. 555; Flamini, *La lirica toscana*, pp. 543-544, n. 4. Bandini, *Cat. cod. lat.*, 5, col. 372, no. 17; col. 373, no. 28. They are related to, but not to be confused with, Giovanni d'Amerigo Benci (general manager of the Medici bank and a confidant of Cosimo de' Medici's, de Roover, *Banco Medici*, pp. 83-85, 44; Rubinstein, *Government*, p. 46, n. 4, pp. 245, 258, 269) and his son Amerigo, the friend and patron of Ficino, *Dizionario biografico*, s.v., della Torre, *Storia* pp. 542, 547, n. 1.

nounced an agreement to rent the half share of a house in San Casciano and at the same time he began to quarrel with his father-in-law about his wife's dowry.[49] Worse, he quarreled with Piero de' Medici about money. In the late summer of 1469 Piero assigned the lease of the house he had allowed Scala to live in without rent to the Bankers Guild.[50] Before leaving Scala raised the question of his expenses with the guild, evidently suggesting that he was entitled to reclaim the money he had spent on the house while living there, which he estimated at about 100 florins. To this the guild replied that it would find out from Piero what he wanted to be done. Immobilized at home with an injured foot, Scala was unable to visit Piero when word came from an acquaintance from Colle that Piero was displeased at his raising the subject of his expenses. Housebound, Scala hurriedly wrote to Piero in Careggi on 12 September to explain: "I told him that it couldn't be true [that Piero was displeased], since I had said or done nothing that you hadn't instructed me to do. But as I am unable to come and visit you, I thought I should write to you about it and remind you that whatever I have has been given to me by you and belongs entirely to you—even my life. The reason I spoke of the expenses was in case this concession should be given to others, since you told me you had given the house for one who supported you. However, I shan't say another word without first talking to you, unless you write to the contrary."[51]

In his 1469 Catasto declaration Scala claimed the house was too small for his family—which now consisted of his wife, a baby daughter, two brothers and a nephew from Colle—but

[49] See Marucell. MS A XVI, fol. 231r (13 September 1469); ASF *Notarile* C 525 (Angelo Cini, 1463-1475, the reference to which I owe to Miss Brenda Preyer), fols. 257v-259r; and Manni, *Vita*, pp. 12-14. On the house in San Casciano, ch. 9, n. 21 below.

[50] On 1 September 1469 the consuls of the guild decided "quod Arma et Insignia Artis predicte apponantur et apingantur in domum dicte artis ab extra positam in Via Largha in qua ad presens habitat dominus Bartolomeus Cancellarius Dominorum," ASF *Arte di Cambio*, 19, fol. 53v.

[51] 12 September 1469, ASF *MAP* 137, 283.

the tone of his letter suggests he was upset at having to leave at this juncture, particularly in view of his financial difficulties.[52] Piero died two and a half months later, leaving Scala economically and politically insecure, still anxious for money and honors. Lorenzo de' Medici was only twenty years old at the time and his "standard," Sacramori had predicted in March, could be upheld in Florence only with great difficulty.[53] But his standard was upheld, and with it, Scala's career. Adjusting himself to serve his young master as family confidant and friend, Scala finally achieved the security and political success he had so far lacked.

[52] ASF *Catasto* 923, fol. 290v: "perchè detta chasa è a nnoi pocha abitazione."

[53] Sacramori to G. M. Sforza (March 1469, postscript to "quella di xiiii," ASMi SPE Fir. 276): "et non senza gran faticha se potrà sostenere el segno de Laurenzo"; cf. his letter of 1 December 1468, *ibid*, Fir. 275: "*l'essere Laurenzo più giovene* [decoded] che non bisognaria," and the words of the cardinal of Rouen reported by Becchi to Lorenzo on 24 November 1470 (ASF *MAP* 61,30): "Disse, io vorrei che Lorenzo havesse xx de' miei anni, che que' canuti da Firenze temo che, etc." On Scala's financial position at this time, see ch. 9 below.

CHAPTER IV

Scala and Lorenzo de' Medici

Lorenzo de' Medici's famous saying about me is still current, in which he asserted that honor had never been better placed in a new man.
Scala to Angelo Poliziano, 1494[1]

Scala served Lorenzo de' Medici as chancellor of Florence for twenty-three years, a far longer period than he had worked with any other member of his family. Inevitably, their relationship changed within this period: the political novice of 1469 rapidly outgrew the tutelage of his father's and grandfather's confidant and Lorenzo must have found Scala's servility and ponderousness increasingly oppressive. Friends like Luigi Pulci and Angelo Poliziano doubtless encouraged him to laugh with them about the gouty and ingratiating Scala and, if we are to believe Poliziano, Lorenzo claimed to have accepted Scala on the basis of someone else's opinion rather than his own.[2] Maybe. As Lorenzo "hoisted his sails" ever higher in Florence,[3] he certainly would not have wanted to admit to being influenced by Scala. But there was more to their relationship than that.

Sacramori, with his usual acumen, put his finger on its true basis. Describing Scala as "a real supporter of Lorenzo's," he defined him as someone "who has, I believe, the measure of politics as well as any man in Florence, because he knows the secrets of the Florentines and is also extremely intelligent."[4]

[1] Poliziano, *Opera*, p. 394: "Extat et illa de me Laurentii Medicis praeclarissima vox, qua nusquam collocatum melius fuisse honorem homini novi testificatus est."

[2] Poliziano to Scala, 1494, see ch. 8, n. 78 below.

[3] S. Sacramori to G. M. Sforza, 3 October 1472 (letterbook), ASMi SPE Fir. 283: "Ma luy [Lorenzo] è de quella natura che *alias* ho scripto: astuto e de gran vedere è ello; ma troppo si reputa et troppo alza le vele per bonaza" (cf. his letter of 16 September, *ibid.*: "molto alza le sue vele quando gli pare havere vento prospero"). Cf. n. 25 below.

[4] S. Sacramori to G. M. Sforza, 3 July 1470, ASMi SPE Fir. 279; Rubinstein, *Government*, p. 179, n. 1: "vero partixano de Laurenzo . . . el quale credo habbia li termini de questo fatto civile così bene como homo de Fiorenza per sapere li loro secreti et per essere sapientissimo homo."

Lorenzo needed Scala's political talents as much as Scala needed Lorenzo's. Moreover, both men shared a common interest in reform. The theme of simplification and reform runs through the whole of Scala's career: in the chancery and the Guelf Party, as a prior in the Signoria and as procurator and member of a lay confraternity.[5] Although this is an aspect of Lorenzo's work that has received less emphasis than it should have done, there can be no doubt that he and Scala worked in close collaboration in all these fields toward the same end: the transformation of the diversified institutions of the medieval state into a unified secular administration.[6] Of course, both men served their own interests in doing so—Lorenzo by increasing his own authority with every constitutional reform of the state, Scala by receiving political rewards to compensate him for the loss (after 1480) of his former position as the one fixture in the government:[7] and Scala's career shows clearly how closely these themes of reform and self-interest were interwoven.

Scala's influence fluctuated: at its greatest from Piero de' Medici's death until the outbreak of the Pazzi war in 1478, low during the war and the years immediately following it, largely restored for the last decade of Lorenzo's life. These three periods form distinct phases in Scala's relationship with Lorenzo and provide the framework in which to describe it. But throughout the whole period we see Scala working with skill and singlemindedness to combine his own interests with those of Lorenzo and of the state for, as he saw it, they all stood or fell together.[8]

The period from 1469 to 1478 saw Scala at his most powerful, working closely with Lorenzo de' Medici and introducing important reforms in the administration of the state. In the event, Sacramori's fear that Lorenzo would be too young to

[5] See especially ch. 7 below.
[6] *Ibid.*, and on Lorenzo's responsibility for reforms in the judiciary, Mercanzia, Guelf Party and Otto di Guardia, cf. n. 24 below.
[7] "uno asso fermo," see ch. 3, n. 30 above.
[8] See below, at n. 100.

succeed to his father's position in Florence proved groundless, although it was some months before he established himself firmly in control of the city.[9] Although Florence, Milan and Naples had been united in their defense of Roberto Malatesta of Rimini against the pope and Venice in 1469, a rift, which was immediately reflected in Florence, began to develop between Milan and Naples after Piero's death.[10] Three years earlier the Mediceans had been united against their pro-Venetian opponents, but now they were themselves divided. By family tradition Lorenzo was more closely committed to the Sforza in Milan than to the House of Aragon,[11] but he was treated by both families as the favored son of a loyal feudatory, and in Florence Ferrante's ambassador, Marino Tomacelli, worked as hard as Sacramori to win his confidence.[12] Scala was on good terms with both ambassadors and was well placed to act as mediator between them and Lorenzo.[13] Al-

[9] On the situation on Piero's death, and the meeting of more than 600 citizens, "el fiore della città," to support him, Guicciardini, *Storie fiorentine*, pp. 20-21; Rubinstein, *Government*, pp. 174-175; Soranzo, "Lorenzo il Magnifico," pp. 44-47.

[10] Soranzo, "Lorenzo il Magnifico," pp. 50-59; cf. Rubinstein, *Government*, p. 176.

[11] The day before Piero died, Lorenzo wrote to ask for Galeazzo Maria Sforza's protection, and on 10 December he wrote: "io sia di cera et potermi disporre et formare a qualunche Suo proposito, secondo che epsa medesima saprà disegnare," *Lettere*, 1, no. 27; cf. Rubinstein, *Government*, p. 175; Soranzo, "Lorenzo il Magnifico," p. 45. On the Medici and Sforza, cf. ch. 3, n. 27 above.

[12] On 5 December in a meeting in the Medici palace, Lorenzo "disse inter l'altre heredità che gli haveva lassato l'avo et patre suo era la servitù et amicitia de Vostra Celsitudine [Galeazzo Maria Sforza] et del Re [Ferrante of Naples], la quale lui continuaria quando da loro el fosse consigliato, et sopra questo molto se extese" (S. Sacramori to G. M. Sforza, ASMi SPE Fir. 283, letterbook, fol. 33r). On 27 February 1471 Luigi Pulci in Naples described Lorenzo as "sopra tutto il cucco del signore Re nostro," and on 2 April 1471 he described Tomacelli as Lorenzo's "gran . . . partigiano et di tutti e fiorentini," *Morgante e lettere*, pp. 965 (cf. Rochon, *La Jeunesse*, p. 230, n. 114), 972. Tomacelli's work is less well documented than that of the Milanese ambassadors because virtually no Neapolitan diplomatic correspondence survives.

[13] On his relationship with Sacramori, see the preceding chapter. One letter survives from Tomacelli to Scala in Florence showing the two men on good terms and Scala also close to the Neapolitan secretary Antonello

though his role in the events of the early summer of 1470 was not as partisan as the Milanese ambassadors implied, it seems clear that the Milanese lobby was reestablished in Florence with Scala's support and connivance, and that he worked in close conjunction with Lorenzo and Angelo della Stufa, using his authority as chancellor to impede the signing of the universal league and peace treaty in December 1470 in accordance with Milanese wishes.[14]

The Milanese were also responsible for helping Lorenzo to establish himself on a firmer constitutional footing at this time. It was Galeazzo Maria Sforza's suggestion that Angelo della Stufa should be elected Gonfalonier of Justice at the beginning of 1471 and, when Lorenzo agreed to try to achieve this (and succeeded), Galeazzo Maria urged Sacramori to get Lorenzo to make the most of this opportunity to secure power, now that he had begun "to understand what medicine he needs."[15] At the same time Sacramori worked to ensure Loren-

---

Petrucci (10 March 1471, ASF *MAP* 101, 209): "No[n] ne scrivo mo[do] a Lorenzo perchè scrivendo a Vuy non è necessario scrivereli, che so ne lo dirite e confortaritelo . . . Lo S[ignor] Secretario vi saluta ed è tanto vostro quanto Vui si[e]te mio. Ève carissimo avere vostra amicitia, et me àve comisso che quante volte ve scrivo, ve lo saluti e pregi lo adoperete in vostro honore e piacere e me àve dicto che di continuo ve tenerà ben recomandato in gratia di lo S[ignor] Re" (Braccesi had commended Scala to Petrucci in 1470, Kristeller, "An Unknown Correspondence," pp. 339 and 355-356). See also Fil. Sacramoro to G. M. Sforza (9 October 1474, ASMi SPE Fir. 288): "Cum Messer Bartolomeo Scala Marino se è rescaldato assay sopra questa tal liga, non cum ira nisuna fra loro, perchè pur sonno confidenti inseme." In 1481 Scala asked Antonio de' Medici to commend him to Petrucci and Ferrante, "dal quale io ho ricevuto tanti beneficii che non può alcuno altro suo servidore essere più obligato et più devoto alla Sua Maiestà di me," ASF *Minut.* 11, fol. 225r (21 August 1481).

[14] See ch. 7, pp. 171-173 below.

[15] G. M. Sforza to Sacramori, 4 January 1471, ASMi SPE Fir. 281: "et parne hora che Lorenzo comenzi ad intendere la medicina che gli bisogna," cf. Soranzo "Lorenzo il Magnifico," p. 70; Rubinstein, *Government*, p. 180, n. 3 (who fails to make it clear, however, that Angelo's election was at the duke's own suggestion). On Galeazzo Maria's responsibility for this, see Sacramori's letters to him of 18 December 1470 (ASMi SPE Fir. 280): "Io ho conferito cum Lorenzo quel pensero de la Vostra Illma. Signoria de fare confallonero d. Angnola da la Stuffa e nettare l'orto . . . Et del fare d. Agnolo Confallonero non me nè da, nè tolle, speranza"; 22 December (*ibid.*): "El me ha pur poy data qualche più speranza che d. Agnolo nostro serrà

zo's success in another direction. Ever since the summer the friendship of Lorenzo and Tommaso Soderini had been turning to enmity, "to their own harm and danger, and to the grief of the wives of the men who love them and of their true friends, among whom you and I [Otto Niccolini had written to Bernardo Corbinelli] are numbered."[16] Now, with the help of money and a secret supper party in his house on 8 January, Sacramori succeeded in winning Soderini's support for Lorenzo[17] and the way lay open for constitutional reform.

The proposals of Angelo della Stufa and his Signoria answered Scala's criticism of Lorenzo's abortive scheme for reform the previous summer. He had then confided in Sacramori that Lorenzo's scheme relied too heavily on a relatively small group of leading citizens (in proposing that accoppiatori should be selected only from a group of about forty citizens, to include all the principal knights, among those who had held the office since 1434) for, although they presented no danger as long as they remained disunited, as at present, they could pose a serious threat if they ever reunited. It was on this occasion, in passing his opinion on to Galeazzo Maria Sforza, that Sacramori praised Scala's intelligence and grasp of the political situation in Florence.[18] The new scheme adopted the second

---

Confallonero, che se cossa seguirà, me sforzarò sdrucilarlo a qualche cosa"; 26 December (*ibid.*): "Et ditto Laurenzo mi confessa che io dico el vero, et credo pur ch'el farà pensero, che per questo el nostro d. Agnolo da la Stufa sia confallonero"; 29 December (*ibid.*, announcing his election); and 30 December (*ibid.*): "Poichè el prefato d. Agnolo è confallonero, a mi pare che haviamo condutto Laurenzo suso el camino dove serrà più agievole a fare qualche bene."

[16] 22 August 1470 (Niccolini Archives, Florence): "a danno loro e pericholo, a sschonsolazione delle donne degli huomini che vogliono loro bene et de' veri amici loro, fra il quale numero siamo tu et io."

[17] On Sacramori's invitation to Soderini to join him, Lorenzo, and Angelo della Stufa "secretamente a cenna" and Soderini's promise "cum sacramenti terribilissimi" to "seguire la via de Lorenzo et de V. Illma. Signoria," see Sacramori to G. M. Sforza, 9 January 1471, ASMi SPE Fir. 281, and on the oath and the duke's gift to Soderini on 15 January of 500 ducats, cf. Soranzo, "Lorenzo il Magnifico," pp. 71, 73, n. 70.

[18] Sacramori to G. M. Sforza, 3 July 1470, ASMi SPE Fir. 279, "cavalleri principali," and Rubinstein, *Government*, pp. 178-179; in general on the reform bills of 1470-1471, *ibid.*, pp. 177-181, cf. n. 4 above.

of the alternatives Scala proposed to Sacramori in July: the restriction of power to a smaller group of reliable supporters. The bill scraped through the Cento by a majority of only two votes and was not presented at all to the Councils of the People and the Commune. Accordingly, on 5 July 1471 the new accoppiatori for the following year were chosen by the pro-Medicean Signoria and the accoppiatori then in office.

The scheme was self-perpetuating, for this favorable Signoria (headed by Piero Malegonnelle) proposed at the same time that a new Balìa should be created: its first forty members to be chosen by the same Signoria and the freshly selected accoppiatori, the remainder by the forty, the Signoria and the accoppiatori. Little wonder that Sacramori confidently predicted it would consist of "picked men," or that these picked men chose to reward Scala by granting him full citizenship. On 13 September 1471 it approved a decree of the Signoria giving Scala all the privileges of a "real, ancient and original citizen of the state of Florence," enabling him to hold offices and honors in Florence although a new man—for, as Juvenal said, "virtue is man's only true nobility." The same decree, as we have seen, enabled the Signoria to decide on 15 October which offices Scala could hold as chancellor.[19]

The work of the Balìa was completed by a scrutiny to revise the lists of those eligible for office—among whom Scala could now be included. The ten accoppiatori elected by the Cento to advise on technical matters included Lorenzo de'

---

[19] Ed. C. Bartolini: "est enim nobilitas sola atque unicus virtus" (Juvenal, *Satires*, 8. 20), cf. ch. 3, nn. 13 and 14 above. On the Balìa of "picked men," Rubinstein, *Government*, pp. 181-183. Thirty years was the statutory period for which taxes had to be paid before holding office without special legislation, as the decree states (cf. n. 21 below), although it had been decreed on 4 April that year (1471, ASF *Provv.* 162, fol. 5r; cf. Rubinstein, "I Primi Anni," p. 190, n. 168) that no one could petition for a decree granting eligibility to office unless he had paid taxes for at least 20 years, and if he had paid taxes for less than this period, he must pay a tax of fl. 50 before his petition could be considered: "Et così faccendo gli huomini non cercheranno tale habilità innanzi al tempo: et se pure la cercheranno, o obtenghino la petitione o no, costerà loro: et il comune sarà se non nelle graveze almeno nella taza beneficato" (fol. 5r).

Medici, his henchman Antonio Pucci, and Piero Malegonnelle. The scrutiny council started work in November and voted Scala eligible for the priorate, leaving it to the accoppiatori to decide in August 1472 which bags (offices) he was eligible for and with how many tickets. Since they broke the rules only to make "some minor concessions to a few leading chancery officials," we will not be surprised to find Bartolomeo Scala prominent among them: he was qualified for the Gonfalonier-ship of Justice, the Signoria and other less important offices; and together with two other members of the chancery he was awarded two instead of a single *polizza* or name ticket for the bags from which names were drawn for the so-called Three Highest Offices (the Signoria and the Colleges of Sixteen Gon-faloniers and Twelve Good Men), a concession that should have been granted only to those whose fathers or who themselves had been qualified in the 1458 scrutiny.[20] Having doubled his chances of being drawn for office in the scrutiny, Scala was elected a member of the Signoria only six months after the bags were filled.[21] Once again he owed his achievement to a Balìa whose main purpose had been to strengthen the Medici regime, and he emerged as one of the regime's most influential members. Anticipating his election to the Signoria by scarcely a month, he acquired the house in Borgo Pinti that

[20] Rubinstein, *Government*, pp. 186-192; ASF *MAP* 86, fols. 320r (cf. 329v), 320v, 328r (where he heads the list for the second *borsa* for the Gonfaloniership of Justice in San Giovanni), and 330r (conceding him 2 *polizze*). For an additional concession granted in August 1473 to the Palace Officials, *ibid.*, fol. 332r; ch. 6, n. 48 below.

[21] For March-April 1473. On the speed of his election, see the list of Gonfalonieri di Giustizia since 1434 in ASF *Tratte* 15 (unfoliated, cf. n. 114 below): "Vinse il priorato nello squittino 1471 et fu poi presto de' Signori. Cominciò a paghare le graveze d'Aprile 1459. *Bisogna a exercitare ufici pagare prima 30 anni interi. Ma fu facto habile a potere exercitare innanzi*" (deleted). For a list of this and other drawn and elected offices, ASF *Tratte* 82, fols. 63r, 3r, 5r, 60r; 83, fol. 25r; 354, fols. 53r, 79v, 99r: Assessor to the Syndics of the Captain of the People (elected in July 1474), Otto di Guardia (July-October 1479), Camerarius of Orsanmichele and the Bigallo (April-October 1485) and Syndic of the Podestà (July-December 1488), in addition to his election as a prior in 1473 and Gonfalonier of Justice in May-June 1486.

was to serve as the foundation for the spacious estate he developed within the third circle of the city walls.[22] At last his position seemed assured.

Lorenzo de' Medici's position was also assured by the work of the same Balìa. The days were gone when Sacramori had to urge Lorenzo to assert his authority more vigorously. While the Balìa was still at work, Sacramori told Galeazzo Maria Sforza that "Lorenzo de' Medici is the head and steersman of these things and we must place our trust principally in him."[23] In December everything—he reported—was decided "by a sign from Lorenzo," who was planning to abolish the office of Judge of Appeal, having already attempted to divert some of the funds of the Guelf Party and the Sei di Mercanzia, and limit the authority of the Otto di Guardia.[24] By mid-September 1472 Sacramori openly criticized Lorenzo's unrestrained display of power as unsuitable for the Florentine way of life and, although Galeazzo Maria Sforza replied that he did not want Lorenzo to say he was being ruled by Milan, "since by now he knows what he is doing and is out of tutelage," Sacramori held to his opinion that "astute and clear-sighted" though Lorenzo was, he "thinks too much of himself

---

[22] See ch. 9 below.

[23] Sacramori to G. M. Sforza, 19 October 1471, ASMi SPE Fir. 282: "L'è vero che Laurenzo di Medici è el capo et timone de queste cose et che cum luy debba farsi el principal fondamento."

[24] To the same, 4 December 1471 (*ibid.*): "sonne redutte le cose de questa ciptà in locho che tutto consiste in uno cenno de Laurenzo, ne crediate che altri ce siano se non per uno zero. . . . A luy pare che hora non ce sia Giudixe di Appellatione, come c'è sempre stato per el passato." And on the introduction on 13 September 1471 of "alchune reformatione et provisione de la Città in redrizare certe intrate de la Parte Guelfa et del' Officio de la Merchantia, che se mangiavano certe officiali et servy deputati a quelle case cum pocho profito del comune, et in limitare le auctorità de li Otto de Balia. . . . Il che è stato molto commendato et ha acresciuto bona gratia a Lorenzo," see Sacramori's letter to G. M. Sforza, 15 September 1471, *ibid.*, alluding to the creation by the *Balìa* on 13 September of 5 officials to sell the possessions, but not the residences, of the Guelf Party and the Mercanzia to create a new Monte de' Castellani e Provigionati, ASF *Balìa* 31, fols. 51v-53v. But in fact this reform was not then put into effect, see n. 54 below.

and hoists his sails too high when things are going well."[25]
Shortly afterward the disillusioned ambassador left Florence,
leaving in his place his nephew Filippo Sacramoro.

The transformation of Lorenzo into this dynamic and ambitious ruler could have threatened Scala as much as Sacramori.
Lorenzo was not more than ten years old when Scala first
knew him. It was Scala who told him he had been elected a
member of the *Opera* (or works' commission) of the monastery of Santa Brigida in place of his uncle Giovanni de' Medici
and who sent him a long *Dialogue of Consolation* on Giovanni's death; and it was Scala again who sent him and his brother
advice and consolation on their father's death.[26] After Piero's
death the two men worked closely together and Scala was rewarded by Lorenzo with political office. What would their
relationship be now?

On one level it was—by our standards—somewhat syco-
phantic. For Scala assured Lorenzo—as he had Lorenzo's father
and his father's cousin Pierfrancesco before him—that everything he had he owed to him, and that during Lorenzo's absence
in Naples he was "blinded without my sun, lost without my
leader, and shipwrecked without my pole-star."[27] When he
made his will in 1484 he declared unequivocally that he wanted
Lorenzo, "to whom and to whose progenitors, that is his father
Piero and his grandfather Cosimo, I owe everything," to be
able to change and dispose of everything as though it were his

[25] Sacramori to G. M. Sforza, 16 September 1472, ASMi SPE Fir. 283
(letterbook): "Altre volte ho scripto . . . che la reputatione et conditione
de Lorenzo in questa cipta non potria essere magiore nè andare più suso s'el
non ne fosse Signore a bachetta . . . Io per my ne voria più presto un pocho
meno . . . che tal volta non si convene a questo vivere"; Galeazzo Maria's
letter in reply, 22 September 1472, *ibid.*: "non voressemo ch'el dicesse che
vogliamo governare: luy hormay intende il facto suo et è fora de tutoria";
and n. 3 above.

[26] ASF *Strozz.* ser. 1, 136, fol. 55: "Erat Ioannes patruus tuus ex Operariis
Sancte Brigidae; tu es a meis Capitaneis in eius locum suffectus"; on the
Dialogue, ch. 2, n. 45 above; the letter to Lorenzo and Giuliano is in BNF
MS Magl. VIII, 1439, fols. 73r-76v.

[27] See n. 92 below.

own, and to inherit his estate should his own son or his brothers die without masculine offspring.[28] Moreover, Scala consistently flattered Lorenzo as his patron and dedicated all his principal writings to him: his *Apologues*, which he later said he used to write as a form of annual tribute to Lorenzo, his dialogue *On Laws and Legal Judgments*, and poems reflecting Lorenzo's own bursts of poetic inspiration.[29]

On another level, however, their relationship was refreshingly pragmatic and realistic. It was Lorenzo's nature, Scala recognized, to "delight in doing where speaking is unnecessary";[30] hence the working basis of their relationship has to be sought in the field of practical politics and administration and not in rhetoric. But even Scala's flattery had a sardonic edge, witness his dry parody of Lorenzo's poem *La Nencia*, and his "annual tribute" of apologues, which cleverly play with the theme of patronage and currently fashionable neoplatonic theory.[31] The letters of recommendation he was inevitably asked to address to Lorenzo are similarly dry: "It will do him a great favor as a new man, a greater one to me," he wrote on one occasion, "since you will free me from continual molestation" or, on another, when the favor concerned his wife's uncle, "fix it with Giuliano or with whomever you want so I can get some peace from my wife, who never leaves off badgering me about it day or night: to tell you the truth,

[28] ASF *Notarile* G 619 (Testamenti 1486-96), fol. 389r: "volo ut Laurentius Petri filius de Medicis, cui ego eiusque progenitoribus, idest Petro patri et avo Cosmo omnia debeo, possit pro arbitrio suo omnia hec mutare et tanquam de rebus suis disponere; quodque ipse mutaverit disposueritque volo mutatum et dispositum esse habeatque effectum. Et si filius aut filii, si item fratres, sine prole mascula decesserint, volo sit ipse aut filii eius atque heredes sint heredes mei."

[29] Cf. ch. 11; and on the poems, ch. 10, p. 272-273 below.

[30] See his letter to Lorenzo of 29 July 1479, ASF *MAP* 37, 588: "che si dilecta del fare dove el dire non è necessario." In letters written in Italian from 1463 to 1473 Scala addressed Lorenzo as "tu" and after 1475 as "voi," suggesting a formal change in their relationship when Lorenzo was about 25 years old.

[31] See n. 29 above. He describes his gift of apologues to Lorenzo "aliquot annos . . . tanquam qui tributum quotannis persolvunt" in a letter to Piero de' Medici (Turin, Bibl. Civica, Raccolta Autografi, Mazzo 34, see below).

there is nothing which would give me greater pleasure at this moment."[32]

In the virtual absence of letters from Lorenzo to Scala,[33] we have to rely on Scala's to Lorenzo for a picture of their working relationship. They reveal the two men in close collaboration, often on a semiofficial basis—Scala transmitting messages that could not be committed to the official letter-book to Lorenzo from the Signoria, consulting him over public letters and showing him incoming mail—and sometimes on a private one. Since Lorenzo held no official position in Florence and had no more right of access to public documents than any other citizen, it was vital for him to have a private means of access, and Scala provided this.

For example, in 1476 Scala wrote to Lorenzo "by order of the Signoria" authorizing him to exceed the amount of money that could legally be spent on honoring an ambassador in anticipation of authorization by the Councils: "The Signoria's letter to you is written, as you will see, in accordance with the

[32] See his letters to Lorenzo of 26 August 1476 and 25 September 1473, ASF *MAP* 33, 693 ("Erit grande beneficium illi novo homini. Maius mihi, quem continua quadam molestia liberaveris"); 29, 804 ("commetti a Giuliano o chi ti paresse, in modo io possi havere pace colla donna, la quale dì et nocte mai resta di sollecitarmene. Io in verità al presente non potrei ricevere maggiore piacere"). His wife's uncle, Banco di Fruosino di Cece da Verrazzano, had been sentenced by the Captain of the People, "precedente il bullettino degli Otto di Balìa," on 5 March 1468 to six months in prison and then exile twenty miles outside Florence for five years. He could only return with the consent of the Signoria, Colleges and Otto di Guardia ("el partito delle 36 fave" Scala refers to in his letter), within one month after completing his sentence (see ASF *Balìa* 25, fol. 112r-v: the vote could not be taken more than six times but it could be repeated at one-yearly intervals); and on 5 October 1473, doubtless as a result of Scala's influence, Banco's sentence was canceled, ASF *Otto di Guardia (repubb.)* 224, fol. 154r.

[33] Dott. Riccardo Fubini suggests that Lorenzo de' Medici's note [of 10-20 (?) August 1470] may have been addressed to Scala (*Lettere*, 1, no. 63). If so, it is the only known letter to survive, apart from one incorporated into Scala's apologue "Beneficium" (*Apologi centum*, p. 30). But it is clear from Scala's own letters that Lorenzo did write to him, probably usually in the form of "polize"—see Scala's letter of 29 July 1479 (ASF *MAP* 37, 588: "Tutto quello m'avete a questi dì ricordato per vostre varie polize s'è facto") —like the one above, but on occasion more formally (see *Protocolli del carteggio*, pp. 8 and 319, letters to Scala of 9 May 1477 and 23 December 1484).

regulations, which they cannot contravene in writing. Nevertheless, the Signoria tells me their intention is that you should honor [the cardinal] freely as you think fit, and that whatever you spend in excess of the amount that can be spent in honoring a legate, which is £260, can be sanctioned by the councils, as is laid down by the laws of the city."[34] The following day he was even more explicit. When the Signoria wrote to Lorenzo yesterday, they did not yet know that Federigo of Aragon was also coming to Pisa; now they knew this, they were still writing to him as before, since they lacked the authority to write in contravention of the regulations: "nevertheless they have ordered me to write to you that despite the regulations, you should honor him as freely as you like and that measures will be taken to legalize whatever is in excess of the regulations."[35] Excessively law abiding, one might say, but nevertheless this letter could not be transcribed in the official register.

On other occasions Scala visited Lorenzo in Careggi or wrote to him to show him letters and ask for his advice. In 1474 he was sent to Lorenzo "with the book in which all the letters written from here and there are copied," reporting Lorenzo's opinion on his return.[36] Here Scala must have been exceeding the bounds of duty for, although Lorenzo had doubtless been officially invited to attend the meeting (or committee) deputed to deal with the matter in hand,[37] it was

---

[34] 12 August 1476, ASF *MAP* 33, 629. It had been decreed on 17 December 1473 that "per Cardinale legato non si passi la somma di lire cclx piccoli" (ASF *SS. Delib. sp. aut.* 34, fol. 132r), completing the program to limit public expenditure introduced by the Signoria of which Scala was himself a member in March-April 1473).

[35] 13 August 1476, ASF *MAP* 93, 259.

[36] See Angelo della Stufa to G. M. Sforza, 6 June 1474, ASMi SPE Fir. 286: ". . . per non ci si ritrovare Lorenzo de' Medici, che è alla villa; et èsseli mandato il nostro cancegliere con libro in su che si copia tutte le lettere si scrivano di là et di qua," and 7 June, *ibid.*: "Il quale Cancelliere per la ritornata sua riferisce Lorenzo riferirsi a tutto quello se ne diterminassi per la pratica." Lorenzo was then at Careggi, Rochon, *La Jeunesse*, p. 641.

[37] The "cittadini della camera" or "della pratica," as they are called by the later 1470s, anticipate the Otto della Pratica instituted in 1480 to discuss foreign affairs, see ch. 6, n. 37 below.

highly irregular for the chancellor to leave the palace and dance attendance on him with the official letter-book of the Commune. Similarly, in May 1477 he sent Lorenzo copies of despatches from Milan and offered to send the postal rider to him with the mandate approved by the citizens as soon as he had it written out in case Lorenzo wanted to comment on it (as perhaps he did, since the date of the Signoria's letter to Soderini with the mandate is altered from "23" to "25" in the official register). In the same letter Scala also discussed how to reply to Louis XI's letters to Lorenzo and the Signoria. After giving his own opinion, he said he thought the Signoria would await his return before replying unless Lorenzo wrote to them about it: "Anyway, think about it, as you do about our other affairs. Giuliano [de' Medici], I think, is going to write to you at greater length." And in the event the Signoria did await his return before replying.[38] In September 1477 Scala again sent Lorenzo certain letters and documents, "by order of the Gonfalonier," and on the following day he wrote to ask him and some other citizens (probably, like Lorenzo, members of the *pratica* deputed to deal with the matter) to return to Florence to join the discussion to be held on Lucca: "They also want you and say that without you they will not hold this discussion. You must come or send your opinion in writing. The Signoria and citizens would much prefer you to come." Later the same day the Gonfalonier of Justice asked Scala to forward Lorenzo a letter just received from Pisa to keep him up to date and make him all the keener to return.[39]

Sometimes Scala wrote to tell Lorenzo about the arrival in

---

[38] See Scala's letter to Lorenzo of 22 May 1477, ASF *MAP* 34, 131, and ASF *Minut.* 10, fols. 436v-437v; *Leg. Comm.* 19, fol. 102r. The Signoria's reply to Louis XI is in *Missive* 49, fol. 29v, dated 31 May 1477 (cf. Canestrini-Desjardins, *Négotiations*, 1:167-8, "30 May"). Lorenzo was in Pisa on 24-27 May and back in Florence by the 29th (*Protocolli del carteggio*, p. 10).

[39] See Scala's two letters to Lorenzo of 9 September 1477, ASF *MAP*, 32, 456 and 35, 710. In fact the *cittadini della camera* replied to the Lucchese ambassador on 11 September (now published as doc. 10 in Lorenzo's *Lettere*, vol. 2) and, unusually, the minutes do not list the names of those by whom the reply "fu consultata" (ASF *SS., Dieci, Otto* 77, fol. 93r).

Florence of ambassadors. On one occasion it was the ambassador of the king of Naples, the bishop of Policastro, "Messer Gulielmo or some such name—there was a letter G for his name in his credential letters," he recalls with disarming vagueness, the ambassador's name being Gabriel da Guidano, who delivered a "very fulsome" speech.[40] On another occasion he wrote to announce the approach of an ambassador whom Lorenzo wanted to honor,[41] and on another he wanted to know what to do about an envoy from Perugia who demanded a letter from Scala to enable him to visit Lorenzo: "I didn't know how to get rid of him as I would have done to save you this bother, not knowing what you had decided. Now he wants to see you and has asked me for a letter. Decide the best thing to do, and let me know if there is anything you would like me to do."[42]

These letters were all written to Lorenzo about state business that concerned Scala as chancellor. On other occasions he wrote to Lorenzo as a member of communal magistracies. When he was a member of the Signoria in 1473, for instance, he wrote to remind Lorenzo that a new Otto di Guardia had to be elected within fifteen days: "It seems to the Gonfalonier, on whose behalf I am writing to you, that you should be informed of this, and he wants you to be here for this and other matters. If you think you don't need to be here, he begs you— as I do—to give us some idea about what you want done." Since the Otto then exercised absolute powers concerning the safety of the state and political offenses, its election was a matter of importance to Lorenzo, who became a member himself in May 1478, "with the authority and power of all the people of Florence," to carry out a program of reform; but before

[40] 25 September 1473, ASF, *MAP* 29, 804. Gabriel da Guidano was bishop of Policastro from 1471 to 1485, Eubel, *Hierarchia*, 2:240.

[41] 6 February 1477, ASF *MAP* 33, 98.

[42] 16 August 1479, "ai Pinthi," ASF *MAP* 37, 633. On 17 August Lorenzo wrote directly to Pietro Paolo de' Ranieri in Perugia to say that "se non si acconciano le cose altrimenti, non è da sperare altro della venuta sua per Podestà" (*Protocolli del carteggio*, p. 95).

he could achieve this, the aftermath of the Pazzi conspiracy forced him to resign.[43]

During the Pazzi war Scala was elected a member of the Otto di Guardia, and in this capacity he reported to Lorenzo on measures taken by the Dieci di Balìa to safeguard markets in the Mugello, "although someone among us was not pleased and said this was beseiging the city": but for this he would not have written to Lorenzo since "all the things you have reminded me to do in your various notes these days have been done, and I know how busy you are and that it is your nature to delight in doing where speaking is unnecessary."[44] Both in this letter and in August Scala asked for Lorenzo's instructions in matters in which he had no brief: "If you have any advice to give me about this, give it to me. If I hear nothing, I shall be guided by what I know your intention has been up to now."[45] We can take it that this was his normal method of procedure, as it had been when he worked for Pierfrancesco de' Medici: to act without instruction when he knew what Lorenzo wanted to be done, otherwise to ask for his advice.

Occasionally we find Scala acting with Lorenzo in the interests of the small group of leading citizens with no reference to the government at all—as in July 1476 when he wrote to chastise the Florentine captain in charge of the fortress of Sarzana on the Ligurian coast. The captain, Domenico Bartoli, had dismissed the man in charge of the castle of Falcinello

---

[43] Scala's letter of 1 April 1473, Rome, Bibl. Nazionale, MS A. 118. 25/1, is edited in *Il Quattrocento negli autografi e incunabuli della Biblioteca Nazionale Roma. Catalogo*, Rome, 1950, pp. 72-73, no. 123. On the Otto's *balìa*, Rubinstein, *Government*, pp. 165, 168; and on its powers in 1478 and Lorenzo's resignation, Morelli, *Cronaca, Delizie*, 19:192 ("con autorità e balìa quanto tutto 'l popolo di Firenze"); Rubinstein, *Government*, p. 220, and n. 8.

[44] 29 July 1479, ASF *MAP* 37, 588, see nn. 30 and 33 above.

[45] *Ibid*.: "Se m'avessi sopra ciò a dare aviso alcuno, lo fate. Non havendo da voi altro, m'adirizerò dove io so che è stata la vostra intentione insino a qui"; cf. *MAP* 37, 633 (16 August 1479): "Voi ne piglierete quel savio partito vi parrà, et me aviserete se harò a fare circa questo o altro alcuna cosa."

[75]

who owed allegiance to the Marchese Gabriele Malaspina of Fosdinovo and not directly to Florence. This had displeased one of the leading citizens—Tommaso Soderini, related to the marchese by marriage, as it turned out—and the captain was asked to let him return. Letters that passed between Domenico Bartoli, Lorenzo de' Medici and Scala show that the affair was dealt with privately without reference to the Signoria and that the captain strongly resented being requested to rescind his orders in this way, without regard, he said, for the honor of Florence and himself, the example it would set, or the peace of the castle.[46]

Scala also mediated between Lorenzo and citizens in his home town of Colle and other towns in the Florentine state. In 1472 he suggested an ideal compromise between the displeasure felt by his compatriots in Colle over the fact that possession of the ancient Benedictine abbey of San Salvadore in Spugna dominating Colle had been given "to an outsider and especially to a cardinal," and the danger to Florence of alienating a nephew of the pope and so powerful a friend as Giuliano della Rovere, cardinal of San Pietro in Vincoli, "which is to let the Cardinal take possession and give the administration to my relation from Colle, if an administrator is needed. He is a good man and a good administrator. And the men of Colle would take the *commendam* less badly if they saw that one of them, and someone they were fond of, was to be its abbot."[47] When the parish church of Colle fell vacant

[46] On this incident, see letters from D. Bartoli to Scala, 25 July 1476, ASF *MAP* 68, 139, Scala to Lorenzo de' Medici, 29 July, and to Bartoli, 30 July, *MAP* 33, 555 and *Minut.* 10, fol. 361r, and Bartoli to Lorenzo, 15 August 1476, *MAP* 25, 439, referring to "questa benedetta restitutione che mi scrive M. Bartolomeo Cancellieri in tuo nome che io debba fare," "et io non n'ò l'autorità . . . et non ha riguardo all' onore della nostra comunità, nè respecto che sia di ghattivo exemplo agli altri nostri, nè alla pace et quiete di quel castello, nè all' onor mio." Marchese Gabriele's *capitoli* with Florence, agreed on 13 January 1469 for ten years, are in *Capitoli*, ed. Guasti, 1:677-678. On Tommaso Soderini's relationship with him, through the marriage of his son Piero to Marchese Gabriele's daughter Argentina, see S. Sacramori to G. M. Sforza, 16 March 1469, ASMi SPE Fir. 276.

[47] 21 August 1472, ASF *MAP* 28, 442 (Scala actually writes "the Cardinal of San Sixto" who was Pietro Riario, also a nephew of the pope, but he

the following month Scala again wrote to Lorenzo to commend a local citizen to succeed as priest, who was favored by his old friend Antonio di Pela Pasci and other leading citizens as well as by himself.[48] He mediated, too, between Lorenzo and the former chancellor of Volterra, Antonio Ivani.[49] He also used his friendship with Lorenzo to commend teachers for the Studio—in April 1473 the famous lawyer Baldo Bartolini, whom he had heard from a relation studying at Perugia would be prepared to teach in the newly established university at Pisa where Lorenzo served as a *provveditore*,[50] and—less successfully—the doctor who had saved Scala himself from dying of mushroom poisoning the previous autumn.[51]

---

evidently confused the two men). The Bull awarding this abbey to Giuliano della Rovere (17 June 1472) is in Rome, ASV Reg. Vat. 554, fols. 184r-185r; the approval of Colle is in Siena, AS, *Comune di Colle*, 163, fol. 152r (25 August 1472); cf. Biadi, *Storia*, p. 268 (but 1472, not 1471), and on the abbey, *ibid.*, pp. 19-20, 268-270.

[48] 21 September 1472, ASF *MAP* 28, 536. According to Biadi (*Storia*, p. 198) Jacopo Bonaparte succeeded to the Pieve instead of Scala's commendation, Niccolò Corbizzi.

[49] See A. Ivani's letter to Scala in BNF MS Magl. VIII, 10, fol. 6r-v ("Non eram nescius tanta fore operam tuam ut me tandem amplissimo viro Laurentio Medici conciliares. Id intellexi non solum ex litteris ad me tuis, redolentibus miram quandam suavitatem, sed etiam ex suis ad hunc ingratum"), and to D. Acciaiuoli, *ibid.*, fol. 8r ("Accepi litteras tuas quibus cognovi quid vir amplissimus Laurentius Medix et Bartholomeus Scala in re mea consulunt. Amice illos et te amico consulere arbitror"). On Ivani, C. Braggio, "A.I., umanista del sec. XV," *Giornale ligustico d. arch. stor. et lett.*, 12 (1885):346-385, 401-463, esp. 402, n. 2; P. L. Ruffo, "L'epistolario di A.I., 1430-82," *Rinascimento*, ser. 2, 6 (1966):141-207, esp. 143; and Kristeller, *Supplementum*, 2:324; and on his relationship with the Medici, cf. E. Fiumi, *L'impresa di Lorenzo de' Medici contro Volterra*, Florence, 1948, pp. 99-101. In 1476 he was appointed chancellor of Pistoia.

[50] 1 April 1473 (see n. 43 above). On Baldo Bartolini and his appointment to teach in Pisa for the unrivaled salary of fl.1,050 a year, *Dizionario biografico, s.v.*, and S. M. Fabbruccio, *Recensio notabilium conductionum . . . quae renovato Pisano Gymnasio cohevae reperiuntur*, in *Raccolta d'opuscoli scientifici*, ed. A. Calogiera, Venice, 1747, 37:3-10.

[51] 16 September 1473, ASF *MAP* 29, 757. On Scala's near death from mushroom poisoning, see also A. Braccesi's letter to the bishop of Forlì, Alexander Numai, 3 October 1472, Oxford, Bodleian MS Auct. F. 2. 17, fol. 146v: "Scala noster ob malos fungos pene periit et morti proximus fuit. Et adhuc medici salutem eius in dubio ponunt, exitum expectabimus."

This is the picture Scala's letters to Lorenzo paint of their working relationship. It embraced official, semiofficial, party-political and purely personal matters, conducted on a practical *ad hoc* basis. The letters throw little light on Scala's administrative reforms (which will be discussed separately in chapter 7) or on the scope of his collaboration with Lorenzo. These were not matters they discussed in their letters, but this is not to say that such collaboration did not exist. Scala's talent lay in acting behind the scenes and his influence is therefore difficult to document, but it is clear that he was inspired by the same motives as Lorenzo in the reforms with which he is closely associated. Take, for instance, the reforms initiated in the Guelf Party during Scala's chancellorship to introduce order and moral probity in their affairs, or the notable program "to restore public morality and cut back unnecessary expenditure" introduced during Scala's office as a member of the Signoria in 1473.[52] The latter reforms reflected very closely both Scala's puritanism and that of the Gonfalonier of Justice, Luigi Guicciardini, but according to Francesco Guicciardini Lorenzo de' Medici was himself extremely "keen to prescribe them and to see that they were observed."[53] Similar motives underlay Lo-

[52] On the legislation of the March/April 1473 Signoria, "a ridurre la gente a buoni costumi e risecare le superfluità delle spese," Rinuccini, *Ricordi storici*, p. cxxi; cf. Guicciardini, *Memorie di famiglia*, p. 24, and *Dialogo*, p. 59 (quoted in the following note). The law of 23 April 1473 on games with its "nuovo modo di punitione et levando le confusioni di tante leggi che sono in tale materia per tanto" was in fact renewed on 24 January 1514 and is printed as part of that law (see British Library, 5359 b 45). On 27 April, "vedendo approximarsi il fine di tale autorità et non volendo tale opera et sì perfecta lasciarla indrieto et . . . cognoscendo che da una grande largheza descendendo a troppo stretteza difficilmente s'observarebbe quello che così si deliberasse," they passed two decrees "pro pompa mortuorum et funerum impensa moderandis" and "pro conviviorum sumptibus moderandis" (ASF *SS. Delib. sp. aut.* 34, fols. 126v-131r), leaving subsequent Signorie to complete their work (e.g. *ibid.*, fol. 131r-v). On earlier sumptuary laws, see, for example, the *Due provvisioni suntuarie fiorentine* (29 November 1464 and 29 February 1472), ed. C. Mazzi, Florence, 1908 (but referring to a law of 1330 limiting marriage banquets Davidsohn calls them "altrettanto frequenti quanto inefficaci," *Storia di Firenze*, 7 (Florence, 1965): 641).

[53] *Dialogo*, p. 59: "Ricordatevi delle legge degli ornamenti e delle spese, fatte quando era gonfaloniere di giustizia messer Luigi Guicciardini, quanto

renzo's plans for the Guelf Party, the Mercantile Court, the judiciary and the Otto di Guardia in the 1470s.[54] Whoever initiated the policy, it evidently reflected a widely shared attitude among the members of the Medici party who put it into practice.

In the field of foreign policy, too, Scala and Lorenzo worked in collaboration. We have already seen how they supported Milan in the latter part of 1470, and it is largely thanks to the reports of the Milanese ambassadors in Florence that we can see this collaboration continuing—although not always in support of Milan. In 1472 Lorenzo turned from Milan to Rome—where his friendship with Sixtus IV offered him the prospect of financial and dynastic advancement—and with him turned Scala, who revived his old friendship with Cardi-

---

Lorenzo fu caldo a ordinarle ed a farle osservare." On Luigi Guicciardini's puritanism, see the tenor of his contributions to *pratiche* in these years (e.g. ASF *Cons. Prat.* 60, fols. 34r (10 September 1468): "Luxuriam vestimentorum conviviorum et superfluorum sumptuum resecandam"; 92r (3 January 1470): "admonuit de luxuria resecanda"; 111r (4 August 1470): "Agendum potius dixit de resecanda luxuria sumptuum superfluorum, de reparando erario et monte et vectigalibus, quae omnia sunt in magna rerum confusione"; 115v (17 November 1470): "Multis verbis quibus in omne genus et negligentie publice vitiorum invectus est"; and 139r (12 March 1472): "super corrigendis moribus civitatis propter homicidia et furta," "arguit in ea re pretores urbanos exemplo antiquorum . . . arguit etiam famulos octovirales et mutandos censuit ut melius servirent . . . Vetanda arma et itiones nocturnas. . . ."

[54] On the attempt to reform the wasteful Guelf Party and the Mercanzia in 1471, see the legislation of 13 September and Sacramori's letter of 15 September 1471 quoted in n. 24 above, also ASF *SS. Delib. sp. aut.* 34, fol. 95r, 1471-1472; Rinuccini, *Ricordi storici*, pp. cxviii-cxix. The Guelf Party was deprived of most of its property in July 1481 (ASF *Provv.* 172, fols. 81v-84v; cf. Rinuccini, *Ricordi storici*, p. cxxxv), whereas the Mercanzia was reformed in June 1477 (ASF *Cento Delib.* 2, fol. 12r-14r; A. Doren, *Le arti fiorentine*, Florence, 1940, 2:70; and in general, G. Bonolis, *Giurisdizione della Mercanzia*). The judiciary was reformed at the same time, the office of Captain of the People being replaced by a Judge of Appeals appointed by the officials of the Studio (ASF *Cento Delib.* 2, fols. 10r, 24v-27v, June-July 1477; cf. Martines, *Lawyers*, p. 137). On the projected reform of the Otto in 1478, see n. 43 above, and on Lorenzo's association with all these reform schemes in 1471 and with the Otto in 1478, see nn. 24 and 43 above and Guicciardini, *Storie fiorentine*, p. 42.

nal Jacopo Ammannati at this time, through whom Lorenzo hoped to win a cardinalate for his brother Giuliano.[55] For the moment, however, their ambitions were thwarted by the rival ambitions of the Riario family in Rome and the Pazzi in Florence, and were to be revived only a decade later.[56] By the beginning of 1474 the old alignment of powers in Italy was changing, Ferrante drawing closer to the pope, Milan to Venice. In February, Lorenzo, "sorrowful and sad," delivered a long criticism of Venice to Filippo Sacramoro while Scala confessed to the second Milanese ambassador in Florence how grossly he had been deceived by that "lord of words and artifice," Ferrante.[57] Although Florence joined Venice and Milan

[55] See Jacopo Ammannati's letters to Scala of 5 March and 10 September 1472, *Epistolae et commentarii*, fols. 227r, 243v, and to Lorenzo of 25 April and 15 May 1473, in Fabroni, *Laur. Medicis vita*, 2:58-60 (cf. Picotti, *La giovinezza*, pp. 161-162, and Palmarocchi, "Lorenzo de' Medici e la nomina cardinalizia di Giovanni," p. 40). On Ammannati's "intrinsechissima amicitia" with Lorenzo, "perchè l'è già stato, *dum erat in minoribus*, in casa loro," see Fil. Sacramoro to G. M. Sforza, 19 September 1474, ASMi SPE Fir. 287. Scala had expressed the hope that Filippo de' Medici would be made a cardinal in a passage added in his own hand to Donato Acciaiuoli's mandate to Rome on 6 March 1471, ASF *Minut.* 9, fol. 256r; cf. his earlier letter to Paul II on 6 December 1466, *Missive* 45, fols. 114v-115v. On the banking interests of the Medici in Rome, see G. Holmes, "How the Medici Became the Pope's Bankers," in *Florentine Studies*, ed. Rubinstein, pp. 357-380; and de Roover, *Banco Medici*, pp. 279-321.

[56] On the events leading to the Pazzi conspiracy, see Lorenzo de' Medici's *Lettere*, vols. 2 and 3; Pastor, *Storia dei papi*, 2:496-504; and Guicciardini, *Storie fiorentine*, pp. 31-32.

[57] See Fil. Sacramoro to G. M. Sforza, 2 February 1474, ASMi SPE Fir. 286: "doglioso et triste . . . me feci un longo et diffuso parlare" and [Gherardo Cerruto] to the same, 28 July 1474, *ibid.*, 287: "Parole di D. Bartholomeo Scala, el quale come sa la Vostra Celsitudine intende tutte le cose de qui, et ha ingegno, sono queste: Compare Gerardo . . . per noi il Re è salito in grandissima reputatione . . . El ce ha tenuto pasciuti de lettere humane, summisse, piene di tanta suavità, che recitate et intese dal populo gli resero una affectione maravigliosa. Ma . . . non l'havimo più nè per il più savio degli altri, nè per bono, nè per sincero, ma per Signore de parole et de arte et del quale pigliare non se posse se non pocha fede." On Scala's relationship with Milan at this time, see also Fil. Sacramoro's letter of 17 July 1474 ("Et hòllo da Messer Bartolomeo Scala in secreto, et non vorria che altri el sapesse, maxime per luy"), 25 and 27 July 1474, *ibid.* On Ferrante's closer relationship with the pope, Pastor, *Storia dei papi*, 2:464-465, 488-489, and in general, 477-483; Rinuccini, *Ricordi storici*, p. cxxiii. A

in a triple alliance in November 1474, Florence had lost her old relationship with Milan. Worried by this, Scala finally decided to raise the matter with Lorenzo in May 1476 and, finding themselves in agreement, they jointly decided what action to take.[58] Since this cannot have been the first occasion on which Scala took such initiative, it provides a useful illustration of how the two men worked together.

This led to a revival of the Milanese lobby in Florence. When Galeazzo Maria Sforza asked Florence and Venice to send a secretary or chancellor to him, Angelo della Stufa did all he could to get Scala elected:

> and up to now I thought I had succeeded [he explained]. I don't know who could have spoilt it. I went to him so that Your Excellency could have the chance of getting to know an outstanding man, as outstanding in his job as any our city has ever had. And I also wanted him because he supports Your Excellency and knows all the nooks and crannies in this city where there are crabs. All our most important secrets pass through his hands, and I think he would have been able to inform you of many things that they would do

---

vehemently anti-Venetian oration drafted by Scala as a speech for delivery in a consultative meeting in Florence, in BNF MS Magl. II, 1, 201, fols. 42r-45r (a volume relating to the Congress of Mantua) might possibly, despite its title and position, relate either to this period or to the 1460s.

[58] Fil. Sacramoro to G. M. Sforza, 12 May 1476, ASMi SPE Fir. 291: "L'adviso qualmente hersera M. Bartholomeo Scala, facendomi lui intendere havea de dirme alchune cose in secreto, fussemo inseme ne la cancellaria sua . . . Examinate adoncha fra se più volte queste cose . . . dice havea pensato più fiate dirne cum Laurenzo, et tandem dice deliberò farlo heri, et così fece . . . Dopoi che Laurenzo gl'hebe resposto quanto queste cose, et suoi penseri gli erano piaciuti tutti, et regratiandolo et rasonando de modi de providerli, li proposi. . . ." On the disagreement between Florence and Milan in 1476, see *Storia di Milano*, 7:301-305. Another glimpse of Scala and Lorenzo together at this time is provided by Fil. Sacramoro (in a letter to Cicco Simonetta, 11 April 1476, ASMi SPE Fir. 291): "Item sento da M. Angelo [della Stufa] che usciendo lui de cancelleria sentì Laurenzo dire a M. Bartholomeo Scala . . ."; cf. the same to Gian Galeazzo and Bona Sforza, 14 August 1477, *ibid.*, 293: "hora essendo in pallatio et usciendo de practica el Magnifico Laurenzo et M. Bartho. Scala me dixerano. . . ."

for Your Excellency, and our Signoria. The man who has spoilt it for me has been able to demonstrate that the Chancellor of our Republic should never be allowed to absent himself because of all the things that might happen in his absence.[59]

More relevant than the fact he was chancellor was perhaps the fact that he was not, strictly speaking, "a notary who understands all about rogations and contracts" as Angelo said the duke wanted. In fact this may have been why Angelo particularly wanted him to go, since Scala was responsible for reforming the style of mandates and ratifications in Florence, and Angelo may have wanted him to discuss this in Milan.[60] Scala nevertheless continued to work closely with Milan, particularly after the assassination of Galeazzo Maria Sforza, hinting frequently—but without avail until 1481—that he would like the decree appointing him a ducal councillor to be renewed by Galeazzo Maria's young son.[61] When a defensive

[59] Angelo della Stufa to G. M. Sforza, 13 October 1476, ASMi SPE Fir. 291 (cf. Fubini, "Note Machiavelliane," pp. 373-375): "Feci ciò che io potetti che questa electione toccassi a Messer Bartolomeo Scala, primo nostro Cancelliere, et fin hora credecti gli toccassi. Non so io altrimenti chi se la guastassi, et io andavo a llui perchè Vostra Sublimità conoscessi un singular huomo, tanto quanto n'avessi a mai la nostra Cipta al suo exercitio. Et disideravolo perchè è partigiano di Vostra Celsitudine et anche sa conoscere in questa Cipta tutte le buche dove è granchio; et tutti li gran segreti nostri vanno per le sue mani. Et credo harebbe saputo ricordarle di molte cose che farebbono per Vostra Sublimità et nostra Signoria. Et chi me l'à guasto ha saputo dimostrare che il Cancelliere della nostra republica non si vorrebbe mai absentarlo per tucti li casi che potessino occorrere." See also Fil. Sacramoro's letter to the same, 11 October 1476, *ibid.*: "del Secretario o Cancellaro recerca la Sublimità Vostra."

[60] See Angelo della Stufa's letter above: "un notaio che fussi bene intendente di roghi et di scripture"; and on Scala's reforms, ch. 7 below.

[61] Fil. Sacramoro to Gian Galeazzo and Bona Sforza, 15 March 1477, ASMi SPE Fir. 292: "Messer Bartolomeo Scala . . . alchuna volta me ha da qualche dì in qua dicto che passati alchuni dì, che gli parerà più congruo el tempo, vorà scrivere alle Excellentie vostre et Quelle pregare li piaccia essere contente de renovarli et confirmarli el privilegio. . . . Hora m'è parso da me scriverne et suplicarne . . . parte perchè concedendogli le Sublimità Vostre questo suo desiderio inante ancho che da luy le siano . . . rechieste . . . a Elle l'habia ad saperglini tante magiori gratie." Cf.

league was signed between Florence, Milan, Venice and the pope on 23 December 1477, Scala was closely involved, and for the first time assumed responsibility for preparing the ratification himself by letters-patent, then an entirely novel procedure.[62] This reconciliation with Rome came too late to deter the Pazzi conspirators in Florence. The crisis their assault on the Medici brothers provoked ultimately proved more serious for Scala than for Lorenzo de' Medici.

The crisis of the Pazzi conspiracy—the murder of Giuliano de' Medici in the cathedral on 26 April 1478 and the two years' war that followed—constitute a second stage in Scala's relationship with Lorenzo. It is a revealing period in which men accustomed to communicate in daily conversation are for the first time forced to declare themselves in writing. We learn more about Scala's character and forcefulness from his letters to the war magistracy as emissary in southern Tuscany in October 1479 than from his daily work in Florence over a much longer period, and similarly from his few but long letters to Lorenzo in Naples toward the end of the war. These years saw a decline in Scala's influence. Perhaps his political virtues were less valuable in war conditions and, as a Medicean, he must have suffered from Lorenzo's own oscillating fortunes. Nevertheless his influence was not negligible, for he still had an important role to play as first chancellor.

There is no evidence that Scala was with the Medici party

the dukes to Sacramoro, 12 November 1477, *ibid.*, 293, Scala to the dukes, 25 November 1477, *ibid.*, and Fil. Sacramoro to the same, 4 December 1477, reminding them of Scala's "singulare desiderio che l'ha ch'el piacesse a Quelle renovarli el Privilegio . . . perchè el vedo et provo tutto el dì andare vero a bono camino." Scala's appointment was renewed on 13 February 1481, ed. Moreni, *Notizie istoriche*, 3:77-79. The following letters from Fil. Sacramoro to the dukes in 1477 provide evidence of his close relationship with Scala in the chancery: 10, 19, 26, 30 January; beg. March (?), 27, 30 March; 24 April; 14 May; 4, 11, 21 June; 1, 13 July; 14 August; 12, 25 November; 7, 12 December 1477, etc., ASMi SPE Fir. 292, 293.

[62] On the Florentine ratification, due within a month of the signing of the treaty and dated 20 January 1478, see ch. 7, n. 39 below. On the treaty and the pope's unwillingness to join, Pastor, *Storia dei papi*, 2:483.

in the cathedral when Giuliano de' Medici was murdered and Lorenzo escaped with his life, nor in the chancery when the archbishop of Pisa, Francesco Salviati, tried to take over the Palazzo della Signoria.[63] However, he was closely involved in the aftermath. He was present at a secret meeting of selected citizens at which one of the conspirators' confession was read out to the Milanese and Venetian ambassadors behind closed doors in the Palazzo della Signoria.[64] And he later incorporated this confession in an open letter to be printed and widely circulated abroad, his so-called *Excusatio Florentinorum*.[65] When the war magistracy, the Dieci di Balìa, was appointed on 13 June 1478 with supreme powers for the duration of the war, Scala acted as its first chancellor, with authority to attend its meetings and write its external letters and ambassadors' mandates.[66] On the very first day of of-

[63] On the events of the conspiracy, see Angelo Poliziano's first-hand account (with full bibliography) in Perosa's edition of his *Commentarium*, also that of the Milanese ambassador in Florence, ed. Mercati, in Pastor, *Storia dei papi*, 2, append. 123:768-769. On the conspiracy in general, *ibid.*, pp. 505-529, and Lorenzo de' Medici's *Lettere*, vol. 3.

[64] Fil. Sacramoro and G. A. Talenti to Gian Galeazzo and Bona Sforza, 17 May 1478, ASMi SPE Fir. 294: "Hogi questa Exc. Signoria mandò per noi oratori . . . et gionti in palazo et reserati insieme el Gonfaloniere di Giustizia [Luigi Guicciardini], messer Antonio Ridolfi, messer Bongiani Gianfigliazzi, messer Bernardo Bonhieronymo, el Magnifico Laurentio e messer Bartholomeo Scala, per el cancelliere del Magnifico Laurentio [Niccolò Michelozzi] ne fece religere el processo de Iohanbaptista de Montesecco scripto *manu propria*."

[65] There is a chancery transcript on vellum dated 11 August 1478, signed by Scala and sealed with the large and small seals, in ASF *Misc. Repubb.* 4, 125 (my knowledge of which I owe to Professor Rubinstein; I am also grateful to Dott. Merendoni for tracing its original location, according to a late copy in ASF *Manoscritti* 167: "Armadio .P. delle Riformagioni," Commissioni vol. 2). The whole document is edited, with subscriptions, by G. Adimari (*A. Politiani Coniurationis Pactianae commentarium*, Naples, 1769, pp. 171-196) and without subscriptions by Fabroni (who dates it "10 August," *Laur. Medicis vita*, 2:167-181), thence Roscoe (*Life*, 1, append. 28: 99-109). The contemporary printed edition (Florence, Nicolò di Lorenzo, after 11 August 1478, *Indice generale*, 5:56) has some slight variants.

[66] The beginning of the register of appointments and letters of the Dieci in June 1478 is missing, but in December 1478 Scala was paid fl. 100 for six months' service in the Dieci (ASF *Dieci Debitori Creditori* 21, fol. 162v) and a year later fl. 200 "per suo salario di uno anno" (*Dieci Delib.* 22, fol.

fice, however, Scala apparently wrote a letter to Milan that had to be corrected the following day by a special messenger. If unintentional, this was an unpropitious start to his office, and by March 1479 the Este ambassador in Florence reported that Scala's influence—"our messer Bartolamio Schala" he calls him— "seems to be waning, since he rarely comes to the Dieci, where his place is taken by another chancellor, although he does occasionally turn up."[67]

Outside the Dieci he still had much to do, however. As first chancellor of the Signoria he must have composed their forceful reply to the pope on 21 July 1478 rejecting his request for Lorenzo's expulsion, a letter which the dukes of Milan described as "most seriously pondered and dictated . . . quite justifiably rebuking the Pope for his error and impiety."[68] This

---

320r). On these occasions Scala is described as "Chancelliere della Signoria" and "Primo Cancelliere de' Signori" and he doubtless played the same role before as after 13 December, when it was stated that he was "Primus Cancellarius dictorum Decem, sed ad eum spectet solum cancelleria rerum externarum, hoc est rogare litteras ad externos dirigendas et ad oratores et eorum commissiones describere et alia huiusmodi" (*Dieci Delib.* 21, fol. 1v, cf. 140v, 14 December 1479). As second chancellor of the Dieci, Niccolò Michelozzi wrote all internal letters (as though he were second chancellor of the Signoria), and was paid fl. 240 a year. Although in theory Alessandro Braccesi replaced Michelozzi as second chancellor in December 1479, with responsibility for internal letters, in practice he seems to have acted as sole chancellor, preparing the ambassadors' mandate of 2 March 1480 as "Cancellarius . . . Dominorum Decem" (*Dieci Delib.* 21, fol. 172v, ASMi SPE Fir. 299).

[67] Antonio Montecatini to Ercole d'Este, 11 March 1479, Modena, AS., Firenze, busta 2: "El nostro d. Bartolamio Schala a me pare molto calare de conditione. Lui pocho viene ne li.X. ed ècce uno altro canciliero. Pure li viene qualche fiada"; cf. G. A. Talenti and Fil. Sacramoro to the Sforza, 14 June 1478, ASMi SPE Fir. 295: "essendosi accorti che in una loro lettera che scripse questa Messer Bartholomeo Scalla sub nomine de li .X. de la guerra . . . era errata l'intentione loro."

[68] Gian Galeazzo and Bona Sforza to Fil. Sacramoro and G. A. Talenti, 21 July 1478, ASMi SPE Fir. 295: "gravissimamente maturata et dictata . . . et debitamente remorde lo errore et impietà del Papa." The Florentine letter was written in reply to Sixtus IV's letter of 7 July (in Florence, Bibl. Riccard. MS 913, fols. 69r-71r, ASMi SPE Roma 86): "Quis est enim ex vobis, qui desiderare non debeat tantam ex ista civitate tyrannidem extirpari? Tum, ut tam praeclara civitas in libertatem restituatur. . . ." (cf. the pope's letter to Federigo of Urbino, 25 July 1478, ed. Fabroni, *Laur. Medicis vita*,

was not the first time, of course, that Florence had attacked the pope with letters as well as arms, but Scala's biting irony won considerable renown throughout Italy: "We were amazed in the first place, most Holy Father," he began, "to find you had suddenly changed the long-established custom of Popes in writing to us." It was clear enough, he went on, why the pope had omitted the names of "Liberty" and "Justice" from his inscription (addressing the government simply as "Priors and Gonfalonier" instead of "Priors of Liberty and Gonfalonier of Justice" as they liked to be called), but it was much more perverse of him to omit the appellation of love with which papal letters were normally prefaced (alluding to the phrase "Dilectis in Christo filiis"), when writing to people for whom he claimed to feel such love and affection. "Could it be that you do not love the people whom you castigate with such censures and whom you attempt to reduce to your path by force of arms? If you deprive us of your love, there will be no reason left for proceeding in this manner."[69] On 11 August Scala signed and sealed his *Excusatio Florentinorum* for dispatch to the emperor and the king of France, and in September he could be found discussing matters of policy with the Milanese ambassador.[70] As first chancellor, he was responsible for reply-

---

2:130-131, referred to by Rubinstein, *Government*: p. 197 and n. 1). The pope's letter was discussed in a meeting on 13 July 1478 (ASF *Cons. Prat.* 60, fols. 162v-163v).

[69] Ed. L. Pignotti, *Storia della Toscana sino al principato*, Livorno, 1820, 4:117-121, on p. 117 (cf. W. Roscoe, *Illustrations of the Life of Lorenzo de' Medici*, appended as vol. 4 to his *Life*, Heidelberg, 1926, append. 5, pp. 199-205; Marzi, *Cancelleria*, p. 401; it was significantly registered in ASF *Missive* 47, "Littere de rebus *magis privatis*," fols. 54v-55v): "Mirati primum sumus, Beatissime Pater, inveteratam ad nos scribendi Summorum Pontificum consuetudinem repente mutatam his literis tuis. . . . An non diligis eum Populum quem censuris castigas talibus? quem armis tuis in viam tuam redigere conaris? Nulla profecto, si Delectionis [appellationem] auferas, causa restabit cur ita proseguare." On Salutati's part in the War of the Eight Saints, Ullman, *The Humanism of C. S.*; on the publicity enjoyed by Scala's letter, quoted in full in the *Commentarius* of the Genoese chronicler Antonio Gallo (*RIS* n.s., 23, 1, pp. 71-72), F. E. Comani, "Spigolature fiorentine in Reggio e Modena (1478-81)," *Studi storici* 10 (1901):73-87, esp. 74-79.

[70] Fil. Sacramoro and G. J. Simonetta to the Sforza, 20 September 1478, ASMi SPE Fir. 296.

ing (at first briefly and four days later in detail) to the large French embassy that passed through Florence in January 1479 on its way to Rome.[71] When the Dieci moved to Fiesole that summer to escape the plague then raging in Florence, it was apparently Scala's duty to remain in the city to dispatch and receive letters, which on at least one occasion we find him taking out to Fiesole.[72] At the end of June 1479 he was elected a member of the Otto di Guardia for four months, which seems to have revived his influence, for it is at this time we find him again attending meetings of the Dieci and writing confidentially to Lorenzo and to other members of his family.[73]

It was doubtless in this capacity that Scala was sent to southern Tuscany on at least two occasions in the autumn of 1479. The fortress of Poggibonsi had just fallen to the enemy in quick succession to the fortress of Poggio Imperiale and, with the enemy advancing on Colle Val d'Elsa, Scala was considered an appropriate emissary to put heart into the army. On 25 September the Florentine commissaries reported to the Dieci that Scala had "demonstrated in his speech with great wisdom and ability how important the territory of Colle was

---

[71] ASF *Risp. verb. orat.* 2, fols. 62r (11 January 1479: "Quod oratio latina fuit, Magistratus iussu Cancellarius breviter respondit"; cf. Fil Sacramoro to the Sforza, 12 January 1479, ASMi SPE Fir. 297: "La resposta li fuo facta per d. Barth°. Scala latine, perchè così loro exposeno le parte sue") and 62v-65r (15 January 1479, ed. D. Godefroy and Lenglet du Fresnoy, *Mémoires de M. Philippe de Comines*, London-Paris, 1747, 4: 184-188).

[72] Fil. Sacramoro to the Sforza, 21 June 1479, ASMi SPE Fir. 298: "essendo cum li Signori .X. M. Bartholomeo Scala, che era venuto da Firenze, referse alle loro Signorie . . . como li era accapitato novamente una littera alle mano del Cardinale de Sancto Petro ad Vincula . . . Dice epso M. Bartholomeo che vedute epse lettere, le lassò poy venire via a epsi oratori."

[73] ASF *Tratte* 82, fol. 3r; 354, fol. 53r: he was appointed for 4 months from 1 July 1479. He was twice elected chairman of the Otto for 4 days (on 29 August and 30 September), and on 15 and 16 September he was appointed with different colleagues to decide the punishment due to a critic of the state and government and to settle a dispute (as well as being sent to southern Tuscany, below), ASF *Otto di Guardia* 53, fols. 10r, 21r-v, 28r. Cf. his letters to Lorenzo and his mother Lucrezia Tornabuoni of 29 July-16 August and 18 October (including two undated notes), ASF *MAP* 37, 588 and 633; 22, 334; 80, 78; 34, 523.

[87]

to your state, and with powerful arguments he urged and exhorted [the army] in your name to defend it in every possible way. He was welcomed and what he had to say was well received."[74] Scala returned to Florence and a week later the inhabitants of Colle were offered full Florentine citizenship if they prevented their town from falling to the enemy.[75] In October Scala was again sent to southern Tuscany, this time to encourage the league camp to move from San Casciano to San Gimignano, nearer to Colle.[76] He stayed in San Gimignano for at least two weeks and his letters to the Dieci in this period paint a vivid picture of his activities, showing him organizing supplies of food and ammunition; on his arrival rousing a captain from his bed to discuss the commission of the captain, who despite finding the hour "late . . . nevertheless came"; mounting his horse and leading everyone he found out of the gate and on to the meadow to display them to the enemy when Colle gave the battle signal, "as one conducts the affairs of wise men"; tipping guides and spies, "and a few others

[74] ASF *Dieci Responsive* 25, fol. 290 (from the League camp at San Casciano): "messer Bart. Schala fu hoggi qui . . . et molto prudentemente et bene mostrò nel suo parlare di quanta importantia era a lo stato vostro la terra di Colle, et con ragioni efficacissime gli confortò et strinse in nome vostro a doverla difendere in tucti e modi. Fu veduto volentieri et con buono animo udito ciò che disse." On the military situation, see Lorenzo de' Medici's *Lettere*, vol. 4, excursus.

[75] See ch. 1, n. 15 above. Scala's return to Florence at the time this offer was made is demonstrated by his autograph in ASF *Dieci Missive* 10, fol. 99v (commission of Jacopo Lanfredini to Bologna, [28 September-2 October, probably 1 October]). Moreover on 30 September he was elected chairman of the Otto di Guardia for 4 days, whereas he is registered as absent from 7 to 29 October (ASF *Otto di Guardia* 53, fols. 28r, 33v-48v *passim*).

[76] See ASF *Dieci Missive* 10, fols. 117v (Dieci to A. Spini, Commissary in Colle, 10 October 1479: "[Scala] domattina parte per esser prima in campo et poi là," i.e. San Gimignano); 119r (the same to B. Gianfigliazzi, 11 October 1479: "et questo ci pare che debbino bastare insino che il campo vi vada . . . et a questo fine vi habbiamo mandato M. Barth° [Scala]"). Scala received two payments from the Dieci: fl. 12, £239 6s ("mandato in campo a San Casciano e a San Gimigniano, per le spese facte per se et famigli et ghuide in tutto dì 33 in più volte") and fl. 58 ("mandato a San Gimigniano da' Dieci: [margin] fùvi mandato pe' casi di Colle"), ASF *Dieci Delib.* 22, fols. 212v, 211r.

as it seemed to me necessary. If I had more money, I could do even more and would think it well spent, investing it for a return of a hundred for one"; interrogating an enemy spy with torture and sending his statement meticulously on to the Dieci after authorizing him to be hanged; and disciplining a cowardly "foreign" foot soldier with the whip and chain, putting him "all beaten up" into prison after the local populace, including children, had had their turn at giving him "a kick and a punch." Not for nothing was Scala a member of a flagellant lay religious company in Florence, and this visit to the war front as a member of the Otto di Guardia evidently gave him an opportunity to indulge his love of discipline, "for if what we needed was sluggards to win, we would be victorious everywhere," he commented drily.[77]

Despite being ambushed and nearly killed on arrival and spending one day confined to his bed, Scala was very active in San Gimignano and his work was approved by the Dieci, even if he failed to get the camp transferred there before Colle fell.[78] Uninhibited by diplomatic formula and protocol, his letters to his colleagues in Florence reveal his vigorous personality and the flavor of his conversation, combining as they do conventional adages with realistic evaluations of people and situations. "Hunger does not wait," he told the Dieci, and—as

[77] See his letters to the Dieci, 13-16 October 1479, ASF *Dieci Responsive* 25, fols. 316-333 *passim*. The captain was Antonello da Forlì. On 17 October the Dieci replied to Scala's letters of 13 and 14 October concerning the interrogation and hanging of a prisoner: "Maraviglanci bene che non diciate alcuna cosa di quelle examine, che non importa mancho che l'altre cose" (but cf. their letter of the 15th, in n. 78 below), *Dieci Missive* 10, fol. 133v.

[78] See Scala's letters of 13 and 14 October referred to above and the Dieci's letter to Scala of 15 October 1479 (ASF *Dieci Missive* 10, fol. 130r): "Havemo hiersera la vostra et restiamo molto satisfatti delli advisi et opere vostre. . . . Commendiamo assai quanto havete fatto nel ritenere et examinare quelli huomini d'arme, etc." They wrote to Scala on 11, 15, 17, 18, 22, 24 and 25 October and jointly to him and P. Vettori on 15 October (*ibid.*, fols. 119v, 128v, 130r, 133v, 136v, 146r, 151r, 152v). In their first letter (11 October, fol. 119v), they wrote: "Ècci paruto darvene adviso, perchè crediamo che la Cresima vostra doppo questo baptesimo harà facto uno buono christiano. Crediamo la difficultà resti negli altri, dove bisogna usiate lo ingegno et industria vostra, et sollecitiate in modo che si facci bugiardo colui che disse il nostro sarebbe il soccorso di Messina."

they (and later Machiavelli) well knew—"the first fortification is always the hearts of the inhabitants." "God does not abandon him who helps himself," he wrote, as he quickly succeeded in getting supplies of bread and flour to the famished town; and, finding himself "at a banquet where more has been spent than we have calculated for," he pressed the Dieci for more money, cannons and workmen.[79] Throughout his embassy he reported frankly on the soldiers and commissaries with whom he worked; praising one constable as worth more than all the rest, he added, "I wouldn't say it if I thought they could hear me, because I would make too many enemies, but your servant must speak the truth." And after making an invidious comparison between two captains, Scala and the commissary in a joint letter commented: "it is our duty to tell your Lordships everything we hear."[80] When Scala finally asked to be allowed to return to Florence on 27 October, he did so because he failed to see that his staying on could "bear any fruit, since—as I have said—everything is well organized here and in the control of men who know their office well."[81]

He returned to Florence in time for the reelection of the Dieci, who were approaching the end of their third six-month term of office. None of the original magistracy—not even Lorenzo—were reappointed, and Scala lost his position as their first chancellor also; times were bad for Lorenzo and his supporters in Florence, and Lorenzo reacted by leaving the city to plead for peace privately with Ferrante of Naples.[82] After

---

[79] See his letters to the Dieci of 13 October (cf. Machiavelli, *Il Principe*, ch. 20), and 16 October 1479, *cit.*: "La fame non aspecta," "la prima fortificatione sempre, come sapete, sono e cuori degli abitatori," "chi ss'aiuta, Idio nollo abandona," "mi sono trovato a tal convito dove s'è speso più che abiamo facto . . . conto."

[80] Letters of 16 and 18 October 1479, ASF *Dieci Responsive* 25, fols. 333r ("Nol dire' se credessi che m'udissono, perchè farei troppi nimici, ma el vostro servidore vi debba dire el vero"), and 334v.

[81] Letter of 27 October 1479, *ibid.*, fol. 331v.

[82] Lorenzo sent an envoy to Naples on the day that the new Dieci was elected on 3 November 1479. A list of the new Dieci is in ASF *Dieci Missive* 12, fol. 1r. On 5 November Fil. Sacramoro explained to the Sforza that "per non passare l'ordini, videlicet, et consuetudine de la terra, che sono che de 6 mesi in 6 mesi se sogliono mutare, nè ad più de 18 mesi, el

Lorenzo's sudden departure and before the new Dieci took office on 13 December, Scala was able to perform one last vital service for him. He prepared a plenary mandate transferring the Dieci's extraordinary authority for war, peace, alliances and treaties to Lorenzo as their absent colleague: "For it seemed to be to the benéfit for the republic that wherever Lorenzo de' Medici was, he should do what he and his ancestors always did and join the public interest to his own private interest and give much greater preference to the public interest: that is to say, that he should forget his own in order to consult the public interest."[83] This was a pious hope, and Lorenzo—doubtless for personal reasons as well as for the formal reason that his mandate had not been approved by the Cento as was customary—later refused to act in a public capacity.[84] Scala, too, would have preferred the mandate to have been authorized by the Cento and had had to bow to the opinion of colleagues who thought it better not to risk it.[85] Although Lo-

quale tempo se trova fu ancho già Cosmo [de' Medici], se trovano quasi mai essere stati reconfirmati" (ASMi SPE Fir. 298).

[83] BNF MS Palat. 1091, fol. 5r: "Mandatum Decemvirorum Baliae Civitatis Florentiae in Laurentium de Medicis" (12 December 1479): "Neque enim visum est e republica esse, ut Laurentius Medices ubi ubi esset, quod semper ipse maioresque eius fecissent, Rei suae privatae publicam quoque non coniungeret, et publicam multo anteferret, idest rerum etiam obliviceretur suarum, ut publicis consuleret. Omnibus id suffragiis deliberatum." The new Dieci confirmed this unanimously on the following day, and it was subscribed by Scala: "Ego Bartholomaeus Scala cancell. florentinus haec omnia rogavi et mandavi litteris his et manu mea subscripsi" (fol. 6r). This plenary mandate or procuration was drawn up in notarial form, dated 12 December, by A. Braccesi, ASF *Notarile* B 2320 (A. Braccesi, 1477-1479), fols. 126v-127r.

[84] See Lorenzo de' Medici to the Dieci, 6 January 1480, ed. B. Buser, *Lorenzo de' Medici als Italienischer Staatsmann*, Leipzig, 1879, p. 151: "che m'è paruto meglo a proposito stare chome privato," adding "non è forse inconveniente, non essendo io electo pel Cento"; cf. Fil. Sacramoro to the Sforza, 30 December 1479 (quoted in Lorenzo de' Medici's *Lettere*, 4, no. 445, n. 7): that to his question as to whether Lorenzo had "titulo de oratore, et tenga grado de ambasatore, m'è facto intendere de non, nè l'havea perchè ha monstro non lo volere."

[85] See his letter to Lorenzo de' Medici, [1]5 December 1479, ASF *MAP* 34, 420, ed. Fabroni, *Laur. Medicis vita*, 2:205-206. The letter is dated "quinto decembris," but as it was written after the 13th and was received in

renzo ceased to be a member of the Dieci on the day this mandate was approved, the new magistracy confirmed it on the following day. Because "some people were very keen" that the mandate and other diplomatic documents should reach Naples after Lorenzo, "in order to emphasize that you left here as a private citizen,"[86] the dispatch was delayed, and on 1 January 1480 Scala sent them off again in case they had not arrived safely, together with a plea to Lorenzo to "adopt our mandate," which would "in time be more honorable for you."[87] When Lorenzo finally received it in Naples, he professed to be pleased with it: "If you are pleased, then so am I," Scala replied to him on 12 January. "The things produced by the chancery used at one time to be very well received down there. That is why I decided to do it in that way. Nothing that you do in the public sector or concerning me has displeased me—nor can it or should it, when I have received everything from you, whose life I want to endure."[88] It is true

Naples on 24 December, "quindecim" must be intended, "*decim*" probably having been elided into "*decem*bris." Since the Dieci enjoyed absolute powers of peace, war, etc., for the duration of their office, they were entitled to delegate them to Lorenzo (although after the 12th he was no longer their "absent colleague"), but normally the authority of the Cento was necessary for approving mandates.

[86] See Scala's letter to Lorenzo de' Medici of 25 December 1479, ASF *MAP* 34, 592.

[87] Letter of 1 January 1480, ASF *MAP* 34, 408, ed. Fabroni, *Laur. Medicis vita*, 2:200-201, and postscript attached to *MAP* 34, 412. This postscript is undated, and although it is attached to a letter dated 5 January 1480, its close resemblance to the "poliza" the Dieci added to their letter of 1 January ("havamo scripto et sugellato questo quando havemo le tue de 23 et 26," BNF MS Palat. 1091, fol. 24r) and its reference to a further mandate to be drawn up by Braccesi suggests it was written after Lorenzo's letter of 26 December had arrived in Florence and was despatched with the letters of 1 January "per le poste del Duca di Milano" on 2 January 1480. Pierantonio Buondelmonti had been exiled on 11 December 1479 and Giovanni Bartoli (not Ridolfi, as Scala—and Francesco del Barone on 4 January—wrote) was committed to the Stinche for 5 years on 27 December 1479, ASF *Otto di Guardia* 54, fols. 38v, 53r-v.

[88] Scala to Lorenzo de' Medici, 12 January 1480, ASF *MAP* 34, 414, ed. Fabroni, *Laur. Medicis vita*, 2:202-204, who mistranscribes "le cose della *cavalleria*" (followed by Janet Ross in her translation in *The Lives of the Early Medici*, pp. 233-234) instead of "della *cancelleria*."

that the language of the mandate as drafted by Scala is unusually extravagant, and Scala must have been harking back to
the days when the Neapolitan secretary, Antonello Petrucci,
admired his letters and he in turn admired the flowing rhetoric of the Neapolitans.[89] Scala also claimed that no one but
Lorenzo could have received so wide a commission and that
he was "one of the first to have christened the *carte blanche*,"
but in fact the Dieci could not give Lorenzo more than the
full powers they possessed themselves in the field of war,
peace, treaties and alliances, and this they transferred not only
to him but also to the two Florentines who conducted the
peace settlement.[90] Nevertheless Scala's collaboration—as well
as his rhetoric—may have been crucial at a time of wavering
support for Lorenzo.

We can already see two themes vying for predominance in
Scala's letters to Lorenzo: one his dependence on Lorenzo,
the other his concern that Lorenzo should "stick as far as possible to what is honorable in the peace negotiations";[91] and if
the former is more evident in his early letters, the second
theme becomes increasingly pronounced as time passed and
Lorenzo failed to return with the promised peace. Scala's first
letter to Lorenzo, written in Latin, confessed the fear he felt

[89] On the rhetoric of the Neapolitans and Scala's relationship with their
chancery, see nn. 13 and 57 above.

[90] Cf. the mandate of A. Biliotti and N. Michelozzi, 2 March 1480, ASMi
SPE Nap. 297. It is true that in both Scala's draft and Braccesi's notarial document, Lorenzo is empowered to treat with Ferrante not only about peace,
alliance, etc., but "de . . . omni republica, ut videbitur, transigatque quicquid
Laurentio Medici visum fuerit," "prout eidem Laurentio libere videbitur et
placebit," and that whatever he did the Dieci promised would be ratified
by the Florentine people, whereas Biliotti and Michelozzi are given a
plenary mandate to treat only of matters relating to peace, alliance, etc. But
as the Dieci themselves possessed only "auctoritatem . . . et potestatem
bellorum et pacis, amicitiarum et foederum . . . maximam" (as all the mandates themselves state), they could not grant away more than the powers
they themselves possessed; in both cases the form was that of a plenary
mandate.

[91] See his letter to Lorenzo de' Medici of 12 January 1480, *cit.*: "Hòvi
scripto questo perchè stiate più che si può in su lo honorevole nelle conditioni della pace."

after Lorenzo left Florence: "I shall be angry with you for a long time, my Lorenzo, my support, that is, until you return —for what could be longer? . . . Let me tell you the truth about myself, I cannot be brave and I cannot but fear as well as admire your decision to go. Indeed, for several days I have been distraught and practically beside myself with fear: if I can pull myself together, I will be able to write to you more sensibly." And after telling him how hard he had labored over his mandate, he asks: "Who should be surprised that I am blinded without my sun, lost without my leader and ship-wrecked without my pole-star?"[92] Ten days later, on Christmas Day, he again admitted that he had been incapable of writing much before because he was distracted with fear, but now he felt reassured and "filled with tremendous hope that you will give us peace and strengthen the state."[93] Scala's hope was fulfilled, but not for several months, and in the meantime he remained nervous, begging Lorenzo not to cite him as the source of the information that Lorenzo's companions in Naples were leaking news, "because we are, as you know [in Latin], *more fragile even than glass.*"[94]

In view of this his advice to Lorenzo was commendably public spirited, not peace at any price but only peace with honor, and although there was inevitably an element of expediency in his argument, he never encouraged Lorenzo to seek his own salvation at the expense of that of Florence.[95] He wanted Lorenzo's mandate to be ratified by the Cento instead of the Dieci; he wanted Lorenzo to negotiate in Naples in a

[92] [1]5 December 1479, ASF *MAP* 34, 420, ed. Fabroni, *Laur. Medicis vita* 2:205-206: "Cui vero mirum est si sine meo sole obcecatus . . . sine duce vager, et sine mea arcto etiam naufragem."

[93] 25 December 1479, ASF *MAP* 34, 592: "ha preso l'animo grandissima speranza che voi ci diate la pace et confermiate lo stato," quoting Petrarch (*Le rime*, no. 53): "Et dicetur id vere de te: 'Se altri l'aiutò giovane et forte, Questo in vechieza la campò de Morte.'"

[94] 12 January 1480: "perchè, come sapete, siamo *vel vitro fragiliores.*"

[95] See, for example, his letter to Lorenzo of 4 January 1480, ASF *MAP* 34, 410, ed. Fabroni, *Laur. Medicis vita*, 2:201-202: "Ma assai avanza chi senza alcuno altro rispecto nè di se nè di sue cose va a fare quel bene che può per la sua patria"; and n. 91 above.

public, not a private, capacity; he was afraid that if the terms were not honorable, peace would not be welcome: "you know our ways," he reminded Lorenzo, "we want and we don't want according to our circumstances and moods, reason has little to do with it."[96] He was one of the first people to suggest that Lorenzo's private interests might conflict with those of the state for, although Lorenzo may have served his own interests very wisely with regard to Girolamo Riario, Scala wrote to him, any payment made to Riario would be very painful and the costs considered that morning were terrifying: "I know that you will give the consideration to everything that you should. . . . It is difficult to divine what you want done, in particular what the public need is, and to be able to do it." He went on to explain that, although outwardly the city seemed unchanged since Lorenzo left for Naples, "yet many different thoughts and words are being expressed both by your friends and by all manner of people": in other words public opinion was turning against him. Scala urged him to return and warned him of strange rumors that were circulating about his return through Rome, which he should avoid.[97] It was on 12 January that he urged him "to stick to what is honourable," and again warned him about the situation in Florence and rumors from Naples. Three days later he reported the confusion being created by merchants' letters from Rome: " 'The Pope will never agree, the Count [Girolamo Riario] would agree.' 'The Pope agrees, the Count on no account,' etc; and even these contradictions they shred into a thousand small pieces: 'Messer Lorenzo da Castello has gone to wreck it all' and 'he has gone to settle,' 'to justify himself' —and infinite opinions and ideas. For God's sake, get us out

---

[96] Letters of [1]5 December 1479, [1 January 1480?], and 1 January 1480: "eventi" and not "venti" as in Fabroni, p. 201.

[97] Letter of 5 January 1480, ASF *MAP* 34, 412, ed. Gentile, "B. S. e i Medici," p. 137, doc. 8; cf. Antonio Pucci's letter to Lorenzo of 11 January, ASF *MAP* 61, 80, ed. Fabroni, *Laur. Medici vita*, 2:211: "Io credo che alla vostra partita di qui le chose erano molto adietro, et qui è chi crede l'andata vostra habbia chonturbato tutto et facto le chonditioni nostre più chattive."

of this with [Ferrante's] good will."[98] In February he warned him that there had been talk of changing the regime in a meeting of citizens: "But the best marksmen aim at the bull's eye. In my opinion it is essential for you to be here, so that by procuring peace down there you don't find yourself with a worse war on your hands here."[99] As consistently as he warned Lorenzo of the internal situation and his duty to Florence, Scala insisted that it was impossible to separate Lorenzo's interests from the public interest, "and have often said as much," that the object of peace and security was identical for Lorenzo, "and for the regime which is joined to you, and for the city which is joined to the regime," hence his duty to Florence and Lorenzo "have always seemed and always will seem identical."[100]

Influenced, perhaps, by Scala's advice and that of other friends, Lorenzo decided to return home on 27 February before peace was finally signed. He was delayed by bad weather for a week, and on 10 March the Dieci asked Scala to write to Lorenzo once more. It was late and some members had already gone home when Scala wrote out and subscribed the letter in their name.[101] But Lorenzo was already on the high seas, and by the time Scala's letter reached Naples on 14 March he was almost back in Florence. He arrived there the following day, and less than a month later he introduced constitutional reforms that strengthened the state—an object Scala as a

[98] Letter of 15 January, ASF *MAP* 34, 415, ed. Fabroni, *Laur. Medicis vita*, 2:204-205, in English in Ross, *Lives*, pp. 234-235.

[99] Letter of 12 February 1480, ASF *MAP* 34, 418.

[100] See his letters of [1]5 December 1479, 5 January 1480 and 12 February 1480 (ch. 14, n. 1 below, cf. N. Rubinstein, "Notes on the word *stato* in Florence before Machiavelli," *Florilegium Historiale, Essays presented to W. K. Ferguson*, ed. J. G. Rowe and W. H. Stockdale, Toronto, 1971, p. 319). Cf. Antonio Pucci's similar interpretation of Lorenzo's role in his letter of 11 January: "Voi siete chostì per fare e fatti della cipta, et del nostro stato, et chome v'ho detto credo n'habbiate più e termini che tutti gli altri, et però mi rendo certo seguitrete tutto quello che farà per la cipta et per lo stato" (ed. Fabroni, 2:212). This view is later reflected in Guicciardini's *Dialogo*, p. 73.

[101] ASF *MAP* 45, 294. On Lorenzo's return, see L. Landucci, *Diario fiorentino*, p. 34.

Medicean can only have approved of, but with results he perhaps did not predict.

On 10 April a Balìa was appointed with full powers to introduce reforms, and for the first time Scala found himself an elected member of this council. Although it was ostensibly appointed to discuss financial and electoral reforms, it rapidly became apparent that its principal purpose was constitutional reform and the creation of the (in effect) permanent Council of Seventy with two magistracies drawn from its members, the Otto di Pratica responsible for foreign policy, and the Twelve Procurators responsible for home affairs and finance.[102] The significance of these reforms for Scala's standing soon became apparent. For, whereas he had previously been the only permanency or "fixture" in the government (although only an executive member) and therefore someone of great importance, he was now only titular head of a magistracy that in effect had been superseded by other longer-term bodies: these bodies had their own chancellors and in 1480 Scala was not one of them.[103]

The creation of the Council of Seventy also threatened Scala's authority in another way. Both it and the two magistracies had developed out of earlier *ad hoc pratiche* and committees over which Scala had formerly presided. However, with its acquisition of legislative functions the Council of Seventy also became the concern of the notary of the Riformagioni, from whom Scala had been trying to wrest authority during the previous decade.[104] The "tiresome," "stubborn" and ambitious Giovanni Guidi was not popular in the chancery, but he was becoming increasingly powerful in the state

---

[102] On these reforms, see Rubinstein, *Government*, pp 197-202.

[103] The Otto di Pratica appointed as their chancellor on 3 July 1480 Alessandro Braccesi, who had in effect succeeded Scala as first chancellor of the Dieci in the last months of the war (ASF *Otto Delib.* 1, fol. 3r), but see below.

[104] See chs. 6 and 7 below. On Guidi, "quella fraschetta del notaio delle reformacione loro," see S. Sacramori to G. M. Sforza, 29 November 1474, ASMi SPE Fir. 288; cf. ser Francesco di ser Barone to Lorenzo de' Medici, 4 January 1480 (BNF MS Ginori Conti, 29, 101, fol. 1): "questo testerello di ser G."

and also close to Lorenzo de' Medici; after Lorenzo's return from Naples he rather than Scala seems to have gained the ascendency. As a Medicean, Scala's position in Florence was assured by the reforms that strengthened the Medici regime in 1480, but it was at the immediate cost of his practical influence.

So the third period of Scala's relationship with Lorenzo begins with Scala's fortunes at a comparatively low ebb. However, it did not take long for him to regain his lost favor with Lorenzo, or his control of the chancery. Although he never fully recovered the authority he had enjoyed in the 1470s, he quickly reestablished his responsibility for external affairs in the Otto di Pratica and Dieci di Balìa and, like the good bureaucrat he was, he secured overall control of all departments of the chancery in an important reform scheme at the end of 1483. Now he increasingly left the day-to-day labors in the chancery to subordinates, but he retained to the end of his life his special interest in diplomacy and was always to be found to the fore in prestigious embassies and negotiations—orating before the pope in Rome in 1484 and negotiating with envoys of the sultan of Egypt[105] and with the ambassador of the king of Poland, Filippo Buonaccorsi (Callimachus), who rewarded him with "a very large white bearskin." In 1481 the dukes of Milan reappointed him their secretary and secret councillor, in 1482 the government of Lucca presented him with a silver dish, in 1484 the pope knighted him, in 1491 the government of San Gimignano gave him sixteen bottles of wine—from each according to his means.[106] Scala had become a figure, one might say, of international standing.

Scala's standing was also high at this time with the people of Florence—unlike that of Giovanni Guidi, who was never

[105] S. M. Stern, *Documents from Islamic Chanceries*, Oxford, 1965 (referring to the draft treaty and addition sealed and subscribed by Scala on 20-22 November 1488: BNF MS Fondo del Furia 49, eighteenth-century copy, quoted by Bandini, *Collectio*, p. 12n., and Riccard. MS 767, fols. 206-207), and ASF *Otto Delib*. 2, fol. 20v (20 February 1488).

[106] On these gifts, see ch. 8 below.

apparently liked by the populace and was the first to suffer their wrath in November 1494. They received the long Latin oration Scala delivered when Costanzo Sforza was appointed captain general in 1481 with shouts of "Long live messer Bartolomeo" and, since they cannot have appreciated the oration itself, their applause must have been a token of general esteem.[107] In January 1485 the critical Council of the People approved his knighthood with a total of 173 votes out of 195, of which Scala was justifiably proud. Given the people's dislike of this discriminatory legislation and the difficulties they created for Angelo della Stufa and others, they must have been genuinely pleased in the case of Scala that one of themselves had been elected to this élite brotherhood.[108]

During this period Scala also achieved considerable political success. Having been voted eligible for the Three Highest Offices in 1471 and having exercised the priorate in 1473, the rest followed with inevitable ease.[109] He was elected a member of the scrutiny council of 1484 by the Council of Seventy with no opposition.[110] Although he was absent in Rome for much of the period it was at work, as a member of the *cerchio* or inner circle of citizens in his district he was not only successful himself in the scrutiny but was able to qualify his brother Andrea, his infant son Giuliano and his wife's first

[107] Manni, *Vita*, pp. 27-28; cf. Benvenuti, *Quadri storici*, pp. 98-99: "a dì iv d'ottobre, la mattina di San Francesco, in su la ringhiera ci fu una lunga e degna orazione fatta per messer Bartolommeo Scala, per la cui eloquenza uno che era accanto a me conciòssiache cominciasse a dire: Viva Messer Bartolommeo! tutto il populo seguitandolo ad alta voce disse l'istesso." On the oration, see ch. 6, n. 51 below.

[108] ASF *Provv.* 175, fol. 167v. The Council of the People approved on 11 January by 173 votes to 22, that of the Commune on the 12th by 132 votes to 31, the Cento on the 13th by 98 votes to 14. The decree is ed. Manni, *Vita*, pp. 31-34. On Angelo della Stufa's difficulties, see ch. 3, n. 36 above.

[109] See n. 21 above.

[110] ASF *Tratte* 15 (unfoliated): "Scrutineum arrotorum pro novo scrutineo celebratum per dominos LXXta. die 29 Sept. 1484." Scala received 50 votes in favor, none against, cf. Giovanni Guidi: 56/0; Lorenzo di Pierfrancesco de' Medici: 64/2; Scala's father-in-law Giovanni di Lorenzo Benci: 4/0. On this scrutiny, see Rubinstein, *Government*, pp. 210-216, and Piero Guicciardini's detailed account of its procedure, *ibid.*, append. 11, pp. 318-325.

cousin Giovanfrancesco Benci for certain offices—graphically
bearing out Piero Guicciardini's analysis of the workings of
the scrutiny.[111] Just over a year later Scala achieved the highest political honor the Florentine state had to offer when he
was elected Gonfalonier of Justice in May 1486, which also
enabled him to be elected a life member of the Council of
Seventy on 24 July 1486.[112] So for the next eight years he
formed a part of the all-important council which has been described as the "pivot" of the Medici regime.[113] A list of names
compiled on 28 August 1493, on the eve of the expulsion of
the Medici, demonstrates how fully Scala had entered the inner ruling group: he himself figures in the *veduti vivi* column
of those alive who had had their names drawn for office, his
son Giuliano in the fourth column of "seekers" or "hopefuls,"
no Scalas with Lorenzo de' Medici in the obituary column of
veduti morti, nor in that of "unsuccessfuls, alive and dead."[114]

[111] See the gathering of nominations (evidently for Leon d'Oro in S. Giovanni) for offices voted on on 9 January 1485 and subsequently, the so-called
Eleven Offices (actually 12, comprising captaincies, vicariates and podestà-
ships in the dominion), the Provedoratichi, etc. in Rome, ASV Fondo
Borghese, ser. 4, 78, fols. 46r-66r. Scala is listed as third member of the
cerchio (on which, see Rubinstein, *Government*, p. 57, and on its preeminent role in the scrutiny, Piero Guicciardini, *ibid.*, p. 318) for the election of the Eleven Offices and Provedoratichi, and as such he nominated
(for the first) Giovanfrancesco di Tommaso Benci and his son Giuliano
(last on the list of 252 names) and (for the second) Giuliano again and his
brother Andrea (numbered 132 and 263 in a list of 270 names), *ibid.*, fols.
46r, 51v; 48r, 51r; 54r, 56r. Bartolomeo Scala stands last in a list of 23 numbered families, the remainder are unnumbered and have their age on 1
January 1485 beside them ("tutti questi sono 203," *ibid.*, fols. 58r-59r).
Guicciardini's description of voting for the Eleven Offices (and his comment that the large number of nominations—as many as "250 and more" in
some *gonfaloni*—was "al tutto contrario a volere che si squittini bene") is
ed. Rubinstein, *Government*, p. 325.

[112] Manni, *Vita*, p. 38; Cambi, *Delizie*, 21: 34. In order to exercise the
Gonfalonierate of Justice, Scala had to resign from his office of councillor
in the Guild of Lawyers and Notaries to which he was elected on 1 May
1486 for 4 months (ASF *Giudici e Notai* 26, fol. 92v). His election to the
Seventy is in ASF *Tratte Deliberazioni Append.* 2, fol. 136v.

[113] Rubinstein, *Government*, p. 203, cf. pp. 200-201.

[114] ASF *Tratte* 15 (a miscellaneous collection of records and memoranda
relating to elections, to which I was kindly directed by Dr. John Stephens,
unfoliated), a gathering of four leaves headed "A dì 28 d'agosto 1493" and

"Alive, successful and hopeful" aptly characterizes their position in 1493, although hopeful Giuliano had to remain for longer than his father can then have anticipated. The following year the Medici regime fell, and, although eligible, Giuliano was too young for the republican Great Council and had to wait until the return of the Medici in 1512 to be chosen for office. The fact that he was then a member of the Signoria on several occasions demonstrates how successful his father had been in inserting his family into the Medicean ruling class.[115]

Bartolomeo Scala's professional and personal success was assured, that seems certain. What is less certain is his relationship with Lorenzo in this last period: was Poliziano speaking the truth when he said Lorenzo often gave him Scala's letters to rewrite and that Lorenzo accepted Scala on the basis of someone else's opinion of him, not his own?[116] Although the circumstances of both men had changed, their characters had not. Lorenzo was now politically secure: as a permanent member of the Council of Seventy and frequently a member of its dependent magistracies, he had little need of Scala's former vital services. Equally, Scala was less dependent on his former value to Lorenzo now that he had acquired status in his own right. Lorenzo remained headstrong and intolerant of advice, Scala ponderous and legalistic. But both men also remained ambitious for power and enthusiastic for reform; and it was this that ensured their continued collaboration. Whereas before they had worked to reorganize and centralize political institutions in Florence, now they turned to the church, looking to Rome for personal rewards and to religious institutions as a field.for their reforming energies. In its wealth and authority, the church threatened the secular state as much as the medieval institutions—such as the Guelf Party or the dif-

---

written in four columns headed: "Veduti vivi," "Veduti morti," "Non veduti vivi et morti," "Cerchatori."

[115] See ch. 9 below. Giuliano was in fact a member of the last Signoria of the republic in 1532.

[116] *Opera*, pp. 396-399; and ch. 8 below.

fused judiciary—that Lorenzo and Scala had already attempted to reform, and it offered itself as an obvious field for both personal and public gain.

Lorenzo de' Medici's marriage to a member of the Orsini family must have encouraged his dynastic ambition in Rome but, as we have seen, his and Scala's early attempts to prepare the ground for his "crazy desire for a cardinalate" were frustrated. By the end of the Pazzi war their friend in Rome, Jacopo Ammannati, was dead and so, too, was Lorenzo's candidate for a cardinalate, his brother Giuliano. Lorenzo's children were still too young to be eligible, yet it was essential to establish a favorable relationship with the papacy, not only to forestall other possible candidates for a Florentine cardinalate[117] but also to recover the large sums of money owed to Lorenzo by the pope and his nephew Girolamo Riario. From the beginning of 1482 we find Scala, through the agency of an Augustinian monk, Fra Santi,[118] undertaking private negotiations in Rome: they partly concerned a benefice Scala had been offered by the bishop of Massa;[119] partly affairs in Em-

[117] Particularly Francesco di Tommaso Soderini, bishop of Volterra, the son of Lorenzo's old rival, whom the dukes of Milan had asked to be promoted to the Archbishopric of Pisa on Salviati's death in 1478 (in a letter to Lorenzo de' Medici, 8 May 1478, ASMi SPE Fir. 294); cf. Fubini, "Note Machiavelliane," pp. 386-387, n. 18, describing the Archbishopric of Pisa as "una sorte di ipoteca sulla candidatura cardinalizia." On Lorenzo's "fantasia del cardenallato," S. Sacramori to G. M. Sforza, 9 February 1473, ASMi SPE Fir. 283 (letterbook).

[118] On Fra Santi, see Scala's letter to the duke of Urbino asking for his release in the course of the Pazzi war (6 January 1479, London, British Library, Add. MS 16,163, fol. 12), and below. Scala describes him as "Priore di Sancto Antonio del Bosco," "molto mio amico," and he is doubtless identical with the "tavolaccino" (= "servidore pubblico," Giannotti, *Opere*, 1:22) who apparently occupied this Augustinian monastery in the name of the Florentine Signoria (or Scala), until it was reclaimed for the Order by Ambrogio Massari da Cora in 1483, A. Landucci, *Sacra Leccetana selva*, Rome, 1657, p. 63 ("fu occupato da alcuni secolari, e particolarmente da un tal Maestro Bartolomeo Scala, Conseglicre della Signoria di Fiorenza, e per lui vi stava un Tavolaccino di detta Signoria"); cf. Manni, *Vita*, p. 25; Perini, *Un emulo*, p. 20. On S. Antonio del Bosco (presumably identical with S. Antonio dei Confini), Repetti, *Dizionario*, 1:94; and below.

[119] See Scala's letter to G. Gianderoni, bishop of Massa, 9 February 1482, and to his secretary, Corrado de Gualdo, 9 May 1482, ASF *Minut.* 11, fol. 400r, and Modena MS, fol. 12r-v.

poli, where Scala was acting as arbitrator between the Augustinian Hermits and the lay Confraternity of the Most Holy Cross;[120] partly reform in the Augustinian monastery of Santo Spirito in Florence;[121] and partly a matter of importance involving Lorenzo de' Medici. In an autograph letter to Scala dated only 17 May the bishop of Massa, referring to Fra Santi's visit, writes: "His Holiness is extremely willing to have the Magnificent L[orenzo] as his son and [to protect] his state, and he will see that the Count Girolamo [Riario] will always be a good brother to him, and this he has sworn on his breast not once, but twice and three times." Although both he and the pope found it difficult to believe that Lorenzo could act without the agreement of Milan, he continued, if things were as Fra Santi said, "the business will be concluded as you want it to be. . . . If you think you can write a letter that can be shown separately, send me a memorandum of the particular matters which I will keep beside me to serve our need better. I have told Fra Santi many things by word of mouth which he will tell you about at length. Nothing else."[122] If this letter

[120] See Scala's letter to the cardinal of Rouen, 9 May 1482, Modena MS fol. 13v (cf. the Signoria to the cardinal of Rouen, 16 November 1481 and 9 February 1482, ASF *Minut.* 11, fol. 5v; *Missive* 49, fol. 103r; and below).

[121] See Scala's letter to Ambrogio Massari of 9 May 1482, Modena MS, fols. 12v-13r (cf. the Signoria to the same, 9 February 1482, ASF *Missive* 49, fol. 103r) and below. The close relationship between Scala's official and private letters at this time can be seen from the fact that his private letters are drafted in the same hand in both his Modena MS and in ASF *Minut.* 11 (see Modena MS fol. 26v: "Sequuntur littere domini Barth. nomine in Minutario Dominorum [listed]").

[122] ASF *MAP* 126, fol. 161: "Messer Bartolomeo, ò inteso ad licteram f[ra] S[anti] et per non stare in su le generali e perchè queste cose volgliano celere expeditione, rispondo per lettera de mia propria mano. La Santità del Nostro Signore è di bonissima volglia da avere el Magnifico L[orenzo] per figlolo e lo stato suo, e farà che el Conte Girolamo gli serà sempre bon fratello. E questo me lo à jurato sopra el pecto suo non una volta, ma due e tre. Pare dificile a Sua Santità e a me Lorenzo possa fare senza consentimento dello Stato de Milano, e per questo non pare si creda facilmente al frate . . . So certo che rispondendo voi come frate Santi dice, le cose avere vostro optato fine . . . Se così vi pare di scrivere, acciochè la lectera la possa mostrare a *partim*, mi mandate uno memoriale delle cose particulare e quello terrò apresso di me pure per fare melglio el bisongno. A frate Santi ò decto a boccha molte cose le quali lui vi dirà *ad longum*, etc. Non aliud." *Verso*:

was written in 1482 as evidence suggests it was,[123] it shows
Scala undertaking important private negotiations on behalf of
Lorenzo de' Medici on the eve of the Ferrarese war, apparently trying to avert war or prevent Lorenzo's personal interests becoming involved in it as they had been in the Pazzi
war.[124]

War did break out and Rome was once more inaccessible
to the Florentines until the pope signed a separate peace with
Florence, Naples and Milan on 12 December 1482. One of the
first to profit from the peace was Bartolomeo Scala. At the
beginning of December 1482, just before it was concluded,
Scala's nephew, Giovanni, was offered the Florentine benefice
of San Jacopo sopr' Arno.[125] On 11 January 1483 Fra Santi
(evidently already in Rome) was sent a sheaf of letters according to his prior arrangement with Scala: two from Scala
to the cardinal of Novara and the papal secretary Leonardo
Griffo, one from Lorenzo de' Medici to Girolamo Riario "in
good ink," one from messer Marino (Tomacelli) to messer
Agnello (Arcamonte), one from Francesco Gaddi to his
brother Taddeo, one from Scala to Taddeo and another to

"insigni et claro. viro domino Barth. Scal[e] Ill. domini Floren. Secretario
ut fra[tri] Carissimo S[uo]."

[123] It fits convincingly with what we know of Fra Santi's itinerary in
1482, when he left for Rome with letters dated 9 May, including one to
the bishop's secretary, to whom Scala commends himself: ten days later
the bishop would have replied to Scala (*MAP* 126, fol. 161?), three days
later (before he would have received the letter, but with Fra Santi still in
Rome) Scala commended himself again to the bishop in a letter to Fra
Santi dated 20 May 1482 (Modena MS, fol. 28v).

[124] On the outbreak of the Ferrarese war and the attempts of Lorenzo
de' Medici and Ercole d'Este to avert it through Giuliano della Rovere in
January 1482, see Pastor, *Storia dei papi*, 2:547; cf. *Storia di Milano*, 7:354-
359.

[125] Rome, ASV Reg. Vat. 624, fols. 63v-64v, Sixtus IV to Giovanni di
Tomè Scala de Colle, "rectori parrochialis ecclesie Sancti Jacobi supra
Arnum Florentin.," 3 December 1482. Giovanni, described in the Bull as
"in vigessimo tue etatis anno constitutus," was to be inducted by the abbot
of the Florentine monastery of San Felice and by Carlo de' Medici and
Manente Buondelmonti (not Baldimonte, as written), Florentine canons.
The previous incumbent, Lorenzo Colonna, was accused of rebellion and
lese maiestatis.

Zanobi Gaddi. In addition Scala had also spoken to Giovanni Tornabuoni to ask him to use his influence with the protonotary in Rome.[126] What was the object of this exercise? According to Scala's letter to the cardinal of Novara, it concerned "a small piece of business of mine," evidently a benefice he hoped to obtain through the cardinal's influence, to whom he also commended the cause in Rome of Girolamo Biondo, son of the historian Flavio Biondo.[127] It seems certain, however, that it also formed the diplomatic prelude to more important matters: Lorenzo de' Medici's revived dynastic and commercial ambitions in Rome.

The former were revealed on the death of the cardinal of Rouen on 22 January 1483, when Lorenzo asked Louis XI if it was possible to obtain any of the cardinal's benefices for his son Giovanni; and although the king was unable to favor him on this occasion, he amiably (but unsuccessfully) offered the seven-year-old boy other benefices that year, Fontdoux and Aix-en-Provence, "a huge office and rarely bestowed on one of his age."[128] In April Lorenzo began to lend the pope considerable sums of money again and to receive from the pope

[126] See Scala's letter to Fra Santi [11 January 1483?], Modena MS, fol. 36r. His letter to the cardinal of Novara and part of his letter to [Taddeo Gaddi?] are *ibid.*, fol. 36r-v. Lorenzo's letter to Girolamo Riario is referred to in *Protocolli del carteggio*, p. 220.

[127] "negotiolum quoddam meum." On Girolamo Biondo, *doctor utriusque iuris* in 1459, see Nogara, *Scritti inediti e rari di Biondo Flavio*, p. 210, cf. pp. cxlix and clxxx. On his attempts to recover his benefice of S. Reparata in Castrocaro, Rome, ASV Reg. Suppl. 807, fols. 136v-137r (14 November 1482) and ASF *Dieci Missive, Leg. Comm.* 5, fols. 406v-407r (letter of 5 July 1483, urging "qualche buono assexto a satisfactione dello utile et honore di M. Hieronimo il più che si potessi").

[128] In general, Picotti, *La giovinezza*, pp. 70-73. The pope's Bull granting Giovanni the *commendam* of Fontdoux on 28 May 1483 "in octavo tue etatis anno" is in ASV Reg. Vat. 630, fols. 229r-230r, confirmed at the end of February and September 1484, Reg. Vat. 677, fols. 189v-191v, and 700, fols. 59r-61v; according to the register of *Obligationes et Solutiones* (ASV 84A, fols. 155v, 173r; cf. *Intr. Exit.* 508, fol. 36r), Giovanni paid 14 carlini for Fontdoux on 2 June 1483 and Antoine Balue (its French incumbent) the same amount on 11 October 1483. Aix-en-Provence is described in ASF *Missive*, 49, fol. 128r-v, as: "ingens munus hoc esse et raro in illam aetatem collatum."

repayments of money owed to him since 1478; on 28 May Giovanni de' Medici was appointed an apostolic protonotary by papal bull and on 1 June he received the tonsure.[129]

Meanwhile Scala's hunt for benefices was proving no more successful than Lorenzo's. He had spent about 100 ducats on the benefice the pope had conceded to him "of his own accord" before it was revoked, and now he wanted "some compensation for the expenses I have incurred," as well as something for his nephew, "to start him off in life." If he did obtain the reservation without payment, he told the Florentine ambassador in Rome, it would be necessary to insert a clause to the effect that in general revocations it should not be revoked without specific mention. "Messer Guidantonio, my friend, the labor of obtaining benefices from [Rome] is so great, as you know, that I would dearly love to derive some profit from all the trouble and money I have spent so far."[130] Although the Florentine chancery did not go to the lengths of Milan, where religious affairs and the concession of benefits became the concern of a separate secretary after 1480,[131] we can see from Scala's and Lorenzo de' Medici's letters how all-absorbing this pursuit was becoming.

Success first crowned Scala's efforts at the end of 1484 when the new Pope Innocent VIII granted his request for the right

[129] Rome, *Intr. Exit.* 508, fols. 6v (9 April 1483, "Lorenzo de' Medicis et socii" lend the pope fl.10,050, to be repaid within a year), 42v (19 June: fl.367; cf. Picotti, *La giovinezza*, p. 123, n. 4), 52v (7 July: fl.6,000), 72r (22 September 1483: fl.3,150), etc. On 13 April 1483 the pope repaid the Medici Bank more than fl.7,000 "pro totidem quos mutuaverunt Camere Apostolice de anno 1478" (*ibid.*, fols. 145v-146r), fl.1,000 on 30 May, 16 and 25 June, fl.2,000 on 28 July, fl.1,000 on 22 August (fols. 163r, 169v, 173v, 180v, 186v). On Giovanni, Picotti, *La giovinezza*, pp. 67-68; Lorenzo de' Medici's *Ricordi*, ed. Fabroni, *Laur. Medicis vita*, 2:299-300.

[130] Scala to Guidantonio Vespucci, Florentine ambassador in Rome, [28 May 1483?], Modena MS, fol. 35r-v. A summary of taxes payable on benefices is contained in L. Schmitz-Kallenburg, *Practica*, pp. 51-62 (cf. pp. 1-15: "de variis supplicationum formis"), and A. Cameron, *The Apostolic Camera and Scottish Benefices 1418-88*, London, 1934 (St. Andrew's University Publications no. 35), esp. pp. xlix-lvi, lx-lxxviii.

[131] *Storia di Milano*, 7:525.

of patronage to the church or chapel of Santa Maria Maddalena at Monte Vasone in Val d'Elsa. This church, like others
with which Scala was associated, had belonged to the Augustinian Hermits before falling into decay and secular usage;
Scala had already restored part of the church, which lay close
to his recently acquired property at Monte Vasone, and the
pope agreed to grant him its patronage provided he endowed
it with land equivalent to an annual income of 20 florins and
allowed masses and other offices to be celebrated there on occasion.[132] He won this favor not as a result of diplomatic pressure, but as a reward for the oration he delivered before the
pope on 15 December 1484 rendering him the homage and
congratulations of the Florentine people.[133] This was Scala's
first official embassy outside the republic and it won him general approval.[134] On Christmas Day the pope invested Scala in
St. Peter's with the insignia of a knight and senator of Rome
and three days later he was awarded the patronage of Santa
Maria Maddalena. As he said himself, he was becoming a citizen well worth knowing and, when he returned to Florence

[132] 28 December 1484, Rome, ASV, Reg. Vat. 683, fols. lxv^r-lxvi^r; cf. ASF
Notarile B 2321 (A. Braccesi, 1481-1489), fols. 202r-203r, *Giornale de'
letterati d'Italia* 23 (Venice, 1716): 366-367. Scala fulfilled the condition of
this grant on 25 February 1485 by endowing the church, or chapel, with 80
hectares of partly cultivated and partly (as yet) uncultivated land at the
foot of Monte Vasone, *Notarile* B 2321, fol. 202v. On Scala's estate at Monte
Vasone, see ch. 9 below.

[133] Cambi, *Delizie*, 21:24-25; ASF *Leg. Comm.* 21, fols. 52v-54r (election
of Scala with five other citizens on 21 October 1484), and Johan Burchard,
Diarium sive rerum urbanarum commentarii, 1483-1506, ed. L. Thuasne, 1
(Paris, 1883):116-117 (arrival in Rome on 7 December and reception in
public consistory on the 15th, where "egregio D. Bartholomeo Scala cancellario florentino, inter eos tertium locum obtinente, orante, prestiterunt
prefato SS. Domino nostro nomine eorum obedientiam debitam et consuetam"). Before leaving Florence, Scala made his will, ASF *Notarile* G 619
(Testamenti 1486-1496), fols. 388r-389r.

[134] Scala's *Oratio* was published at least six times between 1484 and 1490,
four times in Rome, once in Florence [Nicolò di Lorenzo, 1485-1486] and
once in Venice, with copies scattered widely throughout Italy, *Indice
generale*, 5:56-57, nos. 8819-8824. Lorenzo de' Medici wrote to congratulate
Scala on 23 December, *Protocolli del carteggio*, p. 319.

in January (accompanying the young Piero de' Medici), he found his honor had already been confirmed by the Florentine councils with unusually generous majorities.[135]

Hopes of further success in Rome were once again dashed by war, this time between the pope and Ferrante of Naples, whom Lorenzo supported; once again peace saw renewed attempts by Lorenzo to reestablish his favor with the pope by lending him money.[136] Although in 1487 Lorenzo quashed as inopportune the idea of promoting his son Giovanni to the cardinalate, it can never have been far from his mind. For the moment he was content to settle for the rich abbey of Morimondo for Giovanni, the office of depositary for himself, and the marriage of his daughter to the pope's son. However, with the help of a series of persuasively large loans he achieved his wider object of a cardinalate for the fourteen-year-old Giovanni in March 1489 (to be kept secret for three years, however).[137] Profiting from this unique opportunity, Scala worked

[135] ASF *Provv.* 175, fols. 166v-167v, ed. Manni, *Vita*, pp. 31-34; n. 108 above; see Scala's letter to G. Lanfredini, 25 December 1484, ch. 8, n. 1 below. Scala had also sent word to his old rival Gentile Becchi to say he would be returning via Arezzo (ASF *MAP* 137, 468, Becchi to P. da Bibbiena, 31 December 1484). On the date of his return, BNF MS II, V. 12, fol. 300 (anon. letter to G. Lanfredini from Florence, 12 January 1485: "gl'inbasciadori di Roma tornorono in parte: M. Ant[onio Canigiani] e M. Agniolo [Niccolini] e lo Schala, el quale torna chavaliere e chostoro gli daranno le bandiere e domenicha e riterrà in Firenze"); cf. the Priorista quoted by Manni (*Vita*, p. 26: "A dì 16 [Saturday] Genn. MCCCCLXXXIIII ab. Inc. [= 1485] tornò da Roma Messer Bartolomeo di Giovanni Scala da Colle, quale stette all' incoronazione d'Innocenzio VIII Pontifice, e da lui fu fatto Cavaliere." On Piero and Scala, *Protocolli del carteggio*, p. 318.

[136] Rome, ASV *Intr. exit.* 514, fols. 72r (28 April 1487, Lorenzo de' Medici and Company lend the pope fl.5,117); 101r (they pay him fl.166 "in restitutione duarum armatarum dudum per eorum manus solutarum quae non fuerunt sortite effectum," as well as the settlement of other outstanding business); 233r (31 July 1487, the pope pays the Medici bank fl.2,000 'in valore pannorum"). On the Barons' war and Lorenzo's policy when it ended, Guicciardini, *Storie fiorentine*, pp. 63-67, esp. 67; R. Palmarocchi, *La politica italiana*, esp. p. 227.

[137] Picotti, *La giovinezza*, pp. 106-109, and *Protocolli del carteggio*, pp. 364-365 (but "la Depositeria che hanno dato a Lorenzo" was not the General Depositaryship he had previously held, which was now held by Gerhardus Usumaris: A. Gottlob, *Aus der Camera Apostolica des 15 Jahrhunderts*,

equally hard to obtain favors for his own family in Rome: a reservation and a dispensation for the son of his brother Andrea and later an office for Andrea himself. At first he worked through the papal *cubicularius* Antonio Ipoliti,[138] and, only when Ipoliti failed did Scala turn for help to successive Florentine ambassadors in Rome, Giovanni Lanfredini and Niccolò Michelozzi. Using his public authority as chancellor and his private influence as friend of the ambassadors, he appealed for the pope's favor toward "his small slave," "his humble creation," "the work of his hands," but without Lorenzo's success.[139]

In their hunt for benefices and honors in Rome Lorenzo de' Medici and Bartolomeo Scala consulted their private interests more obviously than the public interest. Nevertheless their labors intimately concerned the state, not only because they involved the use of public ambassadors and letters—and on oc-

---

Innsbruck, 1889, p. 112). Maddalena was betrothed to Franceschetto Cibò in November 1487 and married him in Rome at the beginning of 1488. On Lorenzo's negotiations in Rome for Giovanni's cardinalate, Palmarocchi, "Lorenzo e la nomina cardinalizia"; Picotti, *La giovinezza*, pp. 160-207. His loans to the papacy are recorded in Rome, ASV *Intr. exit.* 516, 518, 520, the highest being loans of fl.30,000 on 17 July 1488 and fl.95,000 on 11 August 1489 (*ibid.*, 516, fol. 100v, and 518, fol. 94r-v).

138 See Scala's letters to G. Lanfredini of 17 and 20 July 1487, BNF MS II, V, 20, fols. 211, 219. On Ippoliti's mission to Florence in 1485 with briefs from the pope for Scala, Lorenzo de' Medici, the archbishop of Florence and Francesco Gherardi, Rome, ASV MS armadio 39, 19, fol. 109r-v, 17 December 1485; Palmarocchi, *La politica italiana*, pp. 94-95.

139 See Scala's letters to G. Lanfredini from 28 June-20 July 1487, to Lanfredini and Innocent VIII on 12 November 1489, and to N. Michelozzi on 17 and 30 January 1490, BNF MS II, V, 20, fols. 201, 202, 211, 219; BNF MS Ginori Conti, 29, 64, fols. 52-54, also the Signoria to Lanfredini (18 July 1487, BNF MS II, V, 20, fol. 215: "Piaceci che habbi usato diligentia in nelle cose di Messere Bartholomeo Scala nostro Canciellieri et piaceràcci più continuamente se intenderemo sieno expedite secondo il suo desiderio." On Scala's family, see ch. 9 below. Lorenzo di Andrea was at the time "about 14 or more years old" and "a familiar of the Reverend Giovanni de' Medici" (like the brother of Niccolò Michelozzi). A dispensation was needed to hold two incompatibles ("id est ad duo curata beneficia," Schmitz-Kallenburg, *Practica*, p. 8), for which the incumbent should be 25 years old at least (*ibid.*, p. 13).

casion public arms[140]—but also because they represented the extension of secular authority in the affairs of the church. From this point of view the church (and the monasteries it controlled) was an institution like the Florentine judiciary, the guilds, the Mercanzia or the Guelf Party, which needed to be reformed and molded to fit within a centralized—and Medicean—administration.

Here it is no easier to isolate private from public interest than in Lorenzo de' Medici's and Scala's other reforming enterprises. When the government agreed to reform the Augustinian monastery of Santo Spirito at the request of the general of the Augustinian Hermits, Ambrogio Massari, it did so because of its interest in the monastery as a *studium generale*,[141] but in fact the matter was dealt with by Lorenzo, Scala and his envoy to Rome, Fra Santi.[142] Reform, too, was ostensibly the motive behind Lorenzo's interest in the affairs of the Camaldulensian monastery of Santa Maria degli Angeli. But the general of the order, Pietro Delphin, was distressed when the

[140] See below.

[141] See, for example, the Signoria's letter to Ambrogio Massari da Cora of 20 September 1483, ASF *Missive* 49 ["de rebus . . . publicis"], fol. 136r-v. On S. Spirito and its *studium*, Davidsohn, *Storia di Firenze*, 7 (Florence, 1965): 240-241; della Torre, *Storia*, pp. 185-190, 200-202; also Richa, *Notizie istoriche*, 9:1-67. On Massari, J. F. Ossinger, *Bibliotheca Augustiniana historica*, Ingolstadt and Augsburg, 1768, pp. 260-261; D. A. Perini, *Bibliographia Augustiniana, scriptores Itali*, 2 (Florence, 1931): 194-197; and on his writings, Kristeller, "The Contribution of Religious Orders to Renaissance Thought and Learning," *American Benedictine Review* 21 (1970): 46, reprinted in *Medieval Aspects of Renaissance Learning*, Durham, N.C., 1974. Lorenzo de' Medici was very friendly with another Augustinian Hermit, Fra Mariano da Genazzano, also a reformer and subsequently general of the order, for whom he built the monastery of San Gallo in Florence (Richa, *Notizie istoriche*, 1:264-266); on Fra Mariano, see Perini's biography, *Un emulo*, esp. pp. 20, 55-56, 69; L. Torelli, *Secoli Agostiniani*, Bologna, 1682, pp. 324, 341, 300-400, 437, 450; on his work as a reformer, D. Gutiérrez, "Testi e note sull'ultimo quadriennio del generalato di Seripando,' *Analecta Augustiniana* 28(1065):307-308; and F. X. Martin, "The Augustinian Order on the Eve of the Reformation," *Bibliothèque de la Revue d'Histoire ecclésiastique* 44 (1967):71-104, at 79.

[142] See Scala's letter to Massari of 9 May 1482 (Modena MS, fols. 12v-13r).

seemingly cooperative Lorenzo[143] suddenly decided to replace this order with the Cistercians and impose his own favorite, Guido da Settimo, as their abbot, "since he asserted that the Cistercians had a far more plentiful supply of men suitable for reform than we have and were more influential in so far as they were better endowed to pay off the debts of this monastery."[144] Although he found his advice "extremely displeasing," Delphin was powerless to resist.[145]

The dangers of allowing secular intervention in religious affairs were obvious. The case of Passignano was particularly instructive. The abbey had been promised to the young Giovanni de' Medici in 1484 and confirmed in Rome at the end of the year.[146] On the death of its incumbent the following

[143] See Delphin to Abbot Ventura (23 August 1485, *Epistolae*, ed. Martène and Durand, *Veterum scriptorum et monumentorum . . . collectio*, 3, Paris, 1724, no. 179, col. 1130: "magnifici Laurentii consensu et favore") and to the cardinal of Siena (27 August 1485, *ibid.*, no. 180, col. 1131: "Sed et magnifico Laurentio haud parum certe propterea debemus. Semper enim idem mecum fuit in hoc negotio. Et . . . laetus semper ab eo discessi"). On Delphin, see J. Schnitzer, *Peter Delphin, General des Camaldulenserordens, 1444-1525*, Munich, 1926.

[144] Delphin to Abbot Ventura (2 September 1485, *ibid.*, no. 182, col. 1133) and to the cardinal of Siena (22 March 1486, no. 185, col. 1137): "Persuasus Laurentius Medices, a quibusdam qui nobis adversantur, non posse per nos reformari monasterium Angelorum, hortatus est me per scribam suum ut ipsum permutem cum monasteriolo quodam Cisterciensis congregationis. Si quidem asserebat Cistercienses abundare hominibus ad reformationem idoneis, magis quam nos, et potentiores esse, utpote ditiores ad dissolvendum aes alienum huius monasterii."

[145] *Ibid.*: "Displicuit valde tale ipsius consilium." On subsequent events, see Delphin's letters to the cardinal of Siena of 11 and 15 April and 17 October 1486, *ibid.*, nos. 187, 188, 192, cols. 1139-1147. In April 1487 Scala arbitrated between Guido da Settimo, "prior of the monastery of S. Maria degli Angeli of the Benedictine Hermits," and ser Antonio di Jacopo of Prato, ASF *Notarile* B 2321 (A. Braccesi 1481-1489), fols. 237r-239r (30 April 1487); cf. Manni, *Vita*, pp. 36-37. On the appointment of Guido da Settimo and the change of rule, see Schnitzer, *Peter Delphin*, pp. 80, 83; Weinstein, *Savonarola and Florence*, p. 363.

[146] Picotti, *La giovinezza*, pp. 88-89, BNF MS Magl. XXXVII, 325 (Bernardo Del Serra, "Delle azioni di Don Biagio Milanesi," from which extracts have been ed. De Maio, *Savonarola e la Curia Romana*, append., pp.

year the Florentine government sent an emissary in the middle of the night to arouse the local Florentine magistrates. Supported by a large crowd from Florence, "as though they were destroying a rebel town with more than three thousand troops," they apparently converged on the abbey, which was defended by a mere twenty or at most twenty-five monks, and expelled the "decrepit and venerable" abbot in charge, leaving him to make his way almost naked to Florence.[147] Giovanni was finally granted the abbey, but on conditions that led to protracted litigation between church and state.[148]

Lay control of patronage was the principle at issue here rather than reform, but it was one over which Scala and Lorenzo again collaborated. Scala was himself involved in a semi-official capacity in another conflict between secular and religious, this time between the hospital and the lay flagellant company of the Most Holy Cross in Empoli and the monastery of the Augustinian Hermits where the company held

184-211; my attention was first drawn to this work by Sir Ernst Gombrich as one of the few surviving sources openly critical of Lorenzo de' Medici), fol. 55r: "La qual cosa ottenne sanza fatica, cum sit che li oratori mandati da' Fiorentini ad congratularsi di sua assumptione, fra altre gratie li adomandorono fu questa di Passignano in spetieltà per Lorenzo"; cf. Lorenzo de' Medici's *Ricordi*, ed. Fabroni, *Laur. Medicis vita* 2:300, which also confirm that possession was achieved "col segno della Signoria."

[147] BNF MS Magl. XXXVII, 325, fols. 59v-60r: "Interim publicata la morte dello Abbate et quello era seguito da San Salvi che facea per Messer Giovanni, immo per Lorenzo, a meza notte hauto el maziere con lettere a magistrati circumstanti, cioè Podestà, vicarii et rectori, et con molta gente di Firenze insino al boia, come ad expugnare una terra ribella con più di tremila fanti, concorsono ad questo monastero dato in custodia di monaci xx o al più xxv. . . . Et più lo Abbate loro vocato dom Ricciardo delli Alberti, decrepito et venerabile religioso, così expulso, quasi nudo andarsene ad Firenze pedestre"; cf. Picotti, *La giovinezza*, pp. 88-90. In order to prevent the abbey from being held *in commendam*, the abbot, Don Isidero di Miniato del Sera, described by Picotti as a "reggitore solerte ed austero," had vainly attempted to unite it to the Vallombrosan Congregation before dying on 1 March 1485 (*ibid.*, pp. 89 and 138, n. 97). Don Isidero was godfather to Lucrezia Rinieri with Scala, see ch. 8, n. 25 below.

[148] BNF MS Magl. XXXVII, 325, fols. 60r-63v. According to Picotti (*La giovinezza*, p. 139, n. 102) the Medici finally received the Bull granting possession in July-August 1487. On subsequent events, *ibid.*, fols. 63v-69r.

their meetings.[149] By attempting to deprive the monastery of
the hospital in 1477 and erect his arms on the hospital beside
those of the cardinal of Rouen, protector of the order, Scala
directly challenged the cardinal's authority,[150] and d'Éstouteville wrote angrily to Lorenzo de' Medici to demand their
removal.[151] Later Scala was appointed to arbitrate between the
company and the monastery[152] but, although the monks gave

[149] The history of the society and its relationship with the monastery of
S. Stefano is described in an entry dated 21 October 1471 in ASF *Conv.
Soppr.* 72 (Convento di S. Stefano, Empoli), 31, fol. 35r. On the monastery,
see also Repetti, *Dizionario*, 2:61-62. On confraternities in general, Monti,
Le confraternite, and ch. 13, n. 32 below; on the role of Cardinal Protectors,
S. L. Forte, *The Cardinal-Protector of the Dominican Order (Institutum
historicum FF. Praedicatorum Romae ad S. Sabinae, dissertationes historicae,*
fasc. 15), Rome, 1959.

[150] On events in 1477, ASF *Missive* 49, fols. 24r-v, 30v (Signoria to the
Cardinal of Rouen, Guillaume d'Éstouteville, 15 March, 14 June 1477),
MAP 45, 362 (Consuls of Empoli to the same, 28 April 1477, referring
to the "sola commessione, quanto possiamo comprendere, di messer Bartolomeo, Cancellieri della Magnifica Signoria nostra" authorizing the removal of the cardinal's arms); *MAP* 45, 363 (Fra Basilio of Pisa, "Pisane provincie . . . provincialis," to the same, 28 April 1477), *MAP* 34, 157 (Éstouteville to Lorenzo de' Medici, 25 May 1477: "tanta vergogna sia stata facta a
noi a dilaniare quelle arme nostre con tanto vilipendio et brutte parole")
and following note. I owe my knowledge of this incident to Dott. Riccardo
Fubini.

[151] Éstouteville to Lorenzo de' Medici, 16 August 1477 (ASF *MAP* 46,
468): "vi significamo che con le nostre arme non volemo che si metta altro
che o quelle de la Signoria o de la Magnificentia Vostra. Et però voliate
per amore nostro pigliare questo carico di non lassare mettere quelle del
prefato misser Bartholomeo, et se ce sono poste, fate che si leveno via." Cf.
also his letter to Lorenzo of 6 July 1477 (*MAP* 46, 461), that the hospital
should be given back to the monastery, "et anche che misser Bartholomeo
Scala desista dal impresa."

[152] The erection of the cardinal's arms again acted as an incitement to
trouble, ASF *Missive* 49, fol. 94r-v (Signoria to Éstouteville, 24 September
1481). On Scala's arbitration, ASF *Minut.* 11, fol. 5v (Signoria to the same,
16 November 1481); Manni, *Vita*, pp. 35-36 (referring to the Society of
San Lorenzo Vestis Nigrae as well as that of the Holy Cross, cf. ASF
Conv. Soppr. 72, 31, fol. 35r); and letters quoted in n. 120 above. On
Scala's work for the Company, including the purchase of grain for himself,
see his letters to G. Rucellai, 26 January [1482], Fra Alessandro of Empoli,
18 May 1482, to the priors of the company, same day, and to ——— (incomplete), 13 June 1482, Modena MS, fols. 26v, 28r, 27v, and 14r; cf. Manni,
Vita, p. 36.

him a freshwater pond and 50 florins, they recorded with some bitterness that instead of winning his favor with these *douceurs*, "exactly the opposite has happened and we have entirely wasted the said money."[153] As chancellor, Scala supported the lay company and remained closely associated with it for the remainder of his life.[154]

The church was rich, ripe for reform and influential, and it attracted both Scala and Lorenzo de' Medici as a field in which they could exercise private and public influence.

In March 1492, just before Lorenzo died, the news of Giovanni's cardinalate was made public: two ambassadors were sent to Rome to thank the pope for honoring their city and Scala as chancellor wrote him a brief letter on 10 March.[155] Giovanni was not only "the youngest Cardinal . . . who has ever been created up to now," as his father proudly claimed, but he was also the most expensive.[156] The seeds of discontent sown by the cost were reaped by Lorenzo's successors. Lorenzo died on 8 April 1492 and only two and a half years later the Medici regime fell: what would Scala's position be now? Whatever his personal relationship with Lorenzo had been, Scala had worked closely with him throughout his lifetime and it remained to be seen whether this would prejudice his chances of survival in 1494.

---

[153] ASF *Conv. Soppr.* 72, 31, fol. 51v: "è fatto tutto l'opposto e abbianci perduto detti denari nella malora." On the freshwater pond, which Scala had to protect from the depredations of the local people, see his letter to Carlo da Diacceto, 27 June 1482, Modena MS, fol. 18v.

[154] ASF *Notarile* B 65 (Francesco di Baldese Baldesi 1453-1496), the reference to which I owe to Miss Brenda Preyer), fols. 165r-166r (3 December 1491), 174r-176r (1 November 1496), showing Scala acting as *sindaco principale* for the hospital and society and Matteo di Niccolò Arrighi as his procurator. Arrighi acted as *sindaco* and *provveditore* of the society in 1481 and 1491, when he is described as "spedalinghus" of the hospital and society, and in 1496 as their "factor and administrator," ASF *Comp. relig. soppr.* 704, fol. 81r and above.

[155] Ed. Bandini, *Collectio*, p. 16; cf. Picotti, *La giovinezza*, pp. 325, 352, n. 84.

[156] See Lorenzo de' Medici's letter to his son, ed. Fabroni, *Laur. Medicis vita*, 2:310-311 ("il più giovane Cardinale . . . che fusse mai fatto insino a qui"); and Rinuccini, *Ricordi storici*, pp. cxlviii-cxlix ("per fare il figliuolo in età puerile cardinale, spese più che dugento migliaia di fiorini in corrompere e comperare il consenso de' cardinali e pontefice").

CHAPTER V

Fall of the Medici and the New Republic

I, who am incapable of greater things, would never fail to perform for our Republic the duties at least of orator and scribe. *Scala, 1496*[1]

Scala must have hoped his close relationship with the Medici family would continue under Piero's aegis. Shortly after Lorenzo's death he reapplied his "out-of-practice mind" to apologues, reviving for Piero the annual tribute of apologues he used to pay his father.[2] Scala and Piero had been friends in Piero's childhood when Scala had written a note "in my little old hand, as you wanted" in Piero's translation of Bruni's treatise on the Florentine constitution.[3] However, that was some time ago and recently Scala had dedicated nothing to him. Piero may have been influenced by his tutor Poliziano against Scala,[4] and his "proud and tyrannical nature" would have found Scala's pedantic concern for legality even more inhibiting than Lorenzo had done. Certainly Scala was not a member of his small inner circle of friends—nor were many

---

[1] *Apologia contra vituperatores civitatis Florentiae*, henceforth called *Defense*, Florence, 1496, postscript "eis qui legerint," fol. b5v: "Neque ego non hanc saltem verborum et scripti operam, qui maiora nequeam, rei nostrae publicae praestiterim."

[2] Letter to Piero de' Medici, Turin, Biblioteca Civica, Raccolta Autografi, Mazzo 34: "desuetum animum."

[3] "Vetula manu mea, ut voluisti," BNF MS Pant. 126, fol. 9r (facsimile in C. H. Clough in the *Journal of the Society for Italic Handwriting*, 78 (1974) pl. 2, p. 9), ed. (with Piero's letter to his father, dated 30 May 1484), G. Pesenti, "La scuola di greco a Firenze nel primo Rinascimento," *Atena e Roma* n.s. 12 (1931):93-94. At the end of that year, 1484, Scala brought Piero back from Rome with him after his embassy there, see ch. 4, n. 135 above.

[4] See Piero's note attacking Scala for criticizing Poliziano after his death, ASF *MAP* 72, 88, ed. del Lungo, "Tra lo Scala e il Poliziano," pp. 179-180, dated between 29 September and 26 October 1494 by G. B. Picotti (*Ricerche umanistiche*, pp. 23-24, n. 4, and p. 125, n. 2). Marzi (*Cancelleria*, p. 271, n. 2) suggests Scala may have used this note to protect himself after Piero's downfall, but its tone reflects that of Poliziano's *Ode* against Scala (see ch. 8 below), suggesting Piero may have inherited his tutor's old quarrel with Scala.

of the men with whom Scala had collaborated most closely in the preceding year.[5]

During his lifetime Lorenzo de' Medici had managed to maintain a balance between his interests in Naples, Rome and the rest of Italy, but Piero was not equally successful. By alienating the pope, he encouraged Charles VIII's descent on Italy and at the same time deprived the Florentines of the chance of honors in Rome.[6] It was little advantage to them now to be represented by a cardinal in Rome and, by seizing all vacant benefices for himself, Giovanni de' Medici only increased popular resentment against his family.[7] When Piero made the mistake Scala had tried to prevent his father and grandfather from making—that of surrendering to Charles VIII all the most important fortresses on the Tuscan coast, "not only without any public commission, but without having so much as notified or communicated with either the Signoria or any other magistracy in the city"[8]—the Florentines could stand no more. Incensed by this double usurpation of civil and ecclesiastical authority, they refused him entry to the Palazzo della Signoria on the day after he returned from visit-

[5] See Piero Parenti, "Storia fiorentina," BNF MS II, IV, 169, fol. 195r: "In questo numero [= adherenti allo intrinseco stato di Piero] furono Lorenzo Tornabuoni, Antonio di Bernardo [Miniati], e ser Giovanni [Guidi] da Pratovecchio, ser Niccolò Michelozi, ser Simone Grazini, notaio delle Tratte, e alcuni altri"; cf. Rubinstein, *Government*, p. 231, n. 2; n. 11 below. On Piero's "natura . . . tirannesca ed altiera," Guicciardini, *Storie fiorentine*, p. 84.

[6] Guicciardini, *Storie fiorentine*, pp. 86-89, esp. 88; and in general Pastor, *Storia dei papi*, 3:357-363. On the unsuccessful attempts of the Florentines to win a cardinalate in September 1493, Picotti, *Ricerche umanistiche*, pp. 130-140; letters of their ambassadors in Rome to Piero de' Medici, 19 September-25 October 1493, ASF *MAP* 55, 76-91 *passim*; cf. Pastor, *Storia dei papi*, 3:366-368. See Manni, *Vita*, p. 53, for a "causa" at Rome v. Scala in 1493.

[7] Piero Parenti, "Storia fiorentina," ed. Schnitzer, *Quellen*, 4:7: "Agiugnevasi allo ordinario odio, che il Cardinale de' Medici, quanti benefici vacavano, occupava."

[8] Gaddi, Priorista (British Library, Egerton MS 3764, fol. 227r, partly ed. from another MS by G. Aiazzi, "Sulla cacciata di Piero de' Medici e la venuta di Carlo VIII in Firenze," *ASI*, ser. 1, 4(2)(1853):43; cf. Rubinstein, "Politics and Constitution," p. 148, n. 1): "non solum sanza alchuna publicha chomessione, ma sanza averne pure participato o chomunichato nè cholla signoria nè chon alchuno altro magistrato della città." Cf. ch. 3 above.

ing the king of France at Sarzana, and he fled the city the same night, on 9 November 1494.[9]

Suddenly exposed to the fury of the mob, Piero's most unpopular supporters fell quickly. The all-powerful Giovanni Guidi, notary of the Riformagioni, and Antonio di Bernardo Miniati, *provveditore* of the Monte officials, were the first to have their houses pillaged and, despite their attempts to hide in San Marco and Santa Croce, they were captured and subsequently tortured in prison, Antonio di Bernardo being put to death by hanging on 12 December, Guidi escaping with imprisonment and a heavy fine.[10] Lorenzo Tornabuoni, a relation and close supporter, ser Niccolò Michelozzi, Piero's father's former secretary, ser Simone Grazzini, secretary of the Tratte, and Antonio Malegonelle were also sought by the Signoria on the evening of the 9th. Others, including ser Piero Bibbiena, Piero's secretary, ser Zanobi, notary of the Otto di Guardia, the hated police magistracy, and ser Francesco di ser Barone, critic of Scala and secretary of the Otto di Pratica for internal affairs, apparently fled.[11]

[9] Parenti, "Storia fiorentina," ed. Schnitzer, p. 7: "Così usurpato havendosi lo ecclesiastico et il civile, oramai più sopportare non si poteva." On the events of the revolution, see the bibliography in Rubinstein, "Politics and Constitution," p. 151, n. 2; and especially Parenti's "Storia fiorentina"; Luca Landucci's *Diario*, pp. 73-94; Rinuccini, *Ricordi storici*, pp. clii-clvii; Gaddi, Priorista, above; and the official decrees in ASF *SS. Delib.* 96, fols. 86v-129v.

[10] Marzi, *Cancelleria*, pp. 262-263, n. 4; the chronicles referred to above, especially Parenti, "Storia fiorentina," fols. 195r, 211v; Gaddi, Priorista, ed. Aiazzi, pp. 45-46. Rinuccini (*Ricordi storici*, p. cxlvii) singles out Guidi and Antonio di Bernardo as "sceleratissimi e audacissimi uomini" whom Lorenzo de' Medici used to convert the public-funded debt to his own benefit; cf. Gaddi, Priorista (Egerton MS 3764, fol. 230r), blaming Guidi for having "tenuto mano e dati modi di alterare le borse delli u[l]timi squittini traendone molti cittadini e facciendo molte altre mutazioni e alterazioni" (and Simone Grazzini for agreeing to this).

[11] Parenti, "Storia fiorentina," fols. 194v-195r: "Altri occultamente di Firenze partirono, sichome Giannozzo Pucci, ser Piero Cancelliere, ser Zanobi, notaio delli Octo della Guardia e Balìa, el Capitano de' Fanti, ser Francesco di ser Barone, ministro delli Octo della Practica, et alcuni altri. . . . Etiam nella medesima nocte s'attese a pigliare e cittadini capi di tale congiura, adherenti allo intrinseco stato di Piero" (listed in n. 5 above). These men were also the first to have their property confiscated on 10 November (ASF *SS. Delib.* 96, fol. 87r-v); cf. Landucci, *Diario*, pp. 76-77.

Thanks to a letter from ser Francesco in his place of hiding to Niccolò Michelozzi, we can vividly imagine the state of mind of these fugitives. Writing with the greatest difficulty owing to an attack of trembling and feverish palpitations which had nearly killed him, he begged to be allowed to lie low and reveal himself in his own good time:

> I have not been proclaimed banished and I said nothing except for the good of, and not against, the Palace or the community. And there is no advantage to the Signoria to have me first, because I knew no secrets, nor did I get involved in scrutinies, taxes, or money matters to be disliked by the people. And apart from having been a servant and partisan of the [Medici] house and [regime], like many others, nothing else can be imputed to me. As for Lorenzo and Giovanni [di Pierfrancesco de' Medici], I hope to justify myself with them, but I need time in view of their more important occupations.[12]

Ser Francesco's analysis of the reasons for which he might expect to be attacked was sound, since it was the people primarily concerned with elections and taxes who were the first to suffer. He also offers insight into the position of Bartolomeo Scala. Although Scala knew plenty of secrets, he was not principally concerned with elections or taxes: was he lying low and waiting for the right moment to present himself to Lorenzo and Giovanni di Pierfrancesco de' Medici?

Where Scala was and what he was doing we do not know. He was not apparently in the chancery, where Francesco Gaddi had been summoned to hold the fort since Piero left

---

[12] [17-28] November 1494, BNF MS Ginori Conti, 29, 101, fol. 46: "non sono in bando, et non vi parlai se non in bene et non contra al palagio o alla communità. Et alla Signoria non corre interesse di havermi prima, perchè secreti non sapevo, nè mi sono impacciato di squittini, graveze o danari perilchè il popolo mi habbi havere in odio. Et dallo essere stato servidore et partigiano della casa in fuori, chome molti altri, non mi può essere imputato altro. Del particulare di Lorenzo et Giovanni spero iustificharmi con loro, ma mi bisogna tempo rispecto alle occupationi loro di più momento."

the city, or at least not officially. When Gaddi was appointed second chancellor in place of Antonio Muzi on 1 December, he was made responsible not only for internal letters (the province of the second chancery) but also for "letters and orators' commissions outside [the state]," which were traditionally the responsibility of the first chancellor.[13] Nor is there any trace of Scala's hand in the chancery during this period: *minutarii* used before the revolution stop abruptly and continue only in the course of the following year, and the eighteenth-century copy of letters attributed to Scala (but possibly written by one of his assistants)[14] has a hiatus between 4 November 1494 and 4 January 1495, letters written between 9 November and 31 December (evidently copied by a supporter of the new regime) being bound separately.[15]

Perhaps he, too, was waiting to present himself to Lorenzo and Giovanni di Pierfrancesco. The brothers returned to Florence on 12 November, their name changed from Medici to Popolani. Fortunately, Scala as their father's former secretary

---

[13] ASF *SS. Delib.* 96, fol. 100v (1 December 1494): "in cancellarium litterarum secunde cancellerie . . . loco ser Antonii Mariani de Mutiis"; cf. Gaddi, Priorista, fol. 230v: "obrighandolo anchora oltre alla chura della chanciellieria per il dominio alle lettere e chomessioni delli oratori di fuori sichondo ch'el bisognio ochoriesse di mano in mano tenpo per tenpo," and *Inventario de' Mobili*, ed. C. Bologna, p. 12 (cf. Marzi, *Cancelleria*, p. 265), that he was asked to serve "in palagio alla cancelleria et altre cose necessarie in quei tempi non havendo in palagio altri ministri." Francesco Gaddi also delivered "alcune brevi et accomodate parole in lingua franzese" to welcome Charles VIII on his entry into Florence (Gaddi, Priorista, ed. Aiazzi, p. 47).

[14] ASF *Manoscritti* 58 and 59.

[15] ASF *Minut.* 14 has a gap between 8 November 1494 and 27 July 1495, *Minut.* 16 (containing drafts in Scala's autograph) has a gap between 2 November 1494 and August 1495, whereas *Missive* 50 contains only letters between 9 November and 31 December 1494, with hands drawn in the margins pointing out the following sentences: "Le cose nostre succedono continuamente di bene in meglio et con amore et unione di tucti. Et attendiamo a honorare la prefata Christianissima Maestà" (fol. 15v, to G. B. Ridolfi in Milan, 17 November 1494); "La Christianissima Maestà entrò hieri con tanto ordine et apparato et sì pomposamente . . . che sarebbe incredibile ad chi non lo havessi veduto" (fol. 20v, to the same, 18 November 1494); and "Non vogliamo obmettere significarvi come oggi habbiamo a hore xxii facto parlamento publico . . . et tucto è stato approvato con unito consenso," etc. (fol. 38r, to Florentine orators in France, [2] December 1494).

enjoyed a long-standing friendship with their branch of the family as well as with their cousins. He had witnessed Lorenzo's betrothal to Semiramis, daughter of the lord of Piombino, in 1480, and three years later he had acted as a common friend and arbitrator in a dispute between the Medici cousins over their patrimony.[16] It was after a meeting to discuss this settlement in October 1483 that Lorenzo di Pierfrancesco told Scala he wanted to go on the forthcoming embassy to the coronation of Charles VIII in France. Hearing the ambassadors were to be elected that very day, he begged Scala to get the meeting deferred until Lorenzo il Magnifico could be consulted, and this was arranged, allowing Scala (as well as Lorenzo di Pierfrancesco) time to write to il Magnifico, with a successful outcome.[17] Little can the elder Lorenzo have anticipated that his young cousin would be one of Charles VIII's supporters when the king came to Italy as conqueror in 1494, with his own son Piero a mere supplicant for mercy at his feet. For Scala it was providential. He had been personally responsible for drafting a reply to Charles' appeal for clemency toward Lorenzo and Giovanni after they had been exiled from Florence in April 1494, but the brothers had broken their confines and joined the king of France and Lodovico Sforza in Milan before their exile had been revoked.[18] Lorenzo di Pier-

---

[16] ASF *Notarile* M 530 (N. Michelozzi), fol. 70v (7 October 1480) and *Notarile* G 620 (S. Grazzini, 1472-1494), fol. 198r.

[17] Scala to Lorenzo il Magnifico, 16 October 1483, ASF *MAP* 39, 44; Lorenzo di Pierfrancesco de' Medici to the same, 17 October 1483, ASF *MAP* 51, 265: "Stamani sono stato con messer Bartolomeo Schala, il quale m'à referito vostra risposta d'una vi scrisse iersera. Questa mattina la Signoria voleva raunare i 70, ma non ànno potuto avere il numero, et à gli licenziati et richiesti per oggi. Bisogna la tornata vostra sia inanzi si raunino. La voglia mia è andare quanto che a voi parà." Lorenzo di Pierfrancesco was elected an orator to France with Gentile Becchi and Antonio Canigiani by the Council of Seventy on 17 October 1483; their instructions are dated 8 November, and they left two days later, ASF *Leg. Comm.* 21, fols. 49v-52r; Canestrini-Desjardins, *Négotiations*, 1:193, 200-204. Clothing was normally provided for ambassadors going to the coronations of popes, emperors and kings, Vedovato, *Note sul diritto diplomatico*, p. 44, n. 130.

[18] Scala's draft is in ASF *Minut.* 16, fol. 101r, copied in *Risp. verb. orat.* 2, fol. 108r. On the brothers' exile, and their status as "baroni de Re di Francia, o veramente Lorenzino sagretario de Re di Francia e Giovanni suo fratelo barone de Re," see the *Ricordanze* di Tribaldo de' Rossi, *Delizie*, 23:291 ff.;

francesco is described by Guicciardini as "good-natured" compared with his more restless brother Giovanni, which suggests that he may have inherited his father's country-loving nature. Appropriately, then, after his return Scala sent him a long pastoral poem "On trees," in which he makes his hope for Lorenzo's favor explicit: "And you, Lorenzo, can give my sails a propitious start and bring my boat into port. . . . From you came the beginning of my studies and my first youth; these too are owed to you, and now also my extreme old age."[19]

However necessary Lorenzo's favor was to Scala, the fact remains that the chancery was remarkably untouched by the revolution. Alessandro Braccesi was the first purely secretarial member of the chancery to be dismissed on 16 November.[20] The *parlamento* and Balìa of 2 December initiated a period of more radical reform. One of its first acts was to grant the Signoria full powers to dismiss from office and reelect all the officers and employees of the Palazzo della Signoria—in other words, the civil service. Consequently, the following day a series of officers administering various magistracies were dismissed and on 4 December four members of the chancery: the fearful ser Francesco di ser Barone, his assistant ser Antonio di Bibbiena, and two of the four men appointed in 1487 to accompany orators outside Florence, Bernardo Ricci and ser Antonio da Colle.[21]

---

cf. *Libro di debitori e creditori e ricordanze di Tommaso Ginori*, ed. Schnitzer, *Quellen*, 1:94; Guicciardini, *Storie fiorentine*, p. 90; Landucci, *Diario fiorentino*, pp. 67-68; Rinuccini, *Ricordi storici*, p. cli. Their decree of exile on 29 May 1494 is in ASF *SS. Delib.* 96, fol. 95r. On subsequent appeals by Charles VIII for their release, Canestrini-Desjardins, *Négotiations*, 1:414-416, 421; ASF *Risp. verb. orat.*, 2, fol. 108v.

[19] Guicciardini, *Storie fiorentine*, p. 90: "uomo bonario." Scala's poem "De Arboribus ad Laurentium Populanum Medicem" is in BNF MS Magl. VII, 1195, fols. 102r-117v: "Tuque, o Laurenti, potis es mea vela secundo / Et regere auspicio et portum indulgere carinae / . . . A te principium studiorum et prima iuventa: / Haec quoque debentur tibi, iam et postrema senectus" (fol. 102r).

[20] ASF *SS. Delib.* 96, fol. 94v.

[21] *Ibid.*, fol. 106r-v (3-4 December 1494). On the authority granted by the Balìa to the Signoria concerning the chancery, see ASF *Provv.* 185, fol. 2r; Marzi, *Cancelleria*, p. 260.

Apart from fixing Francesco Gaddi's salary on the same day, no more interest was taken in the chancery until after the constitutional reform bill was passed on 23 December. It was then decided that the new Council of Eighty, the Ottanta, without previous deliberation by the Signoria and Colleges, was to prepare a list of names of men eligible "to serve at the Palace or to serve ambassadors and commissaries," which was then to be voted on by the Great Council.[22] Consequently, on 28 December the three assistants dismissed on 4 December were again dismissed from office together with another of the men appointed in 1487 to accompany orators on outside missions, ser Francesco del Cappello.[23]

On the same day, 28 December 1494, Bartolomeo Scala was dismissed as head of the first chancery—the last appointment to be discussed since the revolution on 9 November.[24] He was replaced by messer Piero di Simone Beccanugi, "a skilled lawyer and well versed in Latin and Greek," with a salary of 325 florins a year. At the same time all the remaining offices in the chancery were filled.[25] Three days later, on 31 December, when the Signoria were "better informed," they "restored messer Bartolomeo to his former position, without altering the election of messer Piero."[26] In asking Scala to return to the

[22] ASF *Provv.* 185, fol. 12v; cf. Marzi, *Cancelleria*, p. 267.

[23] ASF *SS. Delib.* 96, fol. 122r.

[24] *Ibid.*; cf. Gaddi, Priorista, fol. 230v: "Riformorono anchora la chancielleria del palagio avendo sospeso per qualche rispetto Messer Bartolomeo Schala, primo chancielliere."

[25] ASF *SS. Delib.* 96, fol. 122r-v (28 December 1494) and Gaddi, above: "Iurischonsulto perito e bene litterato nella latina e grecha lingua." The other appointments are also in *SS. Delib.* 96, fol. 122r-v; cf. Marzi, *Cancelleria*, p. 268 (but "Ser Lucha Fabbiani de *Fecinis*," not *Felini*, as in Marzi, Scala's former assistant, now appointed as an assistant in the first chancery, also serving the Dieci).

[26] Gaddi, Priorista, fol. 230v: "e nondimeno di poi meglio informati restituirono Messer Bartolomeo Schala in suo primo grado none alterando la elezione di messer Piero," ASF *SS. Delib.* 96, fol. 128r: "attenta necessitate palatii et negotiis eiusdem palatii"; Parenti, "Storia fiorentina," fol. 219v: "A dì 28 la nostra Signoria cassò el principale Cancelliere M. Bartolomeo Scala et in suo luogho Messer Piero Becchannugi elesse . . . il quale l'altro giorno electo fu nel numero de' Signori novelli; nientedimeno rielessono poi detto M. Bartolomeo nel medesimo suo luogho con salario l'anno di fl. 200 di suggello"; cf. Marzi, *Cancelleria*, pp. 270-271; Tommasini, *Vita*, 1:136.

chancery with a salary reduced from 432 to 200 florins a year, the government claimed it was influenced by "the needs and business of the palace." It was probably also influenced by the fact that Beccanugi had been appointed first chancellor only from the beginning of March 1495, after the end of his term of office in the Signoria to which he had just been elected.[27] Since it was a condition of his appointment that he should hold no other offices at the same time (unlike Scala's), the government would have been unwilling to breach it at the very beginning of his office. The appointment of Beccanugi nevertheless stood firm and, although Scala's experience probably gave him greater authority in the chancery, surviving letters show that at least they shared letter writing, some letters being subscribed by Scala, others by Beccanugi.[28] Scala may even have welcomed Beccanugi's assistance in his old age, although in fact Beccanugi died first, providing Scala with the occasion to pen a distich on his "moribund" colleague.[29]

Perhaps Scala was also fortunate that Beccanugi needed a substitute as soon as he was appointed chancellor. But whatever part chance played in his survival, credit is due to Scala himself for being found indispensable to the chancery. It speaks for the professionalism of his regime that, when he returned at the beginning of January 1495, he found himself surrounded by the same men with whom he had worked most closely during his earlier chancellorship. Of his former assistants only Niccolò Michelozzi was missing, having deserted the chancery for Lorenzo de' Medici's personal service many

[27] See preceding note.

[28] E.g. ASMi SPE Fir. 941, letters and letters of credence of 8 and 15 January and 11 April 1495 subscribed by Scala, of 12 and 20 November 1495 by Beccanugi; Modena, AS, Fir. busta 16, letter of 14 April 1496 subscribed by Beccanugi (and in 1497, after his death, by Scala). Venice, Bibl. Marciana, MS lat., X, 177 (= 3624), fol. 15, 27 June 1497, must be one of the last letters for which Scala was responsible. On Beccanugi's office, see ASF SS. Delib. 96, fol. 122r: "Et cum hoc, quod durante eius officio habeat et habere debeat devetum ab omnibus officiis communis Florentie."

[29] Beccanugi died on 23 November 1496, ASF Libro di morti della arte de' medici e speciali, 247, fol. 88v. Scala's distich "In Petrum Becanusum moribundum" ("Elisios moriens venies, Becanuse, recessus. / Ne doleas. Fugis haec. Quin moriamur, ait") is in his Modena MS, fol. 1r.

years earlier, while Alessandro Braccesi (now forgiven), Antonio della Valle and Filippo Redditi all enjoyed positions of importance. These men had been constantly used in different combinations to staff magistracies and offices throughout the preceding years; clearly distinguishable from Piero de' Medici's inner circle of supporters who earned opprobrium for fiddling elections and taxes, they formed the professional secretariat of state, as Scala had intended that they should.[30]

As chancellor, Scala was surrounded by a wide circle of friends and acquaintances who made his transition into the new republic smoother than it might otherwise have been. Even before the death of Lorenzo de' Medici he counted as friends many men who were to become adherents of Savonarola and the new regime: Lorenzo di Pierfrancesco, of course, Jacopo Acciaiuoli and his nephew Zanobi, Ugolino Verino and his pupil Pietro Crinito, who belonged to the group that held discussions with Savonarola and Giovanni Pico della Mirandola in San Marco in the 1490s. His colleague in the chancery, Alessandro Braccesi, became a devoted supporter of Savonarola, losing his office in the chancery on Savonarola's imprisonment. So, too, did friends of Scala's in the Gaddi family, and two lawyers, Bartolomeo Redditi, brother of his former assistant Filippo Redditi, and Domenico Bonsi, with whom Scala often shared the offices of consul and councillor in the Guild of Lawyers and Notaries.[31]

As a reformer himself who never lost an opportunity for limiting extravagance or eradicating vice and a member of a religious confraternity practicing flagellation, Scala must have been in sympathy with the puritan spirit that now prevailed in Florence. One can imagine how Savonarola's carnival of 1495 would have appealed to the man who quoted with approval Cosimo de' Medici's detestation of "the license of carnival time": ten thousand children setting up altars and begging for money, belaboring those who passed by without payment with long sticks, and crying "Long live Christ": "no one

30 Cf. chs. 7 and 8 below.
31 On Scala's friendships, cf. ch. 8 below.

[124]

can remember such a thing ever happening before in Florence, and it's all the work of Fra Girolamo of Ferrara," the Milanese ambassador reported.[32]

So we cannot interpret Scala's loyalty to the new regime entirely as opportunism or professionalism, since like others he must have felt attracted to some aspects of the new republic. His ambivalent attitude to it is summed up in the *Defense against the Critics of Florence*, which he wrote in the autumn of 1496. Like his *Excusatio Florentinorum* of 1478, it had an immediate political purpose. In the spring of 1496 a conspiracy had been discovered, hatched by enemies of Savonarola and the popular party, which planned to reform the government.[33] In the summer further division developed between the pro-French party, headed by Lorenzo di Pierfrancesco and Paolantonio Soderini and supported by Savonarola, and the Milanese party, led by Guidantonio Vespucci and Piero Capponi.[34] The arrival of German ambassadors in Florence in the middle of August 1496 demanding that Florence should support the emperor against France provoked a crisis. On 20 August, the day on which the ambassadors were received by the Signoria, Savonarola preached in the chamber of the Great Council "with the purpose of keeping the Florentines firm in the French alliance": "and so the city was divided," Piero Parenti recorded, "and great disorder and dissension grew toward a

---

[32] P. Somenza to Lodovico Sforza, 14 February 1496, ed. I. del Lungo, "Fra Girolamo Savonarola," *ASI*, n.s. 18 (2) (1863):8-9: "non se ricorda che mai in Firenze ne fusse facta una simile: et è facta per opera di Frate Hieronimo de Ferrara." Cf. Scala's dialogue *On Laws and Legal Judgments*, ed. Borghi, p. 258; and below.

[33] Parenti, "Storia fiorentina," fols. 5v-10v; Guicciardini, *Storie fiorentine*, pp. 125-126; Rinuccini, *Ricordi storici*, p. clx; Landucci, *Diario fiorentino*, pp. 129-130; Rubinstein, "Politics and Constitution," pp. 174-175 (especially p. 174, n. 2).

[34] Parenti, "Storia fiorentina," ed. Schnitzer, pp. 128-130. However, on the relationship of Lorenzo di Pierfrancesco and Savonarola with Milan, cf. Bertelli, "Machiavelli e la politica estera fiorentina," pp. 31-43, esp. 35-36; P. Villari, *La storia di Girolamo Savonarola e de' suoi tempi*, 2 (Florence, 1888): cxxxviii (cf. cxxxix, 7 November 1496). On political sects in Florence at this time, Rubinstein, "Politics and Constitution," pp. 166-174.

climax, from which God save us."[35] These differences were sedulously fostered by the Milanese ambassador in Florence, Paolo Somenza, who showed the Signoria letters said to have been intercepted in Milan from Savonarola inviting Charles VIII to return to Italy, "adding that they ought now to consider the situation they found themselves in, under the rule of a friar." At the same time Parenti reported that citizens were opposing measures introduced by Savonarola, "so that it should not be said abroad that the city of Florence was being governed by a friar."[36]

In his *Defense*, Scala specifically answered the charge that Florence was being governed by prophets and her laws passed by the authority of friars and preachers, made, he said, by those who wanted to make Florence "look ridiculous, particularly among other Italians."[37] Written on 1 September and printed five weeks later, in the middle of the period of crisis between the arrival of the imperial ambassadors on 19 August

[35] Parenti, "Storia fiorentina," ed. Schnitzer, p. 135; cf. Sanuto, *Diarii*, I, cols. 284-285; Villari, *Storia* I (Florence, 1887): 470-471; Rubinstein, "Politics and Constitution," p. 182. On the embassy of the Germans and the Signoria's reply, delivered by Scala, Sanuto, *Diarii*, I, cols. 248-251; Santini, *Firenze e i suoi oratori*, pp. 272-273; Parenti, "Storia fiorentina," ed. Schnitzer, pp. 133-134; Landucci, *Diario fiorentino*, pp. 137-138.

[36] P. Somenza to Lodovico Sforza, 28 August 1496, ed. del Lungo, "Fra Girolamo Savonarola," p. 12: "subjungendo che debono hora considerare in che termino se trovino, sotto il governo de uno frate"; cf. Parenti, "Storia fiorentina," ed. Schnitzer, p. 137: "acciò di fuori non si dicesse che un frate la città di Firenze ghovernasse."

[37] *Defense*, fol. b3v: "qui rem Florentinam apud reliquos Italiae maxime populos ridiculam redderent." On the *Defense*, which deserves to be better known, J. Schnitzer, "Die Flugschriften-Literatur für und wider Girolamo Savonarola," in *Festgabe Karl Theodor von Heigel*, Munich, 1903, pp. 203-204; De Maio, *Savonarola e la Curia Romana*, p. 70; Weinstein, *Savonarola and Florence*, p. 244 (and below). Cf. Sanuto, *Diarii*, I, col. 405: "nè voglio tacer di questo, come in defension di la cità di Fiorenza predetta contra quelli la calomniavano, Bartholameo Scalla canzeller grando de' Fiorentini fece una opereta latina la qual fo butada in stampa." Although the printed edition is dated 1 September and was printed "Florentiae ex archetypo" on 21 September (fol. b5v), Crinito's prefatory letters of 5 and 6 October (fol. a2r-v) date the edition "not earlier than 6 October" (*Indice generale*, 5:56, no. 8817). An autograph draft of some of it, together with letters to various friends to whom he sent copies, is in Scala's Modena MS, fols. 7r-11r, the letters on fols. 1r-2v.

and the destruction of the imperial fleet off Livorno at the end of October, his treatise had a very practical and immediate purpose. Its general defense of Florentine republicanism is followed by rebuttal of specific charges against the new regime: that the Great Council was too large, its meetings too slow, that the opportunities for speaking were too few and its members unfit to govern.[38] As for the charge that Florence was being governed by friars and prophets, Scala argued that religion made a necessary contribution to the good and happy life, while prophecy also had an important role in history; like Machiavelli, he regarded religion as an ancillary but important aid to achieving a stable and prosperous state.[39] Despite its confident republicanism, however, the *Defense* is an ambiguous writing. The naturalistic rationalism of his dialogue *On Laws and Legal Judgments* is replaced by a pessimistic view of man's fallen state: if only we followed nature as our guide, there would be no disagreement about who should rule and we would live in happiness; but having transgressed the divine command, "that is to say, the limits of nature," we live in exile, banished from the country of our birth, inhabitants of the civil republic in which there are as many kinds of people as laws and customs.[40] The contrast with his earlier writing is profound: the state is no longer naturalistic, governed by one man according to the dictates of reason and nature, but is the result of man's fall from grace. For Scala, Medicean paternalism was the natural state, republicanism man's punishment for sin.

[38] *Defense*, fols. b1v-b2v (on government in general and Florentine republicanism, see fols. a6r-b1r, esp. a6v: "Civitas nostra regnum semper abhorruit, utputa quod possit soleatque facile verti in tyrannidem . . . Atque hanc quoque speciam [oligarchy] tantus est tyranni metus abiecimus Populumque Florentinum asservimus in libertatem"). On the building of the new hall and the difficulties encountered by the new Council, Rubinstein, "I primi anni," pp. 174-183; J. Wilde, "The Hall of the Great Council of Florence," *Journal of the Warburg and Courtauld Institutes* 7 (1944):65-81, esp. 67-69.

[39] *Defense*, fols. b3r-b5r, cf. ch. 12 below.

[40] *Ibid.*, fol. a6r: "Et beati viveremus. . . . Sed nos, transgressi divinum mandatum, idest naturae limites, desciscentes a patria exulamus."

At the beginning of November 1496 Scala sent his *Defense* to a few old friends—to Jacopo Acciaiuoli, cousin of Lorenzo and Giovanni di Pierfrancesco and uncle of their close friend Zanobi Acciaiuoli, now a Dominican monk and follower of Savonarola; to Manente Buondelmonti, a Decretalist and Florentine canon; to his old friend Niccolò Borghesi, the republican chancellor of Siena, who had suffered worse vicissitudes in the course of his career than Scala. The letters he wrote to these friends and a few others—Fra Mariano da Genazzano, general of the Augustinian Hermits and Savonarola's opponent in Florence, an Aretine poet in Florence and Pandolfo Collenuccio—show how eclectic the chancellor's circle was at the end of his life.[41] In them we glimpse the old Scala pontificating, commending, fixing as he had always done. Congratulating Fra Mariano on his new office of prior general, Scala wished him well, "For I wish mortals many good things provided they are not elevated to unworthy honors"; paying tribute to his long friendship with Niccolò Borghesi he commented: "It is indeed true what they say, that love lies outside the power of fortune"; writing to the Aretine poet Marco Giannerini, he reflects with Theophrastus and Virgil on the differences to be found between people as well as plants bred in different regions—using this occasion to pay a last tribute to his two famous predecessors in the chancery, Leonardo Bruni and Carlo Marsuppini, for "who can deny that the Aretines are born for writing and elegant speech?"[42] A trace of envy in a letter congratulating his old friend Pandolfo Col-

[41] Modena MS, fols. 1r-4r and 11v. On Jacopo and Zanobi Acciaiuoli, Niccolò Borghesi and Pandolfo Collenuccio, see below; on Fra Mariano, ch. 4, n. 141 above, and following note; and on Manente Buondelmonti, S. Salvini, *Catalogo cronologico dei canonici della Chiesa Metropolitana fiorentina*, Florence, 1782, p. 56, no. 416; and *Angelo Polizianos Tagebuch (1477-1479)*, ed. A. Wesselsky, Jena, 1929, p. 156, no. 294.

[42] Cf. Modena MS, fols. 3v-4r, for the poem accompanying his letter to Giannerini. Fra Mariano was nominated acting prior general on 16 August 1495 and general of the order only on 14 May 1497, after the death of the former general, the general Chapter having been postponed for a year because of his own illness. He was in Florence on 3 August where he stayed "for about five months" and preached the Advent sermons (Perini, *Un emulo*, pp. 55-56).

lenuccio on his change of fortune reminds us how his own life had altered since the days when he and Pandolfo used to discuss law together in the early 1480s. There were no more feasts and jousts now, only religious processions and prophecies of impending doom.[43]

Although Scala had survived the revolution, his way of life must have been altered by it—no longer the esteemed first servant and confidant of the Medici, but joint chancellor of the republican regime, which had no use for the diplomatic services he used to render the Medici. Beccanugi died eight months before Scala, who continued to work in the chancery until shortly before his death on 24 July 1497. It was perhaps fortunate for him that he died when he did, before his new loyalties were too severely tested. An unsuccessful attempt by Piero de' Medici to return to Florence in April 1497 was followed in the next month by Savonarola's excommunication for heresy and disobedience. In June Lorenzo di Pierfrancesco took voluntary exile in the Mugello, and in August a conspiracy in favor of Piero de' Medici was discovered and its leaders —all important men—put to death.[44] Savonarola's excommunication and the persecution that followed were widely believed to have been encouraged by Fra Mariano da Genazzano,[45] and his death at the stake in May 1498 was preceded

[43] On Pandolfo, see also P. Negri, "Le missioni di P. C. a Papa Alessandro VI, 1494-1498," *Archivio della Società Romana di Storia Patria* 33 (1910): 333-439, and letters to Ercole d'Este from Rome, ed. with bibliography by C. Varese in *Prosatori volgari del Quattrocento*, pp. 593-720, cf. p. 707, n. 1. On this period, Weinstein, *Savonarola and Florence*, esp. chs. 1, 4 and 5; E. Garin, "Desideri di riforma nell'oratoria del Quattrocento," *La cultura filosofica*, pp. 166-182; and C. Vasoli, "L'attesa della nuova era in ambienti e gruppi fiorentini del Quattrocento," in *L'attesa dell' età nuova nella spiritualità della fine del medievo* (Convegni del centro di studi sulla spiritualità medievale, 3, 1960), Todi, 1962, pp. 370-432.

[44] Nardi, *Istorie di Firenze*, 1:95-109; S. Bertelli, "Machiavelli e la politica estera fiorentina," pp. 36-38, quoting P. Somenza's letter to Lodovico Sforza on Lorenzo di Pierfrancesco's departure, 29 June 1497 (p. 37).

[45] Riccardo Becchi to the Dieci (30 May 1497), ed. A. Gherardi, *Nuovi documenti e studi intorno a G. Savonarola*, Florence, 1887, p. 167; cf. De Maio, *Savonarola e la Curia Romana*, p. 108; Nardi, *Istorie di Firenze*, 1:101, 116; Landucci, *Diario fiorentino*, p. 160.

by the dismissal of Scala's former assistant and colleague, Alessandro Braccesi, from the chancery.

By then Scala was dead. He was buried in the Cestello, the Cistercian monastery opposite his house in Borgo Pinti, and his body was later transferred to the church of SS. Annunziata where in 1534 his son Giuliano acquired a chapel in memory of his son Cosimo.[46] Giuliano was responsible for ensuring that Bartolomeo's memory was kept alive once a year when mass was said for him and his wife on the day following the Feast of St. Bartholomew.[47] No trace of this chapel now remains; his grandson Giulio was buried in the Augustinian nunnery of San Clemente in Via San Gallo, where his brother's three daughters, the last of Bartolomeo's direct descendants, ended their days.[48] Bartolomeo's fame was briefly revived in the late seventeenth or early eighteenth century in a long and eulogistic inscription for a monument by Giovanbattista Foggini.[49] He died at the wrong moment for immortality. There were no Medici at hand to commission a monument for him as there had been when Marsuppini died, and no tribute to his long chancellorship survives in Santa Croce or elsewhere.[50] There is only the inscription on his house in Borgo Pinti: "Bartolomeo Scala, Chancellor of the Republic, illustrious historian and writer, lived and died in this palace which he built and was

[46] ASF *Libro dei morti della arte de' medici e speciali*, 247 (1490-1515), fol. 104r: "M. Bartolomeo Scali—a dì 24 [July 1497]. R[isposat]o in Cestello"; M. Pocciante, *Catalogus scriptorum florentinorum*, Florence, 1589, p. 25; Manni, *Vita*, pp. 55-56, 61-62 (cf. the expanded version in the first and second MS drafts, Vat. lat. 8225, fols. 342r, 365r); Marzi, *Cancelleria*, p. 273, n. 3. According to Andreucci, *Il fiorentino istruito*, p. 68, art. xvi, Scala was buried in the chapel of the Sposalizio di S. Caterina in the tribune, the patronage of which belonged to Giovanni and Angelo de' Bardi (cf. p. 308), whereas Giuliano acquired the chapel of SS. Cosimo and Damiano, see ch. 9, n. 99 below.

[47] See ch. 9, n. 99 below.

[48] See ch. 9, n. 110 below.

[49] In Florence, Bibl. Marucelliana, MS B. 1. 19, fols. 117r, 118r, inc. "D.O.M. Tumulus Bartolomei Scale / Vetusto Cineri / Sepulchrum recens extructum."

[50] On Marsuppini, see ch. 2, n. 55 above. Bruni, Marsuppini and Machiavelli are all buried in S. Croce.

sold by his descendants in 1585 to Cardinal Alessandro de' Medici, later Leo XI . . ."[51] It serves as a reminder not only of the Scala family's close bond with the Medici but also of their achievement. They had maintained their position in Florentine society far longer than Poliziano or Ugolino Verino had predicted in Bartolomeo's lifetime, and when their line died out they sold their estate to no less than a cardinal and future pope.[52]

[51]"Bartolommeo Scala / Cancelliere della Repubblica / Illustre Storico Letterato / Visse e morì in questo Palazzo / Da lui costruito / E dai suoi posteri venduto / nel MDLXXXV / Ad Alessandro de' Medici Cardinale / che fu Leone XI / Da cui lo ebbe Costanza sua sorella / Moglie di Ugo Conte della Gherardesca / nel MDCV," ed. F. Bigazzi, *Iscrizioni e memorie della Città di Firenze*, Florence, 1886, p. 308; cf. below.

[52] On Poliziano's prediction, see ch. 8, n. 60 below; on Verino's, *De illustratione urbis Florentiae*, bk. 3, fol. 34r: "Scala recens nuper Collensi venit ab agro / suscepitque gradum summum, tunc carmine docti / Vatis et Historici, veteres aequavit honore. / At nihil in terris durat, vix orta, recessit." On Scala's family, see ch. 9 below.

PART TWO
Work

CHAPTER VI

The Office of First Chancellor

. . . it comes from God. *Scala to Agostino Dati, 1466*

You know, at Florence the chancellor is the people's drain; it is to him they speak and reveal their thoughts. *Scala to Tommaso Soderini, 1471*[1]

According to the often-quoted description of Gregorio Dati, the chancellor of Florence: "stays in the palace during the day and writes all the letters which are sent to the princes of the world and to any person on behalf of the commune. Their chancellors are always poets and men of great scholarship."[2] Scala held simultaneously a more exalted and a more pragmatic view of his office than Dati's. It was at its highest God-given and required great moral probity. Within the intimate circle of his Florentine colleagues, however, he defined his work as collecting the outpourings of the Florentines as though he were a drain, "the people's drain," for which a good ear must have been more important than "great scholarship." Typically, he polarizes the extremes of his office, as he did his relationship with Lorenzo: formalizing his status with high-flown rhetoric for an outside audience, deprecating it with Tuscan dryness

---

[1] "id ex Deo est," Dati, *Opera*, fol. 137v; "Sapete il cancelliere a Firenze è la fogna del popolo: a lui parlano molti et aprono il loro concepto," ASF *Strozz.* ser. 1, 136, fol. 244 (15 October 1471).

[2] ed. G. Manni, *Istoria di Firenze di G. Dati dall'anno MCCCLXXX all' anno MCCCCV*, Florence, 1735, p. 137, in G. Capponi, *Storia della Repubblica di Firenze*, 1 (Florence, 1875), p. 646; cf. Marzi, *Cancelleria*, p. 35, n. 1; Luiso, "Riforma della cancelleria," pp. 132-142; H. Baron, *Humanistic and Political Literature in Florence and Venice*, Harvard U.P., Cambridge, Mass., 1955, p. 65, trans. in Holmes, *Florentine Enlightenment*, p. 17, etc. On the chancery in general, see Marzi's basic work; Luiso's article above; Tommasini, *Vita*, 1:137n, 665-670 (text of the 1498 reform); and Rubinstein, "The Beginnings of Machiavelli's Career"; on her chancellors, Garin, "I cancellieri umanisti della repubblica fiorentina"; Bec, *Les Marchands écrivains*, p. 365 (and R. Fubini's review in *Rivista storica italiana* 82 (1970): 227); Aeneas Silvius Piccolomini, *In Europam . . . historias, Opera*, Basle, 1551, p. 454; "Commendenda est multis in rebus Florentinorum prudentia, tum maxime quod in legendis Cancellariis non iuris scientiam, ut pleraeque civitates, sed oratoriam spectant et quae vocant humanitatis studia."

for those who would not make the mistake of undervaluing it. In fact the office of chancellor embraced all these functions. It was—as Dati suggests—primarily practical (writing letters and ambassadors' mandates); it was also confidential (compiling minutes of secret meetings and attending the secret count of votes in scrutinies, as well as listening to the people); and it was honorific (representing the commune and delivering orations on official occasions). Its scope was wide and the talents it demanded diverse.

The chancellor was one of the four men known as "the Palace Officials," who were together responsible for all the paper work of government.[3] Although they enjoyed certain privileges and functions in common—such as attending ceremonial occasions like the two-monthly swearing-in of the Signoria or supervising the secret count of votes of electoral councils—their offices were normally autonomous.[4] The office of notary of the Riformagioni, who was alone responsible for drawing up legislation, always kept itself separate from the chancery. The notary of the Tratte, on the other hand, who was responsible for registering the appointments of officials employed throughout the state (and in this period was also

---

[3] Originally used only for the first chancellor and the notary of the Riformagioni, the title "official of the palace" must have been extended to include the notary of the Tratte when he joined them in the *secretum scrutinei* (by 1415, n. 45 below); but as his office was often combined with that of the notary of the Riformagioni, it is not always mentioned separately (e.g. not in the scrutinies of 1431 and 1434, Pellegrini, *Sulla repubblica fiorentina*, pp. xxxix-xl; Marzi, *Cancelleria*, p. 200). It may have been extended to include the second chancellor by 1459 (Marzi, p. 231), and certainly by 1483, when it is used for all four officials, *ibid.*, pp. 599, 600 (referring to the first chancellor, the notary of the Riformagioni and to the "electio reliquorum Officialium Palatii, qui sunt duo"), *ibid.*, pp. 605, 612 (implying that the privileges of Officials of the Palace now to be enjoyed by two secretaries were those formerly enjoyed by the notary of the Tratte and second chancellor and not that they were extended to them for the first time; but cf. Rubinstein, "The Beginnings," p. 77, n. 47). Cf. "Progetto di riforma alla costituzione" [1484], ed. G. Pampaloni, *ASI* 113 (1955): 265, discussing how many accoppiatori should be added "al segreto" to "i 4 di palagio consueti."

[4] *Statuta*, "Friburgi," 2:501, 486; and n. 45 below.

[136]

often responsible for hiring troops and preparing their contracts, the so-called *condotte e stanziamenti*), was sometimes
attached to the chancery, sometimes to the notary of the Riformagioni and was sometimes independent.[5] In contrast to
these bureaucrats appointed for at least a year and usually
longer, the notary of the Signoria was elected for only two
months with the Signoria whom he served, to whom he was
entirely responsible and had continually to attend.[6]

Although there was a clear dividing line between the functions of these officers of state, in practice they must have collaborated quite closely, for the chancellor's work overlapped
that of the notary of the Tratte in his responsibility for recording the election and despatch of ambassadors and he
needed easy access to the notary of the Riformagioni's legislative records—at least until the time of Scala, who attempted
to liberate the chancery from this dependence. As all his letters had to be commissioned by the Signoria and approved by
them, he must also have been in constant contact with the
Signoria and their notary.[7] According to instructions of 1498,
all members of the chancery, with the notary of the Riformagioni and the notary of the Tratte, had to present themselves
to each new Signoria to initiate them into their duties by administering to them a special oath, addressing them on the dispensation of justice, the rules governing legislation, and so on.
The chancellor's special task was to present them with "certain brief memoranda" containing the rules governing the
writing of letters and with two files in which to preserve the
letters received from outside and within the state.[8] Although
these instructions belong to the period after Scala's death, a

---

[5] *Statuta*, 2:716-720, 721-724; Marzi, *Cancelleria*, pp. 107-112, 207-208, etc.;
Luiso, "Riforma della cancelleria," p. 134.

[6] *Statuta*, 2:699-703; Marzi, *Cancelleria*, pp. 166-168.

[7] Marzi, pp. 372, 373.

[8] ASF *Carte di corredo*, 45, fol. 47r, ed. Marzi, pp. 619-620: "Instructio
data officiali reformationum nuper electo in anno 1498": "certi brievi ricordi
con dua filze dove sono notati gli effetti delle provisioni che dispongono
circa allo scrivere delle lettere, et le filze, overo agetti, si danno uno per
infilzare quelle lettere che vengono di fuori della jurisdictione, nell'altra
quelle che vengono da' subditi." On the "brievi ricordi," cf. n. 21 below.

similar procedure must have been observed in his day to initiate each new Signoria into their office. The rooms of the Signoria and their chapel were on the second floor of the Palazzo
della Signoria together with their audience chamber and the
sala where they and the colleges met and held special *ad hoc*
meetings, and it seems likely that the offices of the first chancellor were close at hand.[9]

Letter writing, as Gregorio Dati said, was the chancellor's
principal task. Until 1437 his office had been undivided, but in
that year Leonardo Bruni delegated the work of writing letters
within the Florentine state, as well as safe conducts and letters
of recommendation, to a second chancellor, who was to have
his own office and assistants. Although the offices were formally reunited under Carlo Marsuppini in 1453 on the death
of his second chancellor, it seems certain that this distinction
between the two categories of work was never lost and that
another chancellor—ser Antonio di Mariano Muzi—was appointed soon afterward to write internal administrative letters
even if he did not always enjoy a separate department. In the
absence of second chancery registers from 1445 to 1470, the
situation on Scala's appointment as first chancellor in 1465 is
unclear. When they begin again in 1470 Antonio Muzi is in-
disputably in charge of the second chancery (where he remained until his death in 1494). But the fact that letters to officials within the state are often drafted by the same hands and
in the same book as external letters suggests that the two chanceries must have worked closely together.[10]

[9] Marzi, *Cancelleria*, pp. 475-478. In the time of Scala's successor, Marcello Adriani, the chancellor's office was on the left-hand side leaving the
Sala dell' Audienza on the second floor of the palace and it is likely that
Scala's office was in the same place (Cambi, *Delizie*, 21:275-276; cf. Tommasini, *Vita*, p. 552, n. 3). On the chancellor's office in the 1437 and 1483
reforms, see Marzi, *Cancelleria*, p. 477; and (in 1437) Luiso, "Riforma della
cancelleria," p. 138.

[10] Ser Antonio di Mariano Muzi is described as "vicecancelliere del
Comune" in the ratification of a treaty dated 5 September 1454 (*Libri
commemoriali*, 5:102). The recommendations of 1456 (see pp. 20-21 above)
would have served to confirm him in this position, which he held in 1459
and was again confirmed in 1461 (Marzi, *Cancelleria*, pp. 221, 231-232; ASF

As for the letters written by the first chancery, which were
Scala's particular concern, they were divided by Bruni into
two categories also. Letters of public business were distinguished from letters of private business commending individual citizens for favors or asking that justice be done to them.[11]
In the course of time this distinction seems to have lapsed, although it was briefly revived by Poggio Bracciolini in 1453,
but as soon as Scala was appointed chancellor a twin series of
registers begins again. They were copied by his assistant, ser
Alessandro Braccesi, who was initiated into chancery business
from the middle of March 1465 and took over entirely from
the late chancellor's assistant, ser Bastiano Forese, on 18 April
1465.[12] The following day he opened a new volume of mandates, a day later a new volume of letters of public business
(*Missive* 45), and a month later a new volume of letters of
private business (now in the Biblioteca Nazionale, MS *Palatino* 1103).[13] In case the distinction between these two series
of registers was not immediately clear, Scala had subsequent
volumes titled in bold rustic capitals: "LITTERAE DE

Cento Delib. 1, fol. 40r, 27 February 1461). ASF *Signori Carteggio, Missive
2a. Cancelleria* 3, begins by listing the priors for January 1470 "vigente
eorum secundo cancellario spectabili viro Ser Antonio Mariani Mutii notario
et cive florentino" (cf. Marzi, *Cancelleria*, p. 244, n. 2). It contains letters,
etc., mainly to Vicars, Captains and Podestà in the Florentine state. Cf. ASF
Minut. 7, fol. 44r, a draft in Scala's autograph to the captain and consuls of
Pisa [August 1466]. *Minut.* 11 is made up of a series of separate gatherings,
some containing external letters of public business, others external letters of
private business and others internal letters. On the 1437 reform, Luiso,
"Riforma della cancelleria," Marzi, *Cancelleria*, pp. 196-197.

[11] ASF *Missive 1a. Canc.* 34 and 33: "De negociis privatorum Epistolarum
[Liber] D. Leonardi Cancellarii Florentini," and "Epistolarum liber secundus," beginning on 1 and 2 March 1430 respectively (cf. Marzi, *Cancelleria*,
p. 366: "applicava la divisione classica per libri alla pari di Cicerone"); and
39 and 40, both beginning on 12 June 1453, in the time of Poggio Bracciolini.

[12] Cf. ch. 3, n. 10 above. On Braccesi, B. Agnoletti, *Alessandro Braccesi*,
Florence, 1901; Kristeller, "An Unknown Correspondence," pp. 313 ff., and
the bibliography in *Supplementum*, 2:338; A. Perosa in *Dizionario biografico, s.v.*

[13] ASF *Leg. Comm.* 16, *Missive* 45 and BNF MS Palat. 1103 (the latter
not used by Del Piazzo to locate the unidentified letters listed in the
Protocollo).

REBUS MERE PUBLICIS POPULI FLORENTINI
BARTHOLOMAEO SCALA CANCELLARIO A MENSE
IANUARIO ANNI MCCCCLXVIII USQUE AD AN-
NUM MCCCCLXXV," "letters of purely public business,"
the sequel to *Missive* 45, and "LITTERE DE REBUS
MAGIS PRIVATIS D[OMI]NI BARTHOLOMEI
SCALE CANCELLARII," "letters of more private business," the sequel to *Palatino* 1103.[14] Unlike his predecessors,
whose initial reforming enthusiasm had waned after introducing this reform, Scala elaborated on it and retained a
double series until replacing it by a different system of registration altogether.[15]

Some of these letters Scala drafted himself and some he left
to his assistant. We can see from the volumes of draft letters,
the *Minutarii*, which letters are in his own hand or have been
corrected by him—in this early period usually, but not always,
mandates for ambassadors or letters to important dignitaries
like the pope or the king of France[16]—although of course they
reveal nothing about the letters he may have dictated to his
assistant. Braccesi described his work in 1470 as "for the past
five years writing out the letters which you [Scala] compose
in the name of the Florentine people,"[17] but in view of all his

[14] ASF *Missive* 46 and 47.   [15] In 1483 and 1487, see ch. 7 below.

[16] For example, from 29 March to 14 May 1466 Scala drafted *inter alia*
letters to the Sienese, to the Florentine orators in Milan (twice), to the
king of France, to Pope Paul II (twice), to the cardinal of Rouen, the College of Cardinals and three cardinal legates, ASF *Minut.* 7, fols. 1r, 10r,
98r-v, 3r-v, 9r-v, 96r, 96r-97r, copied respectively in ASF *Leg. Comm.* 16,
fols. 23v, 24r-v; *Missive* 45, fols. 67r-v, 69v-70v, 71v-72v, 73r-v, 73v-75r; cf.
Munich, Clm. 10781, fols. 178v, 181r, 183v, 185v-187r (but excluding letters to
ambassadors, cf. n. 20 below); the letter to the cardinals is also copied in BNF
MS II, 1, 107, fol. 8v. Only about two letters in Scala's autograph in *Minut.*
7 are registered in Palat. 1103 (14 February 1467, to the Sienese, and 28 April
1467 to Leonardo Dati, *Minut.* 7, fols. 73r, 117v; BNF MS Palat. 1103, fols.
59v, 63r; neither is listed in the *Protocollo*), suggesting that on the whole
Scala left letters "of private interest" to his assistant. We can see that Scala
retained his interest in drafting ambassadors' mandates from his autograph
draft of the commission to G. B. Ridolfi and P. A. Soderini dated 21 July
1494 (ASF *Minut.* 16, fols. 88r-89r).

[17] In a letter to Scala dated 10 November 1470, ed. Kristeller, "An Unknown Correspondence," p. 352, cf. p. 324n.: "respondi ego quinquennium

other duties Scala cannot have composed all external letters himself.[18] Occasionally the *Minutarii* show the sort of instructions he might give to his assistant. He will write, "Report what is being written to the Lord of Imola; about Messer Lodovico's doings," and this is followed by a draft more or less adopted in the final letter, which expands his notes into: "The magnificent Lord of Imola writes that your troops have arrived in the Romagna," "Because we have recent information from an envoy sent from Messer Lodovico," and so on.[19] Since a later copy of these letters in Munich is almost but not absolutely identical with *Missive* 45, it is possible that it was transcribed from yet another exemplar.[20]

---

iam usum te esse opera nostra in exscribendis quas tu Florentini populi nomine dictares epistolas." Scala described Braccesi in 1470 as "saepe coadiutor . . . in scribendo," *ibid.*

[18] Letters subscribed with Scala's name are not necessarily drafted by him, cf. a letter of credence and a letter written out by Antonio della Valle and subscribed with Scala's name, dated 3 and 7 January 1485, when Scala was not yet back at work in the chancery after visiting Rome, BNF MS Ginori Conti 29, 116, fols. 3-8, and ASF *Acq. e Doni*, 352, fol. 177. It emerges from ASF *Acq. Doni* 352 (letters from the Dieci di Balìa to G. Lanfredini, 30 April 1484-22 March 1485, cf. *Sotheby's Sale Cat.* 25 June 1968, p. 26, lot 803) that letters written out by Antonio della Valle are usually subscribed with Scala's name whereas those by Filippo Redditi are not.

[19] ASF *Minut.* 7, fol. 106v (draft of a letter to the duke of Milan, 27 June 1466): "Dare notitia di quello si scrive al S[ignor] d'Imola. De' facti di Messer Lodovico," etc. expanded in *Missive* 45, fols. 80v-81v (cf. *Protocollo*, p. 218) to: "El magnifico Signor d'Imola ne scrive le genti vostre essere arrivate in Romagna . . . ," "Perchè intendiamo nuovamente per uno mandatario d'esso Messer Lodovico. . . ."

[20] Munich Clm. 10781, fols. 101-261 (cf. ch. 3, n. 10 above). Since these letters were copied out in an elegant humanistic hand they may represent the work of one man, but as they apparently contain the "litteras . . . quas ad Compararum protectores Janue degentes illustrissimus Florentinus populus mittit" which Braccesi wanted transcribed, possibly as Kristeller suggests because he had composed it and wanted to provide for its diffusion ("An Unknown Correspondence," pp. 314-315, n. 3; ed. Marchesi, *Bartolomeo della Fonte*, append. p. xxx, probably referring to the letter of 30 September 1465, *Protocollo*, p. 193, ASF *Missive* 45, fols. 31r-32v, Munich Clm. 10781, fol. 134r) it may not necessarily represent Scala's work, but rather letters for which he was responsible. Sixteen letters written in May 1466 and April 1467, all contained in Munich Clm. 10781, are also copied in

The chancellor received his orders from the Signoria several times a week (the dates in the *Protocollo* registering all the letters written by the Signoria from 1459 to 1468 show that they were written on differing days, occasionally even on Sundays, but usually not more than twice or three times a week). Once drafted, the letters had to be approved by the Signoria before being copied in the chancery registers, written in letter form to be subscribed by the chancellor and dispatched. Although the date of the letter in the *Protocollo* is usually the same as that of the copy in the letter-book (*Missive*) and the final fair copy, there is often a delay of at least one day.[21] At the end of 1481 Scala told the Milanese ambassador that he had been commissioned to draft a letter to Venice to agree with the letter of Ferrante, king of Naples. He promised to write it the following day and did so, but when the minute was examined it was not approved, and after consultation with all the ambassadors it was agreed finally that Ferrante's letter

BNF MS II, 1, 107, fols. 6r-8v; as they include some letters which exist in Scala's autograph, they too may have been copied as specimens of his writing. ASF *Manoscritti* 58 and 59, copied in an eighteenth-century hand, are attributed to Scala and complement ASF *Missive* 49.

[21] Letters in their final form also sometimes bear a different date from the one by which they are registered and copied (e.g. a letter to the duke of Milan, registered and copied on 3 December 1465 (*Protocollo*, p. 199, BNF MS Palat. 1103, fol. 26r) is dated 4 December in its final form, ASMi SPE Fir. 272), doubtless because they were copied with the date on which they were approved by the Signoria and not with that on which they were sent. Procedure in the chancery was strictly defined, as can be seen from the "Brievi richordi facti a Voi Magnifici et Excelsi Signori Priori di Libertà et Gonfaloniere di Giustizia del Popolo Fiorentino et per quegli che sono deputati al servigio della Cancelleria," which belong to Scala's period and list the authority required for different kinds of letters and mandates, ed. Tommasini; *Vita* 1:668-669, note, dated [1458-1480?]. Letters needed a two-thirds majority of the Signoria to be approved, letters to the pope, emperor, kings and queens had to be approved by the colleges as well as by the Signoria (*ibid.*, p. 668; cf. Pampaloni, "Gli organi," pp. 265-6). A gathering survives in ASF *Minut.* 11 (fols. 239r-284v) containing agenda and notes of letters to be written in Scala's hand (fols. 240r-257v: "Assi a rispondere," "Assi a sollecitare," etc.), as well as notes of letters received from Florentine ambassadors, audiences with visiting ambassadors, drafts of letters, and so on, April-June 1481.

should be returned to him to be rewritten.[22] Although this was not a typical situation in that it involved states other than Florence, it shows that the approval of the Signoria was not a mere formality. On another occasion Scala showed the emperor's ambassador, at his request, the draft of a letter to be sent to the emperor by the Signoria; the ambassador approved of all but the part praising the duke of Milan, which he thought was overdone and should be changed (for so many commendations were unsuitable in a letter to the emperor, he said), to which it was replied: "that what had been done by the Signoria and Colleges and a *pratica* of citizens could not be changed without holding a new meeting and taking a new vote, and here they would never change."[23]

In addition to writing the external letters of the Signoria (and usually in times of war, those of the Dieci di Balìa as well),[24] the chancellor by 1415 had acquired special responsibility for ambassadors. He had to prepare and register their mandates and instructions (which in 1431 he was instructed to copy in a special book, together with all the letters sent to

[22] Fil. Sacramoro to G. G. Sforza (17 December 1481), ASMi SPE Fir. 303: "e come messer Bartholomeo Scala mi havea dicto, come l'havea commissione de fare la minuta e che el dì seguente la faria, e così fu vero tutto; ma seguì poi che, posta in examinatione dicta minuta, non si accordorno che la stesse bene, nè anche usque hodie ad trovargli forma che paresse a epsi opportuna et conveniente a loro modo."

[23] S. Sacramori to Cicco Simonetta (28 May 1469), ASMi SPE Fir. 276: "El me ha ditto D. Bartholomeo Scala . . . che . . . disse ditto Prospero [Camulius] che non se conveniva tante commendationi scrivendo al Imperatore, et che tutto stava bene da quello in fora et volle che Luy la mutasse; a che li fo resposto che quello se e [sic] era fatto per li Signori et Collegii et praticha de ciptadini non se posseva mutare se non se faceva novo conseglio et novo partito, et quy non se mutaria may." The letter referred to is in ASF *Missive* 46, fol. 11r-v (25 May 1469). Prosper Camulius was received by the Signoria as ambassador of Frederick III on 24 May 1469, ASF *Risp. verb. orat.* 2, fol. 34r-v.

[24] On the authority of the Dieci, *Statuta*, "Friburgi," 3:25-31; Pampaloni, "Gli organi," pp. 270-90; Rubinstein, *Government*, p. 68. On Scala's chancellorship of the Dieci in 1467-1468, Marzi, *Cancelleria*, p. 242, and Venice, *Libri commemoriali*, 5:164; Filelfo, *Epistolae*, fol. 208v; of the Venti in 1472, p. 151 below; of the Dieci in 1478-1479, ch. 4, n. 66 above; and of the Dieci in 1482, ASF *Dieci Delib.* 25, fol. 13r (5 September 1482).

and abstracts of letters received from ambassadors). He was also responsible for registering the dates of their election, departure, prorogations and return in a special book and, on their return, for showing the payments due to them to the officials of the Camera, or Treasury.[25] By the sixteenth century, and probably earlier, the chancellor had assumed responsibility for making departing ambassadors swear on the Gospels that they would observe the instructions given to them by the government.[26]

Mandates for ambassadors at the beginning of Scala's office were written by the chancellor at the request of the Signoria and Colleges, by virtue of authority delegated to them by the Cento when it elected the ambassadors.[27] After 1480, however, the situation was changed by the creation of a new Council of Seventy and a new foreign affairs committee, the Otto di Pratica, who interposed their authority between the Signoria and Colleges and the Cento. Now the Cento decreed that orators were to be elected on the initiative and suggestion of the Council of Seventy, while their mandates were prepared by the Otto di Pratica, the Signoria and Colleges merely confirming them and writing them out in their name.[28]

[25] *Statuta*, "Friburgi," 2:705-707, 711; cf. Luiso, "Riforma della cancelleria," pp. 133-134; and for relevant legislation after 1415, "Costituzione per gli ambasciatori, 1421-1529," in Vedovato, *Note sul diritto diplomatico*, pp. 47-82 (cf. Marzi, *Cancelleria*, pp. 589-590, for the 1431 decree).

[26] Luiso ("Riforma della cancelleria," p. 133) quotes Giannotti's *Discorso* (*Opere*, 1:28), which may describe only the situation in the early sixteenth century. According to Martines (*Lawyers*, pp. 13-14, n. 5), this function passed to the Podestà when the office of Executor of the Ordinances of Justice was abolished in 1435.

[27] See the "Brievi richordi" (n. 21 above), p. 668: "Non si può eleggiere Ambasciadori nè fare lettere di credenza, nè commissione, nè altre lettere che chommettino ad alchuno che dicha o expongha alchuna chosa per parte della Vostra Magnifica Signoria se prima non si delibera per voi insieme co' vostri honorevoli collegii e per Consiglio del Cento." Scala's reforms concerning the formula of mandates are discussed in the following chapter.

[28] There is a very early account of the new procedure in ASF *Leg. Comm.* 21, fol. 2r (27 April 1480): "Centumvirale Consilium duos decreverat legatos paucis ante diebus quam Septuagintavir[or]um Prattica statueretur, ut in libro legationum nostrarum scriptum est. . . . Eorum mandata cum prius Octoviri Pratticae designavissent Septuagintaviri novus

Scala introduced important innovations in the writing of letters and ambassadors' mandates, which formed part of his campaign for modernizing the chancery, to be discussed in the next chapter. Although he wrote to Tommaso Soderini in 1471: "You know my practice, I do not write to ambassadors without a reason,"[29] he often did have a reason for writing privately to them. Without ever claiming the right to communicate freely with ambassadors in a private capacity, his special responsibility for them naturally brought him—as we shall see—into close contact with many of the most influential men in the city.

Moving from the chancellor's primary function of letter writing to his more confidential, or discretionary, functions, his most important task was undoubtedly that of attending the *pratiche*, or secret *ad hoc* meetings summoned by the Gonfalonier of Justice to discuss special problems. The minutes of these meetings, compiled by the chancellor or his assistant, vividly demonstrate how in practice the chancellor's day was divided between attending these consultative meetings and writing letters, sometimes at their request.[30] We know that Scala

---

senatus decrevit. Priores deinde Libertatis et Vexillifer Iustitiae, qui a Centumvirali Consilio eam potestatem habebant, decretum perfecerunt Senatus." As examples of the formulae used before and after 1480, cf. ASF *Leg. Comm.* 16, fol. 4v (10 July 1465: "Electus fuit in Consilio Centumvirorum Dominus D.N. . . . cum mandatis, litteris credentie, etc. per Dominos et Collegia deliberandis," and *Leg. Comm.* 21, fol. 25v (28 June 1481): "Praecedenti Septuagintavir[or]um deliberatione A. M. per Centumvirale Consilium creatus fuit Legatus," *ibid.*, fol. 31v (5 December 1481): "B. G. eques postquam ita inter Septuagintaviros prius deliberatum est, a summo magistratu, Collegis et Centumvirali Consilio creatus est orator Ferrariam. . . . Mandata Octoviri Prattice deliberent, quae tamen Priores confirment et suo nomine inscribantur. Iidem credititias litteras scribant."

[29] Letter of 15 October 1471, ASF *Strozz.* ser. 1, 136, fol. 244: "Sapete il mio costume: non scrivo ad ambasciadori senza cagione."

[30] See C. Salutati, *Epistolario*, ed. Novati, 1 (Rome, 1891): 217: "Ego autem qui quotidie secretis intervenio consiliis. . . ." The relevant volumes of *Consulte e Pratiche* in ASF are 57-60, and [post 1494] 61-63. Extracts from the earliest volumes have been ed. Pampaloni, "Fermenti di riforme democratiche nella Firenze medicea del Quattrocento," *ASI* 119 (1961):

attended in person when we are told that he read out a letter or, as in 1466, read out the formula of an oath to be sworn by all citizens.[31] But it is as difficult to detect his presence from his hand in their minutes as it is to detect which letters he wrote for the commune. Sometimes entries in draft volumes are in his hand, sometimes they are in the hand of his assistant, and at the beginning of his office we find him trying to improve the system of registration by making separate copies of letters authorized by the meetings as well as fair copies of debates.[32]

241-281, and 120 (1962):521-528, discussed in 119 (1961):11-62, and "Gli organi," pp. 32-37. On post-Medicean *pratiche*, F. Gilbert, "Florentine Political Assumptions in the Period of Savonarola and Soderini," *Journal of the Warburg and Courtauld Institutes* 20 (1957):187-214; A. Anzilotti, *La crisi costituzionale della repubblica fiorentina*, Florence, 1912, pp. 85-86; Giannotti, *Discorso*, p. 37.

[31] ASF *Cons. Prat.* 60, fol. 14v (27 January 1468): "ex litteris quae per cancellarium lecte erant"; *Leg. Comm.* 17, fol. 35v (13 April 1470): "fu facto leggere uno scripto al ca[n]celliere"; cf. *Cons. Prat.* 57, fol. 171r, ed. Pampaloni in *ASI* 120 (1962):556 (8 May 1466): "Deinde lecta per cancellarium formula quadam iuramenti." This formula is ed. A. Municchi, *La fazione antimedicea detta del Poggio*, Florence, 1911, doc. 4, pp. 116-117; cf. Pampaloni, "Il giuramento pubblico," esp. p. 224; Rubinstein, *Government*, p. 156; Rinuccini, *Ricordi storici*, p. xcix.

[32] ASF *Cons. Prat.* 57 (20 May 1465-12 May 1466) is apparently a fair copy of debates copied in *Cons. Prat.* 58 (8 June 1465-31 August 1467), whereas *Cons. Prat.* 59 (19 October 1465-12 August 1468) is a slim volume of only five entries written by Scala and his assistant, consisting of letters proposed by small *pratiche* of citizens delegated for this purpose. Usually 57 follows 58 closely, although in April 1467 some long speeches written out by Scala in Italian in 58 are much reduced in the Latin version in 57 (58, fols. 119v-135v, 138r-v, 144r-v; 57, fols. 141v-150v, 153r-v, 158v). Drafts in 58 marked "R[egistrato]!" are usually in 57 or have space left for them, whereas canceled drafts in 58 are usually not in 57; 57 contains one speech for which a blank space is left in 58 (57, fols. 49v-51v; 58, fol. 35r), but normally it is the other way round. *Cons. Prat.* 60 (April 1467-25 February 1480), like 58, contains principally reports of debates but also some letters and speeches of orators. The number of exceptions to any rule suggests the system of registration was not yet fully evolved. As both 57 and 59 were begun in the first year of Scala's office and were not continued after 1468, they may represent a reform he gave up or continued more informally, as in the gathering of verbal replies to orators proposed by *pratiche* of citizens in 1477, ASF *SS. Dieci, Otto* 77, fols. 83r-96r. The practice of making fair copies of debates was apparently first introduced by

The meetings were attended by leading citizens whose opinions on important issues could not be neglected,[33] and in a system of rapidly rotating offices these "senators," as they were called, provided an element of continuity in government as well as one of social élitism, since knights usually spoke first in them and tended to dominate the debate (which the most senior among them apparently enjoyed the privilege of initiating).[34] This élitist tendency was encouraged by Scala, fresh from his office in that last bastion of chivalry in Florence, the Guelf Party, and on 5 September 1466 (at the very moment when the Medici party defeated the Pitti conspiracy) Scala's hand carefully differentiates the rank of knights from that of lawyers by giving them their full title of *eques* instead of referring to both indiscriminately (as hitherto) as *domini*.[35] In the 1470s these *pratiche* exercised increasing influence in the field of foreign policy, often delegating authority to a small committee of their members to draft replies to letters discussed in the meeting. This work closely concerned the chancellor. It was he who read out letters received from other states and Florentine ambassadors, and it was often his responsibility to

---

Accolti, who also introduced the *Risposte verbali d'oratori* and possibly the notebook listing letters written by the Signoria, the *Protocollo*, see the doctoral thesis of Robert Black on Accolti (London University, 1974), pp. 104-111.

[33] They were normally attended only by the Gonfalonier of Justice without other members of the Signoria, cf. N. Tranchedini to G. M. Sforza, 16 August 1468, ASMi SPE Fir. 275, describing a *pratica* to which he was summoned, attended by the Gonfalonier of Justice, "che era solo de la Signoria in la pratica come è de usanza el più de le fiate," cf. 18 August, *ibid.*, and n. 38 below.

[34] On the question of precedence in debate, see ASF *Cons. Prat.* 60, fol. 90v (6 December 1469): Carlo Pandolfini "veniam petivit quod ante locum suum sententiam dixit, et in eo dixit obsecutum se esse Manno Temperano, qui sic petiverat."

[35] ASF *Cons. Prat.* 58, fol. 184r (5 September 1466) in Scala's autograph, referring to the "ordinem equitum" and listing knights with the title *eques* written after their names, a practice subsequently continued by Scala on fols. 188v-189r (3 November 1466, distinguishing between *eques* and *iurisconsultus*, previously described indiscriminately with the title "D[octor]" or "M[esser]") although not adopted by his assistant until 8 January 1467 (fol. 211r).

draft replies together with the committee to whom authority had been delegated for this purpose by the Signoria.[36] The members of this committee are called on one occasion the *cittadini della camera*, on another *della pratica*, and they clearly anticipate the Otto di Pratica, the magistracy of Eight created in the constitutional reform of 1480 to deal with exactly the matters previously discussed by these *ad hoc* committees.[37]

The 1480 reform also institutionalized the larger *pratiche* from which members of the committees were drawn. These advisory councils had been consulted particularly on foreign and financial policy, and now their functions were assumed by the Seventy, which provided from its membership the two magistracies of the Otto di Pratica and the Twelve Procurators dealing with foreign affairs and finance, just as the *pratiche* had previously delegated their authority to smaller committees on the same subjects.[38] Although the system that had

---

[36] *Cons. Prat.* 60, fols. 39v (13 October 1468): "Octoviri: verba fecit Otho Nicolinus. . . . Et nonnullos cives cum Cancellario deligendos ad eas litteras scribendas si ita videatur magistratui"; 119r (8 February 1471): "Infrascripti senatores, quos Magistratus delegerat, ut Cancellario designarent litteras infrascriptas omnes una fere voce rettulerunt scribendum esse ad Mediolanensem Ducem, ut in libro litterarum publicarum registratum est sub die nono februarii fol. 55 [ASF *Missive* 46, now fol. 56r-v] et ad Jacobum Guicciardinum Oratorem Rome ut in ij° libro legationum Barth. Scale patet [fol.] 81 [ASF *Leg. Comm.* 17, fol. 81v-82r]. Cives autem ii fuerunt . . . [listing 10 citizens: 6 knights, 3 lawyers and Lorenzo de' Medici]." Cf. also ASF *Minut.* 9, fol. 249v (8 February 1471), listing the same citizens.

[37] See Scala's letter to Lorenzo de' Medici, 9 September 1477 (ASF *MAP* 32, 456, cf. his letter of 27 June 1477: "hebbe in camera cittadini," *MAP* 34, 170), evidently meaning the citizens who met in the Camera of the Gonfalonier of Justice to reply to the Lucchese ambassador on 11 September (ASF *SS. Dieci, Otto* 77, fols. 93r-94r), who were on another occasion called the *cittadini della pratica*, ASF *Minut.* 10, fol. 426r (April 1477). These *pratiche* and the 1477 register are described by Fubini ("Note Machiavelliane," pp. 377-379 and n. 9) as innovations of the Laurentian period, whereas they date from at least the previous decade, see ASF *Cons. Prat.* 59, fol. 1r (19 October 1465), opening with the report of three citizens who "retulerunt ut scriberetur ad Paulum II in hunc modum." On the Otto di Pratica, see Rubinstein, *Government*, pp. 199-200; and below.

[38] Rubinstein, *Government*, pp. 199-202. Moreover, members of the Seventy like members of *pratiche* were called *senatores*, and the meetings of both were secret (ASF *Misc. Repubb.* 4, insert 117, a fragmentary register of the Council of Seventy, the reference to which I owe to Prof. Rubin-

operated before 1480 was not unconstitutional in that the Signoria was empowered to ask for the advice of specially selected citizens (presided over by the Gonfalonier of Justice), it was—as Scala might have put it—not at all convenient that these meetings and committees had continually to be reconvened when they so often consisted of exactly the same people, and if they did not (since they were chosen by the Gonfalonier of Justice), that could be inconvenient as well. Outside advice could still be sought after the 1480 reform, but in practice it rarely was because the people who were most regularly consulted were already members of the Seventy and its delegated magistracies.[39]

stein, fol. 68r-v: "Hic enim est Florentinus senatus. . . . Tandem quaecunque agentur a vobis secreta, ut sint, curare Vos decet et tanquam in penetralibus quibusdam sacris condita, donec ad alias extra vestrum concilium deliberationes sit perventum: haec sunt quae iureiurando Vos servaturos debetis polliceri et tactis altaribus facere haec promissa vestra augustiora"; cf. ch. 10, n. 19 below). Emphasizing this element of continuity, Rubinstein (*Government*, p. 202) links the Seventy with the permanent nucleus of 40 (plus 7) members of the Cento created in 1471, but this, too, may have been modeled on *pratiche*, which often tended to be composed of about this number (e.g. ASF *Cons. Prat.* 57, fol. 136v, 31 March 1466: "B. L. Vexillifer Iustitiae, convocatis et collegiis, et ad xl senatoribus litteras legi iussit"; ASMi SPE Fir. 275, N. Tranchedini and S. Sacramori to G. M. Sforza (14 September 1468): "havendone de poi la prefata Signoria et collegii cum li Otto et circa xxxx^ta. ciptadini ellecti per la praticha tutti radunati insieme"; *ibid.*, 288, Fil. Sacramoro to the same (2 October 1474): "Lau[renz]o ha facto convocare quaranta cittadini").

[39] Few drafts of advisory meetings survive after 1480, but ASF *Minut.* 11 contains some gatherings (fols. 149r-175v, 358r-378r) describing meetings like pre-1480 *pratiche*, usually consisting of about fifty members who on at least one occasion are described as the Seventy (fol. 161v, 14 April 1481: "Deliberaverunt Septuaginta Viri ut confirmaretur foedus") and on another as a collection of different magistracies, knights and other "private citizens," described as *senatori*, who advised that the Seventy should be convened (fol. 361r, 7 May 1482: "XII Viri Procuratores, Equites et Magistratus" who "monuerunt ut celeriter 70 conveniant et procure[n]tur loca nostra ut tuta reddantur" and "ceteri privati"). Cf. ASF *Missive* 48 (a volume of drafts, despite its title), fol. 99v, July 1480, referring to letters deliberated not only by the Otto di Pratica, "ma etiamdio v'intervenne el consenso degli infrascripti viiij cittadini richiesti a consultare decte lettere," including among them Lorenzo de' Medici; cf. Scala to [G. Aldobrandini, 12 October 1481], ASF *Minut.* 12, fol. 16r-v: "Pare adunche a questi delli Octo et della pratica."

Because of his special responsibility for *pratiche* and their delegated committee on foreign affairs, Scala was intimately affected by the 1480 reform. Although he retained his responsibility for transcribing the deliberations of the Seventy when they concerned state or external affairs, similarly for writing the external letters of the Otto and the Twelve,[40] he lost his sole responsibility for their affairs: as a legislative as well as a deliberative council, the work of the Seventy now also concerned the notary of the Riformagioni, and we shall see what action Scala took in the chancery reform of 1483 to recover his authority. He also lost his position as the one fixture in the government, since membership of the Seventy was for life. Although the historian Jacopo Nardi still valued Scala's successor, Adriani Virgilio, for much the same reasons as Sacramori had once valued Scala, for holding "in his chest the perpetual and unbroken thread of the daily conduct of the affairs of the republic,"[41] the chancellor was no longer the only permanency in the government as he once had been.

Among the chancellor's other discretionary functions was oath taking and the conduct of secret interrogations. It was Scala who read out the oath proposed by the Signoria to the *pratica* of 4 May 1466, and it was probably he who also administered it to "all responsible citizens" summoned by the Signoria to the Palazzo Vecchio four days later. As we have seen, the chancellor became responsible for taking the oaths of departing ambassadors, and in 1495 we find him conducting a secret interrogation after first administering an oath to the people involved.[42] Although it was not one of his *ex officio* duties,

[40] See the "Ordine dei Settanta" (19 April 1480, ed. G. Capponi, *ASI* I (1842):336): the chancellor or his assistant is to transcribe the "deliberazioni" of the Seventy in a separate book "quando fussino di cose di stato o di fuori de' terreni havessino dependentia," similarly to write the external letters of the Otto di Pratica and 12 Procuratori; but cf. p. 179 below.

[41] *Istorie di Firenze*, 1:232: "nel petto di questo uomo restava continuato ... il filo perpetuo e continuo del maneggio delle cose della repubblica che alla giornata seguiva" (1502).

[42] On the chancellor as "quasi depositario de' Signori pe' segreti di Stato," Marzi, *Cancelleria*, pp. 363-364. Scala may also have administered the oath for members of the Seventy (described in n. 38 above). However, the gen-

the chancellor also often acted as an arbitrator in disputes between institutions or citizens: with its plentiful supply of notaries and assistants always to hand, his office was the scene of
innumerable settlements and legal transactions.[43]

The seals of the commune were normally in the zealous possession of two friars in the Camera dell'Arme on the ground
floor of the palace, but in May 1472 Scala was given charge
of "the medium-sized seal with a dove" belonging to the Dieci
di Balìa, which was henceforth deleted from the inventory of
seals kept in the sacristy of the chapel in the Palazzo della
Signoria. This was on the day after the Cento appointed a
balìa of twenty (instead of the usual ten) citizens to conduct
the war against Volterra, and Scala was clearly given the seal
to use as their chancellor. This was less of a concession than
to have held the large communal seal of Hercules or the Signoria's small lily, as both Scala's biographer Manni and Marzi
believed he had been granted, but it nevertheless went entirely
against communal tradition and signified an increase of the
power of the executive.[44]

The chancellor shared with the other Palace Officials and

---

eral oath of 13 August 1495 (published in Florence, 1495) was to be administered by "il cancellieri delle Tracte, oltre all' ordinario giuramento el
quale si dà alla Signoria nella sua entrata" (fol. a1v).

[43] Manni, *Vita*, pp. 35-37; ASF *Notarile* B 187 (ser Francesco Baldesi,
1448-1499, fols. 180r-182r); cf. ch. 8, n. 36 below.

[44] ASF *Carte di Corredo* 66, fol. 51r: "Uno sugello mezano con una
colomba pe' X di Balìa" (deleted) and in the margin, "Die primo maii
1472 fuit consignatum sigillum Domino Bartolomeo Scala, Cancelliere, per
deliberationem Dominorum"; cf. Manni, *Vita*, p. 15 (and Marzi, *Cancelleria*,
pp. 248, 385, etc.) who read the date as "Marzo" not "Maii," which according to Florentine style would have been a year later when Scala was instead
a member of the Signoria. According to Manni, the inventory then (in
1768) belonged to G. P. Baldovinetti, although in a note attached to the
MS draft of his *Vita* (Vat. lat. 8225, fol. 322r) it was in the "Archivio of
the Palazzo Vecchio"; an inscription in the inventory records that it was
given to the "Archivio Segreto di S.A.R." by the Abbot Pier Andrea An-
dreini on 16 May 1729 (fol. 3r). On the friars of the Camera, *Statuta*, "Friburgi," 2:523-525, and Giannotti, *Discorso*, pp. 23-24: "un frate dell'Ordine
Cisterciense, che per antica usanza abitava in palagio e teneva il sigillo della
Signoria." On these seals, Marzi, *Cancelleria*, pp. 377-385.

the friars of the Camera the all-important discretionary function of keeping "the secret of the scrutiny," as the 1415 Statutes define it.[45] Together they attended the secret count of votes cast in the scrutiny councils that qualified citizens for office: since the ballot was secret and none but themselves knew who had been successful until their names were actually drawn for office, this was a duty of great trust. No wonder Scala described his office as "the people's drain," since all must have come to pour out their hopes and fears to the man from whose lips a word would suffice to suggest their fate in the polls. Yet to Scala this was an unwelcome task, and in 1466 he described the small room where the beans were counted, the *secretum*, as "the most irksome prison of the scrutinies."[46]

There were three scrutinies during Scala's chancellorship— in 1466, 1471 and 1484.[47] It was after the second that the Palace Officials were given an additional responsibility, or rather privilege, in connection with elections. It was already their duty to check that the candidates chosen by the accoppiatori for the priorate were in fact eligible for office (since they

[45] *Statuta*, "Friburgi," 2:486: "Et quod secretum scrutinei supradicti retineatur per cancellarium communis Florentiae, et scribam reformationum, et notarium extractionum et Fratres camerae armorum palatii populi florentini"; cf. Rubinstein, *Government*, p. 117, n. 5. In the course of the century, the number of Palace Officials represented in the *secretum* was increased to four; cf. n. 3 above.

[46] Scala to N. Tranchedini, 26 May 1466, Riccard. MS 834, fol. 108v, ed. Gentile, "B. S. e i Medici," p. 136, doc. 7: "Ex molestissimo carcere scrutiniorum." On the atmosphere in the city during scrutinies, S. Sacramori to G. M. Sforza (23 November 1471), ASMi SPE Fir. 282: "Quy è facenda assay a questo scotinare, et quando simile cose se fanno, è usanza che semper la Città bolle perchè chi spera et chi dubita."

[47] Rubinstein, *Government*, pp. 152-153, 186-188, 210-218. On the scrutiny in general, *Statuta*, "Friburgi," 2:481; Rubinstein, *Government*, pp. 4-5. On 4 February 1474, when the powers of the accoppiatori (which had expired in 1472) were restored for one day to complete the imborsation, the Palace Officials were instructed that "fra due mesi allora proximi futuri debbino avere interamente fornito quanto resta et allora restarà a imborsare per dare intera perfectione a tutto per la imborsatione del detto squittino del 1471" (ASF *Cento Delib.* 1, fol. 83v, *MAP* 86, 37, fol. 331v; cf. Rubinstein, *Government*, p. 187, n. 6), demonstrating how long the entire process of imborsation could be drawn out.

alone held "the secret of the scrutiny") before putting their names into bags for election or "to be shown" (*per far vedere*). In August 1473 they were themselves allowed to add one name "to be shown" to the bags of either the priorate or the notariate of the Signoria, and this for the first time entitled them to exercise more than the purely executive authority they had until then enjoyed in elections.[48] The third scrutiny of 1484 began on 29 November, just before Scala set off for Rome with other Florentine citizens to deliver the oration that won him a knighthood from the pope. So on this occasion he must have been at least partially reprieved from his prison sentence in the *secretum*, saved by the life of public fame that was beginning to distract him from his more sober duties as chancellor.

The oration he delivered before the pope on 15 December 1484[49] introduces us to Scala's honorific functions as chancellor. Strictly speaking, of course, this was not one of the *ex officio* occasions when he was required to make a speech—although to have been chosen to deliver the Florentine oration of homage to the new pope was a great honor, since the task usually fell to the most experienced or senior of the ambassadors present. Nevertheless, there were many occasions when the chancellor was expected to deliver orations, and Scala had already enjoyed ample opportunity to prove his skill in this

[48] ASF *MAP* 86, 37 (minutes of the proceedings of the accoppiatori in the 1471/1472 scrutiny, cf. Rubinstein, *Government*, p. 187, n. 6), fol. 332r, 9 August 1473: "e ciaschuno de' presenti uficiali del palagio possa per far vedere ongni dua mesi fare imborsare uno de' priori o per notaro coma vorrà." At the same time the number of candidates for the priorate the accoppiatori could nominate *per far vedere* was limited to five each, and one for the notary, "perchè nel far vedere per de' priori o notaro de' Singniori nel modo chonsueto si rivela inn uno anno o pocho più tutto il secreto, dàssi tedio e mancha la cosa di riputatione." On the influence of the Palace Officials in the 1484 scrutiny, see Piero Guicciardini's account of the scrutiny, ed. Rubinstein, *Government*, append. 11, p. 319. On *far vedere*, *ibid*., pp. 188-189.

[49] Published in six editions between 1484-1490 (see ch. 4, n. 134 above). It is partly ed. Santini, *Firenze e i suoi oratori*, pp. 268-271, from the official copy in ASF *Leg. Comm.* 21, fols. 55r-59v.

art. For example, he delivered three orations before Florentine
military commanders: the first to congratulate Federigo of
Montefeltro, duke of Urbino, on successfully quashing the rebellion in Volterra, delivered on 29 June 1472;[50] the second at
the ceremony of handing over the military standards and baton of command to Costanza Sforza, the new Florentine captain general, on 4 October 1481—when he was applauded not
only by the people, but by the more discerning audience of
foreign ambassadors resident in Florence, who called it "a
very elegant oration and elegantly delivered," and "very
learned and long";[51] the third on 25 June 1485 on the appointment of Niccolò Orsini, count of Pitigliano, to the same

[50] The *Oration* is ed. G. Zannoni, "Il sacco di Volterra: un poema di
N. Naldi e l'oratione di B. Scala," *Rendiconti d. R. Accademia dei Lincei*
5 (1894):239-244; cf. Filarete, "Ceremonie," ASF *Carte di corredo*, 61, fol.
13v. It is dated in the chronicle of G. Giusti, MS Vat. lat. 11760, fol. 130r-v:
"Lunedì a dì 29 di Giugno in Firenze la Signoria donò al Magnifico Messer
Federigo Conte d'Urbino e Capitano della Lega una bella bandiera col
giglio e un'bell Elmetto tutto coperto d'argento e fiorini in un Bacino
d'Argento. Fece la diceria messer Bartolomeo Scala Cancelliere della
Signoria in su la Ringhiera de' Signori alla presenza de' Signori e del Popolo
e questo fecero per rimuneratione della vittoria et acquisto di Volterra."
Apart from this, the duke was to be given a horse, Florentine citizenship
with the right to hold office, "che è uno seguire el modo de' Venetiani,
quando fanno uno gentiluomo a Venesa pro bene meritis" (S. Sacramori to
G. M. Sforza, 26 June 1472, ASMi SPE Fir. 283), and a former property of
Luca Pitti's costing 6,000 florins (Filarete, "Ceremonie," fol. 13v); cf.
Vespasiano da Bisticci, *Vite*, 1:284-285.
[51] See ch. 4, n. 107 above; Fil. Sacramoro to G. G. Sforza (6 October
1481), ed. Magnani, *Relazioni private*, p. xlix: "Fu cominciata per d.
Bartholomeo Scala una oratione molto elegante e eligantemente recitata";
Antonio Montecatini to Ercole d'Este (5 October 1481), ed. A. Cappelli,
"Lettere di Lorenzo de' Medici . . . con notizie . . . ," *Atti e memorie
d. R. deputazione di storia patria per le provincie modenesi e parmensi* 1
(1863):257: "Messer Bartolomeo Scala fece l'orazione molto degna, ne la
quale intesi la virtude del Signor Costanzo. . . . Ho voluto dire questa parte
a V. Excellentia de l'orazione [concerning Costanzo's bravery during the
Pazzi war, when he had been in dispute with Ercole d'Este's son], la quale
fu molto diserta e lunga." The *Oratio . . . pro imperatoriis militaribus signis
dandis Constantio Sfortie Imperatori* was published in Florence by Nicolò
di Lorenzo (*Indice generale*, 5:57, no. 8825). It also exists in Riccard. MS
914, fols. 100r-114r, apparently copied from the printed edition.

office.[52] Although the ambassadors followed his argument closely in 1481, much of what he said would have been incomprehensible to the people since it was in Latin and was delivered while the actual ceremony of handing over the insignia was taking place, suggesting it was Scala's manner of delivery and display of learning that impressed them. However, there is one characteristic of Scala's orations, as well as of his writings, that may help to explain their popularity: they are all clearly arranged and developed, listing at the beginning the points to be made and repeating each point when it was reached, which must have made the task of understanding them much easier.[53]

The ceremony conferring knighthoods on citizens and visiting dignitaries was another occasion when the chancellor might be called on to deliver an oration. Scala did so three times in 1469 and 1470 in lieu of the Gonfalonier of Justice, twice when the Gonfalonier was himself receiving the knighthood, once when he was acting as procurator in the ceremony. As Lorenzo de' Medici acted as procurator when Bongianni Gianfigliazzi was knighted on 30 December 1470, although not a knight himself, the ceremony was clearly intended to convey the Medici regime's seal of approval on the way Bongianni had conducted his term of office.[54] When Jacopo Pazzi

---

[52] Filarete, "Ceremonie," fol. 18v: the baton was given to Orsini "con electione dello astrolago" at 18½ hours on 25 June, and "fè l'oratione Messer B. Scala."

[53] See his 1481 *Oratio*, fol. 2r: "De necessitate igitur habendi imperatoris *primum*; de imperatore ipso *deinde*; *postremo* de utilitate deliberationis huius deque imperatoriis insignibus erit dicendum." His model was doubtless Cicero's *Oratio de imperio Cn. Pompei*, 2.6. Filarete ("Ceremonie," fol. 16v) gives a full description of the ceremony, explaining what happened while "continuava . . . el cancelliere la sua oratione" and "finito l'oratione el Can[celliere]." According to a marginal note the baton was handed over at 17⅓ hours on Thursday 4 [October] 1481. Filarete supports Scala's description of the baton as made "ex rudi inculto atque infabricato trunco more maiorum" (*Oratio*, fol. 5v).

[54] ASF *SS. Delib. sp. aut.* 34, fols. 73v-74v; cf. Salvemini, *La dignità cavalleresca*, p. 136. On this award, see N. Michelozzi's comment to A. Braccesi (Oxford, Bodleian MS Auct. F. 2. 17, fol. 117r-v, *s.d.*) "ob bene

was knighted on 24 February 1469 at the end of his term of office as Gonfalonier of Justice, the ceremony took place in the Baptistery, before all the magistrates raised on a platform and in the presence of the resident ambassadors and many knights. Scala delivered his oration praising the dignity of knighthood and its recipient after Mass had been sung and before the procurator administered a solemn oath to Jacopo Pazzi.[55] When Gabriele Malaspina was knighted on 15 August 1470, the ceremony took place instead in the Duomo.[56]

In addition to these grand occasions, Scala was required to make many other less formal orations, particularly to foreign ambassadors who did not understand Italian. Here we can see how important it was for the chancellor to have a ready use of Latin, and it is unlikely that Scala would have forgotten the occasion when Carlo Marsuppini was chosen to deliver a formal oration to welcome the Emperor Frederick III in January 1452 and was unable to reply spontaneously to the emperor's questions, whereupon Giannozzo Manetti—who Vespasiano da Bisticci thought would have been a more suitable orator than the chancellor in the first place—saved the situation by answering for him, and spoke so well that "all who knew Latin and what was involved considered that messer Giannozzo had spoken much better extempore than messer Carlo

gestum magistratum et eius in rempublicam merita equestri ordine decorasse"; and S. Sacramori to G. M. Sforza (27 December 1470, ASMi SPE Fir. 280): "Credo che questo populo lo farà cavallero prima ch'el escha de offitio: ènne caxone Laurenzo, per fare omne honore ch'el pò a li amici soy" and (29 December, *ibid*.): "Domatina faremo Chavallero el nostro Bonzanne et parmi che el Comune et populo che lo fa, faranno Laurenzo di Medici sindico a farlo, etiam ch'el non sia cavallero, tengono ch'el vallerà per l'auctorità, como ho ditto, che li dà el populo." The decree appointing Lorenzo procurator on 28 December 1470 is in *SS. Delib. sp. aut.* 34, fols. 72r-73v.

[55] ASF *SS. Delib. sp. aut.* 34, fols. 19r-21r; ed. Salvemini, *La dignità cavalleresca*, pp. 135-136; cf. Filarete, "Ceremonie," fol. 14v. The procurator was Tommaso Soderini.

[56] ASF *SS. Delib. sp. aut.* 34, fols. 61r-62r; Salvemini, *La dignità cavalleresca*, p. 136; Filarete, "Ceremonie," fol. 15r. According to Filarete (fol. 14v) the ceremony in his time always took place "ne' luoghi sacri."

had with preparation."[57] On another occasion Scala's predecessor in the chancery, Benedetto Accolti, apparently memo-
rized the entire speech in Latin of a visiting ambassador from
Hungary, wrote it down word for word, and translated it for
the Signoria; then, on being asked by the Signoria to reply and
told what to say, "composed it in Latin extempore and replied so well that the ambassador, a most learned and eloquent
man, was amazed."[58]

The standards were high and it is unlikely that Scala ever
performed such feats, but from his own register of *Risposte
verbali d'oratori* (vol. 2), we can derive some idea of the occasions on which he was called upon to reply to foreign legates
in Latin. Twice, in 1469 and 1470, he replied to the legates of
King Matthias Corvinus in Latin because they had delivered their orations in Latin;[59] similarly to the legates of the
king of France in 1469, 1479, 1483 and 1494,[60] and to the
English legate who visited Florence in 1493.[61] On occasion he
was also asked to reply to Italian legates in Latin, as he was to
the Venetian Pietro da Molin in 1476.[62] If the Gonfalonier of
Justice could speak Latin, he was expected to reply to visiting
orators in preference to the chancellor, as when Donato Acciaiuoli welcomed the king of Denmark to Florence in March
1474—although even so, since the king apparently knew no
Latin, Donato's speech had to be translated, and on the king's
return, perhaps to avoid repetition, Scala was asked to address

[57] Vespasiano da Bisticci, *Vite*, 2:65-66; cf. Cambi, *Delizie*, 20:281-283;
Marzi, *Cancelleria*, p. 213.

[58] *Vite*, 2:238-239.

[59] ASF *Risp. verb. orat.* 2, fols. 34v (25 June 1469) and 36v (29 May
1470).

[60] *Ibid.*, fols. 36r (9 November 1469), 62r (11 January 1479, cf. ch. 4, n. 71
above), 86r (5 September [1483]) and 105r-v (6 May 1494: "Responsum
est pro tempore proque re ipsa paucis verbis lingua nostra a Nicolao
Martello Vexill[ifer]o Iustitie. Deinde per Bartholomeum Scalam Cancellarium responsum uberius latine. . . ." A draft of the formal reply in Scala's
autograph, dated 6 May 1494, is in ASF *Minut.* 16, fol. 37r-39r).

[61] *Ibid.*, fols. 101v-102r (24 April 1493).

[62] Fil. Sacramoro to G. M. Sforza (11 April 1476), ASMi SPE Fir. 291:
"Fu li facto respondere per M. Bartholomeo Scala, el quale pur dixit latino,
respondendo alle parte congruentemente."

him instead.[63] The correct procedure was evidently for the Gonfalonier of Justice to welcome ambassadors whenever possible, and when Scala was chosen to deliver the government's formal and considered reply in Italian to the imperial ambassadors who visited Florence in 1496, he did so only after the Gonfalonier of Justice had made an initial reply to their speech two days earlier.[64]

Closely associated with the chancellor's role of public orator was that of apologist for the state. On two occasions Scala wrote in defense of Florence, both at times of danger: the *Excusatio Florentinorum* of 1478 and the *Apologia* or *Defense Against the Critics of Florence* of 1496. The *Excusatio* is an open letter in the name of the Signoria publicizing the full version of Giovanbattista da Montesecco's confession of his part in the Pazzi conspiracy. Together with the counsels of lawyers proving the invalidity of the papal excommunication,[65] Gentile Becchi's *Synodus florentinus*,[66] and Poliziano's

---

[63] ASF *Risp. verb. orat.* 2, fols. 43v-44r (27 March 1474: "D. A. Vexillifer Iustitie verba fecit latine. Rex quia latine non intelligebat cum benigne admodum per interpretem respondisset"); Filarete, "Ceremonie," fols. 13v-14r (". . . Alla sua tornata da rroma . . . fecesi l'oratione a llui da el nostro excellentissimo Cancelliere messer B. Scala alla quale medesimamente per suo interpetre si fe benignie risposta"). Fil. Sacramoro gives a full account of the king's visit to Florence in letters to G. M. Sforza of 1 April and 3 May 1474 (ASMi SPE Fir. 286).

[64] ASF *Risp. verb. orat.* 2, fol. 121r: "quod autem locuti sunt Ethrusca lingua eadem lingua responsum factum, sed tunc quidem paucis verbis a Thomasio Antinoro Vexill[ifer]o Iustitie et in aliud tempus dilatum est, idest post consultationem publicam ut explicatius responderetur; post duos vero dies rursus vocati in eundem locum magistratus iussu Bart. Scala cancellarius respondit ut infrascriptum est" (viz. fols. 121v-124v, ed. Santini, *Firenze e i suoi oratori*, pp. 272-274). For similar procedure in 1494, cf. n. 60 above.

[65] Referred to by Scala in his *Excusatio*, ed. Fabroni, *Laur. Medicis vita*, 2:181; cf. Cagnola and Visconti to the Sforza (14 March 1479, ASMi SPE Francia 544). Poliziano refers to a counsel written by Bartolomeo Sozzini in a letter to Lorenzo de' Medici, 24 August 1478, ed. Fabroni, *Laur. Medicis vita*, 2:183; others are printed.

[66] Printed in Florence, 1478 (*Indice generale*, 5:130, no. 9245) and in a different version by Fabroni, *Laur. Medicis vita*, 2:136-166; cf. Roscoe, *Life*, 1, append. 27, pp. 75-98. References to its printing and what it should include in letters from Becchi to Lorenzo de' Medici and N. Michelozzi

Commentarium,[67] Scala's *Excusatio* forms part of a comprehensive scheme to counter the propaganda issuing from the papal printing press.[68] By contrast, the *Defense* is a more private document written in Scala's own name against internal critics, yet his purpose of defending the state is identical, supporting with Savonarola the government's pro-French policy against the imperialists, who wanted a change of alliance and regime.[69] By speaking out at this time of political uncertainty, Scala demonstrated that his loyalty lay with the government he served as chancellor.

The scope of Scala's office was wide. He had to be a good and fluent Latinist, as capable of writing letters and transcripts of speeches as of delivering orations and making extempore replies in Latin. He had to be a good organizer in order to cope with the expanding bureaucracy of the second half of

(BNF MS Ginori Conti 29, 81, fols. 60, 174, 179, 19 August 1478 and *s.d.*) suggest that it was a literary composition for which Becchi was held personally responsible by subsequent popes (who refused him a cardinalate on these grounds) rather than an account of an actual synod in Florence (see Antonio da Colle and Antonio da Bibbiena to Piero de' Medici, 20 September 1493, ASF *MAP* 55, 77, quoted by Picotti, *La giovinezza*, pp. 259-261, 289, n. 97: "fece già certa invectiva contro a Sixto, che saria stato meglio che havessi arso il Calamo et il Papiro . . . che penso di farla"; cf. Becchi to Michelozzi, 11 December 1484, BNF MS Ginori Conti, 29, 81, fol. 97: "Sapete in che predicamento io sono a Roma per il Florentina Synodus").

[67] Poliziano published his *Commentarium* in a less tendentious version after the war was over (Perosa, preface to the *Commentarium*, pp. x-xiii). Cf. Bartolomeo Fonzio's criticism of it in a letter to Poliziano (22 August 1483, ed. Marchesi, *Bartolomeo della Fonte*, p. 60).

[68] See Sixtus IV's letter to the duke of Urbino (25 July 1478, ed. Fabroni, *Laur. Medicis vita*, 2:130-131): "Al re di Francia habbiamo mandato multi nuncii con nostre justificationi, similiter alli altri Principi, come lo è l'Imperatore, Re di Ungheria, di Spagna e tutti li altri. Praeterea la Bolla nostra, quale è stata posta in stampa a tutto il mondo, dimostrerà nostra justificatione" (his first Bull of Excommunication, dated 1 June, is ed. Fabroni, 2:121-129; cf. Roscoe, *Life*, 1, append. 26, pp. 68-75). On the pope's use of the printing press for propaganda, see L. Botta to the Sforza (13 April 1479, ASMi SPE Venezia 365): "perchè non seguendo pace, me pare essere certo ch'el Pontefice con le consuete justificationi sue le faria mettere in stampa et le mandaria ad sua justificatione ad tutti li Potentati christiani."

[69] Cf. ch. 5 above, and on the *Defense*, *ibid.*, n. 37.

the fifteenth century. Above all he had to be discreet, for, as Angelo della Stufa said, "all our important secrets pass through his hands."[70] Scala was not equally successful in all these fields: his letters were criticized, his new style ridiculed and the chancery needed to be reorganized several times. Reformers are not always popular men, nor do they always interest themselves in the successful running of the schemes they introduce. But underlying all Scala's work in the chancery, as well as in the Guelf Party when he worked there as its chancellor, was a coherent scheme to reform all the institutions of the state and its administration. Unless we grasp how radical his campaign was, we shall fail to do justice to his significance as chancellor.

[70] See ch. 4, n. 59 above.

CHAPTER VII

From Medieval Chancery to Modern Secretariat

. . . at the beginning of my office I dared to do more as a raw recruit than all those great and famous men [his predecessors] had dared to do . . . even as veterans. Scala to Alessandro Braccesi, 1470[1]

The fifteenth century saw the government steadily increasing its influence at the expense of the medieval institutions that had formerly shared authority in the state: the Guelf Party, the guilds, the Mercanzia, the judicial offices of Podestà, Captain of the People and Executor of the Ordinances of Justice, and not least the church. At the same time legislative and executive authority was restricted to fewer, more permanent experts who came to form a powerful political élite.[2] As the government's right hand, the chancery was intimately involved in these steps towards modernization and centralization. Its structure closely reflected that of the state it served and, in order to be effective in this period of change, it, too, needed reform.

Scala was not the first reforming chancellor. However, as he said himself, he "dared to do more" than his famous predecessors and he saw more penetratingly than they did just what needed to be done in order to modernize the state chancery. It was not merely a question of simplifying procedure and centralizing authority to enable it to discharge the vastly increased business it had to deal with, although that was important. Nor was it merely a question of improving the presentation of letters in order to increase Florentine prestige abroad, although that, too, was an important motive in all Scala's reforms, as it had been of his humanist predecessors. It was

---

[1] 13 November 1470, Oxford, Bodleian MS Auct. F. 2. 17, fol. 125v; ed. Kristeller, "An Unknown Correspondence," p. 353: "principio huius nostri muneris ut tyro plus auderem quam . . . ne veterani quidem multi magni et clari viri ausi sunt."

[2] See Rubinstein, *Government*; Martines, *Lawyers*, esp. pp. 136-139, 397-404; M. Becker, "The Florentine Territorial State and Civic Humanism in the Early Renaissance," *Florentine Studies*, ed. Rubinstein, pp. 109-139; and on particular institutions, cf. ch. 4, n. 54 above.

more radically a question of transforming the status of its functionaries and the legal form of its documents to reflect Florence's position as a sovereign power. In theory, the city was still subject to the emperor and, although in practice her councils exercised sovereign authority within the state, their decrees and legal instruments were written as though they needed imperial authority (conferred by the attestations of imperial notaries) to be valid. According to the statutes, the chancellor as well as the notary of the Riformagioni had to be a notary by profession and all legal instruments had not only to be signed by all the members of the ratifying body (usually the thirty-seven names of the Signoria and Colleges, representing the Councils) but also subscribed by the (equally lengthy) attestations of notaries. This procedure was cumbersome compared with that used by sovereign powers, and it also implied that Florence still lacked the necessary authority to validate her own decrees.

Scala saw this very clearly, and his most important reforms aimed at replacing the old notarial officers by secretaries without legal qualifications, who were quite simply the executive servants of the sovereign government they represented. Emulating the chanceries of France and England,[3] they produced short letters and legal instruments authenticated by the communal seal and the subscription of the chancellor, who acted not as a notary but as the representative of the government. Scala introduced his reforms gradually and not all of them survived, for they met with the opposition not only of dignitaries like the pope, who saw his honor challenged by this new simplified formula, but also of colleagues like the notary of the Riformagioni, who thought his legal expertise was threatened. Nonetheless, the fact that Machiavelli (like Bernardo

---

[3] See T.A.M. Bishop, *Scriptores Regis*, Oxford, 1961 (esp. p. 2, describing the king of England as "more than a suzerain. He had ordinary and absolute power, prefeudal in origin, and he exercised this in written acts which it will be convenient to distinguish as 'precepts' "), P. Chaplais, *English Royal Documents*, Oxford, 1971, and *English Medieval Diplomatic Practice*, London, 1975-; A. Giry, *Manuel de diplomatique*, Paris 1894; G. Tessier, *Diplomatique royale française*, Paris, 1962.

Ricci before him) was appointed a member of this secretariat, although he had no legal qualifications, shows that Scala's reforms were not without effect.

Scala first revealed his reforming zeal as chancellor of the Guelf Party. His appointment had come at a critical moment in the fortunes of the Party, when it was fighting to save its life by assuming some task to justify its existence.[4] From December 1459 to January 1461 it gradually took over responsibility for the affairs of the Sea Consuls as well as for the magistracy of the Six of Arezzo, which won for Scala a pay rise, "in view of the considerable increase of labor" these offices brought with them.[5] It is true that Scala's routine activities as its chancellor (writing letters, statutes and decrees, taking oaths, preparing lists for elections, subscribing payments of money, attending the secret of the scrutiny, as if he were all the communal Palace Officials rolled into one)[6] were greatly added to by the work of the Sea Consuls for the short time that the Guelf Party assumed responsibility for them.[7] What

[4] To be discussed more fully in a forthcoming article in *ASI*.

[5] ASF *Capt. P. G.* 9 rosso, fol. 66r (18 January 1462): "Cumciòsia cosa che al Cancelliere è aggiunto faticha assai pell'Ufficio de' Sei d'Arezo e de' Consoli del Mare," he received an extra fl. 3 a month.

[6] See the 1420 Statutes in ASF *Capt. P. G.* 3 rosso, fols. 7r-8r, 4 rosso, fols. 12v-14r, and the 1335 Statutes ed. Bonaini in *Giornale storico degli archivi toscani* 1 (1857):1-41. In 1439 the chancellor was also made responsible for sending lists of debtors in the Party to the communal notary of the Specchio, *Capt. P. G.* 4 rosso, fol. 56r-v.

[7] On the routine work of the Sea Consuls, Mallett, *Florentine Galleys*, p. 22, in greater detail in "The Sea Consuls," pp. 160-161. In addition, the chancellor and *provveditore* of the Guelf Party were specifically given the function of attending the auction of galleys before the last day (when the captains themselves were to attend), and both officials and the treasurer were also to exercise all the functions previously exercised by their counterparts in the magistracy of the Six of Arezzo (ASF *Provv.* 151, fols. 336r-337r, 23 January 1461, 204v-205r, 27 August 1460). When the work of the Sea Consuls was taken from the Guelf Party in May 1462, Scala nevertheless retained his extra salary, himself quoting the relevant legislation to this effect in ASF *Capt. P. G.* 9 rosso, fol. 66r (from *Provv.* 153, fol. 39v, cf. *Consoli del Mare* 3, fols. 152v-153v, *provvisione* of 17 May 1462). In 1481, divested of most of its property, the Guelf Party again assumed responsibility for the Sea Consuls, their captains retaining this title until their demise in 1769,

was more important, it involved him in the attempt to restructure the Guelf Party to make it capable of carrying out its new charges.

It was soon appreciated that "as men of noble birth, accustomed to living off the fruits of their estates," many of the captains of the Party were ill-equipped to deal with maritime affairs.[8] The solution proposed was the old communal one of creating a small bag of select names, a *borsellino*, to ensure at least some competent captains at each election.[9] At the same time an attempt was made to reform the office of *provveditore* by selecting him instead of drawing him by lot and then by prolonging his office beyond the statutory year—a task in which Scala, as we have seen, collaborated closely with Giovanni de' Medici.[10] The bank of Giovanni and his cousin Pierfrancesco de' Medici was chosen temporarily to replace the office of treasurer, showing how closely the Medici were involved in these reforms.

Apart from preparing the legislation for these reforms, Scala also contributed to a whole series of other decrees intended to reorder the Guelf Party. On the day that they legislated for the creation of the *borsellino*, the councils were also presented with measures to reorganize the Orbatello, the almshouse in their care, which was "in considerable disorder," men mixed with women of different social standing and circumstances in the same house.[11] In future, slaves were to be evicted because they "upset and disturbed the whole place," and Corsicans, too, because their habits were very different from those

---

ASF *Provv.* 172, fols. 81v-84r; Mallett, "Sea Consuls," pp. 159-160; A. Sapori, "I primi viaggi di Levante e di Ponente delle galere fiorentine," *ASI* 114 (1956):83-84.

[8] "utpote nobiles homines ex fructibus suorum prediorum vitam agere solitos," Manno Temperani in a debate on 3 March 1461, ASF *Cons. Prat.* 56, fol. 142v.

[9] *Ibid.*, fol. 143r-v; and on the communal *borsellino*, Rubinstein, *Government*, p. 45.

[10] See pp. 32-33 above.

[11] ASF *Capt. P. G.* 9 rosso, fol. 61r (19-20 March 1461): "in assai disordine . . . et mescolati in una medesima casa huomini con femine di diverse qualità e conditioni."

befitting a charitable institution such as this, which was intended for people of good condition fallen upon hard times and not for "so brutish a people."[12] Later, the same puritan zeal spotted "many and very abominable deficiencies" in the benefices owned by the Guelf Party, which were difficult to reform, however, because of "the great humanity of the prelates and indeed their excessive charity toward notorious sinners."[13]

Badly kept accounts met with the same indignation as badly run almshouses or benefices. In July 1461 it was the building accounts that offended, for being "all muddled up and without any order whatsoever," with debtors listed in them who were not really debtors and similarly creditors; and because it seemed "not at all a fitting thing" that the law had to be broken for lack of a quorum every time officers had to be elected by sortition, a bill was presented on the same day reducing the size of the quorum.[14] In February 1463 it was "the very great defects" in the books registering the ages of members of the Guelf Party that offended their chancellor.[15] His enthusiasm for tidiness and order are also reflected in the phys-

12 *Ibid.*, fol. 61v: "Che per l'avenire non possi essere conceduta habitatione in Orbatello ad alcuna schiava, le quali, quandunche vene alcuna, tucto quello luogho inquietano et perturbano; nè alcuna Corsa, perchè communemente sogliono essere di costumi altrimenti facti che in simile luogho pietoso non è conveniente. . . . Il quale . . . et per le parole del testamento et per le habitationi d'esso più ornate et meglio acconcie che a quella tanto brutta gente non si conviene, s'intenda essere suto facto per persone di buona conditione per alcuna mala fortuna devenuti vergognosi miserabili."

13 *Ibid.*, fol. 68v (8-9 February 1463): "molti et molto abominevoli mancamenti nella maggior parte de' rectori de' vostri benefici. . . . Et volendosi provedere et rimediare . . . si truovano tante dificultà per la grande humanità de' prelati et in verità troppa misericordia loro inverso e notorii peccatori."

14 *Ibid.*, fols. 63r (14-15 July 1461): "Inteso la confusione et il disordine delle scripture de' libri appartenenti alla muraglia . . . per essere in essi molti debitori i quali veramente non sono debitori, et così e converso creditori, et per essere quelli conti tucti inviluppati et senza ordine alcuno"; 63v-64r: "Perchè non pare punto conveniente cosa che ciascuna volta che s'à affare alcuna tracta s' abbi a contrafare alla legge della vostra Inclyta Università."

15 *Ibid.*, fol. 69r (8-9 February 1463): "Perchè e' si truova grandissimi difecti ne' libri della età della Casa vostra."

ical appearance of the register of legislation enacted during his term of office, which is written in neat humanist hands and headed, "Provisiones facte tempore Domini Bartholomei Scale Cancellarii," exactly as he later titled all the volumes for which he was responsible in the state chancery.[16] One normally hesitates to ascribe legislation to particular individuals, but in this case the hatred of confusion and disorder expressed in the Guelf Party reforms recurs so consistently in other reforms Scala introduced in the chancery and elsewhere, as well as in other writings, such as the preface to his *History of the Florentine People*, that it must reflect his personal prejudice.[17] It can have been no coincidence that Scala was appointed chancellor of the Guelf Party at the very moment it was decided to regenerate it. His ability was already known to the Mediceans and they must have chosen him for the express purpose of reforming it under their supervision.

The same motives doubtless encouraged them to support Scala's election as first chancellor in April 1465. Certainly, as he says himself, he made his influence felt as soon as he entered the chancery "as a raw recruit." The outward and visible signs of his "reign," as one is encouraged to think of it, still survive. Titles of registers of diplomatic correspondence are numbered from the first book of his office (the third volume in the series, *Legazioni e Commissarie* 18, bearing the title "LEGATIONUM LIBER III BARTOLOMEI SCALE CANCELLARII," the fifth (vol. 20) "LIBER . . . V") and volumes of *Missive and Verbal replies of orators* also bear his name.[18] Covers change from paper to vellum and so do their

[16] The pages for his chancellorship are in ASF *Capt. P. G.* 9 rosso, fols. 55r-71r (in vellum), titled on fol. 55r. There is a particularly fine humanist hand on fols. 65r-70r.

[17] See, e.g., his letter to A. Massari on the reform of S. Spirito (9 May 1482, Modena MS fol. 12v); *Historia*: pp. 1-2 (cf. ch. 12 below); and on the chancery, below.

[18] See ASF *Leg. Comm.* vols. 16-21 (Registri di elezioni, istruzioni ˙e lettere ad oratori dei Signori). Vol. 16 is referred to as the "primo libro legationum Barth. Scale" in *Leg. Comm.* 17, fol. 35r; vol. 17 as "Liber 11°

pages. Script is humanist round-hand or cursive, and titles are written in rustic capitals. Wherever we look it is impossible to escape the fact that a new reforming hand has just taken over.

Once confirmed in office in 1466, this reforming hand swept into action against the inefficiency and disorder it had discovered in the chancery as in the Guelf Party. Finding that incoming letters were "put into some bundle, which resulted in the said letters getting lost within a short time," it instituted a system of recording these letters, the *Copiari di lettere responsive*, in which Braccesi and other assistants copied letters received since the beginning of 1453 (continuing until 1483 when the system of registration was again reformed). Because letters from ambassadors were no longer being copied into special volumes (as Bruni had decreed), Scala was authorized "to probe past events" and ensure that commissions to ambassadors and their correspondence were copied "in good order in one book or more" by chancery notaries. Above all, "in view of the fact that it is the responsibility of the government of every well-ordered republic not only to preserve the honors and dignities of the Republic but also to increase them as far as it is decently and easily possible, from time to time," it was decreed that henceforth external letters must be written on "beautiful clean leaves of kid or sheep skin" instead of paper as hitherto, and then sealed by the friars of the Camera, in order to keep up with "the many princes and lords and dominions" who wrote external letters on vellum and sealed them.[19]

---

legationum Barth^e1. Scale" in ASF *Cons. Prat.* 60, fol. 105v; the final volume, 21, changes its format and is a large folio volume in vellum. On the titles of *Missive*, see pp. 139-140 above. ASF *Risp. verb. orat.* 2 is titled on the cover "LEGATIONUM EXTERNARUM BARTOLOMEI S[CALAE]."

[19] ASF *Balìa* 30, fols. 31v-32r (3 October 1466), ed. Marzi, append. 2, no. 37, pp. 594-595. ASF *Copiari di lettere responsive* vol. 1 is backdated to 6 January 1453, vol. 2 begins on 5 October 1468 and ends on 18 April 1483. For a reference to a copybook of incoming letters in 1474, see ch. 4, n. 36 above. Scala's first vellum (instead of paper) letter in Milan is dated 23 January 1467, ASMi SPE Fir. 273 (cf. *Protocollo* p. 229, dated 22 January).

This is the first clear statement we have of the motive underlying Scala's reform program: the desire to emulate other states who wrote their external letters on "parchment with their seal." For Florence, the preface to the reform states, "through the grace of God, finds herself in such rank and condition that it would be appropriate for her too to have her letters written and dispatched in the same way." Yet when the duke of Milan, Galeazzo Maria Sforza, tried to introduce exactly the same reform two years later, he was opposed by his Secret Council on the grounds that only the pope and the emperor enjoyed this right, and that the kings of France and of Sicily had been granted it by the pope and the doges of Venice by Frederick Barbarossa.[20]

In the next four years Scala extended his campaign to the formula of state letters. Here he was following in the steps of his humanist predecessors in the chancery, who had already begun to simplify the elaborate diplomatic formulas of address—which Scala said "wrapped and bound one in so many coils" that it was scarcely possible to read one's own name.[21]

---

[20] C. Santoro in *Storia di Milano*, 7: 526.

[21] Scala to A. Braccesi, 13 November 1470, ed. Kristeller, "An Unknown Correspondence," p. 354: "Deus bone, quanta ignoratio, quanta inanitas . . . Nos tot tantisque, ut ita dicam, involucris plicamus et confundimus, ut saepe oppleta foris carta exquisitissimis ampullis vix proprium nomen explicare queas. Extant etiam precepta et libelli circumferuntur de inscriptionibus epistolarum, ut insaniorem efficiant tantam insaniam." As Professor Carlo Dionisotti pointed out to me, and illustrated by generously lending me his notes, Scala refers to works like the *Principia subscriptiones et suprascriptiones litterarum missivarum* (subsequently printed in Rome 1476?), the *Soprascripti et introscripti di lettere a varie persone secundo la degnità loro*, Florence, 1488, or the *Formulario* attributed to Cristoforo Landino and Bartolomeo Miniatore, printed many times between 1485 and 1495. Of these it is in fact the (Rome?) *Principia* that offers the simplest form of address for the pope, which Poggio Bracciolini further simplified after his appointment as chancellor of Florence (see ASF *Missive* 39, fols. 141r, 184r, September, October 1453, etc.; cf. Marzi, *Cancelleria*, p. 413, who, however, quotes as the earliest example of this simplified formula, "Sanctissime ac Beatissime Pater," a letter of 19 May 1458, in the time of Accolti). On the extent of this reform, compare an early fifteenth-century chancery formulary, ASF *Carte di corredo* vol. 58, with the simplified post-1484 formulary of P. A. Nicolucci of Castiglione, *ibid.*, vol. 60, or the collection of

In accordance with classical practice, he wanted to address the recipient in the singular instead of the plural and he wanted to open state letters with the name of the sender followed by that of the recipient—as he and his fellow humanists did when writing to each other, or as the pope did in his bulls.[22] Although his reforms were criticized by the Florentine humanist Leonardo Dati, who accused Scala of treating the pope like a country priest in addressing him in the singular instead of the plural,[23] both his reforms and the style of his letters were warmly applauded by "the leading lights of Roman eloquence," Cardinal Jacopo Ammannati and Giovanni Antonio Campano, who urged him to continue his good work and re-

---

inscriptions *temp.* Scala ("Florentinorum Cancellario"), in Siena, Bibl. Comunale, MS G. VIII, 46, fols. 106r-114r, perhaps collected by or relating to the notary Piero Migliorelli, whose name appears on the last flyleaf (fol. 120r; the volume also contains Scala's *Apologues* and dialogue *On Laws and Legal Judgments*).

[22] See his draft-letter to N. Forteguerri, Paris, Bibl. Nationale, MS *nouv. acq.* 1520, fol. 99v: "cum numero singulari uterer scribens ad unum, ut Latini semper Grecique scriptores omnes fecerunt," and to Braccesi, 13 November 1470, ed. Kristeller, "An Unknown Correspondence," p. 354: "Nihil prius venit in desiderium quam ut qui scribit ad nos intelligamus. Ea de re maiores principio tam Greci quam Latini scriptores nomen suum in epistolis primum posuerunt, post nomen ad quem scriberent." The earliest example of Scala prefacing a private letter with his own name is to Lorenzo de' Medici in 1463 (ASF *Strozz.* ser. 1, 136, fol. 55: "B.S. Laurentio Petri Filio Medici salutem dicit"; cf. letters to N. Tranchedini and A. Dati referred to above, 1464-1466). On the classical practice of signing letters, begun in the Florentine chancery by Poggio and continued by Accolti and Scala (e.g. British Library, Add. MS 21520, fols. 2, 4, 5, and ASMi SPE Fir. 272, Scala's earliest signed letter in Milan, dated 17 December 1465), see Scala in Poliziano's *Opera*, p. 391: "antiquae huius consuetudinis signandarum literarum."

[23] See Scala's letter to Braccesi referred to above: "Et ille obiurgator [ie. Dati, referred to by Braccesi in an earlier letter] cum nos latine scriberemus ad unum numero singulari scribi ad summum pontificem tanquam ad presbiterum quendam rusticanum litteris ab Roma conquestus est," and to Forteguerri, above: "Et cum numero singulari uterer scribens ad unum . . . ausi et sunt quidam ex his, qui doctos se scilicet viros haberi volunt, morem illum scribendi rusticanum dicere." On Dati, Kristeller, "An Unknown Correspondence," p. 338, n. 2; F. Flamini, "L. Dati, poeta latino del sec. XV," *GSLI* 16 (1890): 1-107; *Epistolae XXXIII*, ed. L. Mehus, Florence, 1743.

store Latin letters to their former beauty, "which had so long lain flowerless, enfeebled and prostrate."[24]

In the event Scala brought papal wrath upon his head, not by relegating the pope's name to second place in Florentine state letters but by addressing him without the usual epithets in a mandate read out before a full papal consistory at the signing of a universal treaty of peace and league on 22 December 1470. The pope pronounced that Scala was crazy, exclaiming "Hear this!" when his name was mentioned again, and one cardinal thought the mandate invalid. But Ammannati and Campano still supported him, Scala was reassured by his former assistant Alessandro Braccesi, then in Rome, "even if there are some Florentines here who have not wasted this opportunity of maligning you, whose names I shall reveal to you when I see you."[25] One of these critics was Gentile Becchi, Lorenzo de' Medici's former tutor, according to whom Scala's mandate was invalid, lacked the correct formula and was more than a month and a half out of date:

Your ambassadors and the Milanese did not know where to hide their faces for embarrassment amidst so much laughter.

[24] See A. Braccesi's letters to Scala of 10 and 27 November 1470, ed. Kristeller, "An Unknown Correspondence," pp. 352-353, 354-355. Scala refers to them as the "duo eloquentie Romane lumina" and the "duo maximi duces latine lingue" in letters to Braccesi of 13 November and [end November-beginning December] 1470, *ibid.*, pp. 353 and 355. On Ammannati, see ch. 1, n. 26 above; on Campano, Kristeller, *ibid.*, p. 327; G. Lesca, *Giovannantonio Campano detto l'Episcopus Aprutinus*, Pontedera, 1892; F. R. Hausmann, *Giovanni Antonio Campano (1429-1477)*, Freiburg, 1968.

[25] See Braccesi's letters to Scala of 22 December 1470 (ed. Kristeller, "An Unknown Correspondence," p. 356): "reliquis collaudatis Florentinum dumtaxat plurimum strepitu explosum fuit, quod novo stilo et antea insueto conditum esset ut illi aiebant" and 5 January 1471 (*ibid.*, pp. 357-358): "Quod pontifex ipse ita indigne tulit ut bis in hec verba prorupit: 'Audin quantum scriba iste deliret? quid tibi videtur?' Et cum se rursus nominari audisset, iterum: 'hoc accipe' inquit. . . . Etiam si nonnulli ex nostris sunt qui hanc detrahendi tibi occasionem nacti non desinant te maledictis incessere, eos ego tibi coram nominatim aperiam"; cf. *ibid.*, pp. 339-340. On the general league and peace of 22 December 1470, Dumont, *Corps diplomatique*, 3 (1): 429-430, doc. 296; Guicciardini, *Storie fiorentine*, pp. 22-24; *Storia di Milano*, 7: 264-265, and below.

I had to promise the Cardinal of Rouen I would write to ask you [Lorenzo de' Medici] to have more consideration for public honor and to give him a notary with a formulary for his tutor, since it's not the moment for the "However." The Pope said he is a person who thinks only of doing well for himself. . . . Just think of it, to arrive at such a gathering and to produce only shame for his ambassadors and mortification for himself. They refuse to remove him on the grounds that he came from the Medici household.[26]

Because the Florentine mandate was out of date, its ambassadors had to agree to the treaty on their own personal responsibility and in fact never subscribed the ratification in Rome.[27]

Out of date the mandate certainly was, but not inept, for

[26] G. Becchi to Lorenzo de' Medici, 24 December 1470, ASF *MAP* 61, 19: "uno mandato sine forma, non vallido et che fusse spirato il tempo di tale commessione più uno mese et mezzo"; "che non sapevano *ridente contione* dove si nascondere e nostri et Ducali il viso per la vergogna. Bisognòmmi promettergli di scrivervi havessi più cura all'honore publico et gli dessi uno notaio con uno formulario per balio quando non è il tempo del *Quamquam*. Il Papa disse chostui ha pieno il capo di quello che fa buono tempo. . . . Giugnere in tanto conspecto, et non produrre che loro vergogna et sua moratagine pensate voi, scusansi non si remuove perchè uscì di Casa Medici."

[27] See the letters of the Signoria to Pierfrancesco de' Medici and Iacopo Guicciardini of 27 [December] 1470 ("Ècci dispiaciuto che vi conducessi ad leggere il mandato . . . del quale fussi passato il tempo"), 2 January 1471 ("Oggi habbiamo il Consiglio del Cento, per seguitare nel Popolo e nel Commune domani e l'altro"), 7 January 1471 ("harete havuta la ratificatione senza altro mandato perchè . . . quello per due mesi non può dire per tre, nè il nuovo che fussi fatto dopo xxij dì della stipulatione potrebbe servire") and 18 January 1471 ("et questo basti alla parte del mandato senza haverti altre volte a tornare suso"), ASF *Leg. Comm.* 17, fols. 79r-81r. Although their embassy was prorogued several times (*ibid.,* fol. 57r: on 24 October and 23 November 1470 for one month, on 18 December for 15 days and on 11 January 1471 for 20 days), it was agreed that their mandate had expired (see *Libri commemorali,* 5: 198: "essendo poi spirati i poteri dei rappresentanti fiorentini, questi assumono personalmente la responsabilità del loro operato," cf. above). The text of the ratification is in ASF *SS. Delib. sp. aut.* 34, fols. 75v-77v, "reddita in publicam formam et data dominis dicta die 4ta per ipsos dominos missa fuit Romam ad oratores florentinos die quinta dicti mensis Januarii" (fol. 75v); cf. *Libri commemorali,* 5: 202-203, allegato C, Florentine ratification dated 4 January 1471.

there were good political as well as administrative reasons both
for its formula and for the fact that it was out of date. According to Sacramori, there was a secret clause in the Florentine mandate preventing the ambassadors from reaching any
agreement without further consultation—which would explain
why Scala had had to work so hard for the reward Milan
gave him that "his letters did not please the Neapolitans at
all."[28] Less vulnerable to Turkish assault than Venice or Naples, Milan and the Milanese party in Florence were in no
hurry to agree to the universal peace and league. Francesco
Guicciardini explains in his family memoirs that although his
grandfather, Jacopo Guicciardini, had signed the treaty in the
name of the Signoria, "it was the intention of Lorenzo [de'
Medici] and other members of the regime not to subscribe
these documents in order to please the Duke [of Milan]; but
nevertheless they did not discuss it in *pratiche* in order to avoid
being blamed by the people, who were delighted by the conclusion of the league; instead they saw to it that the Signoria
never replied to Jacopo about subscribing [the ratification].
They—and particularly Messer Luigi [Guicciardini, Jacopo's
brother]—advised him privately to leave it suspended."[29] Jacopo disagreed, but was finally persuaded by their letters and
left Rome without ratifying, being made to wait several
months before being granted payment. "And so, in effect,
things were left in suspense."[30] By preparing the secret clauses

[28] S. Sacramori to G. M. Sforza, letters of 11 October 1470 (ASMi SPE
Fir. 280: "ma secretamente gli danno comissione che non debbano venire ad
alchune conclusione, nè streteza, nè promissa, per minima che la sia, nisi
audire et refferre como alias scripsi") and (on Scala's hard labor) 11 January 1471, quoted in ch. 3, n. 32 above. Cf. also Scala's reference in December
1470 (in a letter to A. Braccesi, Kristeller, "An Unknown Correspondence,"
p. 324n) to the Florentine ambassador acting "suo marte, idest sine litteris
publicis." On the fall of Negroponte and the diplomacy of these months,
Pastor, *Storia dei papi*, 2: 410-415; Soranzo, "Lorenzo il Magnifico," pp.
66-69.

[29] "Memorie di famiglia," *Scritti autobiografici e rari*, ed. R. Palmarocchi,
Bari, 1936, p. 34.

[30] Guicciardini, *Storie fiorentine*, p. 24 (where he gives a more succinct
account of the same events): "e così in effetto le cose rimasono pendente."
In fact the only document cited in Dumont (*Corps diplomatique*, 3 (1):

in the mandate and by expediting or delaying instructions to
the ambassadors, Scala was capable of playing a vital role in
promoting this policy, and it seems clear that on this occasion
he used his influence to support the pro-Milanese policy of
the Medicean party.

Scala's mandate has important legal as well as political implications. He had already claimed privileges for Florence that
were said to have been enjoyed by other powers only by imperial or papal grant, and now he extended this claim to mandates. Unlike letters, mandates or procurations were legal instruments, which to be valid had to be drawn up by a notary
and subscribed with the medieval formula (derived from private notarial practice) that he "had been asked" (*rogatus*) to
prepare it as written. Basing himself on classical precedent,
Scala claimed that as chancellor he enjoyed the prerogative of
asking for the people's assent to his document by virtue of his
office as their scribe, not because he was qualified as a notary
(and in fact, although the chancellor was intended by statute
to be qualified as a notary, Scala himself, like several of his
predecessors, was instead a lawyer): "It is a ridiculous custom
that the notaries who subscribe the mandate are described as
rogati ('having been asked'). The notaries are not asked, but
they themselves ask for (*ipsi rogant*) what they later commit
to writing. For the scribe asks (*interrogat*): 'Is it your will
and pleasure that this be done?' whether it concerns the people [i.e. the Councils], the magistracy [the Signoria], the College [the 12 Buonuomini and 16 Gonfalonieri] or private individuals." There was nothing novel in this, Scala claimed,
"since the Romans whose language we use did the same, hence
the name rogation"—as anyone who read his Livy diligently
would know. "I am the scribe of the Florentine people. I
asked (*rogavi ego*) the magistracy and the college to give that
mandate for peace, the magistracy and the college did not ask
me (*non me rogavit*); and when they replied that they ap-

429-430, doc. 196) is the confirmation of the treaty and general league by
the cardinal of San Marco, although a copy of the treaty and related documents does survive in Florence, see n. 32 below.

proved, I wrote out that rogation (*rogationem*) according to my office and subscribed that I had asked for it (*rogasse*)."[31]

Scala's account of his procedure is borne out by the mandate itself as it survives in a very recently discovered copy of diplomatic documents relating to the treaty of 22 December.[32] Lacking all inscriptions and titles honoring the pope, it opens by simply referring to the pope's desire for a congress in Rome to discuss peace—an object, it says, which could not but be welcome to all free peoples "and particularly those where trade and industry is flourishing." At the invitation of Paul II, "Pontifex Maximus" (the second reference to himself to provoke the pope when the mandate was read out in the public consistory), the Signoria and Colleges of Florence had therefore sent

[31] Scala's draft letter to Cardinal Niccolò Forteguerri, Paris, Bibl. Nationale, MS *nouv. acq.* 1520, fol. 99v: "Et illa consuetudo qua notarii rogati subscribunt vana est. Non enim rogantur notarii, sed ipsi rogant quod postea mandant litterarum monimentis. Interrogat enim scriba: velint iubeantne illud quod agitur, sive cum populo, sive cum magistratu, sive cum collegio, sive cum privatis negotium sit. Idque minime novum est. Romani, quorum lingua utimur, ita factitarunt et rogationum inde nomen est. Quod si quis Livii diligenter legat libros, non indigebit ut ita esse credat assertione nostra. Scriba ego sum Florentini populi. Rogavi ego magistratum et collegium: mandatumne darent illud ad pacem? Non me magistratus et collegium rogavit. Et cum respondissent se dare, et suffragiis quod respondissent comprobassent, scripsi ego rogationem illam ex meo officio et rogasse subscripsi." Cf. also Scala's letter to Braccesi of 27 [December 1470], ed. Kristeller, "An Unknown Correspondence," p. 356: "Non eo inficias mandati formam et stilum aliquid novi inventi habere, quia conatus sum redigere omnia quae in mandato sunt ad meram latinitatem." On *rogare*, see Tommaseo and Bellini, *Dizionario*; A. Pratesi, "Rogus = Rogatus," *Archivum Latinitatis Medii Aevi* 22 (1952): 33-61 (the reference to which I owe to Professor Armando Petrucci, to whose advice on this subject I am indebted).

[32] BNF MS Palat. 1133, containing the text of the treaty and the mandates of the signatories, probably transcribed by ser Piero Cennini. I owe my knowledge of this mandate to the kindness of Professor Kristeller, who discovered it shortly before this book went to press. The Florentine mandate on fols. 119v-120v is the first of the two mandates given to the Florentine ambassadors on 10 October 1470, "uno per la pace et lega d'Italia, l'altro per le provisioni per la difensione delle cose christiane" (ambassadors' commission, Florence, Guicciardini Archive, *Leg. Comm.* 4, no. 308). I shall publish the text with Scala's letters and other writings.

two ambassadors to Rome with full powers to discuss the peace and league of Italian states in agreement with their allies.

Although the pope was upset by the informality of the mandate and doubtless by its self-interested and secular attitude to his plans for a religious crusade against the infidel, its changes in legal formula were more iconoclastic than its style. The grant of powers normally introduced by the formula "Dantes et concedentes" is in Scala's mandate replaced by a sentence referring to the Signoria and Colleges' "will," beginning "Voluerunt," and although their promise of ratification opens traditionally "Promittentes," their commission to the notary to prepare the mandate, in the traditional formula beginning "Rogantes," is replaced by a sentence beginning "Iusserunt": not "asking" but "ordering." For the reasons he explained to Cardinal Niccolò Forteguerri, Scala saw the chancellor's function as that of executing the orders of the Signoria and Colleges and asking them if he was acting in accordance with their will: it was their function to "order" the mandate, not to "ask" for it. And so he repeats here the formula he first introduced in a mandate of 16 June 1470: "I Bartolomeo Scala, chancellor, have asked." On receiving an affirmative answer that the mandate he had prepared was in accordance with their will, he and the second chancellor were then asked (in the traditional manner) to have it transcribed; and since they were both occupied with more important matters, we are told, they delegated this task to the notary ser Piero Cennini.

Scala continued to use his original formula for nearly a decade, in slightly differing form. A typical subscription is: "I, Bartolomeo Scala, Florentine scribe, proposed [or, literally, 'asked for': *rogavi*] these things, and I committed my orders as proposed to these writings."[33] Nor did he confine its use to

---

[33] ASF *Leg. Comm.* 17, fol. 171v ("Ego Barth. Scala Scriba florentinus haec rogavi et uti rogavi iussa mandavi his scriptis die xiii decembris 1473"). The earliest appearance of this formula is in the mandate of 16 June 1470, ed. Dumont, *Corps diplomatique*, 3 (1): 412; cf. ASF *Leg. Comm.* 17, fol. 101v (9 October 1471, "B.S. cancellarius rogavi"), 18, fol. 2v (26 March 1474, "Populus ita iussit et Priores Libertatis et Vexillifer Iustitie ita manda-

mandates. It recurs in appropriate form whenever he executes the orders of the Signoria he serves, although the word *rogare* is correctly reserved for documents like mandates, which had to receive conciliar approval.[34] He authenticates the reply he delivered to visiting ambassadors on the instructions of the Signoria in 1479 with the formula: "I, Bartolomeo Scala, wrote and recited all that is written above at the command of my magnificent and exalted Lords";[35] similarly the ratification of a treaty by letters-patent, for which authority had been delegated to the Signoria by the Councils.[36] On each occasion his signature, with the seal of the Commune and/or the Signoria, and the subscription that as chancellor he is acting as the servant of the Florentine people or their government, is sufficient to authenticate the document without notarial attestations.

There was more to Scala's reform than classical pedantry, or the attempt to gloss over the fact that he was a lawyer rather than a notary by profession.[37] What he was claiming was that his office of 'scribe of the Florentine people' gave him authority to propose documents for their approval, on the analogy

---

verunt. Ego B.S. Scriba florentinus Magistratus iussu rogavi et mandavi litteris die xxvi Martii 1474"); and ch. 4, n. 83 above (12 December 1479).

[34] Mandates had normally to be approved by the Cento, see ch. 6, n. 27 above.

[35] Ed. in Comines, *Mémoires* (*cit.* p. 87, n. 71 above), 4: pp. 187-188, "Ego B.S. Cancellarius Florentinus, suprascripta omnia scripsi et recitavi, iussus a magnificis et excelsis Dominis meis . . . in quorum fidem et testimonium haec scripsi manu mea et sigillum parvum Lilii Populi Florentini apposui hoc die decima quinta Ianuarii anni millesimi quadringentesimi septuagesimi octavi."

[36] See n. 39 below.

[37] Although Scala entered the Guild of Lawyers and Notaries as a lawyer, the Signoria asserted on 17 June 1470 (ed. Dumont, *Corps diplomatique*, 3 (1):412), that Scala, ser Antonio Muzia ("qui de praedicto contractu mandati rogati fuerunt") and ser Niccolò Michelozzi ("qui ipsum scripsit et publicavit") "fuerunt et sunt publici et autentici Notarii descripti in Matricula artis Iudicum et Notariorum nostrae Civitatis." However, there is no other evidence that he was qualified as a notary: in December 1470 Becchi complained that Scala needed "uno notaio con uno formulario per balio" (n. 26 above) and in 1488 he was instructed to have a qualified notary as his assistant (Marzi, *Cancelleria*, p. 611, see below), suggesting his qualification may have been a purely formal one.

of the Roman *rogator* (as it were Scala), who at the instigation of the presiding magistrate (the Signoria) presented a
rogatio (bill/mandate) to the Roman people for approval
(the Councils, and in the case of mandates the Cento alone, or
exceptionally the Dieci with supreme authority or *balìa* in
times of war), using the exact formula quoted by Scala: "is it
your will and pleasure that this be done?"[38] Underlying the
analogy was the implication that the Florentine people, like
the Romans, had the sovereign right to pass legislation and
that they did not have "to ask" a notary to legalize their decrees.

In Florence, however, it was not the task of the chancellor
to introduce legislation as it was the *rogator's*: this was the
province of the notary of the Riformagioni. But Scala was
evidently ambitious to extend the chancellor's authority into the field of all foreign diplomatic documents. On one occasion at least he prepared the ratification of a treaty by letters-patent—a simple and quick document compared with the
traditional cumbersome instrument subscribed with the thirty-
seven names of the Signoria and Colleges—which he subscribed: "I, Bartolomeo Scala, Florentine Chancellor, thus
commanded, have committed these things to letters and have
subscribed them with my own hand."[39] Later the same year,
when Lorenzo de' Medici was acting as procurator of the king
of France, an attempt was made to prepare a treaty by letters-
patent, but on this occasion it was thwarted by the conservative ambassador of the duke of Milan.[40] Scala would probably

[38] Receiving either the answer *uti rogas*, "as you propose," or *antiquo*,
"the old state," see H. F. Jolowicz and B. Nicholas, *Historical Introduction
to the Study of Roman Law*, Cambridge, 1972 (3rd edition), p. 27; and on
the office of *rogator*, T. Mommsen, *Römisches Staatsrecht* (3rd edition),
Leipzig, 1887, 3 (1): 403-405 (the reference to which I owe to Professor
Otto Skutsch).

[39] Venice, Bibl. Marciana, MS lat. X. 174 (3621), no. 34b (20 January
1478): "Ego Bartholomaeus Scala Cancell[arius] Florentinus ita iussus, haec
mandavi litteris et propria manu subscripsi."

[40] See L. Cerioni, "La politica italiana di Luigi XI e la missione di Filippo
di Commines (giugno-settembre 1478)," *ASLomb.* 77 (1950): 131 (Milanese
ambassadors to the dukes of Milan, 10 August 1478: "Sua Magnificentia

have liked to extend its use to all forms of diplomatic document, as in royal chanceries outside Italy and increasingly in
Italy itself.[41] Even though he failed to achieve this, he did
manage to secure for the chancery responsibility for the preparation of all diplomatic documents, from 1475 onward preparing for it its own archive of material relating to leagues,
peace treaties and ratifications, which previously had been the
sole concern of the notary of the Riformagioni.[42]

Scala's campaign for reform was disrupted by the Pazzi war
from 1478 to 1480. This was no time for experimenting with
new diplomatic formulae and, although Scala prepared Lorenzo de' Medici's mandate to Naples with his usual subscription,
this was apparently the last time he used it. The mandate was
written out in notarial form by Scala's colleague in the Dieci,
Alessandro Braccesi, who subscribed both it and the mandate
for the Florentine signatories of the peace treaty with the
formula criticized by Scala.[43] Similarly, although Scala's *Excusatio Florentinorum* takes the form of letters-patent, sealed and
signed by himself, the confession of Montesecco it includes is
subscribed by seven witnesses, with attestations by six notaries
that it had been correctly copied and one attestation that they

---

[Commynes] ne mostrò una forma molto breve facta in lingua loro
franciosa per una littera patente. . . . Noi li mostramo desiderare se facesse
ne la forma de le altre et in latino," 135 (the same, 15 August 1478, that
Commynes, on being shown their draft, "mostrò molto piacerli el tenore,
ma ne fece due exceptione, una de dire volerla fare per littera patente et
non per contracto perchè era così più presto suo costume, et per rasone
che noi allegassemo, non respose altramente se non: li pensarò"). The ratification of the treaty is ed. Dumont, *Corps diplomatique*, 3 (2): 43-44.

[41] On French and English diplomatic, see n. 3 above; on papal and imperial, H. Bresslau, *Handbuch*. The differences within Italy in the fifteenth
century are illustrated by the mandates of the signatories to the peace treaty
of 13 March 1480 (ASMi SPE Nap. 297), the papal mandate being in the
form of an apostolic brief, the Milanese signed and sealed letters patent and
the Florentine and Sienese notarial instruments. Cf. n. 45 below.

[42] See below.

[43] See ch. 4, n. 83 above. Braccesi's notarial draft of the same mandate is
in ASF *Notarile* B 2320 (1477-1479), fols. 126v-127r; his mandate of 2 March
1480 for A. Biliotti and N. Michelozzi is in ASMi SPE Nap. 297.

were *bona fide* notaries: there could afford to be no danger of its legality being called into question.[44]

The constitutional reforms that followed the conclusion of peace threatened Scala's former authority, as we have seen. In the 1470s he had been an energetic reformer, increasing his influence at the expense of Guidi's. Now not only was he no longer the only 'fixture' in the government but his position *vis-à-vis* Guidi in the new Council of Seventy was not at all clear. Their spheres of responsibility had been strictly defined in the decree establishing the Council, but the question of which official was to take precedence in this all-important Council depended on whether it was seen more as a secret consultative body like the *pratiche* it superseded, where Scala had reigned supreme, or as a legislative council needing the constant attendance of the notary of the Riformagioni to draw up its decrees. Moreover, Scala also lost his responsibility for preparing ambassadors' mandates, which were now to be prepared by the Otto di Pratica on the instruction of the Seventy. Before the new system had been fully worked out, mandates were apparently written by the notary of the Tratte using the old notarial subscription of *rogatus*, with Scala acting simply as a witness,[45] and when the Otto di Pratica acquired its own secretariat in July 1480 Scala was not its chancellor.[46] This perhaps marks the nadir of Scala's fortunes. Only four months

[44] See ch. 4, n. 65 above. The document begins: "Singulis atque universis in quos haec scripta inciderint Priores Libertatis et Vexillifer Iustitie et Populus Florentinus salutem" and concludes with Scala's autograph signature flanking the great seal of the Commune, with the small seal of the Signoria below.

[45] E.g. ASF *SS. Dieci, Otto*, 77, fol. 105, written by Francesco di Papi Machietti, *rogatus* by Antonio di Mariano Muzi as scribe of the Tratte, *actum* in the Palazzo della Signoria on 27 April 1480, "presentibus . . . domino Barth° Iohannis Scala, primo cancellario," ser Giovanni Guidi, etc., the notaries being authenticated by the Signoria in a document signed by Scala on 29 April 1480. It takes the form of letters-patent, however.

[46] ASF *Otto Delib.* 1, fol. 3r (3 July 1480) electing ser Alessandro Braccesi "al servigio della loro cancelleria" for the first 6 month period. On 6 October 1480, however, Scala's assistant, ser Antonio della Valle, was paid for six months' service for their office (fol. 12r).

later, however, he recovered his responsibility for communicating with ambassadors (later being paid 50 golden florins for his "long labors" on their behalf), and when the Dieci di Balìa was reconstituted in September 1482 we find Scala back in his old position as its first chancellor.[47] At the end of 1483 he reasserted his authority over the whole chancery in one of the most comprehensive reforms it had ever undergone, in which Scala emerged at the helm, steadfastly pursuing the same objectives as at the beginning of his chancellorship.

From the point of view of modernizing the chancery, the most significant feature of the reform was the abolition of all the old titles and ranks, which were to be replaced by an entirely new grade of "secretaries," placed between the traditional offices of chancellor and assistant. Once again Scala was emulating the example of other states, as the preface to the law makes clear:

It is well known that all nations, all peoples, have kept in attendance on their princes and magistracies men of intelligence and outstanding experience, knowledge and trust . . . hence their names Scribes or Notaries, or even, as some call them, Secretaries (for because of their prudence and outstanding trustworthiness they were involved in the most important matters relating to the government of people, and nothing was hidden from them). Princes have made wide use of them, and even republics (particularly free repub-

---

[47] *Ibid.*, fols. 19r (19 November 1480: "deliberaverunt et concesserunt quod Dominus Bartholomeus Scala possit, prout sibi visum fuerit, expedire et esse e republica, conferre et communicare oratoribus hic existentibus omnes litteras scribendas per officium Octo predictorum, et quecunque alia, etc.," cf. Marzi, *Cancelleria*, p. 248, n. 7), 64v (18 April 1482: "quod Domino Barth. Scale solvantur floreni auri larghi quinquaginta pro remuneratione et aliqua mercede sui diutini laboris quem impendit serviendo eorum officio"); ASF *Dieci Delib.* 25, fol. 13r (5 September 1482: "Prestantissimus vir Dominus B.S. . . . sit primus Cancellarius eorum officii ad commissiones et res spectantes ad Oratores et Commissarios. Itemque deputatur ad litteras Oratoribus et Commissariis predictis et quibuscumque extra Florentinum agrum destinandas aliaque id genus faciendum").

lics), in ancient and present times: they esteemed them highly, and the better their choice, the more profit and honor they have derived from them.[48]

Lest the title "secretary" should conjure up the image of a secret confidant beloved of tyrants, the preamble is at pains to explain that the name derives from the qualities of prudence and trustworthiness required of such an official, and that although they are widely used by princes, "even republics" and "particularly free republics" have used them: meaning, no doubt, sovereign powers "recognizing no superior," like the free republic of Venice, whose chancery, like those of Naples and Milan as well as royal chanceries outside Italy, was already using this title.[49] But there can be no doubt that its real intention was to provide a name for an entirely new class of

[48] ASF *Provv.* 174, fol. 112r, ed. Marzi, *Cancelleria*, p. 599 (28 November 1483). Details of the reform follow on fols. 112v-116r, Marzi, *Cancelleria*, pp. 599-602.

[49] In the papal chancery there had been secretaries since the fourteenth century (Bresslau, *Handbuch*, 1: 311-319) and there were secretaries in the Venetian chancery by the 1440s and probably earlier (*Libri commemoriali*; "Traité du gouvernement de Venise," ed. P. M. Perret, *Histoire des relations de la France avec Venise*, Paris, 1896, 2: 277-280, describing the chancery toward the end of the fifteenth century; on the use of resident secretaries for embassies by the 1460s, G. Mattingly, *Renaissance Diplomacy*, London, 1955, p. 104; "Traité," pp. 292-293). On the chancery in Milan, where Cicco Simonetta acted as Francesco Sforza's secretary from 1444, see ch. 1, n. 53 above, especially Santoro, *Uffizi*, pp. xxi, xxiii, and 49, with lists of "secretarii ad Consilium secretum" and "in cancellaria secreta" from 1450 on pp. 31-32 and 49-52. On the chancery in Naples, where at this time two secretaries (Antonello Petrucci, a friend of Scala's, and Giovanni Pontano) were gradually taking over the work of the chancellor and protonotary, see J. Mazzoleni, preface to the *Regesto della Cancelleria Aragonese di Napoli*, Naples, 1951, pp. ix-xxii, esp. ix-x; and now A. Ryder, *The Kingdom of Naples under Alfonso the Magnanimous*, Oxford, 1976, ch. 7, pp. 218-258. Scala had himself been appointed a royal and ducal secretary by Ferrante in 1467 and by Galeazzo Maria Sforza in 1469, and he was titled "primus Secretarius ac Cancellarius Dominorum Priorum" in the 1471 decree awarding him citizenship (ed. Bartolini, B. Scala, *Vita Vitaliani Borrhomaei*, p. 35), but in the 1483 reform he retained only the title "chancellor" and not "secretary" for himself, perhaps following the example of Venice and Naples where the headship and overall direction of the chancery remained the responsibility of the chancellor or (in Venice) the "Cancelliere grande."

functionary, the lay civil servant, entitled to act in the name of the state he served by virtue of his office and not by virtue of his professional legal qualifications.

For the first time, business requiring notarial qualifications is separated from purely secretarial work. The Signoria and people of Florence are to be served by two officials, "a prudent and well-lettered man" as first chancellor, and "a scribe, Notary or Official of the Riformagioni," responsible with assistants for proposing ("rogating") all legislation and documents needed by the Signoria and other magistracies. Only "some" of the six secretaries and their four assistants (who had also to be "beautiful writers") need be notaries. Otherwise the only requisite for the job is intelligence and experience enough to perform the executive business required of them. Moreover, they are allowed to leave the city on public business by simple injunction of the magistracies, without conciliar assent. The creation of this new rank of lay civil servants and their use as mandatories outside the state are two of the most distinctive features of the 1483 reform, thanks to which Machiavelli was able to enjoy his well-known chancery career.

The first chancellor alone retained his medieval title. The second chancellor became a secretary with responsibility for the second chancery, similarly the notary (or, as he is now called, the secretary) of the Tratte. The remaining four secretaries worked for the Signoria (and the first chancellor), and for the new and increasingly important Otto di Pratica, which in times of war became the Dieci di Balìa. Scala thus regained control over all the various offices associated with the chancery, which had not been so effectively united since the days of Salutati and Paolo Fortini. He himself was given no new powers, nor he did regain his responsibility for "proposing" mandates, which with other foreign affairs documents were now to be prepared by the secretary of the Tratte. But he had won the principle for which he had fought in the 1470s: autonomy in the field of diplomacy and foreign affairs for the chancery, taking from the notary of the Riformagioni responsibility for drawing up treaties, ratifications and leagues. In return for suffering "in the public good" a cut in salary of 168 florins, Scala was reappointed in office for the unprecedented term of twenty-five years.[50]

This reform undoubtedly reestablished Scala's influence in the chancery. It also had the purpose of rationalizing its structure. The creation of new magistracies with their own secretariats had detracted not only from Scala's authority but also from their efficiency, in that they were in practice staffed by the same group of men who had to be elected and confirmed in office every six months with the members of the magistracies they served. With extreme economy the 1483 reform pooled the resources of the chancery to serve all these magistracies as needed. At the same time it rationalized the system of registration. "In order that all the correspondence relating to the Florentine commune may be found more easily," volumes of ingoing and outgoing letters were to be registered according to subject and place: three volumes were to contain letters from Florentine ambassadors in Milan, Rome and Naples and from the rulers of these states; a fourth all other letters; another four volumes were to contain letters addressed to ambassadors and rulers in these places; and a separate volume was to contain letters of commendation directed outside the state (Scala's category of "external letters of more private interest"). There was to be a separate volume recording the elections, commissions, departures, extensions and return of ambassadors to provide information for the secretary of the

---

[50] On 31 December 1483 it was decreed (ed. Marzi, *Cancelleria*, p. 605) that ser Simone Grazzini, secretary of the Tratte, "et sui successores, nisi aliter fuerit deliberatum, roget omnia instrumenta que fieri debebunt Florentie ad Rempublicam spectantia et transmitti deberent ad aliquos extra iurisdictionem florentinam, prout sunt sindicatus ad paces, et ligas componendas, ratificationes pacis alicuius et ligarum, nominationes colligatorum ac caeterorum, et caetera huiusmodi": in other words, all legal diplomatic documents concerning foreign relations, previously shared by the first chancellor and the notary of the Riformagioni, from whom Scala had been attempting to wrest them in the 1470s. Thus Pierfilippo Pandolfini's mandate the following year was *rogatus* by Grazzini, "Imperiali Auctoritate Iudex Ordinarius ac Notarius Publicus et Notarius Florentinus" (29 July 1484, ed. Dumont, *Corps diplomatique*, 3 (2): 134). On Scala's reappointment, see ch. 3, n. 16 above.

Tratte. Internal letters were to be copied after they had been approved and before they were written out and dispatched. The secretaries were to see that taxes on all appropriate documents were paid to the Monte and a record of them kept. Also, "because the chancellor and secretaries often have need of the legal instruments and writings containing the laws and negotiations of the Commune kept by the Official of the Riformagioni," one of the assistants, Filippo Redditi, was instructed to copy into a vellum book all the contracts of peace and leagues signed since 1451—evidently an attempt to complete legislation passed in 1475.[51] With this apparatus at hand, the chancery was equipped to carry out the final task assigned to its secretaries by its historically minded chancellor (then embarking on his own *History of the Florentine People*), that of "describing the daily events of the Florentine People and others in which they were in any way involved, forming them into annals."[52]

The hatred of disorder and badly kept records, as well as its ambition to rationalize and secularize procedure in the chancery, reveal Scala's influence on this reform. In some respects it merely acknowledged and institutionalized reforms he had already introduced or tried out. The distinction between public and private letters was of course an old one, which he first revived in 1465; ambassadors' elections and commissions had been separated from their letters since the creation of the Seventy in 1480, whereas the experiment of dividing letters according to place was tried within the office

[51] 31 December 1483, ed. Marzi, *Cancelleria*, pp. 606-607, cf. *ibid.*, p. 598 for the decree of 27 October 1475. The vellum volume of peaces and leagues, titled \in \a \scroll \on \the\ cover \"PACES FEDERA POPULI FLO-RENTINI CUM EXTERIS GENTIBUS," with a dove and inscription below, is in ASF *Capitoli Append.* 17. As instructed, it is copied "per me ser Philippum And. Rhedditi . . . usque ad presentia tempora 1487 & 1494," "init[iatum] ab anno 1454 usque ad annum 1494" (with additions up to 1512).

[52] Marzi, *Cancelleria*, p. 606: "Describat insuper ex eis unus res gestas Populi Florentini in dies ceterasque quibus Populus Florentinus, aliquo modo, interveniet, redigendo eas in Annales."

of the Dieci di Balìa in the year preceding the reform.[53] The new system of registration was put into practice by at least the Otto di Pratica after this reform.[54] New methods were needed to cope with increased business in these years, although as a practical measure Scala's scheme did not survive long because there were too few men to put it into operation. Undoubtedly its most important and long-lasting achievement was to have won for the chancery responsibility for the whole field of diplomacy and to have created the new lay office of secretary.

By 1487 it was clear that the chancery staff of eleven men was insufficient to cope with the daily work of letter writing, let alone with the additional burden imposed on them by the 1483 reform of staffing new magistracies, going on diplomatic missions, copying out letters, treaties and annals. Even before this reform Scala had confessed that it was the custom of the chancery "to be sometimes somewhat slow in replying,"[55] and after it one of the secretaries, Alessandro Braccesi, complained to a Florentine ambassador, "without any arrogance," of having to bear the whole weight of the chancery of the Dieci di Balìa on his "weak shoulders": "I don't have to tell you how much varied business such a magistracy has to deal with."[56]

---

[53] See p. 139 above on the division of letters; ASF *Leg. Comm.* 21 for the post-1480 registration of mandates, etc.; and ASF *Dieci di Balìa, Missive Leg. Comm.* 5, divided into gatherings of letters to ambassadors in Milan, Rome, Naples, etc., beginning in September 1482.

[54] See the inventory of *Signoria, Dieci di Balìa, Otto di Pratica: Legazioni e Commissarie, Missive e Responsive*, ed. M. del Piazzo (*Quaderni della rassegna degli Archivi di Stato*, no. 1), Rome, 1960, describing vols. 12-29 *passim*, at pp. 16-28. Vol. 12 (p. 16) contains letters of the Otto to ambassadors in Milan in 1483.

[55] In a letter to Guidantonio Vespucci [28 May 1483?] Modena MS, fol. 35v: "Et sapete la consuetudine nostra, che è vero che siamo tardetti qualche volta a rispondere."

[56] A. Braccesi to G. Lanfredini (11 February 1485), BNF MS II. V. 12, fol. 316: "Io posso senza alchuna arrogantia affermare che tutto il pesᴊ della cancelleria de' Dieci si sia da molti mesi in qua posato in su le mie debole spalle. Quante siano le occupationi et faccende di uno simile magistrato non bisogna narrarlo a voi."

In November 1486 Bernardo Rucellai alluded to the need for reform in the chancery, having seen for himself as an ambassador that there were too few men there to supply ambassadors with the information they needed.[57] Thus, a year later the chancery was reformed again, because—the preamble states—"the affairs of both the 1st and 2nd offices of the chancery of the Signoria and of the Otto di Pratica are not in the order they should be in, and there are too few ministers to cope with all the business and paperwork involved."[58]

The first task of the reform was to increase the chancery personnel: a minimum of sixteen was insisted on, although at least nineteen men were appointed to offices in the chancery at the beginning of the following year.[59] The second was to reestablish a more rigid division of labor, suggesting that the fluidity of the earlier reform scheme had not succeeded. The secretaries in charge of the second chancery and the Tratte were given two assistants each instead of one. The work of the other four secretaries was then carefully defined. Cristoforo Landino was given the title of "Secretary of the Signoria," serving the Signoria and Otto di Pratica and deputizing for the three principals in their absence. The chancery of the Otto di Pratica was subdivided into two departments

[57] In a letter to N. Michelozzi, written as Florentine ambassador in Naples (23 November 1486), BNF MS Ginori Conti 29, 101b, fol. 47, the reference to which I owe to Dr. William Kent: "Le nuove mi sono sute care per ogni rispetto, maxime che ne ho carestia a uso di amb[asciato]re fiorentino, sanza giovarmi punto in questo l'essere de' Dieci, e così con cotesti cancellieri come coconpagni: il che credo che sia, quanto a' secretari, perchè tanto più io favorisca la riforma della cancelleria, veduto per effecto che non sono bastanti, nè per supplire di avisi alli amb[asciato]ri" (but according to D. Queller, *The Office of Ambassador in the Middle Ages*, Princeton, 1967, p. 136: "Ambassadors were as apt to complain of the lack of instructions from their governments as the latter were to complain of the lack of information from their ambassadors").

[58] ASF *Provv.* 178, fol. 141r (24-28 December 1487), ed. Marzi, *Cancelleria*, p. 608 (and on the reform, pp. 608-616).

[59] Ed. Marzi, *Cancelleria*, p. 610: "non possint esse pauciores sexdecim" and pp. 610-614 (the appointment of officers by the Signoria, Colleges and Otto on 22 January 1488).

[186]

for external and internal affairs, as the first chancery had been from 1437 to 1478, showing the extent to which the Otto was replacing it in the work it did. The department for external affairs was under two secretaries, Francesco Gaddi and Alessandro Braccesi (its first secretary in 1480), and one assistant, Antonio della Valle, who like Braccesi had formerly assisted Scala in the first chancery and had then become Braccesi's assistant in the Otto. The internal department was in charge of only one secretary, ser Francesco di ser Barone (who had also served as an assistant in the Otto), with one assistant, ser Antonio di Bibbiena. The remaining secretary, Bernardo Nuti, was given the function of writing out the annals, for which he was given no money but instead the title of "Secretary of the Palace of the Signoria."[60]

Also in reaction against the fluidity of the previous reform, when it was laid down that only "some" of the secretaries and their assistants need be notaries, was the decision that all the assistants—or ministers as they were called—of the three principal offices, the first and second chanceries and the Tratte, had to be notaries matriculated in the Florentine Guild of Lawyers and Notaries. Moreover, when Scala was confirmed as first chancellor the following January it was decreed that he had to have as his assistant (whom he could appoint and remove at will) a similarly matriculated notary, "in order that he may duly perform the business concerning the first chancery." Perhaps this was a victory for the guild, who in return for accepting the new non-notarial rank of secretary may now have insisted that notarial expertise was still essential to chancery business. Scala had been successful in winning for the chancery responsibility for all documents relating to foreign affairs, but not in taking them from the hands of notaries. The head of the Tratte reverts to his old title of "Notary" and not "Secretary" of the Tratte, and he is given responsibility for the new men appointed to accompany orators on outside embassies, as well as presumably retaining his former responsi-

---

[60] *Ibid.*, pp. 611-613.

bility for preparing mandates and other foreign affairs' documents.[61]

The greatest novelty of the reform was the appointment of four men with the new and entirely separate function of accompanying orators on outside embassies when necessary, "especially in the most important legations and in which there is the greatest need of secrecy."[62] It was these last appointments of salaried officials sitting in permanent residence in Rome, Naples and Milan like watchdogs for Lorenzo de' Medici that Francesco Guicciardini criticized as one of Lorenzo's methods of exercising political control in Florence.[63] Some political motivation is suggested by the fact that three of the four men appointed for this task in 1488 were dismissed as Mediceans in 1494 and not reappointed—as well as one of the new assistants appointed in that year, a member of the Bibbiena family.[64] Although secretaries were needed for outside embassies,[65] the creation of permanent officials was a complete innovation, as the preamble suggests, and one that went against the communal tradition of electing all ambassadors in the councils for specific and limited periods of time—though this had already been eroded in the 1483 reform.

Despite this, it is clear from surviving records of their work that these secretaries served a very useful purpose during their exile from Florence in recording all the incoming and outgoing letters to the ambassadors they served. As always, the de-

[61] *Ibid.*, pp. 609, 610, 611 and 612, cf. n. 50 above, Filippo Redditi was chosen by Scala as his assistant, *ibid.*, p. 611, n. 2.

[62] *Ibid.*, p. 608. Ser Francesco del Cappello, Bernardo Ricci (not a notary, see n. 66 below), ser Antonio di Piero da Colle and ser Andrea di Jacopo da Foiano were appointed on 22 January 1488, and on 24 January the Signoria, Colleges and Otto decided what their duties were to be, in accordance with authority granted to them on 24 December 1487 (Marzi, *Cancelleria*, pp. 608-609, 613, 614-615, cf. n. 66 below).

[63] *Storie fiorentine*, p. 79.

[64] See pp. 121, 122 above.

[65] For example, Scala's assistant, Alessandro Braccesi, had accompanied the Florentine embassy to Naples and Rome in 1470, see Kristeller, "An Unknown Correspondence," pp. 323 ff. The legislation allowing chancery secretaries to go on external embassies in 1483 and 1487 is in Marzi, *Cancelleria*, pp. 602, 612.

cree lays down with great precision how this is to be done, and surviving registers show how meticulously these instructions were carried out: commissions, instructions and letters containing anything new or any particular commission were to be recorded at the beginning of their register; letters from the ambassador, together with remaining letters to him from the government, in the second half of the register, which was to be presented to Scala or his assistant Filippo Redditi (by 1492 replaced by Luca Ficini) on their return.[66] In this way a solution was found at last to the vast problem of copying official correspondence, for by delegating it to secretaries outside Florence it left the secretaries in the chancery free to attend to more immediate business.

Scala himself exchanged his position as head of a small, fluid chancery of six secretaries and four assistants for a more formal headship of a large complex of more strictly differentiated

[66] *Ibid.*, pp. 614-615. An example of a register arranged exactly as legislated for is ASF *SS. Dieci, Otto*, 21, fol. IIr-v: "Hic liber appellabitur Registrum Petri Victorii [Vettori] oratoris Florentini apud serenissimum Regem Neapolis: et erit bipartitus. In eo autem ego Bernardus Riccius, unus ex Cancellariis publice deputatis ad serviendum oratoribus Florentinis iuxta reformationem Cancellarie factam sub die xxiij Januarii MCCCCLXXXVII [= 1488] in prima parte eiusdem libri transcribam . . . [etc.] In secunda vero parte libri transcribam etiam . . ." etc.; and on fol. 134r, below his subscription, Filippo Redditi, Scala's assistant, wrote: "harum litterarum volumen presenti hac die ix mensis Julii mihi ser Philippo Rheddito fuit exhibitum ex lege a Bernardo Riccio Cancellario suprascripto et in Archivio prime Florentine Cancellarie consignatum"; cf. vol. 28, also by Ricci (described by Jacopo Antiquario to Poliziano as "adolescens in tua schola tornatim expolitus," the first nonlegal member of the chancery, Gabotto and Badini-Confalonieri, *Vita di Giorgio Merula*, pp. 319-320). Other chancellors were not as meticulous in recording their instructions as Ricci, but there are notes in their volumes recording that they were shown and handed over to Scala's assistants, e.g. 17, fol. 140r (2 January 1490) and 22, fol. 143v (13 November 1490) to Filippo Redditi, "Coadiutori Magni Cancellarii Barth. Scale"; 19, fol. 145v (18 April 1492), to Luca Ficini, "Magnifici Cancellarii Bartholomei Scale coadiutori." A single notarial document by Ficini survives in ASF *Notarile* II, 23 (2 September 1516), subscribed "Ego Lucas Fabiani Angeli ex Montegontio de Ficinis, civis et notarius publicus Florentinus . . . scripsi." He was probably the "notaio in cancellaria" who drew up the deed of exchange between Scala and his nephew in September 1494 and may have transcribed Scala's *Historia Florentinorum* (see ch. 12, n. 3 below; he also worked as amanuensis to Marsilio Ficino, *ibid.*).

offices. In contrast to the 1483 reform, in which he and Guidi were apparently given equal status, Scala is now given clear precedence over him.[67] Moreover, Scala is given control over the chancery of the Otto di Pratica where real power was exercised after 1480, and he was also made responsible for seeing that the system of registering letters introduced in 1483 was properly carried out—confirming that this was his particular concern. While being relieved of the day-to-day work of the chancery by his greatly increased staff, he remained firmly in control of its two most important offices.

In decentralizing the chancery, Florence was following the example of Milan, where on the downfall and death of the all-powerful Cicco Simonetta in 1479 the business of the hitherto unified chancery was divided into four different sections with a different secretary at the head of each. Whatever the political motives behind decentralization in Milan and Florence, it was also necessitated by expanding work in both chanceries, particularly in the field of religious affairs.[68] From this point of view the 1487-1488 reform represents yet another attempt to improve the efficiency of government by replacing short-term elected officials by long-term professionals.

This was the last major reform of the chancery before the 1494 revolution, although rivalry continued between the notaries inside and outside the chancery, fomenting dissatisfaction within the state bureaucracy. Chancery officials belonging to the Guild of Lawyers and Notaries thought they were discriminated against by the notary of the Riformagioni, and after a "lightning" scrutiny of notarial offices in the guild car-

---

[67]Marzi, *Cancelleria*, p. 609 ("Et quod praesenti et futuris Officialibus Reformationum semper praeservetur . . . secundus locus, hoc est immediate post primum Cancellarium"), cf. p. 599.

[68] One of the secretaries in Milan "deve occuparsi solo dei benefici" (*Storia di Milano*, 7: 525; cf. Santoro, *Uffizi*, pp. xxiv-xxv); and although Florence did not go to these lengths, one can see from the correspondence of Florentine ambassadors in Rome how much time the search for benefices consumed. On Cicco as "un accentratore" who "aveva diretto da solo tutta la cancelleria," *ibid*. He was granted Florentine citizenship in September 1464 after the proposal was initially rejected by the Council of the People (ASF *Liber fabarum*, 67, fols. 187r-188v).

ried out by the resourceful Guidi in 1489, one of them complained that "the honor and tradition of the Palace Officials has been blemished."[69] An anonymous and undated memorandum, which may have emanated from Guidi in the early 1490s, complains in its turn about the way in which the Palace of the Signoria was run, with offices for sale and nepotism rampant, the best men leaving and impecunious and inexperienced newcomers appointed in their place, often from outside the city.[70] Although the chancery itself was not directly implicated in these charges, it was doubtless responsible for some of the offices referred to. In the event, the chancery had reform forced on it by the revolution in 1494. Afterwards, however, we find it in the hands of exactly the same men who had controlled it during the years of Scala's chancellorship: apart from Scala himself, who was reappointed joint-first chancellor after his three days' dismissal, there were Alessandro Braccesi,

[69] The scrutiny is vividly described in two letters to Niccolò Michelozzi, one from Alessandro Braccesi (13 March 1489, ed. T. de Marinis and A. Perosa, *Nuovi documenti per la storia del rinascimento*, Florence, 1970, pp. 45-47), and the other from ser Francesco di ser Barone (18 March 1489, BNF MS Ginori Conti, 29, 101, fol. 45, describing the "successo dello squittino facto qui all'Arte nostra *in morem fulminis*"; he concludes: "Et io non mondo nespole: in noi s'è maculato l'honore et consuetudine dei ministri di palagio").

[70] ASF *Tratte* 15 (unfoliated): "El palagio de' Signori non può esser peggio servito: sempre fuora ,di Firenze ne molti contro alle leggi gli ufici si vendono, eschonne el più delle volte quegli sono pratichi et servono bene, et venghono novellini con assai debito et bisognia attendino ad altro per vivere. . . . Ogniuno vi vole mettere il figliuolo et sonvi molti smemorati et tol[gon]si di fuora gente non ha praticha nè cognoscenza." Entitled "La Riforma dello stato," it notes: "Pensare al palagio maxime circa le cancellerie, perchè per tutto Dicembre finischono le electioni, et anchora di quegli servono agli Octo della Praticha," suggesting a date at the end of 1490 (when the Otto as well as other members of the chancery, appointed from 1 January 1488 for 3 years, were due for reappointment, Marzi, *Cancelleria*, p. 613), or perhaps three years later, in 1493. Its reference to the "extimo nuovo" and the attempt to "spegner" foreign coins suggest 1490, although many of the reforms concerning "qualche aggiunta alla borsa de' Gonfalonieri della Giustizia" and the administration of justice were in fact introduced by the priorate of September-October 1493, "poi non missono a effetto tali leggi" (Rinuccini, *Ricordi storici*, pp. cl-cli; on the decree against using foreign coinage on 28 August 1490, *ibid.*, p. cxlv). The memorandum also comments: "La cancelleria seconda non sta bene con ser Antonio di Mariano [Muzi] a stare così in commenda."

Francesco Gaddi, Antonio della Valle and Filippo Redditi—
to name only the most important, who included three of
Scala's former personal assistants.

Scala experimented with his most far-reaching ideas for reforming chancery practice in the 1470s and, although he never
recovered the authority he then enjoyed, he continued to work
for his objective of making the chancery independent and its
officials direct representatives of the sovereign state that appointed them. During his lifetime he succeeded in making the
chancery responsible for preparing all diplomatic documents,
formerly the joint responsibility of chancellor and notary of
the Riformagioni, and he created its own archive in which to
preserve the diplomatic material he had so painstakingly organized and had copied throughout his office.[71] He also succeeded in establishing the position of secretary as an independent, non-notarial office. In the year after his death it was decreed that anyone could be nominated as a chancery official,
with the authority to prepare public documents "as if they
were matriculated notaries."[72] This established the principle
that Scala had championed so vigorously throughout his important chancellorship.

[71] On the "Archivio prime Florentine Cancellarie," see n. 66 above, and
on the copying of documents for the first chancery, see p. 184 above. See
also C. Rotondi, "L'Archivio delle Riformagioni Fiorentine," *Fonti e studi di
storia legislazione e tecnica degli archivi moderni* 6 (Rome, 1972): 14-17,
who emphasizes Scala's responsibility for reorganizing the Archivio delle
Riformagioni in the second half of the fifteenth century: while it seems
unlikely that all the inventories she attributes to his influence were in fact
due to him (e.g. that of 2 September 1474, listing documents in the chest
of the notary of the Riformagioni in the hand of Guidi's assistant, ser Piero
Cennini pp. 16-17, cf. Marzi, *Cancelleria*, p. 468), it is nevertheless true that
Scala took a great interest in the order and preservation of documents.

[72] Decree of 13 February 1498, ASF *Provv.* 188, fols. 56v-58r, ed. Tommasini, *Vita*, 1: 666; cf. Marzi, *Cancelleria*, pp. 280-281: "et di quella qualità
et conditione che a llui parrà et piacerà, non obstante alcuna prohibitione
o divieto . . . Tucte le cose che si faranno circa il loro uficio per quegli che
come di sopra saranno electi et durante il tenpo del loro uficio vaglino et
tenghino et observinsi et habbino quella forza et vigore et a quelle si presti
indubitata fede *come se fussino facte per publico notaio matricolato nell'
Arte de' Giudici et Notai della ciptà di Firenze*" (fols. 56v-57r, my italics).

PART THREE

Place in Society

CHAPTER VIII

A Citizen Worth Knowing

And tell him that I am becoming a citizen to whom it will be well worth making himself known, especially with one of his nice little articles from down there, and that I lack gloves, *uselletti* and soap; anything would be welcome. *Scala to Giovanni Lanfredini, 1484*[1]

Scala's message to his old friend Marino Tomacelli in Naples on the very day he was knighted by the pope in St. Peter's shows him at the height of his career: successful and confident enough to laugh about his lack of refinement. He was proud, of course, but also ironic about his achievement, as he had been about his office of chancellor in Florence. His reputation has suffered at the hands of envious rivals like Luigi Pulci and Angelo Poliziano, who lampooned his pomposity and pretentiousness: "messer Bartolomeo of the sweeping obeisances,"[2] moving "with pompous tread, swollen with a crowd of public servants, or borne through the spacious forum on a whinnying horse."[3] To those who pierced his armor of reserve, however, he offered a refreshingly sardonic wit and loyalty. He was always quick to take offense and stand on his dignity, for the miller's son lay close beneath the surface and he was perhaps always too insecure to enjoy as wide a circle of friends as the more effusive Ficino. He quickly litigated with his father-in-law about his dowry and he once confided to Lorenzo de' Medici that hopeful new men "cannot be persuaded that they

---

[1] 25 December 1484, ASF *Acq. Doni* 352, fol. 169: "e li diciate che mi vengho faccendo un ciptadino di natura che buon per lui se mi saperrà cognoscere, maxime con qualcuna di quelle suo gentil cosette di costà, e che sono senza guanti, senza uselletti, senza saponi: ogni cosa m'ataglierebbe." For references to the use of scented gloves and toilet soap at the beginning of the sixteenth century, see A. Luzio and R. Renier, "Il lusso di Isabella d'Este, Marchese di Mantova," *Nuova antologia* 65 (1896):681-682. For *uselletti*, Dott. Giuseppe Frasso suggests "calze ricamate a uccelli."

[2] See Pulci's poem "Messer Bartolomeo dei bell'inchini," *Sonetti del Burchiello del Bellincioni e d'altri poeti*, London (Livorno), 1757, p. 161; cf. V. Rossi in *GSLI* 18 (1891):382-384, and Parronchi, "The Language of Humanism," p. 109; also ch. 3, n. 8 above.

[3] Poliziano, Ode "In Bart. Scalam," nn. 59 and 60 below.

[195]

are not despised by me."[4] Yet "after shrewd enquiry" he did admit a small number of men to his friendship "on a high moral plane"—as one of them put it—provided they were prepared to wait until the evening for him briefly to cast off the cares of the day.[5] Scala was a political animal. His career came first and professional acquaintances were more valued by him than intimate friendships.

As chancellor, Scala's acquaintances ranged from illustrious heads of state and leading citizens of Florence to the poorest men who visited or ran errands for the chancery. Knighted by the pope in 1484, he was much earlier appointed councillor and secretary to King Louis XI of France, Ferrante of Naples and the dukes of Milan, who also gave him gifts of money.[6] The secretary of the king of Poland presented him with a large white bearskin.[7] The lesser Italian nobility,

[4] ASF *MAP* 33, 693 (26 August 1476); on the dowry, see ch. 3, n. 49 above. In a letter to Lorenzo de' Medici of 28 August 1476 (ASF *MAP* 25, 443, the reference to which I owe to Dr. William Kent), Giovanni Rucellai asked Lorenzo to see that Scala was not offended by his own servant replacing the present *tavolaccino* serving the Signoria (whom it had been decreed on 8 November 1475 each Palace Official could appoint "al suo beneplacito," ASF *SS. Delib. sp. aut.* 33, fol. 92v); on the office of *tavolaccino*, G. Rezasco, *Dizionario del linguaggio italiano*, Florence, 1881, pp. 994, 1169.

[5] See Antonio Geraldini's poem to Scala, ed. and trans. by J.F.C. Richards, "Some Early Poems of A.G.," *Studies in the Renaissance* 13 (1966): 129-130, 139-140; on these poems, Kristeller, *Studies*, pp. 154-155. He visited Florence on at least two occasions: in 1468, on his way to Venice (ASMi SPE Fir. 275, 19 October 1468) and in 1483 as ambassador of Ferdinand II of Aragon.

[6] See above. On his relationship with the Sforza, see especially his letter to the Dukes of 25 November 1477, ASMi SPE Fir. 293; and ch. 10, n. 58 below.

[7] Described by Lattanzio Tedaldi, Rome, Bibl. Vat. MS Barb. lat. 2031, fol. 97r: "Preterea donavit domino Bartolomeo Scalae equiti ac Excelse Reipublice Florentine Cancellario maximo, viro quidem aetate sua doctissimo, pellem ursi albam et permagnam." Letters referring to business negotiations between the king's secretary, Filippo Buonaccorsi, called Callimachus, *ibid.*, fols. 99v, 100v, 102v. On Callimachus, see the note and bibliography in Kristeller, *Supplementum*, 2:339; S. Ciampi, *Bibliografia critica delle antiche reciproche corrispondenze . . . dell'Italia colla Russia, colla Polonia, ecc.*, Florence, 1834, 1: 26-37, esp. 28; and *Dizionario biografico, s.* Buonaccorsi. There is a letter from the Florentine Signoria to Callimachus,

too, provided him with friendships if not gifts: Federigo of Montefeltro, duke of Urbino,[8] Costanzo Sforza, lord of Pesaro and his ambassador Pandolfo Collenuccio,[9] Ercole d'Este, lord of Ferrara,[10] and Gabriele Malaspina, marquis of Fosdinovo.[11] So did neighboring republics. Scala corresponded privately with the chancellors and leading citizens of Lucca and Siena.[12] One of the leading citizens of Lucca "spoilt" him with gifts of oranges and orange trees,[13] and in 1482, recognizing the value of demonstrating their gratitude to him, the government of Lucca decided to send him secretly but "as a public and not a private gift" a silver-gilt bowl worth 60 golden ducats.[14] His home town of Colle granted him tax

---

probably drafted by Scala (29 August 1496), concerning a member of the Tedaldi family, in ASF *Manoscritti* 59, no. 618.

[8] See his correspondence with him about fortune (ch. 13, n. 22 below) and his letter asking for Fra Santi's release in 1479 (ch. 4, n. 118 above).

[9] See his *Oratio* to Costanzo (ch. 6, n. 51 above) and letters in Modena MS, fols. 18r, 32r-v (especially fol. 18r, 27 June 1482): "Sono richiesto da altri da chi sa l'amore della Vostra Signoria inverso di me come havete voluto che lo sappi ciascuno"; and on his friendship with P. Collenuccio, see his dialogue *On Laws and Legal Judgments*, ed. Borghi, p. 269, and Modena MS, fol. 11v; also M. Morici, *Per un decennio della vita di Pandolfo Collenuccio (1477-87)*, Fano, 1901, p. 71. On Collenuccio, a humanist, subsequently employed by Ercole d'Este, see C. Varese in *Prosatori volgari del Quattrocento*, Milan-Naples, 1955, pp. 593-720; *Pandolfo Collenuccio umanista*, Pesaro, 1957, reviewed by E. Garin, in *Rassegna della letteratura italiana* 63 (1959):72-75.

[10] See letters in ASF *Missive* 48, fol. 131v, and *Minut.* 11, fol. 115v.

[11] See ASF *Minut.* 12, fols. 15v, 17v; Modena MS, fol. 34v.

[12] See his letters to Agostino Dati and Niccolò Borghesi, chancellors of Siena, and to Borghese Borghesi and Lorenzo Venturini in Siena (Dati, *Opera*, fols. 137v-138r; Venice, Bibl. Marciana, MS lat. XI, 83, fol. 87r; Modena MS, fols. 2r-v, 14v-15v); to Buonaccorso Massari, chancellor of Lucca, and to Martino Cenami, Niccolò Gigli and Jacopo Ghivizano in Lucca (ASF *Missive* 48, fols. 213v, 214r, Modena MS, fols. 27r, 34r, 35r, Siena, Bibl. Comunale, MS K. XI. 49, no. 26). On Massari, see R. Cardini, *La critica del Landino*, pp. 40-61; on Borghesi, L. Zdekauer, *Lo Studio di Siena nel Rinascimento*, Milan, 1894, pp. 119-124, and doc. 26, pp. 195-199.

[13] Jacopo Ghivizano, see esp. Scala's letters to him of 7 December 1481, 10 May and 31 August 1482, Modena MS, fols. 21r-v, 27r, Siena, Bibl. Comunale, MS K. XI. 49, no. 26.

[14] Lucca, AS, ATL Consiglio Generale 21, fol. 189r (22 August 1482): "Item fuit propositum quod sepe fuit commemoratum Magnificis Dominis

concessions and the right to bear its arms and insignia, and San Gimignano gave him wine.[15] Clearly he was "a citizen worth knowing."

He was valued, too, within Florence by patricians and commoners alike, and not only after he became chancellor. Among his earliest supporters were two members of patrician families, Donato Acciaiuoli and Andrea Alamanni, the "academicians" of Argyropoulos who had admired his talent as a student in Florence.[16] His staunchest political supporter was Angelo della Stufa, a member of one of the oldest families in Florence.[17] He also worked closely with Luigi and Jacopo Guicciardini, collaborating with Luigi Guicciardini to intro-

---

esse utile reipublice et valde conveniens ostendere signum aliquod gratitudinis claro et eloquenti viro domino Bartholomeo Scale . . . propter multa merita sua erga nos et pro laboribus quos suscepit prompto animo in decus et commodum reipublice nostre. Ideo si videatur quod sit donandus aliquo munere pro dicta gratitudine ostendenda et pro reddendo ipsum ferventiorem in futurum et pro conservanda benivolentia, etc.": selected citizens recommended "sit obtenta expensa usque in summam duc. sexaginta auri pro argentis donandis . . . ex illa forma argentorum quae decentior videbitur Magnificis Dominis . . . et per modum secretum mittatur munus domino ipse intelligat fore donum publicum et non particulare." On 6 November Scala thanked the government of Lucca for the "inauratam atque insigni celatura, ex puro puto argento, patinam," Lucca, AS, ATL 534 (no. 40), fol. 76r. On the relationship of Lorenzo de' Medici, and Scala, with Lucca, see E. Lazzareschi, "Relazioni fra il Magnifico Lorenzo e la Signoria di Lucca," *La Rinascita* 4 (1941): 323-360, esp. 335, 342; letters in Lucca, AS, ATL 534, reg. 40. The priors of Arezzo also corresponded privately with Scala, e.g. Arezzo, AS, *Delib. Consigl.* 12, fols. 359v, 362v, 363r; 13, fol. 5r; *Delib. Priori* 3, fol. 12v, 13r, etc.

[15] See ch. 1, n. 13, and Scala's letter to the priors of San Gimignano (23 June 1491), Siena, Bibl. Communale, MS K. XI. 49, no. 26, ed. A. Becattelli, *Lettere al Comune di S. Gimignano*, Per Nozze Bacci-Del Lungo (*Misc. Colle Vald.*), Castelfiorentino, 1895, p. 72 (with the date 23 June 1481).

[16] Above. Cf. Donato's letter to Scala when he was Florentine ambassador in Rome in 1471 (BNF MS Magl. VIII, 1390, fol. 57v, 26 April 1471): "Te vero mihi in omnibus rebus fautorem esse scio, ea est humanitas tua et singularis in me benivolentia. Ego vero Papiensi te comendavi, et ubicunque occasio oblata est, amicitie nostre non defui."

[17] Scala was also a friend of Angelo's son Sigismondo, see letters in Rome, Bibl. Corsiniana, MS 582 (45.C.17), fol. 59r-v, ed. Patetta, "La *Nencia da Barbarino*, ecc.," pp. 159-160; Modena MS fol. 37r. He wrote a poem on the death of Sigismondo's wife, Albiera, ch. 10, n. 55 below.

duce a program of reform when they were both members of the Signoria in 1473, and corresponding privately with Jacopo, who in 1483 asked him for a copy of Scala's *Apologues*—or *fumee*—for the papal legate, Cardinal Francesco Gonzaga.[18] It was Jacopo's son Piero who was so critical about the way new men were advanced in the 1484 scrutiny of electoral offices at the expense of old-established citizens,[19] and he in his turn influenced his son Francesco Guicciardini's early *Florentine History*, which was far more critical of Scala than his later *Portrait and Eulogy of Lorenzo de' Medici*.[20] There was one other aristocrat who criticized Scala's appointment as chancellor, Alamanno Rinuccini, but his verdict was probably retrospective, colored by his increasing hostility to the Medici regime.[21] Scala's special responsibility for ambassadors as chancellor inevitably brought him into close contact with the old and prestigious families from whom such men were drawn. Whatever their personal feelings towards him may have been, men like Piergiovanni Ricasoli, Domenico Giugni, Bongianni Gianfigliazzi, Tommaso Soderini, Giovan-

[18] See Scala's letters to Jacopo of 19 April 1483, Florence, Arch. Guicciardini, ASF *Leg. Comm.* V, 26, and [26 April-6 May 1483], ASF *Dieci Missive, Leg. Comm.* 5, fol. 223r ("ingegneròmmi satisfare alla volonta di Monsignore legato delli apologi, o vogliamo dire fumee secondo il Mellino"). I am grateful to Count Piero Guicciardini for kindly allowing me to transcribe the former from his family archives. Cardinal Francesco Gonzaga was papal legate in Ferrara at the time, Pastor, *Storia dei papi*, 2: 564-565.

[19] Piero's account of the scrutiny is in Rubinstein, *Government*, p. 319, cf. 215. On Piero, see Francesco's "Ricordanze" in *Scritti autobiografici e rari*, pp. 71-72. It was partly at Piero's behest that Scala wrote to Jacopo on 19 April 1483 (n. 18 above): "così m'è ricordato da Piero vostro figluolo et da altri."

[20] The *Portrait* is ed. R. Palmarocchi, *Scritti politici e ricordi*, Bari, 1933, p. 226: "exaltato da lui, e quale fece eleggere con onorato stipendio per primo secretario della republica"; on this eulogy, see F. Gilbert, "Guicciardini, Machiavelli, Valori on Lorenzo Magnifico," *Renaissance News* 11 (1958): 107-114; cf. *Storie fiorentine*, p. 79, and his *Dialogo . . . del Reggimento di Firenze*, p. 34.

[21] See ch. 3, n. 6 above. Alamanno attacked Lorenzo as a tyrant in 1479 in his *Dialogus de libertate*, especially p. 301; cf. *Ricordi storici*, pp. cxlvii-cxlix. On Rinuccini, see Giustiniani's biography; Martines, *Social World*, pp. 347-348.

ni Aldobrandini, Antonio and Tommaso Ridolfi—and particularly Pierfilippo Pandolfini and Giovanni Lanfredini, of slightly lower status[22]—corresponded privately as well as publicly with Scala.[23] In retrospect Scala may have appeared more portentous of a changed order of things than he did at the time.

The world of politics, which was the center of Scala's life, was closely associated in Florence with the world of business. Many of the richest and most influential citizens were merchants and bankers like the Medici themselves, and as they played a full part in the political life of the city they ensured that the two worlds were closely interlocked. Scala had himself been involved in trade and shipping early in his life, first as Pierfrancesco de' Medici's factotum and then as chancellor of the Guelf Party when it was responsible for maritime affairs, and it was in this circle of society that his family established its roots. His young brother Carlo—"your Carlo Scala," as Benedetto Dei described him to Carlo Martelli— went on a voyage to the Levant in 1465 with Martelli and Raffaello Carsidoni doubtless thanks to the influence of Bartolomeo, who was listed by that merchant adventurer and

[22] See Pierfilippo Pandolfini's letter to Scala during Lorenzo de' Medici's absence from Florence in 1479-1480, dated 17 January 1480 (ASF *SS. Dieci Otto Missive*, 10, fol. 118v: "Ora per rispondere alla vostra de dì x, dico che ò bene inteso et gustato quanto scrivete (et il dubio et sospetto che avete è ragionevole). . . . Farò quello potrò per rispondervi con qualche fondamento"); his brother Jacopo was married to Scala's niece, Agnola di Tomè Scala, in 1483, see ch. 9, n. 70 below. In 1484 Giovanni Lanfredini wrote to ask for Scala's help as a new ambassador (6 July 1484, BNF MS II, V, 15, fol. 76v, beginning: "Benchè continovamente mi ricordi dell' affectione che sempre m'avete mostro et nelle cose mie sempre operato"); Scala replied on 24 July, and frequently asked for his favors, ASF MS *Acq. Doni* 352, fols. 93, 169; BNF MS II, V, 20, fols. 42, 64, 70, 201, 202, 211, 219; MS Ginori Conti 29, 64, fol. 54. On Giovanni's career, M. Mansfield, *A Family of Decent Folk, 1200-1741; the Lanfredini, Merchant-Bankers and Art-Patrons*, London, 1922, pp. 185-212; de Roover, *Banco Medici*, pp. 361-362.

[23] He also corresponded in a semi-official capacity with Matteo Bartolini, Bernardo Buongirolami, Carlo da Diacceto, Piero Nasi, Francesco Cortegiani, Antonio, Lorenzo and Bartolomeo Pucci, Giovanni di Piero Rucellai, Sigismondo della Stufa, Guidantonio Vespucci, Antonio—and of course Lorenzo—de' Medici.

connoisseur of friendships, Benedetto Dei, as one of his "proven friends."[24] Scala's early friendship with the banker Bernardo Rinieri could have provided him with another entrée into the world of business and commerce and, as godfather to his eldest child, also to the social milieu of Bernardo, who was related by marriage to the Dietisalvi, the Acciaiuoli and the Altoviti.[25] Bartolomeo's marriage in 1468 to Maddalena Benci drew him closer to the merchant community, and he was connected to another merchant family, the Ginori, through his brother Andrea, himself a merchant in the wool trade and a partner of Gabriele Ginori in 1475.[26] Andrea was joined in the wool trade by his nephew, Bartolomeo's son Giuliano, whose will in 1535 refers to his share in a silk company and in a Genoese company with which he became associated through Andrea's second wife. Interestingly, this second generation of the Scala family married into old Florentine merchant families who wrote histories of their city: Giuliano married Francesca Villani, descended directly from Matteo and Filippo Villani, and his cousin Lorenzo di Andrea Scala

[24] On Carlo Scala, see ch. 9, below. Dei's letter referring to "il tuo g[i]ovane Charllo Schali, il quale saria sofficiente a magior cosa che a dar ffine a quello ch'ai qui" (6 December 1462) is now ed. P. Orvieto, "Un esperto orientalista del '400: B.D.," *Rinascimento*, ser. 2, 9 (1969):229-230. His reference to B.S. as one of his "amici provati" (from whom he had also received letters) is in M. Pisani, *Un avventuriero dell' '400, la vita e le opere di B. Dei*, Florence, 1923, pp. 101, 115; cf. Orvieto, p. 220. Dei's career is summarized by Orvieto, p. 205, n. 1.

[25] On Bernardo Rinieri, see ch. 9, n. 5 below. The christening of Lucrezia Rinieri on 17 May 1462 is described in ASF *Conv. Soppr.* 95, 212, fol. 159 right. On Scala's fellow-godfather, Abbot Isidero del Sera, cf. ch. 4, n. 147 above. The husband and father-in-law of two of Scala's daughters are mentioned in the Rinieri accounts, suggesting they formed part of the same business circle (Niccolò da Filicaia and Messer Francesco Gaetani, cf. ch. 9 below).

[26] *Ibid*. In a letter to Ercole d'Este on 20 August 1480 (ASF *Missive* 48, fol. 131v) Scala describes Gabriele Ginori as "a me in luogho di fratello." On Gabriele as a Medicean, see F. W. Kent, *Household and Lineage in Renaissance Florence*, Princeton, N.J., 1977, p. 213, cf. his doctoral thesis (London University, 1971), "Ottimati Families in Florentine Politics and Society, 1427-1530: the Rucellai, Ginori and Capponi," pp. 338-342. On the Benci, see ch. 3, n. 48 above.

(a friend of the historian Benedetto Varchi) married Costanza
Cerretani, the historian Bartolomeo Cerretani's aunt; the Cerretani were in turn related by marriage to the Buonaguisi, the
family into which Bartolomeo Scala's eldest daughter Giovanna married.[27] They formed a small, interrelated group and,
thanks to Bartolomeo's position as a Florentine historian and
humanist as well as chancellor, his descendants were able to
take their place quite naturally among the mercantile intelli-
gentsia of the city.

As a member of the Guild of Lawyers and Notaries, Scala
would have worked closely with another group of men drawn
from a wide social stratum in Florence. Although he did not
practice as a lawyer, he regularly served as a consul and member of the Council of Twelve and often acted as an arbitrator
in legal disputes. We find him as many as five times working
as consul or councillor with Simone di Bernardo Uguccioni, a
patrician, and as often with the much newer Domenico di
Baldassare Bonsi, twice with Tommaso di Guidi Deti and with
Antonio di Piero Malegonnelle, once with his relation by marriage, Giovanni di Niccolò Cerretani, and with the successful
lawyers from new families Battista di Bartolomeo, Nelli, Guidantonio Vespucci and Angelo di Otto Niccolini, as well as
with men as new as himself, Cristoforo Landino and Bernardo
Buongirolami.[28] When he was chosen to make a new scrutiny
of men eligible to serve the guild in 1489, he collaborated with
five other lawyers, Antonio Malegonnelle, Guidantonio Vespucci, Angelo Niccolini, Cristoforo Landino and Marcello
Adriani, three of whom were outstanding Medicean politicians, Scala and Landino prominent Miceceans in the chan-

[27] See ch. 9, nn. 81 and 85 below.
[28] ASF *Giudici e Notai* 26 (cf. Manni, *Vita*, pp. 52-53), fols. 38v-45v,
87v-94v. Scala was also elected a councillor in May 1491 with a "nonjuror"
whose name is obliterated (fol. 94v). On the offices of proconsul, consul and
councillor in the guild, see Martines, *Lawyers*, pp. 17-21, although contrary
to the evidence above and the lists (1385-1505) in *Giudici e Notai* 26, fols.
50r-99v (cf. 50r: "Consiliarii Artis Iudicum et notariorum sunt duodecim,
videlicet, semper duo Judices et reliqui decem notarii per iiij menses"), he
states that in the fifteenth century lawyers held a quarter of the places in
the Councils (*ibid.*, pp. 20-21).

cery, Marcello Adriani the father of Scala's successor in the chancery. Together they probably represented the most influential lawyers in the guild at that time.[29]

Landino was Scala's colleague in the chancery, a fellow humanist and perhaps one of his closest associates. They began and ended their careers together; these ran complementary courses, Landino making teaching his principal profession, the chancery his second, Scala the other way round. They were both commended in 1456 for a combined chancery and teaching job, but whereas Landino was then appointed to teach in the Studio, Scala worked as Pierfrancesco's secretary. In 1458 Landino hinted to Piero de' Medici he would like a job in the chancery while two years later we find Scala delivering classes on Virgil in Pierfrancesco's house. When Scala became first chancellor of Florence, Landino became chancellor of the Guelf Party in his place, continuing to teach in the university and joining Scala in the chancery only in 1488.[30] The temperaments of the two men were very different, Landino the young poet urging Scala to "Stop prescribing laws for our love, stop!" while the earnest young lawyer went on to write a dialogue *On Laws and Legal Judgments* and sardonic *Apologues,* which Landino shrewdly admired as the right vehicle for Scala's intellect, in contrast to his own more poetical nature. Yet they were both humanists who wanted the classical program of liberal arts restored to the curriculum, and they ended their days in the chancery discussing the state of contemporary culture together as they went about "their common task of writing public letters."[31]

[29] See the letter of ser Francesco di ser Barone of 18 March 1489, cited in ch. 7, n. 69 above.

[30] See Cardini, *La critica del Landino,* pp. 1-84; Marzi, *Cancelleria,* pp. 603-606, 607, 612. His letters to Piero de' Medici in 1458 and to Lorenzo de' Medici in 1465 are ed. Perosa, *Carmina omnia,* pp. 187-190, and Bandini, *Collectio,* p. 1 (cf. Marzi, *Cancelleria,* p. 240, n. 3).

[31] Landino's early poems to Scala are in his *Carmina omnia,* pp. 6-7, 24-25 ("Desine iam leges nostro praescribere amori"), and 25-31 ("De suis maioribus"). His letter praising Scala's *Apologues* is ed. Bandini, *Cat. cod. lat.* 2: 637; and by Müllner, in his edition of Scala's *Apologi centum,* p. 6: "Invenisti argumentum in quo ingenium tuum regnare videatur" (cf.

Then there was Alessandro Braccesi, who began his career in the chancery with Scala as his assistant in 1465 and remained there in a series of increasingly important offices until Scala's death, being dismissed from office on Savonarola's downfall a year later, in 1498.[32] He served as Scala's loyal confidant in Rome and Naples in 1470 and on several occasions acted as his private notary, as well as exchanging poems and letters with him as a humanist.[33]

Niccolò Michelozzi, the son of Cosimo de' Medici's favorite architect, was another of Scala's early assistants until he was seconded to Lorenzo de' Medici's private secretariat.[34] He lived next door to Scala in Via Larga for a time and was called upon to draw up Scala's early property transactions and deeds of guardianship for a girl whose dowry Scala had promised to

---

Bandini, *Specimen*, 1: 157). Scala's account of their conversation in the chancery is in a letter to Poliziano, 31 December 1493, Poliziano, *Opera*, p. 135: "commune literarum scribendi publicarum munus." Cf. Gentile Becchi's poem in BNF MS Magl. VII, 1025, fol. 74v: "Postquam iura vobis rapiunt sic premia, o vates / Parcite si novum transfuga quero ducem, / Parcite si vester alia ad stipendia tyro / migrarit. . . . / Ergo duces quondam, o Scala et o Landine, valete. / Ad Christum propero militiamque piam."

[32] See the bibliography in ch. 6, n. 12; on his chancery offices, Marzi, *Cancelleria*, pp. 251, 255-256, 259, 268, 288-289.

[33] On his 1470 embassy, see Kristeller, "An Unknown Correspondence," and above; for his notarial work for Scala, ASF *Notarile* B 2318 (1468-1501), fols. 45r-v, 107r-113v; B 2321 (1481-1489), fols. 178v-179v, 181v, 202r-203r, 237r-239r; his letters to Scala (1470-1471) are ed. Kristeller, "An Unknown Correspondence," pp. 352-358; a letter (1491) and poems to Scala are ed. Perosa, in Braccesi's *Carmina omnia*, Florence, 1944, pp. 100-102, 139, 156-158 ("Orator vehemens dives es historicus / Seu vis in carmen validas effundere vires, / Virgilio similes concinis ore modos," p. 101).

[34] Michelozzi's letters asking to be commended to Scala and thanking Braccesi for doing so are ed. Marchesi, *Bartolomeo della Fonte*, append. 6, nos. 13, 14, pp. xxxi-xxxii; cf. his letter from Chios on 29 April 1467, referred to by N. Rubinstein, "Michelozzo and Niccolò Michelozzi in Chios, 1466-67," in *Cultural Aspects of the Italian Renaissance: Essays in Honour of P. O. Kristeller*, ed. C. H. Clough, Manchester University Press, 1976, p. 219. For the date of his earliest letters in the chancery, see R. Fubini, in Lorenzo de' Medici's *Lettere*, 1, no. 109, n. 1; for his position as Lorenzo de' Medici's private chancellor from 1472, Fubini, *ibid.*, and "Note Machiavelliane," p. 374, n. 2.

pay when she married a servant of the Signoria.[35] At other times the chancery and not Scala's private house provided the setting for their notarial activities, and from 1472 the Medici palace, where one of the first of an increasingly illustrious series of marriage settlements prepared by Michelozzi was for the bethrothal of Scala's brother Andrea.[36] When Scala wrote to Niccolò Michelozzi as Florentine ambassador in Rome in 1490, he declared he thought it unnecessary to commend his affairs to him, for "he errs who thinks he should be commended to his own."[37]

The list of Scala's chancery friends could be continued: Antonio della Valle, another of his assistants who in 1484 asked Scala to act as an arbitrator and "common friend" in a dispute over the division of their family property;[38] Filippo Redditi, the first assistant Scala had been allowed to appoint and dismiss himself, a fellow humanist and historian with whom he shared many views about the state and the writing of history and whose brother Bartolomeo, a lawyer, took charge of Scala's business affairs in Rome in 1489-1490;[39] Si-

[35] On his house, Marzi, *Cancelleria*, p. 313, n. 5, and C. von Fabriczy, "Michelozzo di Bartolomeo," *Jahrbuch der Königlich Preuszischen Kunstsammlungen*, 25, Beiheft, Berlin, 1904, p. 68; his notarial work in Scala's house is in ASF *Notarile* M 530, fols. 3r-9r, *passim* (1470).

[36] *Ibid.*, fols. 1r-10v *passim*, 16r, 17r-v (1469-1472, in the chancery, with Scala sometimes acting as a witness); 15r (22 April 1472, "in domo Laurentii de Medicis": with Lucrezia Tornabuoni, Lorenzo de' Medici's mother, Sigismondo della Stufa and Francesco Albizzi as witnesses). The *notarile* supports Guicciardini's contention (*Storie fiorentine*, p. 79) "che non si faceva parentado alcuno più che mediocre sanza participazione e licenzia sua [Lorenzo de' Medici]."

[37] 17 January 1490, BNF MS Ginori Conti 29, 64, fol. 52: "quoniam peccat qui commendandum se putat esse suis." On Michelozzi's subsequent career, Marzi, *Cancelleria*, pp. 263, 307, 312-314; on his writings, della Torre, *Storia*, pp. 716-719.

[38] See ASF *Notarile* B 2321 (A. Braccesi, 1481-1489), fols. 178v-179v (5 February 1484). On his career, Marzi, *Cancelleria*, pp. 251, 255, 259, n. 2, 268, etc. He was given Florentine citizenship in February 1477, ASF *Carte di corredo*, 8, fol. 240v.

[39] On Filippo, Marzi, *Cancelleria*, pp. 268-270, 604, 607, 611, n. 2; Schnitzer, *Quellen*, 1: 9-10, n. 3. There are legal deeds drawn up by him for Scala and his wife in ASF *Notarile* R 74 (1483-1524), fols. 4v, 22r, 23r (1488-1489). His letters are ed. Bandini, *Collectio*, pp. 86-100. On Bartolomeo, Schnitzer,

mone Grazzini, secretary of the Tratte, who did private notarial work for Scala and drew up Scala's will in 1484;[40] Francesco Gaddi, whose brother Taddeo and Zanobi Gaddi in Rome
were Scala's friends and correspondents.[41] Only ser Francesco
di ser Barone was apparently critical of Scala for asking the
Florentine ambassador in Naples to commend his own affairs
to the king's secretary, Antonello Petrucci: "I would have
thought—correctly, in my opinion—that it would have been
better to say nothing than to speak like that. Yet . . . the servant must tie up the donkey in his master's way."[42] Ser Francesco was also the only secretary to be dismissed in 1494 and
not reappointed. Loyalty was evidently demanded of members of the chancery and, apart from ser Francesco, Scala
seems to have commanded it.

Although the chancery formed its own community, it was
closely linked to the cultural as well as the political life of

---

Quellen, 1: 7-84; Martines, *Lawyers*, p. 495; and Scala's letters to G. Lanfredini of 12 November 1489 and to N. Michelozzi of 17 and 30 January
1490, BNF MS Ginori Conti, 29, 64, fols. 52-54.

[40] See ch. 9, nn. 84-87 below. On his career in the chancery, Marzi,
Cancelleria, pp. 254-255, 263, 270.

[41] See Scala's letters to [Taddeo Gaddi] and fra Santi [11 January 1483],
Modena MS, fols. 36r, 37v. On Francesco Gaddi, see J. Gaddi, *Eliographus
scilicet elogia omnigena*, Florence, 1638 (esp. p. 202: "Nec minor huic
[F.G.] gratia et existimatio apud Barthol. Scalam equitem"); Bandini, *Cat.
cod. lat.*, 4: iv-xiii; *Inventario de' mobili*, ed. C. Bologna; L. Sozzi, "Lettere
inedite di P. de Commynes a F.G.," in *Studi di bibliografia e di storia in
onore di T. de Marinis*, Vatican City, 1964, 4: 205-223; Marzi, *Cancelleria*,
pp. 256, 265-267, and his "Ricordi," Florence, Bibl. Laur. *Acq. Doni*, 213,
fols. lxxxx-96, describing his double role as Medicean and public ambassador,
1478-1496.

[42] Letter to N. Michelozzi, 2 May 1481 (BNF MS Ginori Conti, 29, 101,
fol. 13): "Io crederrei con vera ragione sostenere, et piglatela ad che verso
voi volete, che meglo era tacere che così dire. Nolo tamen sapere plus
quam sit sapere, et chi è servo debbe legare l'asino a modo del padrone."
As secretary to Piero Nasi, the Florentine ambassador, he mistakenly took
it upon himself to act on a private letter from Lorenzo de' Medici which
he had to decipher (*ibid.*, fols. 23r-24v, 19-21 May 1481). On his career,
Marzi, *Cancelleria*, pp. 251-252, 255-256. As a boy, the Florentine Signoria
petitioned for his release from prison in Siena (BNF MS Palat. 1103, fol.
5v, 18 June 1465). He drew up at least one legal document for Scala, referred to in Scala's 1495-1498 Decima (ASF *Decima Rep.* 26 A-F, fol. 358v).

the city. Cristoforo Landino, Alessandro Braccesi and Niccolò Michelozzi were all humanists who formed part of the
circle that gathered round Marsilio Ficino in the second half
of the fifteenth century. Scala had been a friend of Ficino's in
his student days, when they were both interested in Lucretius
and Epicureanism and wrote short accounts of the different
philosophical schools of antiquity. It was during this period
that Scala acquired the knowledge of Platonism he reveals in
his dialogue *On Laws and Legal Judgments*, while Ficino in
his turn admitted to being helped by Scala, as well as by Landino and Poliziano, in his work of translating and commenting
on Plato's *Dialogues*.[43] To judge from his letter to Scala ap-
praising Landino's *Camaldulensian Disputations*, he regarded
Scala as someone who would share his own opinions.[44] Not
only did he admire Scala's *Apologues* and write his own "Apologue" about them, but when they were being discussed in the
house of George of Cyprus, doctor to Ficino and the Medici,
Ficino spoke out first because he had recently read them. He
recorded later that he was laughed at at the time for praising
them as "learned and masculine," but his own multiple birth
of apologues proved how right he had been to call Scala's
Apologues "masculine," since it was thanks to them he had
been fertilized.[45] There is no evidence that Scala ever joined

[43] On Ficino's debt to Scala, Kristeller, *Supplementum*, 2: 105; cf. Marcel,
Marsile Ficin, 1433-99, Paris, 1958, p. 465, n. 3; della Torre, *Storia*, pp. 606-
607, n. 3, quoting from the 1st [1484] edition of Ficino's *Opera*: "usum
praeterea acerrimo Angeli Politiani doctissimi viri iudicio; usum quoque
consilio Christophori Landini et Bartholomei Scale, virorum clarissimorum";
on Scala's Platonism, cf. ch. 13 below.

[44] Ficino, *Opera*, 1: 667; cf. della Torre, *Storia*, p. 580, n. 1: "Legi quae-
stiones Christophori Landini Camaldulenses. . . . Lege illos et tu, scio, mecum
senties. Vales. Sed quare in laudando Christophoro tam brevis es, Marsili?
Quia habet nescio quid, quod exprimere nequeam. Iterum vale."

[45] Ficino's "Apologus de apologo" is in his *Opera*, 1: 847, and his letter
to George of Cyprus, *ibid.*, p. 865 (and in the preface to the 1677 edition
of Scala's *Historia Florentinorum*). On George of Cyprus, della Torre,
Storia, pp. 779-780. It is true, as Professor Kristeller pointed out to me, that
some of Ficino's apologues "de voluptate" predate Scala's, if they were, as
Ficino told Martin Brenninger, composed at the time of his commentary on
the *Philebus* (*Opera*, 1: 921 and Kristeller, *Supplementum*, 1: cxxii). How-

Ficino's gatherings at Careggi, but we know that the two men remained on friendly terms with each other from Ficino's letter to Scala on 11 November 1490, "An act of thanks for the gift of a home received": "Greetings, dearest Scala, almost my *alter ego*, four times my brother, in Cosimo, in genius, in love, in Lorenzo. We were once both reborn from great Cosimo. We both share the same genius Mercury. Divine love has for a long time melted us into one. We both have the same patron Lorenzo the Magnanimous, who is also the savior of our country. Therefore we are indeed a unit, indeed we are one person." Evidently Scala had invited Ficino to stay with him in Borgo Pinti: separated by fortune no longer, Jupiter had succeeded in decreeing that one man should inhabit one home and, whereas it would have been wrong for Ficino to have attempted to receive so great a man as Scala in his small and humble dwelling, it was right for him to be admitted to Scala's spacious abode and to be received by the Pinthian *penates*. "Here, therefore, under the pleasant shade of the laurel [Lorenzo] we shall together worship the splendor of Phoebus; under Apollo, the Muses; and in the company of the Muses, Plato. And both the Muses and Plato thank you for your kindness to me. Indeed bountiful Jupiter with Phoebus will one day give you thanks."[46] How different from Ficino's friendly effusion was Scala's dry and serious manner, expressed in a series of short fables instead of long punning letters and discourses. Scala lacked Ficino's philosophical originality and poetic inspiration, and he disliked the art of astrology that was so basic to Ficino's beliefs. Yet they evidently enjoyed each other's respect and affection, and gradually it became the

---

ever, he seems to have had a second burst of writing apologues (in his *Opera*, 1: 847-849, 855), seven in all, beginning with his "Apologus de apologo," referring to Scala's "Pinthian gardens" (which follows a letter dated 18 October 1481) and ending on p. 865 with his "Proemium in Apologos" to George of Cyprus: and these may well have been provoked by the completion of Scala's *Hundred Apologues* for Lorenzo de' Medici on 20 September 1481 (see ch. 11 below).

[46] Ed. Kristeller, *Supplementum*, 1: 60 (11 November 1490), "Gratiarum actio pro dono accepte domus."

fashion among aspiring poets and writers of Ficino's circle to praise Scala as one of the leading lights of their day.[47]

In themselves, the eulogies of Naldo Naldi, Ugolino Verino, Bartolomeo Fonzio, Bastiano Forese or Benedetto Colucci would mean little were they not supported by other evidence. However, Bartolomeo Fonzio demonstrates the admiration he expresses for Scala's learning in his *Annals* by quoting several long passages from Scala's writings in his *Dictionary*.[48] Similarly, Ugolino Verino's poem praising Scala's history and his poem about the secrets of nature "in the manner of Lucretius" seem to derive from his son Michele's letter describing a visit he had made to the house of Antonio Geraldini, ambassador of the king of Spain, where he read not only Scala's *Apologues*, which pleased him so much he read them in one go, but also his "History of our people," "described with amazing Livian simplicity," and his poem "De rebus naturalibus" in the manner of Lucretius (now lost): "And I marveled at his versatility in being able to write so well in prose and verse—but better in prose."[49] Since he had all these examples of

---

[47] Scala's debt to Ficino and the neoplatonism expressed in his writings are discussed in ch. 13 below. There are eulogies of Scala in Naldo Naldi's *Elegiae*, ed. L. Juhasz, Leipzig, 1934, p. 37, and in his *Epigrammaton liber*, ed. A. Perosa, pp. 9, 35-36, 37 (cf. ch. 9, n. 51 below; on 23 December 1460 Scala paid Naldi fl. 1, ASF *Conv. Soppr.* 95, 212, fol. 79 left); in Ugolino Verino's *De illustratione urbis Florentiae*, fols. 13r, 34r; cf. Bottiglione, *La lirica latina*, p. 116, n. 5 (and n. 49 below); in Bartolomeo Fonzio's *Opera*, Frankfort, 1621, p. 385 (poem to Scala); in Bastiano Forese's *Trionfo della virtù*, *Nozze Pellegrini Marchesini*, Ancona, 1883, preface, p. 13 (cf. BNF MS Magl. VII, 816, fol. 52v: "Lo Scala monstra che virtù 'l conduce / far degne pruove nel suo fatal raggio"); in Benedetto Colucci's *Declamationes liber*, in *Scritti inediti di B.C. da Pistoia*, ed. A. Frugoni, Florence, 1939, p. 47; cf. della Torre, *Storia*, p. 808.

[48] *Annales*, ed. G. C. Galletti, *Philippi Villani liber de civitatis Florentiae famosis civibus*, Florence, 1847, p. 156; cf. Marchesi, *Bartolomeo della Fonte*, p. 11, n. 3; his *Dictionary* is in Florence, Bibl. Riccard. MS 837, see fols. 44r, 73v, 84r and 100r, quoting words from Scala's treatises *On Whether a Wise Man Should Marry* and *On Laws and Legal Judgments*.

[49] Michele to Ugolino Verino, Bibl. Laur. 90 sup., cod. 28 (L), fol. 50r-v (cf. Bibl. Riccard. MS 915, fol. 62v (R), in Italian in MS 2621, fols. 73v-74r); cf. Lazzari, *Ugolino e Michele Verino*, p. 49, n. 2: "Cum essem apud Antonium Geraldinum Legatum Ferdinandi utriusque Hispanie Regis, qui Florentie commorabatur, legi librum Apologorum Bartholomei Scalae,

Scala's writings in his house in the 1480s, Geraldini evidently retained the admiration he had felt for Scala when he lived in Florence nearly twenty years earlier.[50] Another admirer in the city was the Greek scholar and soldier Michele Marullo, who subsequently married Scala's daughter Alessandra. Marullo was a friend of Lorenzo and Giovanni di Pierfrancesco de' Medici and Zanobi Acciaiuoli, and he shared Scala's interest in Lucretius. He wrote poems praising both father and daughter and died only three years after Bartolomeo, helping to defend Forlì against Cesare Borgia in 1500.[51] Another was Pietro Crinito. Taught by Ugolino Verino and Poliziano and by Savonarola in the Convent of San Marco, Crinito was also a friend of Marullo's and, like him, was one of Scala's literary adherents after the 1494 revolution, printing for him the *Defense Against the Critics of Florence* in 1496.[52]

Scala's literary circle extended outside Florence by the 1480s. We have seen how Cardinal Francesco Gonzaga, papal legate in Ferrara in 1483, wanted his *Apologues*. So did the

---

disertissimi viri, qui usque adeo mihi placuit ut totum uno haustu antequam deponerem pellegerim. Quod si Aesopus Phrigius lepidior est, Scala gravior. Illico Geraldinus Historias nostri populi ostendit, quas miro et Liviano candore descripserat: porrexit et carmen de rebus naturalibus [R; L = *moralibus*] instar Lucretii. Miratus sum versatile ingenium, et in utroque bene, sed prosa melior incedit"; cf. his father's poem (above): "Scala quoque Historias et Lydia gesta leonis / Explicat Hetrusci: Naturaeque abdita versu / Aggreditur vates docti de more Lucreti." Michele died at the age of 17 on 30 May 1487; on his education, Lazzari, *Ugolino e Michele Verino*, pp. 109-118.

[50] See n. 5 above and on his tetrastich praising Scala as Gonfalonier of Justice in 1486, see ch. 13, n. 1 below.

[51] *Carmina*, ed. A. Perosa, Verona, 1951, pp. 56, 61, 82-83, 91 (poems to Bartolomeo and Alessandra Scala, his "Sappho"). On the influence of Lucretius and Stoicism on his "Hymni Naturales" (*ibid.*, pp. 105-165), see P. L. Ciceri, "M.M. e i suoi 'Hymni Naturales,'" *GSLI* 64 (1914): 289-357; and on his friendships, *ibid.*, p. 299; A. Perosa, "Studi sulla formazione delle raccolte di poesie del Marullo," *Rinascimento* 1 (1950): 125-156, esp. 133-134 (and p. 261, n. 3, on Marullo, Scala and BNF MS Magl. VII, 1025).

[52] On Crinito, see Angeleri's preface to Crinito's *De honesta disciplina*, esp. pp. 7, 14; his letter to Scala is printed with the *Defense* (1496), fol. a2r, Manni, *Vita*, pp. 44-45: "Et hercle tu unus Florentiae, cuius eruditioni non auctoritas, auctoritati non eruditio, desit."

Sienese humanist Giovanni Lorenzo Buoninsegni, and they were admired by Alessandro Farnese (later Pope Paul III) for blending "sweet with sour" and "the serious with the humorous."[53] The Pistoiese poet Tommaso Baldinotti found "the serious, clever and impressive discourse" delivered by Scala when taking the waters invigorating enough to revivify a dead man.[54] In Venice he and Alessandra were admired by the young humanist Cassandra Fedele.[55] In Milan he corresponded with a former friend in the chancery, Carlo Barbavaro, who sent him a copy of Giovanni Simonetta's "Commentaria Sfortiana" in 1482.[56]

The one dissenting voice in this chorus of praise was that

[53] *Carteggio umanistico di Alessandro Farnese*, ed. A. Frugoni, Florence, 1950, p. 30: "Vero te Platonicum esse dixerim ita congrue dulcia amaris et iocis seria lepidissima quadam permisces." He was in Florence from August 1487 to mid-1489 to complete his education; according to the order of letters in the *Carteggio*, his letter to Scala must have been written at the beginning of 1488. On his youth, see his *Carteggio*, pp. 70-72, and A. Frugoni, "Per uno studio sulla giovinezza di Paolo III," *Annali d. R. Scuola . . . di Pisa*, ser. 2, 9 (1940): 202-210. On Francesco Gonzaga, see n. 18 above; for Scala's letter to Buoninsegni, ch. 11, n. 4 below.

[54] In a poem addressed to Scala, Pistoia, Bibl. Comunale Forteguerriana, MS A 58, fol. 218v: "Lieti, sacri, felici e sancti bagni / Che m'han di vero amor con voi congiunto/. . . Ricordomi de' gravi, accorti e magni / Sermon: da suscitare un hom defunto. / Hora io son vostro a tanto bene assumpto/ Fin che l'alma dal corpo si scompagni." I am indebted to the Director, Dott. Giancarlo Savino, for a copy of this poem. On Baldinotti, *Dizionario biografico, s.v.*; Poliziano, *Prose volgari*, ed. del Lungo, pp. 231-232; A. Chiti, *T. Baldinotti: poeta pistoiese*, Pistoia, 1898. His poem to Scala may represent an attempt to restore himself to favor in Florence after his expulsion in 1485.

[55] Cassandra Fidelis, *Epistolae et orationes postumae*, Padua, 1636, letters 109 and 110, pp. 165-166, to Bartolomeo, n.d. and 18 January 1493; and 107, 108 and 111, pp. 248-252, from and to Alessandra, 6 October 1492-18 January 1493; cf. Pesenti, "Alessandra Scala," pp. 248-252; Kristeller, *Supplementum*, 2: 281. Their friendship may have been brought about by Poliziano, who met Cassandra in Venice in 1491, and it is to her he describes Alessandra's performance of Electra in Borgo Pinti in [1493], see ch. 9 below.

[56] See Scala's letter to Barbavaro of 7 August 1482, Modena MS, fols. 32v-33r. He refers to the *Rerum gestarum Francisci Sfortiae commentarii*, ed. G. Soranzo, *RIS* 21 (2) (first printed in 1480, preface, pp. xxv-lxxxiii). Barbavaro worked in the Secret Chancery in Milan under Cristoforo Cambiago, Santoro, *Uffizi*, p. 56.

of Angelo Poliziano,[57] the teacher of many of these young admirers of Scala's, and the teacher, too, of Scala's own daughter Alessandra, his admiration for whom was apparently unaffected by his feelings for her father.[58] In his "Ode" against Scala, written probably after Scala's election as Gonfalonier of Justice in 1486,[59] Poliziano maliciously ridicules his achievement: his pomposity, his mad town villa in Borgo Pinti, where the elderly man "putrid with gout plays the Greek amidst overflowing cups" and "disports himself with prostitutes or worse." Fortune, not noble birth or virtue, bore him to the top, covered with bran from the mill where he was born: "But he has already forgotten his origins and spatters with poison and bites with his rusty teeth those who are ennobled with a long ancestry or outstanding endowments. He is drunk with success and buffeted by violent winds is teetering on the slippery summit, doomed to fall at any moment, and not *gradatim* either."[60] The last lines, playing on Scala's motto, recall the anonymous epigram written of him in 1472, the year in which he was made eligible for public office in Florence: "They are raised up high so their descent will be the more violent when they fall."[61] Scala's spectacular rise to power in-

[57] Angelo Ambrogini from Montepulciano was the son of a lawyer, of higher social status than Scala but, because his father was assassinated when he was 10 years old, as badly off and in need of patronage as Scala when he entered Lorenzo de' Medici's household as tutor to his children in 1477. On his early life, see Maier, *Politien*; del Lungo, *Florentia*, pp. 3-90; Picotti, *Ricerche umanistiche*, pp. 3-86.

[58] See ch. 9 below.

[59] On the *Ode*, see following note. It is dated by Parronchi before 1479 because it describes Scala's house as "being built" (*struit*) ("The Language of Humanism," p. 110); but the reference to fortune carrying him "ad usque supremos gradus" and to his motto *gradatim* makes it more probable it was written after his knighthood and election as Gonfalonier of Justice and a member of the Council of Seventy in 1486. Cf. E. Bigi (*La cultura del Poliziano*, p. 150n.), who dates it "non molto prima della polemica del poeta con lo Scala" (= 1493/4); on similarities with the 1493/4 correspondence, see n. 76 below.

[60] Ed. del Lungo, *Prose*, pp. 273-274.

[61] Ed. G. Corti, "Una lista di personaggi del tempo di Lorenzo il Magnifico caratterizzati da un motto o da una riflessione morale," *Rinascimento*

evitably made him a target for contemporary satirists like Poliziano, Pulci or Gentile Becchi, and in all satires there is a basis of truth. A fellow member of the chancery had criticized Scala for overcommending himself, and it is true that his language is often ingratiating and far removed from the brevity and simplicity he professed to admire.[62] Like his touchiness, his readiness to commend himself whenever an opportunity offered was another facet of his ambition and insecurity as a new man. Yet the very men who criticized him most vehemently were themselves hopeful Medici clients, as anxious for patronage as Scala and jealous of his success. Far from being chastened by their attacks, Scala retaliated with well-matched weapons of wit and irony, ridiculing the popular nonsense Luigi Pulci and his brother Luca printed about "nymphs, Morgantes and Dryads,"[63] triumphantly visiting poor Becchi in Arezzo in 1484 with his own knighthood instead of the cardinalate Becchi had been hoping to win from the Florentine embassy to Rome,[64] and engaging Poliziano in a long and equally fought duel. He had done much better for himself than his critics and they did not lightly forgive him.

The quarrel that broke out between Scala and Poliziano in 1493-1494 began as a professional squabble between humanists—one of several Poliziano conducted with his contempo-

---

3 (1952): 155; "Tollantur in altum ut lapsu graviore ruant," dated 5 January 1472. Cf. L. B. Alberti, "mai caduto alcuno giacere se none chi saliva troppo alto," *I libri della famiglia* in *Opere volgari*, 1: 182, repeated in Rucellai, *Zibaldone*, p. 41.

62 On his love of "brevitatem, quae sine obscuritate sit rerum dicendarum," see his letter to Niccolò Forteguerri, Paris, Bibl. Nationale, MS *nouv. acq.* 1520, fol. 99r; but cf. his letter to the dukes of Milan of 25 November 1477, ASMi SPE Fir. 293.

63 See Scala's letter in Poliziano, *Opera*, p. 137. Luigi Pulci's *Morgante* was printed in at least two editions in the early 1480s and others later (Hain, 13586-13589, *Indice generale*, 4, Rome, 1965, pp. 343-344, nos. 8227, 8228); his *Nenciozza da Barberino e la Beca* in one (Hain 13584) and Luca's *Il Driadeo* in many editions from 1479 (Hain, 13575-13582, *Indice generale*, 4, pp. 341-342, nos. 8212-8217).

64 See ch. 4, n. 135 and ch. 6, n. 66 above.

raries over matters of literary style.[65] What is striking is the amount of common ground the two men shared: Poliziano the philologist and university "reader . . . of ancient literature to young people, [who] has learnt to be discriminating about words and sentences" (as Poliziano described himself), and Scala, the practical man of affairs (in Poliziano's opinion), "a public scribe accustomed to writing letters, [who] must approve most of that style which is least abhorrent to common practice."[66] As a literary critic and scholar Poliziano outclassed Scala, but Scala never sank to the level of Poliziano's invective and was as urbane and amusing as Poliziano and his match in argument. Scala began it all by laughing at Poliziano and Ermolao Barbaro for using such an obscure and precious verb as *ferruminare* (meaning "to glue" or "solder"), about whose derivation and spelling he was, with good reason, suspicious, nicknaming them "ferruminators."[67] Poliziano raised the question of literary imitation, to which Scala responded with an anecdote about Theodore Gaza and St. Jerome's Ciceronianism: "But why this tale, you ask me, Poliziano, delight of the city? Because I, too, need some Theodore to remove me from the Ciceronian flock."[68] On the contrary, replied Poliziano; no

[65] See particularly his controversy with Cortese (*Opera*, pp. 250-257, trans. I. Scott, *Controversies over the Imitation of Cicero*, New York, 1910, pp. 17-22; cf. R. Sabbadini, *Storia del Ciceronianismo*, pp. 33-34, 37-42) and with Merula (n. 75 below). Cf. his letter to Piero de' Medici describing the replies he would make to those who called him too like or too different from Cicero or Pliny, *Opera*, pp. 1-3.

[66] *Opera*, p. 138.

[67] *Ibid.*, p. 129: "me quoque esse quendam . . . ferruminatorem," trans. in Scott, *Controversies*, pp. 14-16; drafts of this and another letter contained in BNF Aut. Pal. II, 57, fols. 2r-7r, are referred to by A. Perosa, "Due lettere inedite di P.," *Italia medioevale e umanistica* 10 (1967): 348-349, 374. The discussion continued in *Opera*, pp. 134-135, 142; cf. E. Bigi, *La cultura del Poliziano*, p. 101, n. 67. On the etymology of *ferrumen*, A. Ernout and A. Meillet, *Dictionnaire étymologique de la langue latine*, Paris, 1967, p. 230, *OLD*, fasc. 3. Ermolao Barbaro used the verb *ferruminare* in a letter to Poliziano, *Opera*, p. 17. On Barbaro, an eminent philologist like Poliziano, who published his *Castigationes Plinianae* in 1492-1493 and died probably in September 1493, see E. Bigi in *Dizionario biografico*, s.v.

[68] *Opera*, pp. 132-133 (31 December 1493). On St. Jerome's dream, *Epistulae*, ed. I. Hilberg, *Corpus scriptorum ecclesiasticorum latinorum*, 54

one ever took Scala for a Ciceronian and he therefore had no need of a Theodore.[69] Disagreement over "certain minutiae concerned with orthography"[70] provided Scala with the opportunity of citing his *risqué* four-line poem about the derivation of *adulescens*, spelt by Poliziano with a *u* instead of an *o*: "Surely *adulescens* will not come from the tail, like *adulor?* Surely the name will not come from the name *cauda?* That is a shameful name; so, say I, take away the pudendum, Papirianus, and call it what grows (*adolet*)."[71] Brushing off the joke that Scala's friends told him was lying in the tail of the epigram, Poliziano later reciprocated Scala's verse with an epigram criticizing Scala for using *culex* ("mosquito") in the feminine instead of the masculine gender, in which he wittily describes the mosquito in the role of a lover, rising like Venus from breeding waters and flying like airborn Cupid to suck the blood of heavily sleeping women as he sings his rousing Bacchic song: "in fact, what man bears as many marks of love

(Vienna-Leipzig, 1910) pt. 1:190 (no. 22); cf. P. Crinito, *De honesta disciplina*, ch. 10, pp. 72-73. On Gaza, *P.G.* 161, cols. 971-1014, Voigt, *Wiederbelebung*, 2: 143-146: he translated Cicero's *De senectute* and *Somnium Scipionis* from Latin into Greek.

[69] *Opera*, p. 137. The question of Scala's Ciceronianism has monopolized scholarly interest in his dispute with Poliziano, from Erasmus onwards, but scarcely deserves such emphasis: *Dialogus . . . Ciceronianus sive de optimo dicendi genere*, in *J. C. Scaligeri adversus D. Erasmum orationes duas eloquentiae romanae*, Toulouse, 1621, p. 71; cf. Sabbadini, *Storia del Ciceronianismo*, pp. 35-36, 100-102; Manni, *Vita*, pp. 40-44; F. O. Menchen, *Historia vitae . . . Angeli Politiani*, Leipzig, 1736, pp. 358-365, etc. The dialogue is also discussed by L. Ruberto, "Studi sul Poliziano filologo," *Rivista di filologia e d' istruzione classica* 12 (1883): 212-260.

[70] *Opera*, pp. 133-134 and 137-143: "minuta quaepiam, quae ad orthographiam potissimum pertinent"; cf. Sabbadini, *Storia del Ciceronianismo*, pp. 102-103. Poliziano had discussed "Quo argumento dicendum Vergilius non Virgilius" in his *Miscellanea*, ch. 77 (*Opera*, pp. 645-649). On Landino's change from Virgilius to Vergilius in 1488, alluded to by Poliziano, see Cardini, *La critica del Landino*, p. 312, n. 1.

[71] *Opera*, p. 134. According to Priscian, Papirianus wrote a work "De Orthographia," Pauly-Wissova, *Real-Encyclopaedie*. On the derivation of *adulescens*, OLD fasc. 1; on *adulor*, Ernout-Meillet, *Dictionnaire étymologique*, p. 9.

as the mosquito?"[72] Since Poliziano was lecturing on the *Organon* in the university at the time, Scala was quick to accuse his poem of illogicalities and Poliziano replied in similar vein; the combatants were well matched.[73]

To prevent their quarrel degenerating into a petty squabble Scala imaginatively conceded victory once again to Poliziano. He decided to defer replying to Poliziano's last communication from Fiesole, since he was troubled with gout in his right hand and had no amanuensis with him:

> I had already had supper and was trying to go to sleep. But before sleep came to me, I lay turning over in my mind (as I usually do when anything is worrying me) such thoughts as: "I shall reply thus, I shall do this, I shall solve that. That was right, and the philosopher knows it. But nothing can wound Poliziano. Surely he is a friend and a good man? Surely too, he is extremely learned. Did he not come from the common bosom of the Medici, and if with unequal merits at least with equal fortune should he have raged against us—but [paraphrasing Virgil]: 'Let the gods divert the omen on to our enemies first.' "[74]

And so his thoughts continued to chase each other until at last he fell asleep, and in his sleep he dreamt that Giorgio Merula came to him to say he was crazy to engage in a literary battle with Poliziano: "It is lethal and I come to you as a shade from yonder. Indeed Lorenzo de' Medici, fearing for you, sent me from the high heavens to give you this warning."[75] This ref-

---

[72] *Opera*, pp. 380-381. Poliziano's epigram is translated into Latin in his *Opera*, p. 381; and by del Lungo, *Prose*, p. 224. *Culex* is in fact in the feminine gender in Plautus, *Casina*, 2. 3, p. 239: "cana culex"; since he uses it to describe a licentious old man, it may have contributed to Poliziano's verse, but cf. Manni, *Vita*, p. 43.

[73] *Opera*, pp. 382-384 and 386-387, cf. 399-400. Poliziano lectured in 1492-1494 on books of the *Organon*, listed in del Lungo, *Florentia*, p. 180; Bigi, *La cultura del Poliziano*, pp. 70-71. Cf. C. Vasoli, "Il Poliziano maestro di dialettica," *Il Poliziano e il suo tempo, atti del IV Convengo Internazionale di studi sul rinascimento*, Florence, 1957, pp. 161-172.

[74] *Opera*, pp. 389-390, quoting from Virgil, *Aeneid*, 2.190.

[75] *Ibid*. Giorgio Merula, a humanist from Alessandria near Milan and

erence to Lorenzo de' Medici served to transform their dispute into a bitter quarrel about their standing with Lorenzo, with each man's honor at stake. Poliziano immediately returned to themes of his "Ode" against Scala, which he now told Scala Lorenzo had refused to allow him to destroy. Reacting to the repeated insult that his success had been due to fortune alone,[76] Scala delivered his famous account of his achievement, a classic statement of a new man's rise to fame:

> I came to the republic naked, disadvantaged, of the lowest parentage, full of confidence but absolutely penniless, without reputation, patrons or kinsmen. However, Cosimo, Father of our Country, embraced me and received me into the service of his family. Meanwhile the Florentine people elevated me to the Priorate, then to the Gonfaloniership, and finally voted me a member of the Senate and Equestrian Order so unanimously that many thought nothing had ever been done with more popular support. Lorenzo de' Medici's famous utterance about me still survives, that honor had never been better placed in a new man. It is with him that the question of my honor must be discussed, and with all the people of Florence. This I would affirm: I achieved a great deal, more than I would have thought possible or hoped for. Nor did I have anything to bring with me except loyalty and integrity, but these—if I may say so— were always of the highest quality.[77]

---

historian of the Sforza in the court of Lodovico il Moro, had been accused by Poliziano of criticizing his *Miscellanea, Opera*, p. 327 (and Merula's reply, *ibid.*, pp. 331-333, etc.). Their dispute was terminated by Merula's death on 19 March 1494, Gabotto and Badini Confalonieri, *Vita di G. Merula*, pp. 318-332, 339-349; M. Santoro, "La polemica Poliziano-Merula," *Giornale italiano di filologia* 5 (1952): 212-233, discussing unfavorably Merula's recently discovered criticism of Poliziano; Picotti, "Marullo o Mabilio," in *Ricerche umanistiche*, pp. 141-176.

[76] *Opera*, p. 391: "Non enim credo reputasti fortuna dulci nimis ebrius, tantundem te descendisse in literis, quantum ascenderis in honoribus, ut compensatione quadam paria tecum literati fecerint." This, and his reference to bran (below), recall the *Ode*.

[77] *Opera*, pp. 393-394.

As incensed by Scala's account of his relationship with the
Medici and his popularity in Florence as Scala had been by the
slur on his honor, Poliziano attacked Scala more virulently,
mixing schoolboy invective with more damaging criticism of
Scala's relationship with the Medici. On the one hand he repeated his charge that Scala was "a bran-filled monster,"
"monster because you are composed from the droppings of
a monster, filled with bran, because born among the filth of
a grinding mill and therefore entirely worthy of a mill"; referring to Scala's criticism of the present age, he said he was
not surprised that Scala's age displeased him since he also displeased his age, and that Scala should have added to his statement that he came to the republic deprived of all the good
things of life "and rich in all evils." On the other hand, and
more damagingly, he denied Scala's account of his close relationship with the Medici by quoting what Lorenzo de' Medici
used to say to him about Scala:

> Certainly Lorenzo (with whom I lived as part of the family)
> often used to speak to me about you, and he made it plain
> enough that he was keeping alive someone else's opinion
> about you, not his own. You know, however, he often re-
> jected your official letters and gave them to me to rewrite,
> which was why you disliked and envied me in the first
> place. Nor did he allow me to tear up that iambic poem I
> wrote against you, for someone might say it was a pity for
> so good a poem to be buried.[78]

As a final barb, he accused Scala of adulterating the Roman
language by using such unclassical titles as "Vexilliferate" or
"Priorate" and a thousand other such expressions he was unwilling to publish lest it be said that so famous a city as Florence had a scribe who was completely ignorant of Latin literature.[79]

[78] *Ibid.*, p. 398.
[79] *Opera*, pp. 398-399; cf. Kristeller, "An Unknown Correspondence," p.
341. On Scala's use of new names, see ch. 10 below.

What began as a literary dispute ended as bitter rivalry between two Medici partisans who came, as Scala said, "from the common bosom of the Medici." Far from being unequal, their merits, if different, were well matched. They enjoyed the same jokes and used the same weapons of irony and empirical argument.[80] As lawyers interested in law reform and humanists who studied philosophy within the discipline of the liberal arts, they had more in common with each other than with Marsilio Ficino, whom Poliziano accused Scala of maligning.[81] Despite this, Scala's last letter shows how sensitive he still was in matters concerning his honor and achievement, and perhaps the last word should rest with him: "I achieved a great deal, more than I would have thought possible or hoped for." Such achievement inevitably brought its critics, but they were fewer than his posthumous reputation suggests.

[80] On Poliziano's empiricism, see C. Mutini, "Ritagli in materia di umanesimo Laurenziano," *Trimestre*, 2, nos. 3-4 (1968): 14-23; and in general E. Garin, "Poliziano e il suo ambiente," in *Ritratti di umanisti*, Florence, 1967, pp. 131-162; cf. also *Opera*, pp. 141-142 (to Scala), using an inscription in Rome as evidence for correct ancient spelling.

[81] *Opera*, p. 397: "instauratori Platonicae familiae." Ficino may have been one of the followers of astrology whom Scala criticized, and Scala laughed at his description of Poliziano as Hercules (*Opera*, pp. 136 and 392; cf. Ficino's "Apologia" in his *Opera*, 1: 574, 15 September 1489; Poliziano to Ficino, *Opera*, p. 191, and to Scala, *ibid.*, p. 396; Kristeller, *Supplementum*, 2: 281); but on Scala's friendship with Ficino, see above. On Poliziano as a humanist, see his inaugural lecture, the "Lamia," ed. del Lungo, *Florentia*, pp. 133-174; A. Scaglione, "The Humanist as Scholar and Politian's Conception of the *Grammaticus*," *Studies in the Renaissance* 8 (1961): 61-70; Bigi, *La cultura del Poliziano*, pp. 68-79.

CHAPTER IX

Property and Family

To the many debts I owe your Exalted Republic it would add the further one of not being condemned to oblivion by my descendants. *Scala to the officials of the Balìa of Siena, on the purchase of land in Monte Vasone, 1483. (See n. 60 below.)*

Scala's climb to social and economic success was as slow but sure-footed as his climb to political success, and equally shrewd. Both his property in Borgo Pinti and his estate in the Elsa valley were bought in depressed areas when prices were low. But by the time of his death in 1497 Borgo Pinti was the center of large-scale development, so fashionable now that a grandiose palace for the Medici family was designed on the site of Scala's own property.[1] Nearly a hundred years after his death it was sold by his last descendants to a Medici cardinal, subsequently elected Pope Leo XI. Far from crashing from his pinnacle of success as Poliziano had augured, he and his fam-

[1] The plan for this villa at La Crocetta in the hand of Antonio di San Gallo il Vecchio (?) is in Florence, Uffizi, Gabinetto dei Disegni, 282 A, "piantta del sitto de lo Schala in Firenze" and "disegni de lo palazo de' Medici nel sitto de lo Schala e misure d'alttri sitti." It is reproduced by K. von Stegmann and H. von Geymuller, *Die Architektur der Renaissance in Toscana*, 5, Munich, 1885-1908, pt. 3, facing p. 20. The problem of its attribution and date is still unresolved, but the most recent contribution to the debate (G. M. Mariani, "Il disegno per il complesso Mediceo di Via Laura a Firenze," *Palladio*, n.s. 22 (1972): 127-162, with relevant bibliography) favors an early date in the time of Lorenzo il Magnifico (cf. the earlier opinion of Sanpaolesi, "La casa fiorentina," p. 278, as opposed to the post-1512 date suggested by Professor G. Marchini, *Giuliano di San Gallo*, p. 101). If the palace was designed for Lorenzo il Magnifico by Giuliano di San Gallo, it would have involved the destruction of Scala's palace in his lifetime (*pace* Mariano, p. 159, n. 46, although it is true that the full implications of the plan might not have been worked out). But this in itself does not rule out an early date and may on the contrary support one, since Scala would undoubtedly have been expected to sacrifice his large and convenient site for the family to whom he "owed everything" and who helped him to acquire it in the first place. I am grateful for suggestions from Miss Caroline Elam, currently working on the subject of the development of the Innocenti area.

ily maintained the secure place in Florentine society that he—and the Medici—had procured for them.

Bartolomeo first started to pay taxes with his young brother Carlo in April 1459.[2] As Carlo was only a boy at the time, the brothers' tax of 3 *soldi* must have been based on the salary Bartolomeo received from Pierfrancesco de' Medici, and it placed them in the lowest bracket of taxpayers, below whom were only the *miserabili* who paid nothing at all.[3] In October 1459 Bartolomeo was appointed chancellor of the Guelf Party with an annual salary of 96 florins a year for himself and his notary.[4] Thanks to the survival of a ledger of his banker and accountant, Bernardo Rinieri, the next five years are the best documented years of his life and graphically demonstrate Scala's rise from poverty to material and cultural prosperity.[5]

[2] According to his 1469 Catasto, ASF *Catasto* 923, fol. 290r, and ch. 4, n. 21 above. The return itself apparently does not survive: if Scala was living in Pierfrancesco de' Medici's house, his return may have been included in that of the Medici family, although he is not mentioned in it (ASF *MAP* 82, no. 182, 24 December 1458, listing only the 14 intimate members of the family of 50 *bocche* for whom tax concessions were allowed, cf. de Roover, *Banco Medici*, pp. 37-38).

[3] On the distribution of wealth in the 1458 Catasto, de Roover, *Banco Medici*, table 4, p. 43.

[4] ASF *Capt. P. G.* 9 rosso, fol. 55r.

[5] ASF *Conv. Soppr.* 95, 212, my knowledge of which I owe to the generosity of Dr. William Kent, to whom I am deeply indebted. In 1446 the Rinieri were one of only 4 Florentine bankers, apart from the Medici, to whom the Medici manager Giovanni Benci advised giving credit, de Roover, *Banco Medici*, pp. 133, 562. Bernardo separated his capital from his brother Filippo's in 1456 and in 1460 formed two companies with his brothers Filippo and Luca and with Piero Neretti, one in Florence in the names of his brothers (which held Scala's money), one in Pisa in his and Piero Neretti's names; they were replaced in 1463 by one company consisting of the three brothers but trading under the former names, and at the same time Bernardo bought a 5th share in a silk company in his name and that of Niccolò Bartolini (*Conv. Soppr.* 95, 212, fols. 150 left, 156 right, 160 left and right). On 18 May 1456 Bernardo married Bartolomea di Dietisalvi di Nerone di Nigi Dietisalvi (dowry fl. 1500); in 1463 and 1486 he was a member of the Sei di Mercanzia; in 1464 of the Signoria and in 1465 of the college of 12 Buonuomini, refusing to serve as Podestà of Pistoia in 1486 (*ibid.*, fols. 151 left and 161 left).

At first clothes and books receive equal priority, but after Scala rented a house in 1460, household goods, food, wine and the sartorial needs of himself and his brothers compete for his salary: little wonder he complained to Pierfrancesco de' Medici in May 1460 of his "need," having done his "duty in finding a house as I was told to."[6] Professing his dependence on the Medici, he was rewarded then or later with Monte shares worth 500 florins, which were given to him by Cosimo not, as Scala thought, in perpetuity but merely for his lifetime.[7]

Scala opened his account with Bernardo Rinieri on 28 April 1459 by paying in the sum of some 20 florins, supplemented in June by two further payments totaling about 24 florins, 16 from "things of his own which he sold," the remainder presumably from Pierfrancesco de' Medici, for whom he still worked. With this money he spent 17 florins on material for a black gown or *lucco*, drew out 3 florins 15 *soldi* for himself, paid for a lute lesson and made a payment to Cristoforo Landino.[8] For the next five and a half years the Guelf Party provided his basic but not his total income: in 1460 and 1461 he exceeded his Guelf Party salary by about 60 florins, in 1462, after his rise, by about 30 florins, and in 1463 he paid in less than his official salary, suggesting that he continued to work for the Medici at least until 1463, but for less money.[9] In the four complete years described in the account book Scala averaged an annual income of 148 florins and an annual expenditure of 145 florins. He overdrew his account in two years, in 1462 as the result of buying a house in Colle, but the

---

[6] See ch. 2, n. 23 above: "mio debito d'avere trovato casa come mi fu decto"; and on his acquisitions, below.

[7] See ch. 2, n. 41 above.

[8] *Conv. Soppr.* 95, 212, fols. 29 right and 29 left. The money for his own use "gli porttò Carllo suo fratello." Here and subsequently I quote prices to the nearest florin.

[9] See following note and on his Guelf Party rise, ch. 7, n. 5 above. Since the payer is not normally specified, it is not always possible to identify Guelf Party payments in his account, but Scala appears to have been paid fl. 18 every 2 months until 1462, and then, with increasing regularity after the Medici Bank became responsible for administering their finances, fl. 24 every two months (for himself and his notary).

following year he reduced his expenditure to 62 florins and ended it again in credit. Over the total period he spent 89 florins less than he earned.[10]

If these accounts illustrate Scala's financial caution and good husbandry, they also illustrate his youthful poverty. Comparison with the period before 1459 is impossible, but it is clear from the extent and nature of his purchases in the Rinieri accounts how much he had to buy: not only books like Justinian's *Digest* or Cicero's *Orations* but a whole wardrobe of essential clothes and household accoutrements. For himself he bought material for a long black gown for office wear, purple cloth for a cloak, shoes, a scarlet overgarment, a rough linen gown, a simple purple gown to wear in his study, and eleven and a half yards of scarlet taffeta. For his youngest brother Carlo he bought two doublets, a pair of hose, gray cloth and rough lining for a gown. For Andrea, who joined them in Florence in 1461, a doublet and dark red cloth for a cloak. For his house he acquired a set of cutlery, chests, a cupboard, a sideboard, a dining table and tablecloth, a desk, beds, mattresses and bedding, a pair of buckets with chains and a pulley, pots and pans. He had his cesspool emptied, built a well and paved the forecourt of his house. He bought grain, wine, oil, salt and wood. His principal extravagance was books, but although Scala revealed himself to be an early patron of scribes and illuminators who subsequently became famous in Florence, the manuscripts he bought and had copied were classics no humanist and teacher could afford to be without.[11]

The death of Cosimo de' Medici in 1464 and Scala's appointment as first chancellor the following year should have enabled him to sever his dependence on the Medici. But in September 1466, after the Medici regime had been confirmed

[10] The figures are, quoting credit, debit, then balance, in florins, *soldi* and *denari*: *1459* (April-December): 45. 8. 5; 45. 2. 4; 0. 6. 1. *1460*: 157. 8. 11; 167. 10.4; −10. 1. 5. *1461*: 152. 2. 8; 126. 19. 3; 25. 3. 5. *1462*: 163. 5. 7; 224. 1. 10; −60. 16. 3. *1463*: 121. 5. 11; 62. 8. 1; 58. 17. 10. *1464* (January-June): 93. 16. 7; 18. 0. 8; 75. 15. 11. *Total*: 733. 8. 1; 638. 12. 6; 89. 5. 7. The account continues in "Libro B" which has not survived with "Libro A."

[11] See Brown and de la Mare, "Bartolomeo Scala's Dealings."

in power by a *parlamento* on the 2nd, Scala was given a rent-free house in Via Larga by Piero de' Medici, which kept him closely bound to the family.[12] He had already bought a house in Colle, and now he increased the supply of food and wine so vital to a town dweller by buying a piece of land at Bacchereto in Carmignano, which provided him with five and a half barrels of wine and half a barrel of oil a year, as well as other small pieces of land and property in and around Colle.[13] In September 1467 he bought from Angelo di Rinieri del Pace a small house in Via San Gallo, but as he was still living in Piero de' Medici's house in Via Larga nearby, he rented it out and then gave it away as a gift *in causa mortis* in August 1468.[14] At about the same time he rented a farm from the Guelf Party just outside the Porta alla Croce in Florence (now Piazza Beccaria), paying £226 *affiorino* a year for a four-year lease for which his banker Bernardo Rinieri stood surety.[15] Rinieri also acted as Scala's guarantor when he rented a house and farm at Montughi in August 1468 from Nigi di Nerone Dietisalvi for three years. The brother of Dietisalvi, Bernardo Rinieri's father-in-law and one of the exiled leaders of the

---

[12] ASF *Catasto* 923 (Scala's 1469 return), fol. 290v: "Insino a qui, cioè da settenbre 1466 in qua, siamo stati in una chasa di Piero di Chosimo de' Medici . . . sanza nome alchuno di pigione"; cf. Scala's letter to Piero de' Medici of 12 September 1469 (ASF *MAP* 137, 283): "Mi dicesti havevi data la casa per quello stava a voi."

[13] ASF *Catasto* 923, fol. 290r and ch. 1, n. 16 above.

[14] *Ibid.*, and ch. 2, n. 23 above. Angelo and his father Rinieri del Pace had been among the 150 citizens ordered to their villas after the arrest of Girolamo Machiavelli in August 1458 (Rubinstein, *Government*, p. 103, n. 6). On the *donatio causa mortis*, see B. Nicholas, *An Introduction to Roman Law*, Oxford, 1962, pp. 266-267, 269-270; and the *Formularium Modernum et Universale*, Florence, 1488(?), fol. cxxxxi. Scala gave the house to Madonna Lisa di Papino da Bagniano. By 1480 he had sold the house for fl. 140, ASF *Catasto* 1015, fol. 269r.

[15] ASF *Catasto* 923, fol. 290r; *Capt. P. G.* 28 rosso (Locazioni di Beni, 1467-1490), fol. 6r, transaction dated 27 April 1467, to take effect from 1 August; cf. *Capt. P. G.* 29 rosso, fol. 33v (1st series), no. 65: "Uno podere con chasa da llavoratore posto nel populo di Sancto Anbruogio fuori alla porta alla crocie . . . alloghato a messer Bartolomeo Schala chancelliere per anni iiij inchominciati a ddì primo di novembre 1467 per £226 l'anno." Bernardo Rinieri agreed to stand surety for an annual rent of £220 on 6 November (*Conv. Soppr.* 95, 212, fol. 162 left).

Pitti conspiracy in 1466,[16] Nigi was himself deprived of office in 1466. He did not want Scala's name to be mentioned in the contract, and it was doubtless Rinieri who arranged the deal and promised to guarantee the 500 florins deposit Nigi demanded from Scala in addition to an annual rent of 35 florins.[17]

Scala's reasons for wanting to rent Nigi's former residence on such conditions must be connected with his marriage to Maddalena Benci earlier that year.[18] Once again he had been helped by his friend and banker Bernardo Rinieri, who had chosen Scala to be godfather to his first-born child in 1462 and who now lent him and stood surety for a headdress decorated with 320 pearls, "which he said was to work for the wife."[19] But although Maddalena brought with her a dowry of 1,200 florins (1,000 in the Monte, the remainder in nuptial gifts), she involved Scala in heavier expenditure than he could afford and he soon found himself in debt.[20] Their first child was born the following year and in August 1469 Scala renounced an agreement he had signed at the beginning of the year to buy the half-share of a house in San Casciano.[21] Evicted from his rent-free house in Via Larga by Piero de' Medici, he tried to recover from the Bankers' Guild the sum of 100 florins he

16 See Rubinstein, *Government*, pp. 165 and 166, n. 1, also his article "La confessione di Francesco Neroni e la congiura antimedicea del 1466"; *ASI* 126 (1968): 373-387.

17 ASF *Conv. Soppr.* 95, 212, fol. 163 left, 8 August 1468: "E perchè detto Nigi non volle il chontratto dicessi in detto messer Bartolomeo, dice in Nicholaio di Bartolino Bartolini [Rinieri's partner], che lo fu a chonpiacenza di detto messer Bartolomeo . . . e quando riarà la detta posizione, arenderà detti fl. 500."

18 See ch. 3, n. 48 above.

19 ASF *Conv. Soppr.* 95, 212, fol. 162 right, 10 March 1468: "Richordo chome questo dì sopradetto io prestai a messer Bartolomeo di G[i]ovanni da ccholle chancelliere della Signoria di Firenze acchatto da me uno frenello di perle grosse di perle 320 . . . disse per operare per la donna." On the christening, *ibid.*, fol. 159 right.

20 ASF *Catasto* 923, fol. 290r; cf. n. 22 below. His difficulties were increased, he says in his tax return, "per non avere potuto avere del Monte e danari della dote nè lle paghe." On the crisis of the Monte delle Doti in 1470, see L. F. Marks, "The Financial Oligarchy in Florence under Lorenzo," *Italian Renaissance Studies*, ed. Jacob, pp. 128-131.

21 ASF *Notarile* M 530 (Niccolò Michelozzi), fols. 1r and 2r (4 February and 23 August 1469); cf. ch. 3 above.

claimed to have spent on the house, and at the same time he litigated with his father-in-law over Maddalena's dowry: little wonder, perhaps, that he "almost seemed to exceed his office" in his desire to be honored by the duke of Milan that year, or that Galeazzo Maria Sforza's gift of 200 ducats made him "happier than ever before in my whole life."

Scala's financial position is summarized in his 1469 tax return. Apart from his shares in the Monte (valued at only 1,162 florins), and a mule valued at 18 florins, his only other taxable property was the small piece of land he had bought in Carmignano in 1466. He was in debt to the sum of 600 florins on account of "the money he had expended on his wife" and his loan to Nigi Dietisalvi. His household now consisted of himself, his brothers Andrea and Carlo, Maddalena his wife, Giovanni, the ten-year-old son of his eldest brother Tomè, and his five-month-old baby Giovanna. His total *valsente* or estimated capital value was reckoned as 1,181 florins, from which he was allowed to deduct 200 florins for each member of his family, at first counted as four and then as six mouths or *bocche*, and in addition 86 florins for his place of habitation, reckoned from the rent of his house opposite "the large house" for which he had paid nothing.[22] Since his deductions totaled more than his capital, he fell into the category of citizens who had no taxable wealth or *sovrabbondante* and were taxed by agreement with the catasto officials. At first he was charged no more than 1 florin, but the supplement of 19 *soldi* 3 *denari* they subsequently added suggests that they may have suspected the chancellor was not quite as poor as his return indicated: more affluent than in 1458 but not one of the richer citizens.[23]

---

[22] ASF *Catasto* 923, 290v. Maddalena's dowry of fl.1,000 in fact consisted of Monte shares totaling fl.4,341 11s; but in view of their low value, Scala's total investment, including Cosimo de' Medici's fl.500, was valued at only fl.1,161 19s 6d. According to Marks ("The Financial Oligarchy," p. 129, n. 1), the market price of ordinary Monte stock stood at 35 in 1470.

[23] On citizens taxed "per composizione," de Roover, *Banco Medici*, p. 37, who comments that they were not among the wealthy or even the well-to-do and rarely paid more than fl.1. On the Florentine catasto in general,

More purchases of land followed: a farm at Scandicci in October 1470 (the one toward which Galeazzo Maria Sforza probably contributed 200 ducats),[24] a month later a small piece of land in Montevarchi, which supplied him with two barrels of Trebbiano wine at his door each year,[25] and more land and houses in Colle.[26] But they did nothing to solve the problem of where Scala and his growing family were to live in Florence. Finally on 22 January 1473, scarcely a month before being elected to the Signoria, he acquired: "a house for my habitation with gardens in the parish of San Piero Maggiore in Via di Pinti near the gateway [Porta Pinti]. . . . It is here that I have built and spent my money."[27] This was the nucleus of Scala's extensive property in Borgo Pinti that survives today, reduced in size and transformed by the work of later genera-

---

G. Canestrini, *La scienza e l'arte di stato*, Florence, 1862, pp. 108-116, and on the *composizione*, p. 116. A direct comparison with 1458 is impossible because the 1469 returns are incomplete, but on the basis of the 1458 returns, Scala in 1469 would have ranked among the 661 families (6.21%) paying a tax of fl.1-2, with at least 1,255 families paying higher assessments, see de Roover, table 4, p. 43.

[24] See Scala's 1480 Catasto, ASF *Catasto* 1015, fol. 260r; cf. ASF *Notarile*, M 530 (N. Michelozzi), fols. 7v-8r (15 October 1470). R. Fubini suggests that the duke of Milan contributed toward the purchase of Scala's house in Borgo Pinti ("Note Machiavelliane," p. 376, n. 5 *bis*), but this transaction did not take place for another two and a half years, nor was it purchased with money at that time, see below.

[25] ASF *Notarile* M 530, fol. 9r-v (29 November 1470). By a separate deed, the land was leased by Scala to the vendor for 3 years in return for "barilium duorum boni et puri tribiani positi Flor[entiae] ad domum habitationis dicti locatoris ad omnes expensas dictorum conductorum" (fol. 9v.).

[26] See ch. 1, n. 16 above.

[27] ASF *Catasto* 1015, fol. 260r: "Una chasa per mio abitare, chon orti . . . è el luogho dove ò murato e dove mi sono chonsumato"; cf. Manni, *Vita*, p. 18; Sanpaolesi, "La casa fiorentina," pp. 275-288, where he publishes an incomplete and inaccurate version of Scala's catasto (p. 280, n. 4). Scala's house is also referred to in C. von Fabriczy, "Aus dem Gedenkbuch Francesco Baldovinettis," *Repertorium für Kunstwissenschaft* 28 (1905): 544; W. Limburger, *Die Gebäude von Florenz*, Leipzig, 1910, p. 156; and L. Ginori Lisci, *I Palazzi di Firenze nella storia e nell' arte*, 1 (Florence, 1972), no. 80, pp. 529-536.

tions, but still impressive in its extent and concept.[28] Built around an atrium, with a classically inspired frieze running round its walls, it provided in addition to the normal rooms a chapel where masses could be said, a study and a loggia; outhouses for cooking and washing; stables; a garden with a fishpond, mound, streams, paths and a lawn; and land for growing grain and wine—*rus in urbe* on the Albertian model or, as Poliziano mockingly described it, "open fields and an urban villa in the safe pomerium inside the city walls."[29] It combined elegance with practicality and, like everything else, it was achieved *gradatim*, if not with public money, as Poliziano suggested, at least with all the influence at Scala's command.

The land inside the third circle of city walls, left undeveloped after famine and plague had halved the population in the middle of the fourteenth century, consisted of market gardens and tumbledown cottages owned by monasteries and religious corporations. In 1462 the Monte had been authorized to buy property belonging to churches and hospitals not paying taxes to provide houses for the people, who were suffering from a shortage of housing, and in April 1474 a law was passed allowing tax exemption for twenty years to anyone "building

[28] On the originality of the house, Sanpaolesi, "La casa fiorentina," esp. pp. 275-276; Parronchi, "The Language of Humanism," p. 108. The house was transformed by the della Gherardesca in the seventeenth century and the garden by the architect Giuseppe Cacialli, 1770-1828 (see E. Brües, "Palazzo Capponi—Incontri, der neue Sitz des Kunsthistorischen Instituts in Florenz," *Mitteilungen des Kunsthistorischen Instituts in Florenz* 12 (1965-1966): 323, nn. 25 and 26; and F. Fantozzi's *Pianta geometrica di Firenze* (1843), contrasting with the layout in S. Bonsignori's plan of 1584, both in R. Ciullini, *Di una raccolta di antiche carte e vedute della città di Firenze* [Florence, 1924]; cf. G. Boffito and A. Mori, *Piante e vedute di Firenze,* Florence, 1926). I am indebted to the help and interest of Professor Middeldorf, former director of the German Institute, and to the hospitality on more than one occasion of the Società Metallurgica Italiana, present owners of the palace.

[29] L. B. Alberti, *De re aedificatoria,* ed. Orlandi and Portoghesi, 5.6.14, vol. 1, pp. 356-359, 400-403; and n. 46 below; cf. Poliziano's "Ode," ed. del Lungo, *Prose* p. 273; "Intraque tutum moenibus pomerium / Agros patentes possidet; / Villamque Dives publico peculio / Insanus urbanam struit" (but cf. n. 64 below).

houses from their foundations in open places."[30] Later, in 1489, the government appealed to the pope to allow land still owned by religious institutions to be built on, in a further attempt to release this land for domestic purposes,[31] but by then Scala had acquired all he needed from the religious institutions surrounding his estate. Property development, like benefice hunting, was another field in which Scala and the Medici could combine public and private interest in fighting to establish the authority of the secular state over the church.

Scala acquired the original piece of land and house that formed the nucleus of his estate from the Silk Guild of Por Santa Maria on 22 January 1473, at a price to be fixed by Giuliano de' Medici.[32] It was owned by the Ospedale degli Innocenti, Brunelleschi's Foundling Hospital, but as it was held for her lifetime by a widow, Madonna Piera di Frosino della Volpaia, it was arranged by Giuliano de' Medici that Scala should pay her an annual rent of £108 during her lifetime and only after her death should he pay the sum of 500 florins to the Silk Guild acting on behalf of the Foundling Hospital—a convenient arrangement for Scala, short as he was of capital, especially as he was apparently outlived by Madonna Piera.[33]

---

[30] Rinuccini, *Ricordi storici*, p. xc; and ASF *Provv.* 165, fols. 26v-27r (26 April 1474), summarized in *Carte di corredo* 8, fol. 220v, as a law allowing "domos edificare a fundamentis cuique liceat in locis apertis et habeat beneficium exemptionis annorum xx."

[31] 2 April 1489, ed. Bandini, *Collectio*, p. 14; cf. Sanpaolesi, "La casa fiorentina," pp. 278-279, n. 3.

[32] ASF *Notarile* B 732 (Antonio di ser Battista Bartolomei, 1472), fol. 216v: "pro illo pretio et quantitatem pretii solvendum . . . prout declaratum fuerit per Magnificum virum Julianum Pieri Cosmi de' Medicis" (22 January 1473); cf. fols. 230v (29 January) and 243v (9 February 1473) declaring the price to be "florenorum quingentorum sigilli . . . solvendum eisdem . . . prima die mensis proximi seguentis post obitum domine Piere filie Fruosini de Volpaia, quae debet et potest tenere talia bona durante eius vita."

[33] See Scala's 1480 Catasto, ASF *Catasto* 1015, fol. 260r; 1495-1498 Decima, ASF *Decima Rep.* 26 A-F, fol. 359r; and on the initial transaction, ASF *Notarile* B 732 (above), fol. 216r-v; Florence, Ospedale degli Innocenti, *Libro di debitori e creditori 1472-1479* (which Professor Richard Goldthwaite kindly helped me to find), fol. 79r (=78v), 1473, giving the bounda-

While the house was being rebuilt, Scala acquired other pieces of land and houses adjoining it. On 7 June 1475 he bought from the Foundling Hospital a small holding to the north of the property toward the city walls, for which he had to pay "by way of exchange . . . the equivalent in Florence of a return of 52 florins a year," in other words, by exchanging it for other property to avoid the prohibition against the sale of land and property by ecclesiastical institutions. This time the Medici were less directly involved in the transaction, but among the properties Scala exchanged for land in Borgo Pinti was a shop he bought, doubtless for this purpose, from Alamanno de' Medici, with money provided by his father-in-law Giovanni Benci.[34] The previous tenant of the holding, a sand merchant, was heavily in debt but stayed where he was because of the shortage of dwellings in Florence. The land produced thirty bushels of wheat, thirty bushels of barley and twenty-five barrels of wine a year, of which Scala, farming on a *mezzadria* basis, took half. It also provided the land for "the freshwater pond, the mound, the streams, the paths, the lawn, the loggia and the study," of

ries as the road, property belonging to the Innocenti on two sides, and property of the Cestello, with the condition "che detto Messer Bartolomeo non possa addimandare detto podere se non dopo la morte di detta Madonna Piera, nè a llui possano essere addimandati e detti fl. 500 se non dopo la morte di detta Madonna Piera mesi ii et allora sia tenuto paghargli a nostra richiesta, e fatto detto paghamento il podere sia suo libero e chome di sua chosa ne possa disporre."

[34] ASF *Notarile* B 734 (Antonio di Battista Bartolomei, 1474-1476), fols. 347r-349v, describing the property ("una domus . . . et duobus peciis terre") as in the parish of S. Piero Maggiore, bounded by the city walls, Via Pinti, property of the Innocenti, Scala's house and by "wheat"; cf. ASF *Catasto* 1015, fol. 260v, where the date is given as 1 June, also the account book of Alamanno di Bernardo di Messer Salvestro de' Medici, 1475-1483 (Philadelphia, University of Pennsylvania, Van Pelt Library, MS Lea 482, the reference to which I owe to the kindness of Dr. Gino Corti), recording the sale to Scala on 7 June 1475 of a shop in the parish of S. Leo, "sotto la volta degli Anglucci," for fl.150 provided by his father-in-law, Giovanni Benci: "E aquista 'l bottegha detto messer Bartolomeo insieme chon altri bene dette in canbio allo Spedale de' poveri Innocenti di Firenze per beni da loro auti dentro alla Porta a Pinti."

which only "the most beautiful vivaio" with its crystalline waters filled with "a great quantity of different fish" (as it was described in the time of Alessandro de' Medici) now survives: the garden has been relandscaped according to eighteenth-century taste, and the loggia and study must have been subsumed in later additions to the house on the north side.[35]

Nearly two years later, in March 1477, Scala added another strip of land with a laborer's cottage to his property, this time on the south side of the main house, "toward the corner at Monteloro." He bought it with papal license from the Cestello, but only eight days later the monastery petitioned to be allowed to construct houses itself on its property, to avoid its neighbors using their influence to occupy its possessions and convert them to their own use "by fair means and foul."[36] Legally or illegally, Scala put his new possession to

[35] "Un bellissimo vivaio che sta in detto giardino fatto a mo[do] di pozzo poscia che l'acque sieno sempre cristalline e . . . vi si vede gran pezza di vari pesci che quei che gli vanno a vedere . . . reprenderanno gran contento," BNF MS Targioni Tozzetti 56 (2) (Agostino del Riccio, Agric. sper.), fol. 170r. Since the loggia was built on the piece of land to the north of the main house, it cannot be the one now filled in to the south of the building, and it and the study were doubtless destroyed or incorporated into the second courtyard to the north of the principal one, which first appears in a map of 1783. At the bottom of this piece of land, among the trees, is a small single-roomed building with a chimney, its two windows and door surmounted by a classical frieze, which probably dates from the time of Cacialli. As for "el monte," the larger of the mounds which now survives was evidently constructed from ruins of an earlier period, possibly when the third city walls were destroyed after 1870, with steps made from stone engraved with (15th-16th cent.?) lettering.

[36] ASF *Notarile* M 227 (Amanzo Martini 1476-1477), fol. 125r-v (13 March 1477): "unum praedium cum terris laborativis . . . cum duabus domibus" (but lacking boundary descriptions), and following note (the "canto a Monteloro" was below Scala's house on the corner of Borgo Pinti and the Via de' Pilastri, now Via della Colonna, *Stradario storico e amministrativo della città e del comune di Firenze*, Florence, 1913, p. 91, no. 645); ASF *Diplomatico, Cestello*, petition dated 21 March 1477 (my knowledge of which I owe to the generosity of Miss Alison Luchs), referring to the "bona seu possessiones et funda propter vicinitatem nonnullorum civium florentinorum cupientium huiusmodi bona propter eorum potentiam occupare et per fas et nephas ad eorum utilitatem convertere." On the Cestello, or S. Maria Maddalena de' Pazzi as it was called after 1628, Paatz, *Kirchen*, 4:90-121.

good use, the cottage he made into a kitchen, laundry and stable to serve his house while the land added a half share of thirty bushels of wheat and barley and fifteen barrels of wine to his annual harvesting of supplies.[37]

Two months later he bought "a little old holding along the walls, with a ruined house" in which to house his servant and the gardener who was constructing his mound and pond. This holding, subsequently called "the poderino," belonged to San Michele Bisdomini and was in its parish, running along the northern boundary of Scala's property beside the city walls apparently as far as the present Via Gino Capponi. It consisted of "an attic, living room, cellar, courtyard and well, with a garden and a piece of cultivated land with fruit trees and some vines," and even its vendor admitted it was in a bad condition because it was in "a solitary position and only paupers were willing to live there." Once again the sale was transacted by means of an exchange "for the greater benefit of the church," which Scala effected by giving San Michele Bisdomini the right of entry to a shop beside Orsanmichele acquired by him only a week earlier.[38]

Apart from a house and garden in Borgo Pinti below the present Via G. Giusti, which Scala and his brother Andrea first rented from the Guelf Party in 1479 and Bartolomeo then acquired,[39] the Borgo Pinti estate was complete. The rebuilding of the principal house must have been well advanced by March 1475 when Scala was granted permission to build an oratory with an altar in the house he had "recently constructed

[37] See ASF *Catasto* 1015, fol. 260r: "e lla chasetta da llavoratore ò ridotta a cchucina e a buchato e stalla, a servigio della mia chasa dell' abitazione."

[38] ASF *Notarile* B 2318 (A. Braccesi, 1468-1501), fols. 107r-113v ("unam domum cum terreno, palcho, camera, cella, curia, puteo et orto et cum uno petiolo terre laborative fructate et cum aliquibus vitibus," bounded on two sides by the "via communis," and on two by Scala's property: "cum dicta domus ruinam fere minetur et male culta sit et eius habitatio sit quasi deserta et posita in loco solitario, non reperitur aliquis qui dictam domum et bona conducat, nisi quaedam pauperes persone e quibus pensio nunquam exigitur integraliter," fols. 109r-110r); cf. ASF *Catasto*, 1015, fol. 260v.

[39] See n. 75 below.

in the parish of San Piero Maggiore."[40] Later a separate oratory was built within the precincts of the Cestello opposite at the instigation of Scala or his son Giuliano, which was given in an incomplete state to the Florentine Academy of Design in 1568 by Giulio Scala.[41]

Both the house in Borgo Pinti and the oratory in the Cestello have been attributed to Giuliano da San Gallo on stylistic grounds.[42] The design and proportion of its inner courtyard resemble a Roman atrium more closely than the loftier colonnaded courtyards of other Florentine palaces of this date, while the barrel vaulting of the arcade, decorated with small highly decorated boxes (*a cassettoni*), employs a new technique also used by Giuliano da San Gallo in his villa for Lorenzo de' Medici at Poggio a Caiano.[43] If the whole house was designed by him and not merely the atrium, it must have been one of the architect's first commissions in Florence, the

[40] ASF *Notarile* B 2318 (above), fol. 45r-v (23 March 1475); ed. Manni, *Vita*, pp. 22-24: "in aedibus tuis, quas nuper in B. Petri Maioris Parrochia construxisti." Manni dates it as it is subscribed, "20 May 1477," but as Patetta convincingly demonstrates ("La Nencia da Barberino," pp. 162-163, n. 2), this disagrees with both the indiction and papal year as given, as well as with its position in the *notarile* and the date at the head of the document, and must therefore be incorrect. Manni was also wrong in identifying this chapel with the rotonda in the Cestello (see Sanpaolesi, "Una rotonda sangallesca scomparsa," *Palladio* 7 (4) (1943): 52; cf., however, the draft of his biography, Vat. Lat. 8225, fol. 330v: "huius oratorii domestici verba faciens Pocciantus, nescio quo pacto erraverit, inquiens," etc.).

[41] Sanpaolesi, "Una rotonda," pp. 51-58; cf. ASF *Accademia del Disegno* 25, fol. 40 left (the reference to which I owe to Mrs. Mary Gibbons), concerning a common wall between the Cestello and the "capella o principio di capella che oggi tenghono li Accademici," which "l'avessero fatta o frati overo Bartolomeo Scala" before 1544 when the Cestello rented a house to Giuliano Scala (whom the document confuses with Giulio). There is also a seventeenth-century reference to "quella Cappella principiata dalli [inserted above: *Bartolomeo*] Scali" in ASF *Comp. Relig. Soppr.* C XVIII, 396, 18-S, fol. 51 (the reference to which I owe to Miss Alison Luchs).

[42] Sanpaolesi, "Una rotonda," and (on the house) "La casa fiorentina," esp. pp. 275, 281-283; Marchini, *Giuliano da San Gallo*, pp. 31-32, 88-89; Chastel, *Art et humanisme*, pp. 137, 155, 174-175.

[43] Sanpaolesi, "La casa fiorentina," pp. 282-283; Marchini, *Giuliano da San Gallo*, p. 89.

harbinger of several other buildings in Borgo Pinti, including his own family palace.[44] Without relevant documents the problem remains unresolved, but in the light of what we now know about Scala's patronage of scribes and illuminators who subsequently became famous, it would not be surprising for him to have employed one of the commune's architects who only later achieved fame.[45] The design of Scala's house may also have been influenced by Alberti, who was working on plans for the tribune of SS. Annunziata nearby at the time of his death in 1472.[46] Perhaps Scala remembered, too, the simple two-storied Borromeo palace where he lived for a year as a young man, decorated with illustrations of Aesop's *Fables*, which could have inspired the frieze of fables decorating the atrium of his house—except that his were fables of his own invention from his *Hundred Apologues* and not Aesop's.[47]

This stucco frieze has been compared to the frieze at Poggio a Caiano and given an autobiographical significance.[48] Cer-

[44] On his other buildings, Marchini, *Giuliano da San Gallo*, pp. 11-12, 84-85, 89; and 42, 91-92. Sanpaolesi ("La casa fiorentina," p. 275) describes Scala's house as "fra le sue prime opere," but Marchini places it chronologically later than he told me he would now accept.

[45] See Brown and de la Mare, "Bartolomeo Scala's Dealings." Although Giuliano da San Gallo's work on the fortifications of Colle di Val d'Elsa (which Scala may well have been instrumental in procuring for him) is generally attributed to the year 1479, following Milanesi in his edition of Vasari (*Vite*, Florence, 4: 269-270n.), he cannot have worked on the new walls at least until after the town was restored to Florence by Alfonso of Calabria in June 1481 (Biadi, *Storia*, p. 142), and n. 58 below.

[46] Cf. n. 29 above; and Sanpaolesi, "La casa fiorentina," p. 275 (and on the influence of Brunelleschi, pp. 281-282). On Alberti's influence on the Rucellai garden at Quaracchi with its pond, lawn, paths and "pogiuolo," see B. Patzak, *Die Renaissance- und Barockvilla in Italien*, 2 (*Palast und Villa in Toscana*), Leipzig, 1913, 2: 97-98.

[47] Professor Parronchi has convincingly demonstrated that the frieze illustrates Scala's own *Apologues* in "The Language of Humanism," pp. 122-125.

[48] Parronchi, "The Language of Humanism," and Chastel, *Art et humanisme*, pp. 277-278 (cf. p. 175), quoted by Parronchi. Both writers provide a plan of the courtyard and Parronchi quotes the texts of the relevant apologues, Parronchi, pp. 112-122; Chastel, p. 278. On the frieze at Poggio a Caiano, Chastel, pp. 217-225. Cf. the roundels in the Medici courtyard, given a Lucretian and neoplatonic interpretation by U. Wester and

tainly the panel Negligentia showing Poverty before the Portico of Apollo begging to Mercury, the god of trade and business, is autobiographical, bearing as it does Scala's *impresa* of a slanting ladder on the Portico of Apollo immediately above the figure of Poverty. Had Scala known Petronius' satirical account of dinner with the *nouveau riche* Trimalchio, whose walls were decorated with a mural of Trimalchio, "holding a wand of Mercury and being led into Rome by Minerva . . . drawn in great detail with descriptions underneath," he might have hesitated to lay himself open to similar parody—or was he again being ironical at his own expense?[49] Irony is present in many of the panels portraying different facets of human life. Although the precise meaning of the frieze as a whole is not perhaps clear, it illustrates a Stoic attitude to life that was very much Scala's own.[50]

By the end of 1480 Scala was installed in his house in Borgo Pinti with his wife, six children and a substantial number of servants. It was in this year that his wife at last gave birth to a son, Giuliano, his last child and sole heir.[51] Scala's brothers

---

E. Simon, "Die Reliefmedaillons im Hofe des Palazzo Medici zu Florenz," *Jahrbuch der Berliner Museen*, 7 (1965): 15-91, esp. 49-91.

[49] Although the *Cena Trimalchionis* from Petronius' *Satyricon* was discovered by Poggio in 1423, it disappeared again apparently without trace until about 1650, when it was rediscovered in Trau, see A. Rini, *Petronius in Italy from the 13th Century to the Present Time*, New York, 1937, pp. 10-17; Sabbadini, *Le scoperte*, 2: 240; and now A. C. de la Mare, "The Return of Petronius to Italy," *Medieval Learning and Literature: Essays Presented to R. W. Hunt*, ed. J.J.G. Alexander and M. T. Gibson, Oxford, 1976, pp. 220-254. On Mercury as the god of traders, Pauly-Wissova, *Real-Encyclopaedie*, p. 978; and on Minerva as the "conduttrice del trionfatore che torna nell' Urbe," F. Magi, "L'adventus di Trimalchione e il Fregio A della Cancelleria," *Archeologia classica* 23, pt. 1 (1971): 88-92.

[50] Discussed more fully in ch. 13 below.

[51] See ASF *Catasto* 1015, fol. 269r (where he is described as "one month old"). The birth of this son is alluded to in a letter from ser Piero Cennini to Tommaso Ridolfi (4 November 1480, ASF *Strozz.* ser 3, 247, fol. 138r, the reference to which I owe to Dr. William Kent): "A Messer Bartolomeo Schala è nato uno fanciul maschio, se ve ne volete con lui rallegrare"; cf. Naldo Naldi's epigram, "Ad Bartholomeum Scalam de puero sibi nuper nato," *Epigrammaton liber*, pp. 36-37.

and nephew no longer lived with him, and in their place we find a fifty-year-old lady companion for his wife (a respected figure mentioned in his will) who was paid 9 florins a year plus shoes and clothing;[52] for himself a secretary who also had the task of teaching his five daughters to read, expenses and clothing paid by Scala with any additional payment at Scala's discretion,[53] and a servant boy on the same basis.[54] In addition he employed a servant girl,[55] a gardener and a nurse for his baby son.[56]

The building of his house and birth of five daughters had taken its toll of Scala's money. His estimated taxable wealth in the 1480 catasto was less than half what it had been ten years earlier, 463 instead of 1,181 florins. But like a modern capitalist he had shrewdly converted his taxable wealth into liabilities and nontaxable trusts, and as a result he was taxed only 2 florins 7 *soldi* and 8 *denari* on the basis of the new progressive scale introduced by this catasto. The scale ranged from 7 percent for taxable incomes below 50 florins to 22 percent for incomes of 400 florins and more. Since Scala's taxable income was assessed at only 31 florins 4 *soldi* and 11 *denari*, taking no account of his salary and the perquisites of his office, he was accordingly taxed at the lowest rate of 7 percent.[57]

[52] Madonna Lisa, see n. 84 below.

[53] Ser Chimenti "di Piero nostro di casa," as Scala calls him in a letter to Fra Santi (January 1483 (?), Modena MS, fol. 37v), in which he refers to his hope of acquiring the Pieve of S. Andrea a Doccia for him.

[54] "quello che ò a presente a nome Durante," son of an "arotatore di rinpetto alla Zeccha" who was living free of rent in Borgo Pinti in 1495-1498 (see Scala's Decima, ASF *Decima Rep.* 26 A-F, fol. 358r: "padre di Durante mio familiare").

[55] Although "non dicho el nome perchè si mutano," he divulges that the present girl was called Costanza, aged 25, from Castellina in southern Tuscany, paid fl.10 a year with a shirt and pair of shoes.

[56] The gardener was paid 1 large florin a month, the nurse £8 a month and expenses. In addition, Scala declares, "tengho una chavalchatura chontinovamente."

[57] On the 1480 Catasto, see de Roover, *Banco Medici*, pp. 39-41; Canestrini, *La scienza e l'arte di stato*, p. 235. By taxable income is meant 7 percent of the *valsente* or capital worth of the taxpayer, which did not include salaries or monetary payments, leaving Scala's relatively high salary as chancellor and other payments (such as his fl.200 salary as chancellor of

After 1480 Scala acquired land to develop as a country estate on the borders of Florence and Siena. The land had been ravaged by the Pazzi war, which had been fought over this territory, and the signing of peace between Florence and Siena in 1481 was a politically as well as economically good moment to invest there.[58] Lying between the range of hills that used to separate the Florentine state and the Elsa valley from Siena, at the foot of the green wooded slopes of Monte Vasone, is a villa that must be where Scala's house once stood with its small chapel of Santa Maria nearby.[59] It was here, "below Monte Vasone and almost in its roots" that Scala endowed the small Augustinian Hermit church of Santa Maria Maddalena with land after he was granted its patronage by Innocent VIII in 1484, having one year earlier asked permission from the government of Siena to acquire land from them a few yards from the house "he had begun to build" at the foot of Monte Vasone.[60] Scala still owned it in 1492, but two years

the Dieci or money received for private letters, see Marzi, *Cancelleria*, pp. 99, 139) untaxed. His principal house in Borgo Pinti counted as a liability instead of an asset during Madonna Piera's lifetime, but as it was "the house of his habitation," it would in any case have been untaxed.

[58] On the state of the town of Colle after the war, see ASF *SS. Delib. sp. aut.* 35, fols. 115v-116r (24 August 1481); *Provv.* 173, fols. 12r-13r (26 April 1482) helping the "fessi Collenses" to repair their walls; Matteo Franco's letter of 12 May 1485 (translated by Ross, *Lives*, p. 268), describing the town as "tumbledown and ruined."

[59] According to inscriptions in the chapel, the villa of S. Chimento and the chapel formerly belonged to the Accarisi family of Siena, who bought back and restored them after "bellica patriae incendia" in the sixteenth century. It had been decreed on 25 April 1471 (Siena, AS *Colle di Val d'Elsa* 8, "Capitula super Finibus Collensium et Senensium," fol. 26r; cf. Rinuccini, *Ricordi storici*, pp. cxiii-cxiv) that "nel sopradetto poggio di Monte Vasone per alcuna di esse Communità non si possa nè debba per alcun tempo edificare alcuna fortezza nè casa per alcun modo."

[60] Scala to the priors of Siena (13 October 1483, London, British Library, Add. MS 21, 519, fol. 5): "presso alla casa che ho cominciata a poche braccia," in order that "non sarei dato a oblivione da' miei posteri"; ASF *Notarile* B 2321, fol. 202v: "quae quidem terra est sita sub dicto Monte Vasonis et in ipsius pene radicibus"; cf. ch. 4, n. 132 above. On the chapel, see Repetti, *Dizionario*, 3:551: "un convento di Romitani . . . eretto in Monte Vasone fino dal sec. XIII"; and Innocent VIII's bull of 28 December

later he may have exchanged it for a small farm at San Martino la Palma and a house in Montughi belonging to his nephew Jacopo di Tomè, the eldest surviving member of his family to remain in Colle.[61]

Scala is reputed also to have owned a villa at San Domenico at Fiesole on the old road from Porta Pinti to Fiesole.[62] It was while the villa belonged to the Guadagni in the early eighteenth century that it was apparently first associated with Scala, and subsequently with the composition there of his *History of the Florentine People*.[63] The accounts themselves disagree as to whether the villa was sold soon after Scala's death to the widow of a Venetian mentioned by Vasari, or whether its contents were inherited by the convent of San Clemente

1484, Rome, ASV, Reg. Vat. 683, fol. lxvr: "ecclesiam eiusdem Sancte [Maria Magdalena] de Monte Vasone . . . que ut ab aliquibus asseritur olim ad domum Sancti Augustini de Colle Vallis Else Ordinis Fratrum Heremitarum . . . pertinebat."

[61] ASF *Decima Rep.* 26 A-F, fol. 358v, referring to his exchange of property with Jacopo di Tomè, to whom he gave "le mia posesione da Colle." Scala still owned the estate in 1492 according to a letter from the Florentine Signoria to the government of Siena asking for its help in recovering goods stolen from it, 14 November 1492, in Manni, *Vita*, pp. 15-16; the letter was taken to Siena by Andrea Scala.

[62] The reconstruction of this villa, previously called the Villa Pisa or delle Lune, is described by G. Marchini, "Aggiunte a Giuliano da Sangallo," *Commentarii*, 1 (1950): 34-38, who accepts on Manni's authority (*Vita*, p. 20) that it belonged to Scala and suggests it may have descended from Scala to Cornelia Salviati, widow of Girolamo Martini, the "Venetian" who figures in Vasari's account of it (*Vite*, 4:275).

[63] S. Salvini in *Giornale de' Letterati d'Italia* 22, Venice, 1715, art. 11, p. 413. He was cited in 1753 by Zeno, *Dissertazioni Vossiane*, 2:259; followed by Richa, *Notizie istoriche*, 5 (Florence, 1757): 257-258, according to whom the convent of San Clemente received among other things from Scala's heirs, the "Villa della Luna sotto Fiesole, che inoggi è dei Marchesi Guadagni da Santo Spirito"; in 1768 by Manni, *Vita*; in 1800 by A. M. Bandini, *Lettere XII della città di Fiesole e suoi contorni*, Siena, 1800, p. 45: "Di questa villa fù il fondatore il celebre B.S. . . . et dalla di lui vita scritta da D. M. Manni . . . sappiamo che quivi scrisse la sua Istoria Fiorentina"; and in 1856 by F. Fantozzi, *Nuova guida della città di Firenze*, Florence, 1856, p. 747, etc.

on the death of Scala's grandson in 1585, and without further evidence the question must remain an open one.[64]

Before he died in 1497 Scala prepared a final statement of his economic position for the 1495-1498 Decima. He had already sold a piece of land from his Borgo Pinti estate in 1490, and by 1495 he no longer possessed his property in Scandicci, but these losses were compensated for by vineyards and land bequeathed to his wife by her mother Alessandra Benci in 1486.[65] He may have had other investments not recorded in his return, quite apart from his official salary and extra payments, but to judge from his land holdings, which were valued in the 1495-1498 Decima at only 182 florins, Scala was not a rich man when he died.[66] His salary had been halved by the repub-

---

[64] See Marchini and Richa, nn. 62 and 63 above. I have been able to find only a "breve ristretto" of Giulio di Giuliano Scala's will drawn up by Francesco Parenti on 13 October 1585 (ASF *Conv. Soppr.* 125, 72, no. 62; cf. n. 110 below), but it does not refer to this villa or its furnishings. Apostolo Zeno (*Dissertazioni Vossiane*, 2: 259), followed by del Lungo in his edition of Poliziano's "Ode" against Scala (*Prose*, p. 273; cf. n. 29 above), suggests that the "Villamque Dives publico peculio Insanus urbanam struit" refers to the Villa Guadagni, but Borgo Pinti is surely intended.

[65] ASF *Decima Rep.* 26 A-F, fols. 358v-359r; Manni, *Vita*, p. 20; *Catasto* 1015 recording on fol. 26or that in 1495 the Scandicci property was taxed in S. Spirito in the name of Tomaso di Pagolo. On 22 February 1488 Scala purchased another vineyard at Gattaia from Marco Bettini for fl.27, ASF *Notarile* R 74 (F. Redditi, 1483-1524), fol. 4v. On a property at Filettole outside Prato offered to Scala as a pledge for a debt of £400 on 13 April 1484, see ASF *Notarile* B 2321 (A. Braccesi, 1481-1489), fol. 181v.

[66] The Decima, unlike the catasto, did not list investments in the Monte, trade or industry, and since both Scala's son Giuliano and his brother Andrea were merchants, Scala may have invested his money in their businesses (cf. p. 243 below). The first Decima of 1495-1498 failed to include land in the *distretto*, although this was subsequently rectified, E. Conti, *I catasti agrari della repubblica fiorentina e il catasto particellare toscano*, Rome, 1966, p. 132 n. 4. On the Decima, cf. also de Roover, *Banco Medici*, p. 35; Canestrini, *La scienza e l'arte di stato*, pp. 319-320; and G. F. Pagnini, *Della Decima e di varie altre gravezze imposte dal comune di Firenze*, 1 (Lisbon-Lucca, 1765): 39. It is also possible some of Scala's dealings were unrecorded, like Antonio Pucci's (described in Conti, *I catasti*, pp. 129-131). Cf. Poggio Bracciolini's *valsente*, which increased from fl.566 in 1427 to almost fl.8,500 at the time of his death in 1459 (Martines, *Social World*, p. 124).

lican government, and of the eight small houses and one bakery attached to his Borgo Pinti estate, two were leased for no rent (to the father of his servant Durante, and to his daughter Francesca and her husband); two were rented without any written agreements (to the wife of his brother Andrea and to a baker); and the remainder were rented for small amounts, paid when the poor men who lived there wanted to pay them, "since they often fly by night when I ask for the rent."[67] Even without accepting this expression of charity entirely at its face value, the manner in which the property was let suggests a great change in Scala's position since the 1480s. But surrounded once more by his family, he cannily managed to keep his estate intact for his son and grandsons to inherit.

Although Scala had left his family behind in Colle when he set out to make his fortune in Florence, he soon found himself the center of a re-formed family group, living with two of his brothers and a nephew from Colle even after his marriage. Increasing prosperity resulted in greater independence in the 1480s, but from the evidence of Bartolomeo's 1484 will the brothers remained closely united. Of his four surviving brothers, two stayed in Colle all their lives and two followed Bartolomeo to Florence. Tomè, the eldest,[68] and Domenico,[69]

[67] See ASF *Decima Rep.* 26 A-F, fol. 358v: "che sco[m]b[ar]ono spes[s]e volte di notte quando chiegho la pigione." In 1488 Scala had given land to Antonio Battista da Piamonte to build a house "iuxta domum ipsius domini Bartholomei," to revert to the donor on his death, ASF *Notarile* R 74 (F. Redditi, 1483-1524), fol. 23r (3 June 1488).

[68] Tomè was 9 years old in March 1429 (Dini, "Bartolommeo Scala," p. 61). On his offices in Colle, see Siena, AS *Comune di Colle* 164, fol. 87v; 165, fols. 54v, 199v, 205v, etc.; ASF *Tratte* 15: "Registrum reforme terre Collis 1474 Giugno" (unfoliated). He acted as Bartolomeo's procurator in the 1470s for deeds quoted in ch. 1, n. 16 above and in ASF *Notarile* L 169 (Giovanni di Piero Lippi), fol. 10r. On Scaligero, who probably died young, and on deeds ratified by Tomè and Domenico in 1466-1467 on behalf of all the surviving brothers, see Dini, "Bartolommeo Scala," pp. 61-62, n. 6, and ASF *Notarile* G 109 (Gentile di Pela Pasci, 1466-1469), fols. 25r, 59r-60r.

[69] "alias Menico," the second youngest brother. On his marriage and offices, see ASF *Notarile* G 109 (1466-1469), fol. 6or-v; Siena, AS *Comune di Colle*, 164, fol. 58r. Since he is not mentioned in Bartolomeo's will of 1484, he may have died by then.

stayed in Colle and so did two of Tomè's sons, Jacopo, to whom Bartolomeo gave his Colle possessions in 1494, and Francesco; while another, Giovanni, joined Bartolomeo in Florence to benefit from his uncle's influence there.[70] His other two brothers, Andrea and Carlo, went to live with Bartolomeo in Florence, and it is in Florence that we have to pursue their careers.

Carlo, the youngest brother, was the first to join him, probably to complete his education, and we find him living with Bartolomeo and performing errands for him by 1459 at the age of about fourteen. Three years later he was working for the merchant Carlo Martelli, and it is clear from his letters to Lorenzo de' Medici from Candia and Chios in 1465 that he already knew Lorenzo and hoped for his patronage on his return, like his brother confessing he was "extremely poor, as you know; and if I don't commend myself to you, I have no one else in whom I can hope."[71] In 1478 he was described as a

[70] On Jacopo, see n. 61 above; on his offices, ASF *Tratte* 15, Siena, AS *Comune di Colle*, 164, fol. 86r; 165, fols. 54v, 61r, 228r; he married Bartolomea di Jacopo Vecchietti in 1487, Marucell. MS A 161, fol. 382v; BNF MS Magl. XXVI, 143, p. 31, no. 27. On Francesco, referred to in the tax returns of his son Alessandro and grandsons Lorenzo and Antonio as "Francesco Scala da Colle," ASF *Decima Rep.* 26 A-F, fol. 14r and *Decima granducale* 3631, fol. 133r-v. On Giovanni, see ASF *Catasto* 923, fol. 290v; and ch. 4, n. 125 above. Tomè had at least two daughters, Antonia, married to Giovanni Battista di Giovanni Lippi of Colle, whose grandson, a notary, married into the distinguished Colle family of Beltramini (F. Dini, "Aggiunte e correzioni: i Lippi del Biadi," *Misc. Stor. Vald.* 9 (1901): 207-208; and on the Beltramini, Biadi, *Storia*, pp. 238, 240); and Angelica, married to Jacopo di Giannozzo Pandolfini in 1483, BNF MS Poligrafo Gargani and Marucell. MS A 161, fol. 382v; according to Andrea Scala's catasto (below): "Madonna Angelucha vedova, figliuola di Tomè di Giovani Schale" was living with her uncle Andrea in 1480 (aged 28, with fl.250 dowry still in the Monte); in B. Benvenuti's genealogy (in the 1677 edition of Scala's *Historia Florentinorum*) she is married to Zanobi Forestani.

[71] ASF *MAP* 21, 29 (9 September 1465, from Candia: "Sono poverisimo chome sai, e s'io non mi rachomando a tte, non ho altro in chi avere speranza"), *MAP* 7, 427 (14 December 1465, from Chios: "perchè ti sono obligatisimo per più chagione e dovunche mi farò un servo fedelisimo quando ti piacerà di chomandarmi"). Cf. ASF *Conv. Soppr.* 95, 212, fols. 29 left (5 June 1459), 70 right, 79 right and left ("per comperare legne," 15 December 1460; "disse per dare al medicho," 2 January 1461), 103 right (26 September 1461); and ch. 8, n. 24 above.

Florentine citizen and merchant, and he was evidently still alive, but otherwise undistinguished, in the 1490s.[72]

Andrea, who was three years younger than Bartolomeo, we know more about. He had joined his brothers in Florence by 1461, when he was about twenty-eight years old. He, too, became a merchant,[73] and while less successful than Bartolomeo, on whom he relied heavily, he achieved a more permanent place in society for himself and his family than Carlo. In April 1472 he was betrothed to Bice del Biada in the Medici palace.[74] In 1474 he bought a house in Piazza San Giovanni, which he rented out in 1479 when he fled from the plague to a house in Borgo Pinti rented from the Guelf Party.[75] By 1489

[72] ASF *Missive* 47, fol. 73v (cf. *Minut.* 10, fol. 577r, in the hand of B.S., completed by Antonio della Valle), Signoria to the Grand Master of Rhodes, 7 February 1478: "Grave fuit quod intelleximus Carolo Scalae Civi et Mercatori nostro impediri iura quedam quae sententia etiam consilii tui assecutus fuerat." Manni (*Vita*, p. 61) refers to a MS of Carlo Scala's in his possession, mentioning property in Via di Pinti dating from 1 December 1490.

[73] ASF *Missive* 47, fol. 10r-v, Signoria to the government of Lucca (11 May 1475): "Gabriel Ginorus et Andreas Scala, socii, cives et mercatores Florentini" (cf. ch. 8, n. 26 above); *Catasto* 1015 (S. Giov. Leon d'Oro), fol. 128r-v, Andrea's 1480 return, describing his first partnership "a una bottegha . . . di lana in Samartino" and the second, agreed on 15 March 1478, "al fondacho e lasciessi la bottega di San Martino a fassi sopradetto fondacho ce[r]ti panni di gharbo in mio nome, cioè Andrea di Giovanni Schala e conpagnia." Cf. B.S. to N. Michelozzi (30 January 1490, BNF MS Ginori Conti 29, 64, fol. 53): Andrea "soleva fare bottegha di lana." In fact in 1480 his *valsente* of fl.488 11s 5d, reduced to fl.464 2s 1d, was slightly higher than Bartolomeo's. He is first mentioned in the Rinieri accounts on 14 August 1461 when Bartolomeo had a doublet made for him, acting as Bartolomeo's messenger in October and on seven occasions in 1462 (ASF *Conv. Soppr.* 95, 212, fols. 103 left, 109 left and right, 131 right). He was first taxed in his own name in 1474.

[74] See ch. 8, n. 36 above; BNF MS Magl. 26, 145, pp. 157, 171, 222 (Gabella de' contratti, in 1472, 1473 and 1478).

[75] ASF *Catasto* 1015, fol. 128r. He paid for his house in 2 instalments, fl.200 on 3 May 1474 and fl.350 on 10 January 1477. At the time of the catasto "perchè fuggi la moria," he was living in a house with a garden rented from the Guelf Party in Borgo Pinti opposite the Cestello. It was rented to Bartolomeo and Andrea from 1 May 1480 for four years at £75 p.a.; on 28 February 1482 Bartolomeo acquired it in exchange for "una vel plures alie domus vicine illi," for the same value (ASF *Capt. P. G.* 28 rosso, fols. 25v and 140v). It was presumably this property which Bartolomeo

his business had failed and Bartolomeo (apparently unsuccessfully) commended him to the pope for an office in Rome.[76]
He later acted as Bartolomeo's emissary, and when he formed
a partnership in a wool company with Giuliano Scala he was
doubtless helped by Bartolomeo's money.[77] His first wife had
died by 1480, leaving him with two sons, Bartolomeo, then
aged six, and Lorenzo, aged five, and two unendowed daughters, Lucrezia, aged four, and Camilla, three, who were cared
for by his widowed niece, Angelica di Tomè Scala.[78] He re-
married in 1487 and ten years later he and his second wife,
Leonarda di Luca Formiconi, were living in a house in Borgo
Pinti (presumably the one acquired from the Guelf Party),
which was rented by his brother Bartolomeo to Leonarda for
her life.[79]

Andrea's house in Piazza San Giovanni was inherited by his
son Lorenzo, evidently by then the sole surviving son.[80] In
1489 Lorenzo formed part of the household of the young Giovanni de' Medici, subsequently Pope Leo X, and his uncle

leased to Andrea's second wife for her life and which afterwards formed
part of his Borgo Pinti estate, see n. 79 and below.

[76] Scala to Innocent VIII (12 November 1489), BNF MS Ginori Conti
29, 64, fol. 54.

[77] See n. 61 above and ASF *Notarile* G 619 (Simone Grazzini, 1489-1490),
fol. 145r (20 September 1490): "per Andream Iohannis et Iulianum domini
Bartholomei Scale et socios lanaiuolos." Andrea returned to Colle in 1479
and sent reports of the siege to his brother and the Dieci di Balìa in Florence (ASF *Dieci Missive* 10, fols. 92v, 93r, 26 September 1479). In the
Florentine scrutiny of 1484-1485 Bartolomeo nominated Andrea for one
of the offices of *provveditore* (ch. 4, n. 111 above). Andrea had failed to be
elected a prior in Colle in 1483 "quia ad speculum," Siena, AS *Comune
di Colle*, 165, fol. 199v.

[78] See ASF *Catasto* 1015, fol. 128v. Andrea describes himself as 45 years
old. On Angelica, see n. 70 above.

[79] BNF MS Magl. XXVI, 143, p. 31; ASF *Decima Rep.* 26 A-F (S. Giov.
Leon d'Oro, Andrea's 1495-1498 return), fol. 14v: "Una casetta posta nella
via di Pinti . . . la quale hebbi da detto Messer Bartolomeo Scala mio
fratello d'aprile 1492 a vita di Madonna Lionarda mia donna"; cf. Bartolomeo's 1495-1498 Decima return, *ibid.*, fol. 358r. On the house, see n. 75
above.

[80] ASF *Decima granducale* 3631 (S. Giov. Leon d'Oro, Lorenzo Scala's
1534 return), fol. 71v.

busily attempted to procure benefices and dispensations for him in Rome. As a clerk in Holy Orders he was appointed procurator for Bartolomeo's only son Giuliano in 1499, but he renounced his vows and in 1525 married Costanza di Messer Giovanni Cerretani, daughter of the eminent lawyer and a member of an old and distinguished Florentine family.[81] Lorenzo was a scholar who corresponded with the historian Benedetto Varchi and other writers.[82] He had two sons by Costanza, Giovanni and Andrea, and lived until at least 1553.[83]

Bartolomeo Scala's will of 1484 demonstrates the unity of the Scala family. Tomè, Andrea and Carlo were to inherit his estate equally if his son Giuliano or subsequent legitimate sons died without male heirs, and they were also to be the guardians of his children, together with his wife Maddalena and his father-in-law Giovanni Benci. They could take no decision, however, unless Maddalena was present and gave her approval and unless her mother Alessandra Benci had also been consulted. Maddalena on her own was to administer all his affairs until his son or sons came of age, provided she did not remarry and his male offspring survived; after that she was "to perform the office of good mother and prudent matron, and exercise her usual compassion toward my children to whom she gave

[81] See ASF *Notarile* B 2323 (A. Braccesi 1498-1500), fol. 110r, 3 August [1499]; cf. Manni, *Vita*, pp. 59-60 (although he mistakes "Dom Laurentium Scalam Clericum Florentinum," referred to in Braccesi's *notarile*, as a second son of Bartolomeo; see also following note); BNF MS Magl. 26, 133, p. 254; Marucell. MS A 161, fol. 382v. According to ASF *Grascia Morti* 8, Costanza was buried in Ognissanti on 24 October 1586.

[82] Manni, *Vita* (but see n. 81 above); G. Pesenti, "Alessandra Scala," p. 244, n. 1, referring to "un Lorenzo Scala, che . . . fu grande amico di Agnolo Firenzuola e primo editore della parafrasi dell'Asino d'oro d' Apuleio, che egli dedicava a Lorenzo Pucci con lettera del 25 Maggio 1545, e delle Rime, che per sua cura venivano in luce con dedica a Francesco Miniati del primo decembre 1548." Antonfrancesco Grazzini, "Il Lasca," dedicated the 1st edition of his *Opere burlesche* (Florence 1548) to him and wrote sonnets and "capitoli" to him "in lode" and "in dispregio de' Zoccoli," *Le rime burlesche*, ed. C. Verzone, Florence, 1882, pp. ix, xii, 59, 506-512.

[83] Manni, *Vita*, p. 59. Andrea di Lorenzo had a son, Giuliano, whose tax return of 1534 is in ASF *Decima Granducale* 3630 (S. Giov. Leon d'Oro), fol. 398v.

birth." Alessandra Benci, "a prudent and serious woman," was to enjoy the proceeds of his home during her lifetime or as long as she wanted to, and his wife's faithful servant, Lisa da Cepparello, was to live there to be fed and paid for by his heirs for the rest of her life.[84]

Scala's five daughters, whether married or unmarried and in addition to their dowries, were to receive 200 large florins each and the income from his home if his male offspring died without male heirs and his brothers inherited the estate. At least four daughters did marry, the two elder and better endowed (with 1,000 florins each) into the Florentine mercantile class, the younger (with 800 florins each) less prosperously. The eldest daughter Giovanna married Cristoforo Buonaguisi, related by marriage to the Cerretani,[85] and Battista married Niccolò di Antonio da Filicaia, member of a well-established Medicean family in San Giovanni whose relationship with Bartolomeo Scala was cited in favor of Niccolò's son in 1515.[86] The next daughter Francesca, however,

[84] ASF *Notarile* G 619 (S. Grazzini: Testamenti 1486-1496), fols. 388r-389r. Scala had nominated his wife's cousin, Giovanfrancesco di Tommaso Benci, with his own son for the bags of the Eleven Offices in his *gonfalone* in 1484-1485, ch. 4, n. 111 above. By an act of attorney, Maddalena appointed her brother-in-law, Andrea Scala, and son-in-law, Cristoforo Buonaguisi, her procurators concerning her Monte stock on 8 February 1489, ASF *Notarile* R 74 (F. Redditi, 1483-1524), fol. 22r. Maddalena's nephews inherited her father's estate, see Marucell. MS A 137, fol. 222r (12 January 1512), settlement of accounts signed by Giuliano Scala, "come rede in tutto del detto Messer Bartholomeo" and Lorenzo, Giovanni Francesco and Tommaso di Tommaso Benci, "chome redi in tutto tra tutti e 3 di Giovanni di Lorenzo Benci et de' fratelli, abiano fatto saldo el chonto chon Giuliano di Messer Bartholomeo Schala, nostro parente, chome rede in tutto di detto Messer Bartholomeo."

[85] Cristoforo was the nephew of Bernardo Buonaguisi (from whom B.S. bought a farm at Scandicci in 1470), who was married to Francesca di Niccolò Cerretani, connecting the Scala doubly to the Cerretani, see Manni, *Vita*, pp. 16-17; Scala's letters to G. Lanfredini of 25 December 1484, 21 June and 23 July 1485, ASF *Acq. Doni* 352, fol. 169; and BNF MS II, V, 20, fols. 42 and 64; ASF *Notarile* G 619 (S. Grazzini, 1489-1490), fols. 145r-146r (20 September 1490).

[86] Marucell. MS A 161, fol. 382v: "1487"; ASF *Notarile* G 619 (S. Grazzini, 1484-1488), fol. 125r, 10 June 1488 (cf. Marzi, *Cancelleria*, p. 273, n. 3): "recepisse pro dote . . . domine Baptiste . . . florenos mille

married the son of a relatively new lawyer, Donato di Messer Francesco Gaetani, who turned out to be a spendthrift and was housed rent-free by his father-in-law on the Borgo Pinti estate after failing to behave "in a fitting way" toward his wife.[87] And the fourth daughter Alessandra, a bluestocking, appropriately married the roving soldier-poet Michele Marullo.[88]

As a student Alessandra was taught and admired by Iohannes Lascaris and Angelo Poliziano, who sent gifts and wrote Greek epigrams praising the beauty and talent of their pupil—to which Alessandra responded as dryly as her father would have done, quoting Homer to cast aside the compliments.[89] A gift of flowers from Alessandra to Poliziano drew forth more epigrams and finally a bone comb for her tresses from her father's antagonist.[90] Poliziano was probably responsible for introducing Alessandra and her father to the Venetian humanist Cassandra Fedele, and it is in a letter to Cas-

ducentos" (on the representation of the da Filicaia in all post-1434 *balìe*, Rubinstein, *Government*, appends. 2-9, pp. 252-314; Scala was a colleague of Alessandro di Antonio da Filicaia in the Otto di Guardia in 1479); ASF *MAP* 117, 37, 28 May 1515, Giuliano de' Medici commends Niccolò's son Pietro to Lorenzo de' Medici as a Medicean, and "maxime per essere nepote di messer Bartholomeo Scala" (the reference to which I owe to Dr. John Stephens). On Niccolò, cf. ch. 8, n. 25 above.

[87] ASF *Notarile* G 619 (S. Grazzini, 1490-1494), 29 March 1491, fols. 11r-12v: "Cum exorte essent dissensiones inter [B.S. and Donato Gaetani] ex eo maxime quia ipse Donatus non se gerebat erga uxorem suam filiam ipsius domini Bartolomei ut decebat"; cf. Marzi, *Cancelleria*, pp. 273-274, n. 3; and Scala's 1495-1498 Decima, fol. 358r. On Messer Francesco, cf. ch. 8, n. 25 above; Martines, *Lawyers*, p. 494.

[88] On Alessandra, see G. Pesenti, "Alessandra Scala"; on Marullo, ch. 8, n. 51 above.

[89] Pesenti, "Alessandra Scala," pp. 252-259; cf. del Lungo, *Prose*, pp. 200-203; G. Pesenti, "Le poesie greche del Poliziano," *Memorie del R. Istituto Lombardo di Scienze e Lettere* (cl. lett. sc. mor. e stor.) 23 (1915): 74-80: "neque enim contra elephantem bombum excito"; cf. Poliziano to her father, "ne fiat Elephantus e culice," *Opera*, p. 387.

[90] Pesenti, "Alessandra Scala," pp. 255-256, epigrams 48 and 50 (ed. del Lungo, *Prose*, pp. 214, 215). Epigram 29 (pp. 199-200) praises Alessandra's performance and purity of accent as Electra, see n. 91 below.

sandra that Poliziano describes the performance of Sophocles' *Electra* in Borgo Pinti, "recently given in her father's house before a large gathering of literati," in which Alessandra, "being a virgin, chose the part of the virgin Electra," performing with such grace that she dominated the evening: "So Alessandra Scala alone is on the lips of everyone here at the moment, that is to say, the Florentine Electra."[91] After Marullo's death in April 1500, Alessandra entered the convent of San Piero Maggiore where she died six years later, scarcely thirty years old.[92]

Giuliano Scala, a young man of "excellent disposition" also took part in the performance of *Electra* in Borgo Pinti, causing Poliziano to be "transfixed by jealousy" when he saw him in his sister Alessandra's arms.[93] At this time he was a partner in a wool company with his uncle Andrea, and he later invested money in the retail silk trade.[94] As the son of one of the charmed circle of politically privileged men, the *beneficiati*, Giuliano's political future seemed assured. But after the 1494 revolution, although qualified for the Great Council, he was

[91] Ed. G. Pesenti, "Lettere inedite del Poliziano," *Athenaeum* 3 (1915): 300-301 (translated into Italian and dated in the year 1493 in his article "Alessandra Scala," pp. 250-251): "Ac superioribus diebus, cum graeca tragoedia Sophoclis in ipsius paternis aedibus maximo doctorum conventu virorum exhiberetur . . . ipsa Electrae virginis virgo suscepit . . . nunc in ore omnibus apud nos Alexandra Scala, hoc est Florentina Electra."

[92] Pesenti, "Alessandra Scala," pp. 263-264. On the Convent of S. Piero Maggiore, Richa, *Notizie istoriche*, 1: 124-161.

[93] Pesenti, "Lettere inedite": "ac studiosi aliquot, inque his etiam frater ipsius praeclarae indolis adulescens, personas alius aliam substineret"; Epigram 29, ed. del Lungo, *Prose*, p. 200: "me invidia autem stimulavit, Ut germanum eius vidi in ulnis"; cf. Pesenti, "Alessandra Scala," p. 254.

[94] See n. 77 above and Giuliano's 1535 will, ASF *Notarile* B 956 (Bastiano di Carlo da Firenzuola), fols. 492v-493r (referring to money belonging to Giuliano, "tam capitale quam fructus et utilia . . . super apoteca et traffico . . . in arte et exercitio setaiuoli minuti in civitate Florentie et in societate quae cantat sub nomine dicti Antonii [olim ser Francisci] de Ginoris et sociorum"); 497r ("quamdam Societatem seu trafficum quod cantat in dominum Leonardum de Fornariis Januensem et socios de Florentia qui habitat Florentie in domo dicti testatoris et in qua seu quo dictus testator est socius").

too young to attend and had to wait for the restoration of the Medici before enjoying office.[95]

Bartolomeo was not alive when Giuliano married Francesca di Girolamo Villani in 1504, but he would have approved of his son's marriage to a direct descendant of the historians he had admired and followed in his *History of the Florentine People*.[96] Giuliano was not a scholar like his cousin Lorenzo, but he was consulted on Paolo Giovio's behalf about his brother-in-law Michele Marullo's death,[97] and he was included in the literary and artistic circles of his day. On one occasion the fashionable Company of the Cazzuola held a supper party in his house that contrasted strikingly with the cultural fare offered in Bartolomeo's day: the conflict of passions illustrated, not in *Electra* or an atrium frieze, but in a series of vivid tableaux showing Mars covered in blood, Mars and Ve-

[95] To enter the Great Council it was necessary to be 29 years old and to have been qualified, or for a direct ancestor ("per recta linea") within the last three generations to have been qualified, for one of the Three Highest Offices, ASF *Provv.* 186, fol. 7r. Giuliano was fined for disobedience and contempt on 22 July 1505 (ASF *Otto di Guardia e Balìa* 132 (repubbl.) fol. 223r-v) and was absolved only on 22 August 1520 (ASF *Provv.* 205, fol. 19v); cf. Marzi, *Cancelleria*, p. 274. In 1520 he delivered an oration on justice as one of the Sixteen gonfalonieri (ASF *SS. Delib.* 122, fol. 38r, 15 March 1520, the reference to which I owe to Dr. John Stephens), he was a member of the Signoria in July-August 1521 and March-April 1532 and a member of the Balìa to elect the new Council of 200, Cambi, *Delizie*, 22, Florence, 1786, p. 199; Gaddi, Priorista, fol. 263v; B. Varchi, *Storia fiorentina*, ed. G. Milanesi, Florence, 1858, 2: 453, 457 (bk. 12, chs. 64, 67). He was fined fl.10 by the Sindachi del Commune on 13 November 1527 (ASF *Balìa*, 46, fol. 235v), demonstrating how closely his career was associated with the Medici regime.

[96] Marucell. MS A 161, fol. 382v; cf. Manni, *Vita*, p. 60. On Scala's use of Giovanni Villani's chronicle (Matteo's brother and Francesca's great-great-granduncle), see ch. 12, n. 26 below. On Giuliano and other members of the Scala family, see the anonymous account in BNF MS Magl. VIII, 1490, fol. 12v; Manni, *Vita*, pp. 59-61; Marzi, *Cancelleria*, pp. 273-274, n. 3, and B. Benvenuti's genealogy, cf. Marucell. MS A CXVII, fol. 8v. ASF *Decima Granducale* 3630 (S. Giov. Leon d'Oro), fols. 62r-63r, contains his 1534 return with reductions and adjustments until December 1559.

[97] P. Giovio to Pier Vettori (16 January 1545), *Opera*, 2 (Rome, 1958): 7: "e da Julian Scali ne arete lume quando se [Marullo] affogò in Cecina."

nus naked in bed, Mars and Venus ensnared by Vulcan, who called on the gods to witness this outrage.[98]

On 20 July 1534 Giuliano acquired a chapel in SS. Annunziata, renaming it the chapel of SS. Cosimo and Damian in memory of his son Cosimo. In it masses were to be said four times a year on the Feasts of SS. Cosimo, Bartolomew (for the souls of his father and mother), Julian (for his children and other relatives and himself) and Francis (for his wife).[99] It was decorated with the Scala arms of a blue ladder on a field of gold[100] and a half tondo of an Annunciation by Andrea del Sarto, associate of the Company of the Cazzuola. After Giuliano's death Cardinal Ferdinand de' Medici asked first Giulio Scala for the painting and then the prior of SS. Annunziata, ordering Bronzino to replace it with a new one, "which is beautiful," the prior said, "but not the same."[101]

In his will of 1535 Giuliano settled the problem of the inheritance of the Borgo Pinti estate, which in a country where there was no law of primogeniture he had been lucky to inherit as sole heir.[102] He then had three surviving sons, Lorenzo and Giulio, the offspring of his marriage to Francesca Villani,

[98] Vasari, *Vite*, 6:618-619.

[99] ASF *Notarile* B 2341 (Scipione Braccesi, 1534-1535), fols. 4v-5v. According to Biffoli ("Notizie delle cose memorabili spettanti al Convento di SS. Annunziata: 1587," ASF *Conv. Soppr.* 119, 59), the chapel was previously called the chapel of S. Simone and was in the tribune, the third on the right-hand side; cf. also Andreucci, *Il florentino istruito*, p. 67, art. xv, according to whom Bart. Scala was buried in the chapel of the Sposalizio di S. Caterina (*ibid.*, p. 68, art. 16) and Manni, *Vita*, pp. 61-62, quoting the inscription on Cosimo's tomb.

[100] *Il Santuario della Santissima Annunziata di Firenze*, Florence, 1876, pp. 178-179. Giuliano Scala is listed among the "cives nobiles florentinos qui sepulchra pro se et eorum heredibus fodere et construere possint in solo et terreno dicte capelle," 6 September 1544, W. Braghirolli, "Die Baugeschichte der Tribuna der S. Annunziata in Florenz," *Repertorium für Kunstwissenschaft* 2 (1879): 279. His chapel passed to the Brunaccini family, Andreucci, *Il florentino istruito*, p. 67; cf. n. 113 below.

[101] See Biffoli, "Notizie," *Conv. Soppr.* 119, 59, fol. 17r: "la quale è bella ma la non è quella"; on Andrea del Sarto, Vasari, *Vite*, 6: 613.

[102] ASF *Notarile* B 956 (Bastiano da Firenzuola), fols. 492r-497v, dated 10 November 1535.

and Bartolomeo, or Giovanni Battista as he was baptized, his
natural son.[103] He left the principal estate, with its gardens,
orchards, stables and adjoining farm, to Giulio and Bartolomeo, to be divided equally between them; it was not to be
alienated and if either died without masculine heirs their share
was to go to the other, and if both died without such heirs it
was to go to Lorenzo. To Lorenzo he bequeathed his house
in Via di Pinti "opposite the houses of the da Firenzuola and
the Braccesi" with a garden as wide as the house (the property originally rented from the Guelf Party) and the house
and land called "el Poderino" situated "along the walls as it
is commonly said" (bought by Scala in 1477).[104] Other dis-
positions concerned his company and Monte shares, which
were mostly inherited by his wife Francesca, who was also
granted the use of the furniture found at his death in his
"large room," the chapel and the antechambers "dell'asse"
and "delle palle."[105]

[103] See Manni, *Vita*, p. 62 (Francesca Villani's will of 1556, appointing
Lorenzo and Giulio her heirs); ASF *Notarile* P 166 (Francesco Parenti,
1547-1572), fol. 9r-v, codicil dated 15 December 1551 to a will dated 26
May 1548: "Adlegavit . . . ei prole ma[sculino] iure naturali . . . Johanni
Battiste in baptismate deinde vocato Bartolomeo eius filio . . . flor. 350.
Item predicto legavit alios florenos 250." He also had one daughter (Lena?),
perhaps the child born on 16 February 1511, whose immediate baptism is
announced in Giuliano's letter of that date in ASF *MAP* 71, 174.

[104] ASF *Notarile* B 956 (Bastiano da Firenzuola), fols. 494r-495r ("Item
. . . reliquit et legavit Bartolomeo et Julio eius filiis legitimis et naturalibus
et cuilibet eorum pro dimidia . . . Palatium sive domum sue habitationis
positam Florentie in Via de' Pinti simul cum suis ortis, pomeriis, stabulis,
vendemmiis et aliis efficaciis . . . et simul cum podere annexo et contiguo
dicte sue domui cum vineis, terris aratoriis, cannetis et pomatis et aliis suis
adiacentibus"); 496v ("Domum dicti testatoris positam in via di Pinti . . . et e
conspectu domos illorum de Florentiola et de Braccesis cum orto eiusdem
latitudinis quanta est latitudo domus [cf. Manni, *Vita*, p. 61, who reads "et
specialiter" in place of "et e conspectu," adding that according to a MS of
Carlo Scala's in his possession, "domos eorum de Florentiola in Via di
Pinti . . . inceptos fuisse Kal. Decembris MCCCCIC"]. . . . Domum et
predium positum ut vulgare dicitur lungo le mura situm in parocchia
S. Michaellis de Bisdominis nuncupatum el poderino"); cf. p. 232 above,
and n. 106 below.

[105] *Ibid.*, fols. 492r-493v and 497r (leaving the brothers a third part of his
share in the company of Leonardo de Fornariis and the residue of his
estate).

Lorenzo evidently died first, and his share of the estate was inherited by Bartolomeo, who alone of the brothers had children and increasingly won his father's favor. But Bartolomeo was predeceased by his two sons, Giuliano and Cosimo, and his three daughters became nuns in the Convent of San Clemente in Florence,[106] leaving the celibate Giulio to inherit the estate. Of all the descendants, Giulio apparently most resembled his grandfather Bartolomeo, "who by the favor of the leading members of the Medici family was for a long time retained as Secretary of the principal magistracy of the Republic, whose rudder he held, and he went on an embassy to Rome."[107] He was a friend of Alessandro de' Medici, subsequently Pope Leo XI, to whom he gave first option of buying his estate, and an enemy of Jacopo Salviati's. He was a man of witticisms that recall Bartolomeo's cast of mind if not his style, he patronized the arts and was a friend of the historian Benedetto Varchi.[108]

[106] Giuliano di Baccio Scala died on 14 August and Cosimo on 29 September 1561, and both were buried in SS. Annunziata (ASF *Grascia Morti* 7, fols. 151v, 66v). On his daughters, see Manni, *Vita*, p. 62; and below. Bartolomeo is named as owner of both the lower house in Borgo Pinti and the Poderino along the walls in the 1561 Ricerca delle Case (ASF *Decima granducale* 3783, fols. 126v, 119v, the reference to which I owe to Miss Caroline Elam), no. 1959: originally adjacent to the garden of Scala's palace, but divided from it by the Via del Mandorlo, now Via G. Giusti, after it was constructed; and no. 1842. It appears that after Bartolomeo's death the house in Borgo Pinti was sold to Girolamo Pazzi on behalf of the nuns of S. Clemente (ASF *Conv. Soppr.* 125, 72, no. 38, 17 June 1572; cf. ASF *Decima granducale* 3745, no. 789, where it is listed among Giulio Scala's "sustantie," "per la portata del Cavaliere Messer Girolamo di Alamanno de' Pazzi").

[107] Manni, *Vita*, p. 63, quoting the inscription from Giulio's tomb in S. Clemente erected by his nieces (revised from the draft in Vat. lat. 8225, fol. 343v).

[108] For his witticisms, BNF MS Magl. VIII, 80, fol. 203r (including "Quando moriva: 'io muoio volentieri perchè non sarò più vicino d'Jac°. Salviati'," evidently referring to Jacopo di Alamanno Salviati, cousin of Grand Duke Cosimo I de' Medici, see P. M. Brown, *Lionardo Salviati*, Oxford, 1974, p. 24, etc.); 81, fol. 236r-v; for his patronage of Domenico Puligo, Vasari, *Vite*, 4: 465-466, describing Giulio as a "uomo non meno di bellissimo giudizio nelle cose delle nostre arti che in tutte l'altre migliori e più lodate professioni"; and *Opere di B. Varchi*, Trieste, 1859, 2: 996,

Giulio died at the age of sixty-two on 13 October 1585 and was buried the following day in the Augustinian convent of San Clemente in Via San Gallo, where his three nieces were nuns. Although he had earlier planned to be buried in SS. Annunziata with his parents and to leave bequests to the Opera of S. Maria del Fiore and the Foundling Hospital of the Innocenti,[109] he finally bequeathed everything to San Clemente. "The palace where Messer Giulio lived" with all its appurtenances, garden, fresh-water pond and other land, "but without the small houses which are leased out" was to be offered to Cardinal Alessandro de' Medici for 6,000 *scudi*, to be paid within sixteen years; the money was to be invested by the convent in "secure real estate" and on no account was it to sell any property to the Salviati family on pain of losing its inheritance, nor could the cardinal sell the palace to the Salviati. Three houses attached to the property were to be leased to his female servants and his gardener for their lifetimes with an annual supply of grain and wine, another to the so-called "master-shoemaker."[110]

Cardinal Alessandro de' Medici accepted this opportunity of buying the Borgo Pinti property and paid his first six-

---

Sonetti spirituali, no. 121: "A Messer Giulio Scali," playing more charitably on the family name than Poliziano once had done.

[109] ASF *Notarile* P 166 (Francesco Parenti, 1547-1572), fol. 157r-v, 1 March 1561. Adjustments to Giulio's tax return (1559-1578) are in ASF *Decima granducale* 3630, fol. 349v; 3745, nos. 606, 789; cf. 3783, fol. 122r.

[110] ASF *Conv. Soppr.* 125, 72, no. 62: "Breve ristretto di quanto devono osservare le Reverende Monache di San Clemente per exequtione del testamento et ultima volontà di Messer Giulio di Giuliano Scali rogato Messer Francesco di Ser Niccolò Parenti addì xiii di Octobre 1585": "il Palazzo che habitava Messer Giulio con tutte sue appartenenze con giardino, et altre terre e vivaio senza però le casette che si apigionano . . . per prezzo di sei mila scudi a mezza gabella delle Monache e del Cardinale" (clause 9), "in beni stabili securi" (clause 10). If the convent did lose the inheritance by selling property to the Salviati, one-third was to go to the Gran Camera Ducale, one-third to the Camera Apostolica, and one-third "alla Fabrica di San Piero di Roma" (clause 8). Giulio's death is recorded in ASF *Grascia Morti* 8 (1584-1601): "Giulio di Giuliano Scala sepolto in San Clemente 14 Oct. 1585." On the convent of S. Clemente and the "ricchissima . . . eredità della Famiglia Scala," Richa, *Notizie istoriche*, 5:256-258, 262.

monthly installment of 100 *scudi* in June 1586.[111] A year later Sister Maria Francesca Scala was appointed treasurer of the convent, and appropriately it is her hand that records the payments received from Cardinal Alessandro for the estate founded by her great-grandfather, Bartolomeo Scala, an able administrator like herself.[112] In 1599 the prioress of San Clemente was awarded 50 *scudi* by SS. Annunziata for the removal of the coat of arms and paintings of the Annunciation and SS. Cosimo and Damiano from the Scala chapel.[113] Alessandro de' Medici died shortly after being elected pope in 1605 and the palace descended to his sister Costanza, wife of Count Ugo della Gherardesca, who transformed the building and erected the arms and inscription to Bartolomeo Scala that survive there today.[114]

[111] ASF *Conv. Soppr.* 125, 15, fol. 32v (22 June 1586): "Ricevuto 100 scudi di moneta dal Illustrissimo Reverendissimo Cardinale di Fiorenza . . . quali danari sono mediante le persone di Suor Giulia Eletta, Suor Maria Francescha e Suor Contessa Schali," for six months ending on 13 April 1586.

[112] *Ibid.*, fol. 41r (June 1587): "Qui si scriverrà fidelmente le entrate del nostro M[onaster]o per ma[no] di Suor Maria Francesca Schali al presente camarlingha."

[113] ASF *Conv. Soppr.* 125, 72 (no. 68), 20 August 1599. According to Richa, the Scala arms are painted in a fresco in a chapel in the garden of the convent.

[114] See ch. 5, n. 51 above. One room survives that was restored by Alessandro de' Medici with the following inscription: "Instructas aedes, hospes, quas cernis et hortos/areolis varios limitibusque suis/ horrere et partim arboribus frondentibus umbram/ et partim ramos fundere poma graves,/ praeses Alexander Medices principesque sacerdos/ Florae inter latios lectus et ipse patres/ΜΝΗΜΟΣΥΝΩΝ Scalae quo longe illustrius esset/ in faciem voluit sic parare novam." On the garden in Alessandro's day, cf. n. 35 above.

PART FOUR
Writings

CHAPTER X

Apprenticeship

For—if you want to know me—I am simply one of the people, a devotee of Latin eloquence, an enthusiastic supporter of the liberal arts, yet a man of little learning and scarcely trivial ability. *Scala to Poliziano, 1494*[1]

Scala was as deprecating about his literary achievement as about everything else. At the end of his life he is still, to friends, the unlettered man of the people, the people's drain, who needs gloves and soap and every kind of refinement on being knighted in 1484. By now we should recognize his irony. Yet there was a basis of truth in what he said. Compared with Poliziano he was not primarily a scholar, but a man of affairs who had to conform to common practice in his public writings.[2] It is true that "there was a great shortage of books and teachers" when he was a student in Florence, and unlike some of his contemporaries he did not even study all the subjects of the old *trivium*, achieving, as he put it, "scarcely trivial ability."[3] Primarily a lawyer, he followed the humanistic program then in vogue. Rhetoric, history, poetry, Latin and Greek were his principal subjects apart from law, and as we shall see they formed the basis of his culture.

Although Scala's early writings are not original in form, however, they contain the seeds of ideas that anticipate Scala the reformer and apologist of the sovereign state. Roman civil

---

[1] In Poliziano, *Opera*, p. 133: "Sum enim quispiam de populo (si nosse me vis), eloquentiae latinae studiosus, assectatorque atque admirator bonarum artium, ipse tamen trivialem vix aliquam eloquentiam doctrinamque consecutus."

[2] Cf. ch. 8, n. 66 above.

[3] Cf. ch. 1, n. 23 above; in general, Kristeller, "The Modern System of the Arts," *Renaissance Thought II*, pp. 163-227, esp. 178. Definition of the liberal arts differed, cf. Cicero, *De oratore*, 3.32.127 and fifteenth-century treatises in W. H. Woodward, *Vittorino da Feltre and Other Humanist Educators*, repr. New York, 1963, pp. 195-234. Scala never studied logic, which formed part of the *trivium*.

law and Greek and Roman philosophy provided ideal com-
post for his secularism and authoritarianism. Like any young
Florentine, he stresses the importance of the state and correct
social behavior in his "Oration on justice" and other early
writings. But he combines this with an interest in mythology
as human history and psychology, in natural law as the expression of individual reason, and in language as a conventional
instrument for correctly naming things, all of which express
a naturalistic approach to the problem of authority and the
state. These ideas culminate in his dialogue *On Laws and Legal Judgments*, in which his two worlds of politics and letters
converge.

Law and humanism found common ground in the study of
rhetoric, which was as necessary to aspiring advocates as to
politicians. It was certainly one of Scala's early subjects,
taught to him in 1451 by Carlo Marsuppini whose influence is
reflected in Scala's "Oration on justice" dated 1 January
1452.[4] Delivered every two months to incoming magistrates,
the oration or *protestatio* on justice was uncompromisingly
public-spirited,[5] and predictably Scala draws on Justinian's
Institutes, St. Augustine and Cicero to demonstrate the importance of administering the state justly, quoting the assurance
of Scipio Africanus to his son in the *Somnium Scipionis* that
a special place is reserved in the heavens for those who have

[4] Laur. MSS 90 sup., cod. 52, fols. 129v-132v, subsc. "finis mccccli die
primo Januarii D. Bart.," and 90 sup., cod. 47, fols. 85r-87r; Rome, Bibl.
Corsiniana, MS Rossi, 230 (36 E 19), fols. 127r-129v (the latter both anonymous). It was tentatively attributed to Scala by Bandini, *Cat. cod. lat.*, 3,
col. 632: "forte Scala"; cf. Benvenuti, *Quadri storici fiorentini*, p. 103; and
on the grounds of its subscription, style and the absence of other more
likely "domini Bartolomei" I accept the attribution. It was clearly written
as a practice oration (like those described in Landino, *De vera nobilitate*,
ed. Liaci, p. 32; A. Rinuccini, *Lettere ed orazioni*, pp. 3-10; D. Acciaiuoli,
BNF MS Magl. VIII, 1390, fols. 22r-v, 27r-v; cf. della Torre, *Storia*, pp. 358-
359, 345-346), and not for delivery.

[5] See E. Santini, "La Protestatio de Iustitia nella Firenze Medicea del sec.
XV," *Rinascimento*, ser. 1, 10 (1959): 48-54. According to the Statutes
("Friburgi," 2: 501; cf. Santini, p. 35), the *protestatio* was to be delivered
"vulgari sermone cum auctoritatibus divinae Scripturae, vel poetarum, vel
legum."

"aided and advanced their fatherland."[6] More original is the exordium in which Scala invokes the aid of those heroes who had been helpful to mortals. In itself there was nothing novel about this euhemeristic view of myth, which is based closely on Cicero's popular *Tusculan Disputations*.[7] But it provides a useful clue to a more immediate source for his attitude, which was shared by Scala's friend and contemporary Donato Acciaiuoli and by Cristoforo Landino, but not by other generations of Florentines in the fifteenth century.[8] This was not Bruni, despite the fact that Scala quotes him,[9] but Marsuppini, professor of poetry and rhetoric in Florence in 1451 and teacher of these three men.[10] His teaching in its turn may reflect the influence of Gemistus Pletho, who would have been an obvious source for Marsuppini's reputed paganism and interest in ancient music and hymn singing—as well as for the practice of invoking the help of the gods, whose names rep-

[6] Laur. MS 90 sup., cod. 52, fols. 130v-132v, quoting from the *Institutes*, 1.1.1-3; 4.18.5 and 7; *City of God*, 4.4 (*P.L.* 41, col. 115); Cicero, *Tusc. disp.* 5.2.5 and *De repub.* 6.13.13.

[7] *Tusc. disp.* 5.3.8. Cf. Boccaccio (*Genealogia deorum gentilium, Opera*, 10, Bari, 1951, pp. 4, 8-10, 19) and Salutati (*De laboribus Herculis*, ed. B. L. Ullman, Zurich, 1951, 1: 116-117, etc.) who both contrast fictitious with historical myths in analyzing interpretations of ancient poets. On these different traditions, cf. J. Seznec, *The Survival of the Pagan Gods*, New York, 1953.

[8] See Donato Acciaiuoli's "Oration on justice," ed. Santini, above, pp. 48-54; and on Landino's attitude to myth, Cardini, *La critica del Landino*, pp. 31-32. Although delivered in 1469, Donato's oration must reflect his early education, and contrasts with the orations, for example, of Giannozzo Manetti, born 1396, Pierfilippo Pandolfini, born 1437, or Bernardo Canigiani, born 1443, ed. Santini, pp. 54-59, 65-74 and 59-65. Cf. also the oration of Matteo Palmieri, born 1406, *Una prosa inedita di M.P.* (1437), Prato, 1850.

[9] "rem ipsam quam [Bruni: *quia*] fictam esse scio nequaquam attendo. Nam fabulosa non movent, sed aliud pro alio significantes intelligo," MS Laur. 90 sup., cod. 52, fol. 130r, quoting from Bruni's *De studiis et litteris*, ed. Baron, *Schriften*, p. 18. On Bruni's attitude to poetry, cf. his letter to G. Cirignano, *Epist.*, 2: 161: "Ego enim non te ad fabulas Poetarum . . . voco"; and C. Rinuccini, *Invettiva*, ed. A. Wesselofsky, *Il Paradiso degli Alberti*, Bologna, 1867, 1, pt. 2, p. 310, where Bruni and his friends are said to regard poets as "compongtori di favole e sviatori di giovani."

[10] See Cardini, *La critica del Landino*, p. 80, n. 20, cf. p. 296; and Landino, *Carmina omnia*, ed. Perosa, pp. 103-113, 181-187 (Cardini, pp. 11-12, n. 15); and ch. 1 above.

resent cosmic Ideas or principles of reason, if only we interpret their names correctly, as Scala said.[11]

Although this is the only oration that survives from Scala's
student days, he put his training to good use in the numerous
orations he delivered as chancellor of Florence.[12] In form they
were closely modeled on Cicero, but they depended for their
success on the moving force of oratory which, Scala recalled
in 1481, was greater than the power of Amphion to move
stones or Orpheus to tame wild animals.[13] Unwilling as he was
to admit that history had anything to do with rhetoric, he
nevertheless used orations in his *History of the Florentine
People*, like Thucydides, to express opposing points of view as
in a court of law.[14] His letters, too, were masterpieces of rhet-

[11] On Pletho, Masai, *Pléthon*, and his *Traité des lois*, ed. C. Alexandre
and A. Pellissier, Paris, 1858, esp. bk. 1, ch. 3, p. 43: "C'est donc aux Dieux
arbitres de la raison que nous devons . . . adresser nos prières," 1.4, p. 45;
3.35, pp. 203-229; cf. Scala's Oration, fol. 130r-v, referring to the Muses:
"Quarum si nomina recte interpretemur, singulas sapientiae proprietates
intelligemus earum adnotationibus indidisse . . . sacrosanctum sapientiae
nomen in omni re primitus invocandum est"; and on his attitude to myths,
ch. 13, n. 16 below. On Pletho as a source for Ficino's hymn singing,
D. P. Walker, *Spiritual and Demonic Magic from Ficino to Campanella*,
London, 1958, pp. 60-63. On Marsuppini's interest in music, see his official
letter dated 19 March 1446, ed. G. Zippel, *I suonatori della Signoria di
Firenze*, Trento, 1892, pp. 29-30, partly ed. Garin, "I cancellieri umanisti,"
p. 25, n. 1; and Porcellio's poem to Marsuppini referring to his lyre,
Carmina illustrium poetarum italorum, 7:510-511. The arguments for and
against Marsuppini's paganism are summarized by G. Ferretti, "Manifesta-
zioni religiose di un umanista," *La rassegna nazionale* 156 (July-August
1907): 393-401; cf. P. G. Ricci, "Una consolatoria inedita del M.," *La
rinascita* 3 (1940): 387; however, his 1433 *Consolation* is irrelevant to the
question of Pletho's influence on him: Marsuppini was accused of dying
"sanza chonfessione e chomunione e non chome buono christiano" by N.
Ridolfi, "Priorista," in *Delizie*, 20: 311; cf. the contemporary evidence of
Francesco di Tommaso Giovanni (not referred to by Ferretti or Ricci),
ASF *Strozz.* ser. 2, 16 bis, fol. 16v; Marzi, *Cancelleria*, p. 216; also di Napoli,
Lorenzo Valla, Rome, 1971, pp. 188-189, n. 28.

[12] See ch. 6 above.

[13] See his 1481 *Oratio*, fol. 3r: "Magna vis est, mihi credite, compteque
atque erudite orationis. . . . Que si movere lapides, quod de Amphione ad
Thebas poete tradiderunt, Si ut de Orpheo silvasque et feras demulcere
potest, multo quod habeat vim maiorem in nostris mentibus est vero maxime
consentaneum." On the influence of Cicero, cf. ch. 6, n. 53 above.

[14] See ch. 12 below.

oric, and although he professed to love brevity and clarity he adroitly adjusted his style to suit his correspondents.[15]

History, in fact, was closely associated with rhetoric and Scala's second extant writing, his *Life of Vitaliano Borromeo*, belongs clearly to the epideiktic tradition. It was written to praise the father of his patron in Milan and reflects the influence of Filelfo, Marsuppini's predecessor in the Chair of Poetry and Oratory in Florence in the early 1430s.[16] Its opening topos on the author's inexperience and ensuing account of the Borromeo family is entirely conventional, although its description of Vitaliano as "profoundly unlettered" and his fondness as a young man for the pleasures of hunting and love contrast with Scala's later eulogies stressing the value of wisdom and following the hard path of virtue at an early age.[17] It contrasts more strikingly with Florentine tradition and is more original in its declared intention of "using new names" for contemporary institutions instead of adopting their ancient Roman equivalents, like *aediles curules* for "magistrates": "for this is not to refuse to cultivate antiquity, nor to want to speak differently from the ancients, but to adhere to current practice and to speak in order to be understood." Here he was following the lead of Valla and Flavio Biondo, but such radicalism was not approved of in Florence, and Scala did not escape Poliziano's criticism for adulterating the Latin language with

15 His style ranged from terse in communications to Rome, courtly to states (like Milan and Naples) with whom his relationship was most feudal, self-consciously literary to fellow humanists and chancellors (as to Agostino Dati and Niccolò Borghesi in Siena, or Buonaccorso Massari and Jacopo Ghivizano in Lucca), lighthearted to the chancellor of the feudal Count Amorato Torelli, more pompous to subject communes like Galeata, and to friends and colleagues in Florence witty and ironic.

16 *Vita Vitaliani Borrhomaei*, ed. C. Bartolini, Rome, 1677. On the dedication manuscript to Piero de' Medici, see ch. 2, n. 8 above. Despite the close relationship of history and rhetoric, all humanists knew of course that "aliud est historia, aliud laudatio" (Bruni, *Epist.* ed. Mehus, 2: 112; cf. Cicero, *De orat.* 2.15.62). On Scala's apologue on this subject, see pp. 306-307 below.

17 *Vita*, pp. 10, 18. On the modesty topos, Curtius, *European Literature*, pp. 83-85. Hannibal's comment on Phormio (p. 6) comes from Cicero, *De orat.*, 2.18.75.

modernisms.[18] As chancellor he followed his predecessors in classicizing the names of new institutions like the Cento, which he called the "Centumvirale consilium," or the Seventy, which he called "the senate": "For this is the Florentine senate, if, as Livy writes, the senate is the public council of each individual state. The Romans were astonishingly painstaking in inventing names. . . ."[19] Scala was no less painstaking in inventing names in his own writings, as he explains in a letter to Sigismondo della Stufa, referring to the names in his poem, "La Nencia": "I make a practice of doing something I see neglected by many, that is, inventing names with great care so that they agree with the things they variously describe, which is often much more difficult than inventing the poem."[20] This concern for the correctness of names is of course a facet of rhetoric, but more deeply it reveals an awareness of change and transition. Language, like people and their laws, as Scala later said, changes and is different in different parts of the world, and like them it must be free to adapt itself to contemporary circumstances.[21]

The development of these ideas lay in the future, although

[18] *Vita*, pp. 11-12; cf. Gilbert, *Machiavelli and Guicciardini*, p. 215. On Valla, A. Besomi, "Dai 'Gesta Ferdinandi Regi Aragonum' del Valla al 'De ortographia' del Tortelli," *Italia medioevale e umanistica* 9 (1966): 75-121; on Biondo, Nogara, *Scritti inediti e rari di Biondo Flavio*, p. cviii; cf. E. B. Fryde, *The Revival of a "Scientific" and Erudite Historiography in the Earlier Renaissance*, Inaugural Lecture, Cardiff (University of Wales Press) 1974, p. 11. For Poliziano's criticism, p. 218 above.

[19] ASF *Misc. Repubb.* 4, insert 117, fol. 68r (cf. ch. 6, n. 38 above): "Hic enim est Florentinus Senatus, si ut Livius scribit Senatus est uniuscuiusque Civitatis publicum Consilium. Mira fuit Romana industria in nominibus fingendis. . . ." As Scala was so intimately involved with the Seventy, as well as concerned with the problems of correct nomenclature, it seems safe to ascribe this preface to him, especially as it shows the same use of Livy and the same interest in the origin of law in antiquity as Scala shows in his dialogue *On Laws and Legal Judgments* (discussed in ch. 11 below). For the "Centumvirale consilium" see ch. 6, n. 28 above.

[20] Ed. Patetta, "La *Nencia da Barbarino*, ecc.," p. 160, discussed on pp. 176-182.

[21] Cf. ch. 11, esp. nn. 24 and 36, and ch. 13, n. 50 below. On Scala's concern for "correctly" naming things, cf. n. 11 above: this, too, may reflect the influence of Pletho.

the seed was sown in Milan. Back in Florence in 1455 Scala continued to work in the field of rhetoric, which was now being taught by his friend Cristoforo Landino as Marsuppini's successor.[22] To judge from the titles of his next essays, the treatises *On Philosophical Sects* of 24 April 1458[23] and *On Whether a Wise Man Should Marry*,[24] he seems, as he himself says, to have "completely given himself up to the study of philosophy," which was then being taught to enthusiastic audiences in Florence by Iohannes Argyropoulos.[25] But in fact it was probably Landino rather than Argyropoulos who inspired

[22] Gherardi, *Statuti*, p. 467 (appointment to read oratory and poetry in January 1458). According to D. Acciaiuoli's letter of 15 April 1455 to A. Alamanni (BNF MS Magl. VIII, 1390, fol. 96v: "Biennio publice lectitasse"), he must have been teaching since Marsuppini's death in 1453; cf. M. Lentzen, *Studien zur Dante-Exegese Cristoforo Landinos*, Vienna, 1971, p. 8; Cardini, *La critica del Landino*, p. 11, n. 14, p. 310, n. 8.

[23] The treatise exists in 3 versions, the 2nd and 3rd being anonymous: (1) an autograph and incomplete draft in Scala's Modena MS, fols. 38r-40v, headed "MCCCCLVIII" and ending: "Ita usque in hodiernum diem vetus exsuscitata academia perdura maiore ex parte"; (2) an intermediate version in BNF MS Magl. VII, 1161, fols. 119r-129r, addressed to "Philippo Bartolomeo Comiti" (probably Count Filippo Borromeo, Scala's former patron in Milan, is intended) and subscribed "Ex Florentia viii kal. maias [24 April] mcccclviii"; (3) a fair copy on vellum with autograph corrections and an identical subscription, but without an addressee, in Laur. MS 76, 55, fols. 28r-46r (which also contains another work of Scala's, see following note). This last version was published as the work of Giovanbattista Buoninsegni by L. Stein, *Archiv für Geschichte der Philosophie* 1 (1888): 540-551 (to which I was directed by Prof. Kristeller); cf. della Torre, *Storia*, pp. 731-732, n. 2; Kristeller, *Supplementum*, 1: cxxxix; Garin, "Ricerche sull'Epicureismo," p. 72, n. 1; and now, rejecting this attribution, Kristeller's article on Buoninsegni in the *Dizionario biografico*, s.v. I quote from Stein's edition.

[24] *Ducendane sit uxor sapienti*. It exists in an incomplete version in BNF MS Magl. VI, 166, fols. 92r-95r, and Benvenuti, who described it in his *Quadri storici fiorentini*, pp. 103-104, supposed the remainder to be "almost certainly lost." However, the missing half is in BNF MS Magl. VIII, 1439, fols. 85r-92v, subscribed "Ex Trebio Mediceo Mugellano, iiii kalendas Ianuarias" (29 December), while the complete dedication copy to Piero de' Medici is in Laur. MS 76, 55, fols. 47r-66v.

[25] Ed. Stein, p. 540: "Scribis audivisse . . . philosophari me coepisse, nec paucis . . . sed hisce studiis totum esse deditum." On Argyropoulos' lectures, Cammelli, *I dotti bizantini*, 2, esp. pp. 85-90; Gherardi, *Statuti*, pp. 264-265, 467, and Rinuccini, *Lettere ed orazioni*, pp. 18, 189.

Scala's budding interest in philosophy at this time. Landino had made it clear in his inaugural lecture on the *Tusculan Disputations* that he, too, intended to give his lectures within a philosophical framework, and it is the framework used by Landino (following the threefold Stoic division of philosophy attributed by Cicero to Plato) and not the Aristotelian framework employed by Argyropoulos that Scala and at least two other Florentines—notably Alamanno Rinuccini and Marsilio Ficino—adopt in their writings at this time.[26] At the same time Ficino also wrote a short treatise describing ancient philosophical sects,[27] and so did Francesco Patrizi, a young Sienese humanist then living near Florence with the family of the Milanese ambassador in Florence.[28] Two years later the very same question of ancient philosophical sects was the subject of a letter given by Cristoforo Landino to his pupils for translation

[26] Ed. Müllner, *Reden und Briefe Italienischer Humanisten*, Vienna, 1899, p. 121, and *La critica del Landino*, p. 297 ("Sapientiae studium, quam Graeci philosophiam vocant, tripartito dividere plurimi consuevere," here contrasting with Argyropoulos' inaugural oration on Aristotle's *Ethics*, bks. 5 and 6: "Philosophia itaque in duas distribuitur partes," ed. Müllner, pp. 10 and 19); cf. Scala, *On Philosophical Sects*, ed. Stein, pp. 540, 547-548; Rinuccini, *Lettere ed orazioni*, p. 29; and Ficino, *Opera*, 1: 757-759 (cf. della Torre, *Storia*, pp. 511-512): "Oratio de laudibus philosophiae," dated by Kristeller *c.* 1457, *Studies*, p. 49, contrasting with the Aristotelian division of his early writings, *ivi*, pp. 56-60, 95-96. On the ancient division of philosophy, see the bibliography quoted by Kristeller in "The Modern System of the Arts" (n. 3 above), pp. 169, n. 27, and 175, n. 73.

[27] "De quatuor sectis philosophorum," ed. Kristeller, *Supplementum*, 2: 7-10. A comparison between the two letters is made by Garin, "Ricerche sull'Epicureismo," pp. 72 and 74, n. 1 (making the point that Ficino characterizes Epicurus more fully, Ficino quoting from Lucretius, 2. 646-651, and 3. 269-274, and Scala from Virgil, *Aeneid*, 4. 379-380, to illustrate Epicureanism). Ficino's letter is undated and Kristeller associates it with a group of other treatises written in 1457, *Studies*, p. 49.

[28] Patrizi's letter is edited by Schmitt, *Cicero Scepticus*, pp. 172-177. On his visit to Montughi, from where he could well have attended Landino's lectures on the *Tusculan Disputations*, see D. Bassi, "L'Epitome di Quintiliano di F. P. Senese," *Studi storici* 22 (1894): 399-401. The influence of Florence is also suggested by the reference to the rumor that Cosimo de' Medici had recently acquired a complete MS of the *Academics* from France (ed. Schmitt, pp. 172-173).

from Italian into Latin, suggesting this topic is to be associated with Landino's teaching in the Arts faculty rather than with Argyropoulos' more strictly philosophical lectures.[29]

Scala begins his account by outlining the proliferation of ancient sects before describing in greater detail the four principal sects that developed from the school of Plato: the old Academy or Peripatetics, the Stoics, the Sceptics and the Epicureans. Here his early draft breaks off, to resume in the completed version with an analysis of the principal beliefs of three sects, the Peripatetics, Stoics and Epicureans according to the threefold division of philosophy into ethics, physics and logic described in Cicero's *Academics*, which Scala closely follows. As to the question of what sect he himself belonged to, Scala replied with a profession of his Christian faith, which provides the basis for his criticism of Plato:[30] like St. Basil, he said, he intended to visit all the flowers to make the best honey, walking through the meadows of the gentile philosophers as

[29] Laur. MS Acq. Doni, 82, fols. 47v-49v: "Epistola quam ex etrusca discipulis suis exercitationis causa latinam faciendam dedit annis 1460." Landino's introduction of the Epicureans compares closely with Scala's (fol. 49r: "Restant Epicurei, qui ab Epicuro huius familie auctore cognominati sunt"; cf. Scala, ed. Stein, p. 547: "Restant autem Epicurei quos fluxisse ab Epicuro omnes norunt") making the same distinction between Epicurus' life and words (cf. Allen, "The Rehabilitation of Epicurus"). Both Scala's and Patrizi's letters refer to the *Tusculan Disputations* (on which Landino was lecturing in 1458), which Landino may have used to initiate a fuller discussion on ancient philosophy based on the *Academics* in which Cicero professes to find the truth "by putting the case for either side" (2.3.7).

[30] Ed. Stein, pp. 550-551, criticizing the transmigration of souls into animals and the return of the purified soul to the corrupt body, which Virgil makes Aeneas amazed by (*Aeneid* 6. 719-721), the idea that punishment was temporary and not in some cases eternal, as the Christians believe (*City of God*, 19. 28, *P.L.* 41, col. 658, although in quoting from the *Phaedo* (62 E) as well as the *Aeneid* (6. 617-618), Scala shows he is aware that this is not Plato's view), the idea that the soul comes from God and the body from secondary gods, and that when released from the body the soul is released from every disturbance. Laur. MS 76, 55 (and Stein) has "vigesimo" for "undevigesimo" (p. 551, line 11) and transposes *c.* 8 lines from "Aberrant etiam" to "addere rursus" (p. 551, lines 2-10), which in MS Magl. VII, 1162 correctly follow "Augustino adhesimus" (line 17).

a Christian, continually expecting to step with his bare feet on a deadly snake hiding among the grasses and the blooms.[31]

If not original in treatment, the essay is important on account of the novelty of its sources, many of which had recently been rediscovered or translated and others little used hitherto. Diogenes Laertius' *Lives of the Philosophers*, for instance, had been translated by Ambrogio Traversari for Cosimo de' Medici earlier in the century, Lucretius had been rediscovered in 1417, St. Basil's *Homily to Young People on Reading the Books of the Gentiles* had been translated and dedicated to Salutati by Bruni.[32] The *Aeneid* and St. Augustine's *City of God* and *Contra academicos* were more familiar, but not Cicero's *Academics*. Borrowing as heavily as it does from both the *Prior* and the *Posterior Academics*, Scala's treatise helped to put back into circulation the physical and logical as well as the moral tenets of the principal ancient sects.[33] As Scala's sources reveal, his interest was not strictly philosophical but belonged to the wider field of humanistic studies, which concerned itself with early patristic texts almost as enthusiastically as classical.[34]

[31] Ed. Stein, p. 551 ("ex singulis id assumunt quod melli faciundo aptum vident"); cf. St. Basil, *Sermo de legendis libris gentilium, P.G.* 31, col. 570, with a somewhat different emphasis however: "ex eis quantum idoneum est ad opus, semel collegere, reliquum dimittunt."

[32] Traversari's translation was printed in Venice in 1475; on its dedication to Cosimo, see Holmes, *Florentine Enlightenment*, p. 124; on Lucretius, discovered by Poggio in Fulda, see Sabbadini, *Le scoperte*, 2: 233; ch. 13, n. 13 below; Bruni's translation of St. Basil is in Laur. MSS. 65, 15 and 90 sup., 52, printed in 1475; his preface to Salutati is in Baron, *Schriften*, pp. 99-101.

[33] On the *Academics*, Sabbadini, *Le scoperte*, 2: 212-213; Schmitt, *Cicero Scepticus*, esp. pp. 43-54. On Salutati's MS of the *Prior Academics*, B. L. Ullman, *The Humanism of C.S.*, pp. 223-224. The *Posterior Academics* is much rarer.

[34] On interest in Greek patristic literature in the fifteenth century, see Kristeller, "Paganism and Christianity" in *Renaissance Thought* [I], pp. 70-91, esp. 80-81; and "Augustine and the Early Renaissance" in *Studies*, pp. 355-372; Trinkaus, *"In Our Image,"* 1: 18-28, 57, 179-199; H. H. Gray, "Valla's Encomium of St. Thomas Aquinas and the Humanist Conception of Christian Antiquity," *Essays in History and Literature presented to Stanley Pargellis*, ed. H. Blum, Chicago, 1965, pp. 37-51. On the transmis-

On Whether a Wise Man Should Marry shows the same combination of interests. Its opening attempt to define the concept of wisdom in antiquity is misleadingly philosophical, for it rapidly reveals itself to be based almost entirely on St. Jerome's treatise against marriage, *Adversus Jovinianum*, supplemented by the equally misogynistic Juvenal.[35] Quintilian had proposed the topic "On whether to marry" as an exercise in oratory in his *Institutio Oratoria*, which makes it likely that this treatise, too, was associated with the school of rhetoric rather than philosophy in Florence. By recanting halfway through his wittily sardonic account of the perils of matrimony—like Plato in the *Phaedrus*, he says, or Stesichorus, translated "by our Leonardo Aretino"[36]—Scala declares himself to be the disciple of the early generation of civic-minded humanists who had advocated matrimony on social grounds.[37]

In the preface to his *Life of Vitaliano Borromeo* Scala promised Piero de' Medici—if he approved—to write a similar account of his father Cosimo, but he never did so, doubtless be-

---

sion of classical culture by the Church Fathers, H. Marrou, *St. Augustin et la fin de la culture antique*, Paris, 1938; C. Cochrane, *Christianity and Classical Culture*, rev. ed., Oxford, 1944.

[35] St. Jerome, *Adversus Jovinianum*, P.L. 23, cols. 215-351, esp. bk. 1, ch. 41-49, cols. 282-293; Juvenal, *Satires*, 2. 6: "On Getting Married"; see P. Delhaye, "Le dossier antimatrimonial de l' *Adversus Jovinianum* et son influence sur quelques écrits latins du xiie siècle," *Medieval Studies* 13 (1951): 65-86; and on Juvenal, G. Highet, *Juvenal the Satirist*, Oxford, 1954, pp. 91-103.

[36] Laur. MS 76, 55, fol. 58r-v; *Phaedrus*, 243 A, which had been translated by Bruni in the 1420s. Cf. Quintilian, *Institutio oratoria*, 3.5.8: "Quod ut exemplo pateat, infinita est, 'An uxor ducenda,' finita, 'An Catoni ducenda' ideoque suasoria potest," and Curtius, *European Literature*, p. 155: "A question of universal interest is: Ought a man to marry? In the Middle Ages it was usually answered in the negative."

[37] E.g. Poggio Bracciolini, *An seni sit uxor ducenda*, *Opera*, ed. Fubini, 2: 685-705; cf. his letter to Pietro del Monte, *ibid.*, 3 (2): 119-121: "Hominem si quidem in communem usum atque in publicum utilitatem procreatum esse sapientis volunt, quae maxime duo in conjugio servantur"; Bruni, *Vita di Dante e Petrarca*, *Schriften*, pp. 53-54; Francesco Barbaro, *De re uxoria*; Guarino Guarini, letter to A. Corbinelli, *Epistolario*, ed. R. Sabbadini, 1 (Venice, 1915): 213-215.

cause it would have been tactless in republican Florence.[38]
Instead he wrote a *Dialogue of Consolation* on the death of
Giovanni de' Medici in 1463 and after Cosimo's death the following year he prefaced a collection of writings in his praise,
which together served the same purpose: a eulogy of Cosimo
in other dress.[39] They both belong to the epideiktic tradition,
but nevertheless provide valuable evidence of Scala's intellectual development at this time.

The *Dialogue of Consolation* contains some familiar themes,
such as a euhemeristic interpretation of myth, emphasis on the
importance of justice and the social virtues, and a strictly
Christian conclusion. Scala's argument in favor of a plurality
of gods and his "Stoicity" is firmly rejected by Cosimo, who
asserts that the ancient Magi as well as Plato and the Sybils all
believed in one God, and that: "nature is better known to us
by experiment and practice" than by the force of Stoic rhetoric, later crying out to Scala in a raised voice: "are you one
of those who dare accuse Nature and God, who is the author
of Nature? How blind can we be."[40] The argument ranges
widely over a number of topics, enriched now by a knowledge
of Argyropoulos' lectures on Aristotle's *Ethics* and by the
Palinode of Orpheus, newly arrived in the Medici library in
Eusebius' version, as well as by a number of other classical and

---

[38] *Vita*, preface, p. 7: "Paolo enim post si tibi haec non desplicuerint,
clarissimi Patris tui magnifica facta atque etiam tua aggredi est animus."
On Machiavelli's inhibitions about writing about the period from 1434 to
1492, see D. Giannotti's letter to M. Michieli of 30 June 1533 (referred to
in ch. 12, n. 37 below).

[39] Laur. MS 54, 10, fols. 104r-122v, 1r-5r. In the preface (fol. 4r) Scala
again alludes to the need for a history of Cosimo's deeds: "Itaque com-
primam orationem meam haecque ipsa, quae nunc quoque me magnopere
ad scribendum inflamant, ad aliud oportunius fortasse tempus reservabo."

[40] *Ibid.*, fols. 111v ("ut experimento ipso atque usu rerum natura melius
nobis innotescat") and 122r ("An tu . . . ex his unus es qui naturam et
Deum, qui naturae auctor est, audeas accusare? Quae est enim haec cecitas
nostra"). On Cosimo's anti-Stoicism, cf. Marsuppini's *Consolation* (n. 11
above), pp. 389-433. On the identification of God and nature in the writings
of the canonists in the Middle Ages, B. Tierney, "*Natura id est Deus*: a
case of juristic Pantheism," *Journal of the History of Ideas* 24 (1963):
307-322.

patristic texts:[41] man's origin is discussed, the nature of the
gods, the rival merits of Stoic fortitude and Epicurean pleasure, human happiness in Aristotelian terms as a blend of external, bodily and mental advantages, and life in Platonic-Chris-
tian terms as a preparation for death. The flowers sampled
were richer and more varied than those distilled for Scala's
1458 essay and the snakes lurking in the grasses more plentiful,
so perhaps for this reason Scala felt it necessary to make its
orthodoxy unambiguous.[42] Nevertheless, what is striking is the
common ground shared by Cosimo's and Scala's empiricism
and rationalism, which clearly show the direction in which
Scala's thought was developing.

The preface to his collection of praises of Cosimo, the *Collectiones Cosmianae*, is more openly eulogistic.[43] Two themes
predominate: the importance of education and hard work, and
praise of Cosimo. Its argument that success is due less to our
nature or fortune than to personal application provides a suitable introduction to his eulogy of Cosimo, who was a paragon
of wisdom and industry, his house a gymnasium of the liberal
arts whence no one left without being wiser than when he arrived, thanks to Cosimo's instruction. The outline Scala gives
of the biography he would write of Cosimo suggests that little
more originality could be expected from it than from his pref-

---

[41] On the *Palinode*, trans. George of Trebizond in Eusebius, *De preparatione evangelica*, and its arrival in Florence, D. P. Walker, "Orpheus the
Theologian and Renaissance Platonists," *Journal of the Warburg and Courtauld Institutes*, 16 (1953): 110-111 (now reprinted in Walker, *The Ancient
Theology*, pp. 26-29), to whom I owe the identification of Scala's quotation
from the *Palinode*. It is also to be found among Maffeo Vegio's translations
of Orphic writings, Lodi, Bibl. Comunale, MS XXVIII A 11, fol. 19v:
"Orpheus ex Greco in Latino." On the same theme of the unity of God,
Scala also quotes from the Asclepius in the translation attributed to Apuleius
of Madaura (*Corpus Hermeticum*, 2 (Paris, 1945): 338-339, cf. F. Yates,
Giordano Bruno and the Hermetic Tradition, London, 1964, pp. 2-3) and
words attributed to Zoroaster, also in Eusebius, *De preparatione evangelica*,
in Trebizond's translation, 1, ch. 7.

[42] On S. Antoninus' attempt to combat the heretical influence of Platonism in Florence at this time, R. Morçay, *St. Antonin*, Paris, 1914, pp.
310-319; Masai, *Pléthon*, p. 342, n. 1.

[43] Laur. MS 54, 10, fols. 1r-5r.

ace.[44] But we would be wrong to dismiss the first of his themes as merely a topos. Quoting from Hesiod, Homer and Sallust, his growing insistence on the importance of education, illustrated first by the simile of the Choice of Hercules, then by the Pythagorean *bivio*, and finally here by the image of Hesiod's steep path to virtue must reflect his own growing interest in this subject.[45]

The themes of this preface are anticipated in Scala's "Elegy" in praise of Pius II which he probably wrote between 1459 and 1460.[46] Poetry formed an important part of the humanistic curriculum, and although Scala was less accomplished a poet than an orator or historian, he nevertheless practiced the art to praise his friends and patrons and vindicate his claim to the name of humanist. His "Elegy" in praise of Pius II is one of his longest extant poems and is conspicuous for its interest in ancient philosophical sects and the importance of choosing the hard path of virtue when confronted by the choice of

[44] Scala's emphasis on Cosimo's wisdom is also due to the fact that, as a new man and *uomo disarmato*, Cosimo could only be praised for the *sapientia* and not the traditional *fortitudo* of the ruler (Curtius, *European Literature*, pp. 176-179); on the problem posed for eulogists by Cosimo's role in the state, Gombrich, "Renaissance and Golden Age," now in *Norm and Form*, p. 33.

[45] Laur. MS 54, 10, fol. Iv, referring to Hesiod, *Works and Days*, 788-790. On the Choice of Hercules (to which Scala refers in his *Apologi centum*, ed. Müllner, no. LXXVIIII, p. 32, and in a poem ed. Dobelli, "Alcune rime," pp. 122-123, as well as his "Elegy," n. 47 below), see T. E. Mommsen, "Petrarch and the Story of the Choice of Hercules," *Medieval and Renaissance Studies*, Ithaca, 1959, pp. 175-196; E. Panofsky, *Hercules am Scheidewege und andere antike Bildstoffe in der neueren Kunst*, Leipzig and Berlin, 1930. The Pythagorean *bivio* (in Scala's *Dialogue of Consolation*, Laur. MS 54, 10, fol. 118v) was known to the Middle Ages through Servius' *Commentary on the Aeneid*, 6. 136; Isidore of Seville, *Ethymologiae*, 1. 3. 7, and in a short poem "De Y Pythagorica" attributed to Virgil or Ovid.

[46] "Bartholomei Vopisci Schale Elegia in laudem Pii II. Pont. Max.," Rome, Bibl. Vaticana, MS Chigi J. VII, 260, fols. 89r-93r, part of a collection of poems addressed to and by Pius II, described by R. Avesani, "Epaeneticorum ad Pium II Pontificem Max. liber," in *Enea Silvio Piccolomini Papa Pio II, atti del convegno per il quinto centenaio della morte e altri scritti*, ed. D. Maffei, Siena, 1968, pp. 15-97, esp. 48, no. 31.

Hercules in early life.[47] Predicting the rule of justice and "the abundance of the golden age" that would follow Pius' election as pope, Scala continued:

> And will Epicurus still persist in abolishing the gods, while he says that they are free of care and watch over nothing and hear not the voices even of those whose prayers are just, because they look in the same way on the just and unjust alike? For as the poems of the learned Lucretius Carus say, when he sings of the nature of things and the gods: *For the gods must, by their nature, take delight in peace, forever calm, serene.* Ah, how much better, how much more wisely does the masculine sect of Zeno dare to tell us that man and god are ruled by supreme reason—for it must be that the world is governed by supreme reason. Now at last the gods look down on us kindly. The random behavior of atoms does not make such great gifts.[48]

Scala's comment on Lucretius, still relatively unknown in the middle of the fifteenth century, is of the greatest interest and it marks the beginning of his lifelong fascination with this

[47] Fol. 91r: "Felices igitur qui te genuere parentes / Et qui preceptis instituere bonis. / Matrone[s] posthac veniunt quando Herculis ad te / Has etenim ad cunctos arbitror ire duas. / Cum veniunt igitur procul a te it blanda voluptas: / Virtutis mores plus placuere tibi. / Te duce difficiles contendit vincere calles / Virtus, angustum te duce carpit iter."

[48] Fol. 90r-v: "Iusticia reget hic populos, rursusque reducet / Pacem (si placitum est): aurea secla fluent / . . . Et persistet adhuc Epicurus tollere divos / Dum quid securos invigilare negat / Aut voces audire aliquas vel iusta precantum / Quod paribus spectent equa et iniqua modis? / Nanque ut habent docti Lucreti carmina Cari / Naturam rerum cum canit atque deos: / *Omnis enim per se divum natura necesse est* / Perpetuos peragat cum requiete dies. / Ah, quanto melius, quanto sapientius audet / Tradere Zenonis mascula secta virum / — Mundus enim constet summa ratione necesse est — / Atque deum summa cum ratione regi. / Nunc ad nos superi tandem aspexere benigni. / Non atomum casus munera tanta facit." He quotes from *De rerum natura*, 2.646-647 (transl. R. Humphries), the 1st line exactly, the 2nd in paraphrase. The same lines were quoted by Ficino in his letter "De quatuor sectis philosophorum," p. 9, see n. 27 above.

Epicurean poet, whose rationalism and atheism both attracted and repelled him.[49]

Scala did not pay such a learned compliment to his other patrons, but to each he attempted to make his verse appropriate. To Pierfrancesco de' Medici, the horse dealer, he wrote in praise of his champion racer Swallow.[50] To Cosimo, statesman and Maecenas, he wrote a series of Virgilian poems praising his political achievements and his patronage: "O Cosimo, O celebrated glory of our time," "You are strong in counsel, you are strong in wisdom, O Cosimo," "If you are wise, Poets, sing of Cosimo with full voice, for he will ennoble your efforts," "On the appearance of Cosimo" (in old age more like a god than a man) and, not included in his *Collectiones Cosmianae*, a poem "To Cosimo, with the roses born at the end of September."[51] To Lorenzo, himself a poet, he wrote in friendly rivalry: no longer capable of completing one poem in ten days when once he had composed ten in one day, he nevertheless took his mind off his building worries in the 1470s by writing his own version of a poem attributed to Lorenzo and his friends about the nymph Nencia;[52] and in 1484, hearing that

---

[49] See ch. 13 below.

[50] BNF MS Conv. Soppr. G 8. 1438, fol. 20v: "Carmina in laudem equi Petrifrancesci de Medicis: Ex re cui dederat pernix bene nomen hyrundo / Aspice quam nihil est nunc nisi marmor inhers. / Et poterat quondam levibus contendere ventis / Et par cum rapidis currere fluminibus / Qui totiens claros tulit certamine palmas / Cum longe ante alios cursibus iret equos."

[51] Laur. MS 54, 10, fols. 164r-v, 163v, 135r and 152v (the last autograph), all published in *Carmina illustrium poetarum italorum*, 7: 489-491. His poem "Ad Cosmum cum rosis natis in fines septembris" is in his Modena MS, fol. 20v.

[52] See his accompanying letter to Sigismondo della Stufa, ed. Patetta, "La *Nencia da Barbarino*, ecc.," p. 159: "qui paulo ante plura etiam quam decem heroica carmina singulis quibus diebus conderem" (on the distractions which like birds steal the corn from the poet's field, cf. his apologue Carmen, ed. Müllner, *Apologi centum*, no. XXXVII). Scala's poem and letters are ed. and discussed by Patetta, "La *Nencia da Barbarino*, ecc.," pp. 159-189; cf. A. Perosa, "La Nencia dello Scala," *Rinascimento* 2 (1951): 459-460. The poem describing the *giostra* of 1475 in Vienna, Nationalbibliothek, MS lat. 3198, attributed to [Bartholomaei] Scal[ae] in a later hand, is in fact Naldo Naldi's *Hastiludium* (see now Naldi's *Bucolica, Volaterrais, Hastiludium, carmina varia*, ed. W. L. Grant, Florence, 1974, p. 17).

Lorenzo had again begun to write poetry, he sent him a poem about the nymph Amorba who presided over the fashionable baths where both Scala and Lorenzo went to cure their gout.[53] To Lorenzo di Pierfrancesco, the patron of his last years, he sent a long pastoral poem "On trees," which he said closed the circle by returning him to the port whence he set out under the protection of Lorenzo's father, Pierfrancesco de' Medici.[54] In 1473, like many other Florentine poets, he wrote an epitaph on the death of Albiera degli Albizzi;[55] he wrote a four-line stanza in praise of the organist Antonio Squarcialupi;[56] he wrote a distich about the fountain of King Matthias Corvinus of Hungary.[57] He wrote poems included in a volume belong-

[53] The letter and poem are in ASF *Strozz.* ser. 1, 136, fols. 57-59; the poem and part of the letter are ed. Bottiglioni, *La lirica latina*, pp. 223-224; both are translated into English by Ross, *Lives*, pp. 255-258. It is referred to as evidence of Lorenzo's second phase of writing poetry by M. Martelli, *Studi Laurenziani*, Florence, 1965, p. 55.

[54] BNF MS Magl. VII, 1195, fols. 102-117; cf. ch. 5, n. 19 above.

[55] "Epitaphium B.S. pro Albiera," Bibl. Riccard. MS 152, fol. 101r, ed. del Lungo, *Prose*, p. 145; see also F. Patetta, "Una raccolta manoscritta di versi e prose in morte di Albiera degli Albizi," *Atti della R. Accademia di Scienze di Torino* 53 (1917-1918): 290-294, 310-328. Other poems were contributed by Naldo Naldi, Ugolino Verino, Bartolomeo Fonzio, Francesco da Castiglione, Ficino, Alessandro Braccesi, and Poliziano. Both Manni (*Vita*, pp. 11-12) and Benvenuti (*Quadri storici*, pp. 77-78) state that Scala loved Albiera before his marriage, on the basis of two lines in a poem by U. Verino (*Flametta*, ed. L. Mencaraglia, Florence, 1940, p. 64): "Quid lacrimae, quid vota pii valuere mariti / Quid, quod eras Scalae vatis amica tui?" This is convincingly refuted by G. Zannoni, "Un elegia di A. Poliziano," *Rendiconti della R. Accad. dei Lincei* (cl. sc. mor. stor., fil.) ser. 5, 2 (1894): 153-154. Albiera was the daughter-in-law of Scala's patron Angelo della Stufa.

[56] Laur. MS Med. Pal. 87, fol. iiir, ed. Bandini, *Cat. cod. lat. suppl.* 3, col. 249: "Amphion Lapides cantu, Styga moverat Orpheus/Incurvos delphinas Arion; / Praedocte Antoni, traxere in carmina cannae/Sic homines, sic numina Divum." The volume is prefaced with other poems, by Lorenzo de' Medici, Gentile Becchi, Ficino, Poliziano, Marullo, etc.

[57] Florence, Seminario Arcivescovile Maggiore, MS B.V.2. fol. 82r (the reference to which I owe to Professor Kristeller): "B.S. disticum in fontem Ungari Regis. Et spectare volunt oculi: et dormire iubentur./ Aut sit pulchra minus: aut sonet unda minus," transcribed with a similar distich by Poliziano: "Usque Fluentina vectum est hoc marmor ab urbe/ Matthiae ut regi largior unda fluat."

ing to Nicodemo Tranchedini, Milanese ambassador in Florence,[58] and an eclogue *Eritus*.[59]

Scala sampled every genre of poetry. He wrote sonnets in Italian on the theme of love.[60] He wrote a poem in imitation of Lucretius.[61] He wrote Latin and Greek epigrams.[62] At the end of his life he wrote a series of taut distichs on a series of miscellaneous subjects—the Romans, his dying co-chancellor Piero Beccanugi, his own apologues, a representation of Love beside a fountain, death, and a longer poem on the theme of the diversity of men and plants in different countries.[63] Michele Verino had admired Scala's versatility in being able to write so well in verse and prose but, although he was probably right in considering Scala better at prose, these distichs, like his apologues, suit his talent particularly well.

Scala's knowledge of Greek was such, Poliziano thought, that he would not be wasting time if he went back to study it at school, like Cato the Censor. Scala himself admitted that he

[58] BNF MS II, X, 31, fols. 102v-103r: "B.S. ad Malumbram," "Ad omnes poetas mediolanenses eiusdem," "Eiusdem ad Cerusium compatrem et amicissimum" (Gherardo Cerruto?), "Disticon in Luciam Principis matrem eiusdem" (Lucia da Torsano or Trezzana, mother of Francesco Sforza, see L. Bignami, *Francesco Sforza (1401-66)*, Milan, 1938, pp. 17, 19).

[59] "Vopisci Bartholomaei Scalae Egloga Eritus," Laur. MS Ashb. 1703, fols. 142r-145r (autogr.), ed. Bottiglioni, *La lirica latina*, pp. 219-223. It is dated 1480-1484 by W. Welliver, *L'impero fiorentino*, Florence, 1957, p. 117, n. 1, despite the presence in the title of Scala's nickname "Vopiscus," which elsewhere seems to have been used only in the 1450s or early 1460s (see ch. 1, n. 2 above).

[60] In his Modena MS, ed. Dobelli, "Alcune rime di B.S.," pp. 120-123.

[61] "De rebus [natur]alibus," see ch. 8, n. 49 above.

[62] See his correspondence with Poliziano, ch. 8 above. It is not clear whether some of Scala's poems were entirely in Greek or "verba . . . graeca latinis admiscens" as Poliziano describes Scala's verse on *adulescens* (*Opera*, p. 140). Scala apparently said his verse describing *culex* in the feminine gender was written "ad imitationem . . . graeci cuiusdam epigrammatis" (*ibid.*, p. 380).

[63] Modena MS, fols. 1r-2v (mainly autogr.) and 3v-4r, with his letter to Giannerini (autogr.). Scala also sent a distich "in mortem" to Piero de' Medici after Lorenzo's death, together with two apologues which he describes as "minus fortasse argutum minusque improbum, ut ita dixerim, quam huic generi conveniret," Turin, Bibl. Civica, Raccolta Autografi, mazzo 34; cf. ch. 11, n. 9 below.

was incapable of reading the Greek poem Poliziano had sent him, saying he wrote to amuse himself and his friends in the heat of the summer, not to amaze posterity or to enrich clamoring printers.[64] But despite his irony, he was clearly aware of his limitations in the language. He was probably taught by Filelfo in Milan, who wrote to him in Greek and may have lent him a Greek history, but unlike many of his contemporaries he never translated from Greek or achieved great proficiency in it.[65]

As for Latin, this was the language in which Scala wrote his early treatises, his histories and his poems, as well as all official letters and orations for the republic. Private letters he usually wrote in Italian unless he was writing to fellow-humanists or needed to be particularly formal. He also used Latin when he wanted to write confidentially.[66] He was accused of Ciceronianism by Poliziano but, although he was certainly influenced by Ciceronian rhetoric, he could write very succinctly when the occasion demanded it—as his *Apologues* and distichs show.[67] Poliziano also said that Lorenzo de' Medici often asked him to rewrite Scala's official writings. It is true they were criticized, and it seems likely Scala was speaking autobiographically when he makes his interlocutor in the dialogue

[64] *Opera*, p. 140: "ne perdidisse operam te credamus, quod homo senex, in graeca schola sedere coeperis sub magistro, Catonem puto illum Censorium aemulatus"; and p. 383: "sic cum amicis in istis aestatis fervoribus, cum otium est, non quod posteritas custodiat et miretur, cudo, aut quod ditet informatores hos librorum, quorum tam cupide quidam implorant operam."

[65] Francesco da Castiglione taught Greek in the Florentine Studio in the late 1440s (della Torre, *Storia*, p. 350, n. 3, and ASF *Monte* 1652, fol. 462v, back payments of £29 5s 8d and £22 in May and December 1452), but as Donato Acciaiuoli claimed he knew "grecarum litterarum vix prima elementa" in 1455 (letter to Lianoro de' Lianori of Bologna, 6 October 1455, BNF MS Magl. VIII, 1390, fol. 89v), it seems likely that Scala, who never translated from Greek (unlike Donato), learnt even less Greek in Florence, probably learning what he knew from Filelfo in Milan; cf. ch. 1 (n. 47) above.

[66] Cf. ch. 3, n. 29 above.

[67] Poliziano himself comments on the variety of Cicero's styles: "ut non omnia perinde quae scribit eiusdem prorsus esse auctoris videantur," *Opera*, p. 131.

On Laws and Legal Judgments say: "there is nothing so arduous, so laborious and difficult as to declare yourself to be an author and writer. . . . Unless you write what you know learnedly and briefly, clearly and with style, you will scarcely find any one willing to read you, rendering all your labors and sleepless nights in vain."[68] Nevertheless, however difficult he may have found Latin composition, it was an art he mastered on the whole successfully. His periods are often long and involved and his style on occasion grandiloquent, but his thought is always lucid, and at his best—particularly in Italian—he is a powerful and incisive writer.

The humanistic bias to his early education is confirmed by a list of texts he read as a student. On the basis of works quoted in his early writings, in addition to those he bought, he evidently knew Cicero's *Tusculan Disputations* and *Academics* very well, also the *De officiis* and *De oratore*, buying Cicero's *Orations* and *Letters* in 1461 when he earned a regular salary; Virgil's *Aeneid*, on which he delivered a series of lectures in 1460, and possibly Donatus' *Commentary* on the *Aeneid* and Macrobius; Lucretius; Plato, the *Phaedo* and the *Phaedrus* in Leonardo Bruni's translation and possibly the *Timaeus* and *Republic* as well; Juvenal, *Satires*; St. Augustine, *City of God* and *Contra Academicos*; Lactantius, *Divine Institutes*; St. Jerome, *Adversus Jovinianum*; St. Basil, *Sermon to Young People* in Bruni's translation; Macrobius, *Saturnalia*; Aulus Gellius, *Attic Nights*; Diogenes Laertius' *Lives of the Philosophers* in Traversari's translation; and Diodorus Siculus, *History* (borrowed from Filelfo but not quoted); also two writings of his own near-contemporary Leonardo Bruni, *De studiis et litteris* and the *Isagogicon*. Through Filelfo's *Commentary* he was probably already acquainted with Petrarch's *Canzoniere* and he later quotes Petrarch's poems in his letters. He acquired a manuscript of Boccaccio in 1461.

[68] Ed. Borghi, pp. 279-280. Scala is often vague or confused about names, transposes letters and on at least one occasion apparently miswrote a letter (see pp. 84-85 above). The constant changes of phrase and word-order in successive drafts of his early writings may reflect difficulty in Latin composition.

As well as the manuscripts of Boccaccio and Cicero's *Orations* and *Letters* referred to above, Scala also acquired in 1460-1463 manuscripts of Livy's *Decades*, Martial, Homer, Lactantius and Justinian's *Digest*.[69] In the same period the list of works quoted extends to include Homer's *Iliad*, Hesiod, more Roman writers—Sallust, Terence, *Andria*, Ovid, *Metamorphoses*, Seneca, *Troades*, Horace, *Satires* and *Epistles*; also Aristotle's *Ethics*, which he read to Cosimo from Donato Acciaiuoli's notes on the lectures delivered by Argyropoulos; Eusebius, *De preparatione evangelica*, probably in George of Trebizond's translation, *De morte Hieronimi*; and the Hermetic Asclepius in the translation attributed to Apuleius. By 1464 he had also borrowed a Ptolemy from the Borromeo family in Milan.[70]

It is clear from this list that the range of Scala's reading was neither original nor wide. Compared with antiquity he thought we were but little men: "And what happens when I consider our military affairs, literature, philosophy, painting, our sculpture and the other adornments of our age and compare them with the ancients? My spirits fall and I begin to be ashamed of our studies." As for himself, he had indeed written too much and published nothing, "except what slipped out imprudently when I was scarcely more than a boy or what necessity demanded."[71] He speaks as a humanist, well aware of his limitations. But in fact his education laid the foundation for the writings of his maturity, in which he achieved important and original reinterpretations of classical ideas with contemporary relevance.

[69] See Brown and de la Mare, "Bartolomeo Scala's Dealings," p. 245.
[70] See ch. 1, n. 47 above.
[71] Scala to Poliziano, 31 December 1493, *Opera*, pp. 135-136: "At ipse cum rem militarem, cum literas, cum philosophiam, cum picturas sculpturasque nostras, reliquaque aetatum ornamenta considero, et confero cum vetustioribus, quid putas? cadunt animi, pudereque incipit nostrorum studiorum. . . . Quae scripsi ego quidem parum multa sunt, edita vero nulla nisi quae aut imprudentiore in aetate pueriliter pene exciderunt aut extorsit necessitas." Cf. Crinito to Scala, *Defense*, fol. a2r.

CHAPTER XI

Years of Maturity

You have found a form of expression in which your talent seems to reign supreme. *Landino to Scala* (*1481*)[1]

The first fifteen years of Scala's chancellorship left him little time for nonofficial writing, but by the 1480s he enjoyed leisure enough to take up his private pen again, completing the *Hundred Apologues* for Lorenzo de' Medici in 1481 and the dialogue *On Laws and Legal Judgments* in 1483. In these two writings his public and private ideas about life and the state join to form a coherent whole. As a student he gradually evolved toward a naturalistic and rationalizing philosophy of life, showing greatest affinity with the Stoics but still sitting on the fence, like Cicero in the *Academics*, presenting his arguments in the form of dialogues in which there is no final statement of beliefs. The same is still true of his later writings, the allusive *Apologues* and the 1483 dialogue about two opposing views of law, but hiding beneath classical clothing is a coherent philosophy that must be Scala's own.

HUNDRED APOLOGUES, 1481

The *Apologues*, as Landino said, provided an ideal vehicle for Scala's talent: terse, ironic and allusive, they allowed him to express his opinion on a wide range of topics as freely but obscurely as the Delphic Oracle.[2] They were widely admired

---

[1] See ch. 8, n. 31 above.

[2] Antonio Sinibaldi completed the dedication copy containing a hundred apologues to Lorenzo de' Medici, Laur. MS 54, 3, on 20 September 1481, "veloci calamo," which was used, with Laur. MS Strozz. 107, by C. Müllner for his edition of the *Apologi centum Bartholomaei Scalae*, Vienna, 1896; on the colophon, see Müllner, p. 4; B. L. Ullman, *The Origin and Development of Humanistic Script*, Rome (Edizioni di Storia e Letteratura), 1960, p. 120 (no. 8) with an illustration of fol. 11r on pl. 66; on Sinibaldi, one of the foremost scribes of his day, Ullman, pp. 118-123. In Laur. MS 54, 3 the title "EQU[ITIS] AUR[ATI] ET SECR[ETARII]" is added to the heading; there are corrections in Scala's own hand on fols. 5r, 9v, 16r, 24r, 28r, 31r, 33r. The same apologues are also to be found with Scala's dialogue

at the time, not only by Landino, but by Ficino, whom they inspired to write more apologues of his own,[3] by Cardinal Francesco Gonzaga and the Sienese humanist Giovanni Lorenzo Buoninsegni, who wanted copies of them,[4] by Alessandro Farnese, later Pope Paul III, who thought the way Scala blended "sweet with sour" and "serious with the humorous" was very Platonic,[5] by the young Michele Verino, whom they pleased so much that he "downed them all in one draught" (Aesop was wittier, he thought, but Scala more serious),[6] and by Antonio Geraldini, perhaps their shrewdest critic in appreciating how Scala gave "new life to the ancient world" by mastering the paradoxes of continuity and change, nature and customs.[7]

There was an increasing vogue for such fables in the fifteenth century. There are fables attributed to Filelfo; Leon Battista Alberti wrote a collection of 100 Aesopian fables, *Apologi centum*, as well as a series of longer satires, the *Intercenali*, modeled on Lucian; and Ficino wrote apologues as prefaces to some of his Platonic commentaries.[8] Scala's fables are on the whole longer than Alberti's very short apologues and shorter than his *Intercenali*, but although they were influenced by them both, as well as by Ficino's, they reflect Scala's

---

On Laws and Legal Judgments in Siena, Bibl. Comunale, MS G VIII 46 (fols. 1-57r) and with Alberti's *Apologi centum* in Bibl. Riccard. MS 717 (on additional apologues, see n. 9 below).

[3] See ch. 8, n. 45 above.

[4] See ch. 8, n. 18 above and Venice, Bibl. Marciana, MS lat. XI, 83 (4360), fol. 114r (Scala to Buoninsegni, 1486: "Apologos meos esse apud Antonium Vitellium nostrum reor. Si is tibi fecerit illorum copiam, pergratum mihi fuerit. Ceterum nisi inde sis quod deest nactus et id feceris me certiorem, mittam ad te exemplar quod apud me est").

[5] See ch. 8, n. 53 above.   [6] *Ibid.*, n. 49.

[7] See ch. 13, n. 1 below.

[8] The *Fabulae* attributed to Filelfo were printed in 1480, Alberti's *Apologi centum* are printed in his 1500 *Opera* (for a MS of them, see n. 2 above), with a prefatory letter to (and from) Aesop, "scriptori vetustissimo" (fol. 6r; cf. especially fol. 7r: "Sol ex calice vitreo pleno aqua Irim in Are pinxerat"; his *Intercenali* have been variously ed. Mancini, Grayson and Garin (see his *Intercenali inedite*, ed. E. Garin, Florence, 1965, from *Rinascimento* (1964), p. 9, n. 2). On Ficino's *Apologues*, see ch. 8, n. 45 above.

own interests as faithfully as Alberti's reveal his interest in science or Ficino's his neoplatonism. We will not be surprised to meet many familiar items from Scala's literary stock in trade, such as his 288 philosophical sects and Hercules' Choice, for although the form was new, it was used to convey ideas Scala had been formulating for some years. He later told Piero de' Medici that he wrote the apologues as a form of annual tribute to Lorenzo, which he revived after Lorenzo's death in order not to "defraud" Piero of his inherited right. But although he wrote scattered apologues after 1481—seven more in the summer of 1482, one on "Immortality" by 1484, another on "Letters" which he described to Poliziano in 1494, another illustrated on the walls of his courtyard in Borgo Pinti, and two others titled "The Kingdom of the Dead" and "Dead and Alive" for Piero after Lorenzo's death—he never apparently added them to the first hundred, which remained the definitive collection.[9]

Because of their form—short, disconnected comments on a wide range of topics, not a single developed argument or a *summa*—it is difficult to expound them as a whole. Nevertheless, two main themes predominate: Scala's interpretation of human nature and personal philosophy, and his view of man in society and the nature of politics. Because of the genre, which was intended originally for popular consumption, many fables express sympathy for the plight of the underdog and highlight life's unfair paradoxes. Here Scala was able to combine his role of unlettered man of the people with his stoicizing attitude to life, stressing the importance of individual effort and acceptance of what lay outside man's power to alter. Nature is essentially benign, but her dictates must be obeyed. In four consec-

---

[9] Scala's draft letter to Piero with two apologues (my knowledge of which I owe to Professor Kristeller) is in Turin, Bibl. Civica, Raccolta Autografi, mazzo 34. The seven apologues are in the Modena MS, fols. 29r-30v. His apologue on "Immortality" is in a letter to Lorenzo de' Medici, partly ed. Bottiglioni, *La lirica latina*, p. 223, transl. into English by Ross, *Lives*, pp. 255-256; that on "Letters" is described in a letter to Poliziano, *Opera*, pp. 146-147. "Ebrietas" is illustrated in Borgo Pinti, see Parronchi, "The Language of Humanism," pp. 113, 123-124.

utive apologues, *Day* and *Light* (LXXXV-LXXXVIII), Scala emphasizes the inevitable victory of Day over Night, Dawn and Dusk, and the victory of Light over Darkness, and in *Nature* (XC) he confirms in the mouth of Jove, "the leader of the senate of the gods" that the animals, birds and fish who complain to the gods about their nature would consult their interests better "if they obeyed Nature."[10]

So what is man's nature and what limitations must he be prepared to accept? Scala's view of man is entirely realistic: neither made in God's image nor utterly corrupted by sin, his man is a battleground of conflicting forces where reason has to fight hard to conquer sensual appetite, which he can do by his own efforts with hard work and constant vigilance. By far the largest number of apologues consist of comments on the weaknesses of human nature: *Boasting* (XVI) wherein animals professing boldness quail at illusory dangers; in *Theft* (XXXI) we are told that what the flowers do not give, the king bee will steal; *Jealousy* (XXXII) is felt by a lover on hearing his mistress talking to her sparrow; *Rumor* (LII) is a useless monster welcomed by the people; *Health* (XXV) is not compatible with sloth; *Marriage* (XIV, cf. *Strife*, XL) is always accompanied by quarrels and worries; *Parsimony* (XCVII) warns mortals that "in the time of greatest affluence one should be most mindful of one's affairs."[11]

Life is unfair and hard work and suffering are not necessarily rewarded: in *Prison* (XIII) the cage and the nightingale

[10] Here and subsequently I identify the apologues simply by the title and number in Müllner's edition. Throughout, Scala refers to his apologues affectionately as his children, using them to express his views on flattery (*Assentatio*, XXVII), fame (*Posteritas*, XXXIV, *Fatum*, XXXV), *Glory* (XLIV), *Avarice* (XCV), neatly suggesting his desire for both fame and riches from them, while countering it with the humanist argument that true glory comes from virtue and that immortality lies in the hands of the gods.

[11] In this category, see also *Metus* (XLIII), *Prudentia* (XLV), *Quies* (XLVIII) |*Perseverantia*|(LIII), |*Magnanimitas*\(LIV),*Odium*\(LVI), *Vita* (LVIII), *Patientia* (LXI), *Cupiditas* (LXVII), *Temptatio* (LXVIII), *Loquacitas* (LXIX), *Fortitudo* (LXXI), *Corona* (LXXIV), *Invidia* (XCII) and *Vanitas* (XCVI).

are told that the Fates prevent them from changing places with each other;[12] *Chance* (XXI) strikes unwary people in identical situations differently; in *Vengeance* (IX, cf. *Malice Aforethought*, LXII) the ensnared sparrows are told the fowler will catch the fowler and they will die happy—but they will die all the same; in *Ambition* (XII), *Ostentation* (XV) and *Utility* (XXIII) different flowers, plants and birds complain that beauty and not utility is rewarded; in *Praise* (III) the feet take it badly that the head is crowned for the race which they have won, to be told that true praise is of virtue, which would always be theirs; in *Nobility* (XCIII) the man in the street, watching money, rank, honors, occupation and antiquity of birth contending for nobility, cries out: what about me, am I to be left ignoble?

Scala's own career, of course, provided the answer to the last question. Here the man of the people, whose decree of citizenship quoted Juvenal's line "virtue is man's only true nobility,"[13] speaks autobiographically, as he does in other apologues. In *Condonation* (LV) the tongue is angry with the teeth for biting the tongue, to whom they give daily food to savor. In *Desperation* (LXXXI) the beams of a roof collapse, exhausted and eaten away by woodworms who refuse to give them respite, and are unjustly blamed by the tiles who have weighed them down. In *Ingratitude* (XIX) teeth die and desert when refused a holiday by the palate:

> The teeth, which had spent their life chewing food and squeezing out flavors, asked the palate, whom they served, for a holiday. . . . Many comrades who could withstand the work no longer died ingloriously; some fell, worn out by disease or broken by fighting. To refuse rest to those few who remained, weak and exhausted as they were and with-

---

[12] Cf. *Res familiaris* (LXXXII).

[13] See ch. 4, n. 19 above; cf. Dante, *De monarchia* 2. 3. 18. On true nobility as virtue, see Dante, *Il Convivio* 4. 19; Poggio Bracciolini, *De nobilitate*, *Opera*, ed. Fubini, 1: 64-83; Landino, *De vera nobilitate*, ed. Liaci, etc.

out any other possible reward for their loyalty, could only be a notable sign of ingratitude. When it was refused, however, one by one they fled from the camp

—like those of the "rusty-toothed" Scala himself,[14] who concludes that the palate learnt at last, but too late, that the duties of love must be mutual. Elsewhere we are told that there is no fortress against *Hunger* (VI). In *Negligence* (XXXVI, one of the twelve illustrated in the courtyard of his own house and bearing his own emblem),[15] Poverty is promised success if she forgets her parents Negligence and Sleep and follows Mercury, god of trade and industry.

So man is not entirely helpless in the face of life's hardships. He must not only recognize mutual obligations but work hard to acquire wisdom. Wisdom as an antidote to poverty is the subject of *Destitution* (IV), *Misfortune* (LXXXIX) and *Fortune* (V). In the latter we are told that Misery can change her condition if she lives in the Kingdom of Minerva and, in a later unpublished apologue with the same title, Fortune says it is men and not herself who should be portrayed as blind;[16] in *Providence* (XXVIII), that it is necessary to look ahead in time.

Wisdom is also an antidote to man's other enemy, the passions and his natural sloth. *Victory* (XXIX) is illusory until the passions have been curbed; *Soul* (LXVI) is incapable of doing more than guiding the five sons (the senses) of Mother Earth through the mediation of reason (which in the neoplatonic scheme of things can alone communicate with the sensory or lower soul),[17] and in *Perturbations* (LIX) it is the

[14] See Poliziano's "Ode," *Prose volgari*, p. 274: "rubiginosis dentibus," and Scala to Poliziano, *Opera*, p. 143: "Dixin tibi edentulum esse me? Sum ante protestatus . . . sum verus."

[15] See pp. 234-235 above.

[16] Modena MS, fol. 29r: "Caecos vos potius finxisse oportuit." On fortune, cf. p. 322 below.

[17] On Florentine neoplatonism, N. A. Robb, *Neoplatonism of the Italian Renaissance*, London, 1935; Kristeller, *The Philosophy of Marsilio Ficino*, New York, 1943 (and on the five senses, p. 234); Walker, *The Ancient*

well-armed mind that conquers feeling. Venus and Apollo are consistently contrasted as symbols of carnal love and reason. Are the anonymous maidens singing and playing musical instruments on the marble wall of the temple of Venus Sirens or Muses, the puzzled spectators ask in *Song* (LXXVII): "Do you not know," the artist who painted them replies, "that Muses dwell in the temple of Apollo and not in the temple of Venus?" Love is *Madness*;[18] *Love* (LXXXIII) and business do not go together; the enticements of *Pleasure* (LXXVIII) are lethal:

> In the middle of the sea there are several projecting rocks, you would easily take them for little boats as they float here and there at random. Sitting upon them is one of the two matrons (the Greeks call her Hedone) who came to Hercules as he pondered at the dividing of the ways. If you sail the sea, human fate requires you to approach them. Once there, the rocks surround you as if in a dance. She has several ranks of servants, among the first of whom are said to be the Gorgons and the Sirens; and among the Gorgons Medusa, who fought with Perseus without yielding. Unless you block your ears as in the story of Ulysses and look the other way, they will turn you into stone or drown you.

The counterpart of the Temple of Venus with its Sirens is the Temple of Apollo with its Muses. A young man who enters the temple of Apollo in *Perplexity* (LXXIX) is confronted by images of the nine Muses each with different names and duties and faces; as he approaches the tripod of Apollo in the innermost cavern of the temple, he hears a murmur which with dif-

---

Theology, pp. 1-62; Panofsky, "The Neoplatonic Movement in Florence and North Italy," *Studies in Iconology*, pp. 129-169, especially 136-137; E. H. Gombrich, "Botticelli's Mythologies," rev. edn. in *Symbolic Images*; cf. E. Wind, *Pagan Mysteries in the Renaissance*, rev. edn., London, 1967.

18 Modena MS, fol. 30v: "Insania"; cf. Ficino, *Opera*, 2: 1357: "Cordis autem morbo eam proprie insaniam fieri arbitramur, qua affliguntur hi qui perdite amant."

ficulty he distinguishes as "Return when more advanced." "Do you mean to say the gods, too, speak obscurely?" he complains as he emerges.

Obscurity and uncertainty are symptomatic of Scala's own questioning approach to the changing world. How did he resolve the paradoxes of change and continuity, nature and customs, as Geraldini supposed he had? The answer is revealed by *Time* (XLI): on reading the inscription in the temple of Apollo at Delphi, "Most wise time," a statesman sought the world to find it, eventually to be shown a swift chariot which he was told contained a divine power propitious to our affairs: evidently the rational soul, or Zeus himself, who in heaven "drives his winged team" of horses.[19] The theme that wisdom is acquired only with advancing years (familiar from the preface to the *Collectiones Cosmianae*)[20] recurs in *Wisdom* (LXIII), where Cosimo de' Medici himself figures as one of the principal devotees of the white-haired goddess Wisdom who is admired most by the more elderly; since Scala had lived as a member of Cosimo's household, he asks Cosimo about the goddess: "Wisdom" Cosimo answers benignly, "is the queen of all human affairs. Tell my people that they should worship her continually, for if you sacrifice to her intermittently, she turns aside her face." *Knowledge* (XCVIII), "the goddess and leader of human affairs" is described as Pythagoras used to describe philosophy, as a woman clad in a dazzling mantle made by the nine Muses (to two of whom, *Poetry* (XXXVII) and *History* (XXXVIII) Scala devoted separate apologues) and served by Poverty, Chastity, Conti-

[19] On time, see Panofsky, "Father Time," *Studies in Iconology*, pp. 69-93; F. Saxl, "Veritas filia temporis," in *Philosophy and History: Essays presented to E. Cassirer*, New York, 1963, pp. 197-222, esp. 213-214; and below. Cf. also Scala's *De legibus et iudiciis*, ed. Borghi, p. 269: "Si quid inest in lege vitii, tempus arguit, quod etiam philosophi solent ob eam ipsam causam appellare sapientissimum." Plato's description of the tripartite soul as a charioteer driving two horses and his reference to Zeus is in the *Phaedrus*, 246A-247C.

[20] Laur. MS 54, 10, fols. 1v-2r; cf. *Dialogue of Consolation*, ibid., fol. 109r, where Cosimo approves the precept of the Delphic oracle "ut nosmetipsos cognoscamus" (cf. *Tusc. disp.* 5.25.70).

nence, Vigilance, Thrift, Industry, Study, Promptitude, Judgment and Truth who fight battles with her enemy Love on her behalf. *Truth* (LXV) is also a woman, but less adorned than Knowledge: she is accompanied on the right by written authority (a woman bearing huge tablets of cedar wood followed by armed and unarmed kings, emperors, leaders and governors of peoples, among whom Cosimo de' Medici is foremost) and on the left by music and poetry (a woman with a lyre and laurel mantle, followed by gods, nymphs and satyrs); she gazes kindly on both, though seeming to prefer the lyre and song, but disparages their learning, pomp and ceremony; the powers above and below award her the first prize.

Truth is not identical with the written word or with music, but is evidently to be discovered by the self-knowledge that comes with age. It has nothing to do with the superstitious trappings of *Religion* (XXII) (which tells us, like the late apologues *On the Kingdom of the Dead* and *Dead and Alive*, that most of the gods have their origin in *Fear*, XVII) or with *Astrology* (L). *Gods* (LXXII) like to receive *Gifts* (LXXIII) and be worshiped, and according to the atheist Diagoras there may be rational grounds for believing in them, "but who can believe they are gods with these morals?" Unlike mortals, they are not apparently subject to *Necessity* (II). *Happiness* (XCIV) lies not in external blessings, such as *Riches* (X), but within oneself.

Nowhere does Scala relate his ideas to conventional religious thought, but there is nothing in the *Apologues* that is incompatible with Christianity. Unlike Ficino, however, he never describes love as the motive power of the universe and he is a stoic rather than a neoplatonist in the primacy he gives to reason over love (which man can achieve through self-control and learning) and to the existence of a rational Providence, revealed through nature to the wise man in the course of time.

Scala's view of politics and law in the *Apologues* is as realistic and paradoxical as his view of human nature. The reality of *Justice* (LXXXIV) is very different from its two representations outside and inside the law courts urging the praetor to forget earthly considerations and exercise equity and humanity in delivering his sentence, and the corrupt Verres laughs when he sees the admiration they arouse.[21] Power thrives on *Injustice* (XLIX), which breeds *War* (LX). *Laws* (XXVI) are spiders' webs, which trap only the smallest and weakest insects, as Scala repeats in his dialogue *On Laws and Legal Judgments*.[22] The true art of politics lies in making agreements and compromises, not in battling for right over wrong: in warfare there is no ultimate *Victory* (XXIX); *Military Glory* (XXIV) is awarded to counsel, not to prowess in battle;[23] the art of *Generalship* (XXX) lies in agreeing to a truce; *Union* (XI) and treaties based on mutual *Trust* (XX) are essential for survival; peace and unity are paramount.

Such being the nature of politics, what form of government does Scala favor? Not absolute democracy, despite his popularism. *"Liberty* [XLII] costs too dearly that is bought with one's life," the parrot escaping from luxurious captivity cries as he dies in the talons of a hawk. *Republics* (VII) lack constancy and stability, like the flight of birds constantly changing their formation and leadership. Not the jeering populace

[21] Outside the law courts Justice is represented eyeless and handless gazing to the heavens, inside, with a raised drawn sword in her left hand and a pair of scales in her right, her eyes directed to the right. On the blindness of Justice, see E. von Müller, "Die Augenbinde der Justitia," *Zeitschrift für Christliche Kunst* 18 (1905), no. 4, cols. 107-122; Panofsky, "Blind Cupid," *Studies in Iconology*, p. 109, n. 48. Verres, the rapacious governor of Sicily (73-71 B.C.) was impeached by Cicero in a series of orations, "the Verrines," which he then published.

[22] See n. 34 below.

[23] *War, Victory, Military Glory, Generalship* and *Sovereignty* (below, cf. n. 43) are all illustrated in Scala's house and are transl. Parronchi, "The Language of Humanism," pp. 113-121. On this theme in his official letters, see for example, ASF *Minut.* 7, fol. 94r-v (in Scala's autograph, copied in *Missive* 45, fol. 136r-v, and Munich Clm 10781, fols. 243v-244r): "cum inter bellorum furores et tumultus neque auctoritati amplius neque relligioni sit locus. Omnia versat Mars, viribus, non rationi, homines parent. Atque ex odio, ex ambitione, ex vindicta, ex insania tandem omnia deliberant"; on the theme of the utility of peace, see, e.g., *Missive* 45, fol. 137v (23 March 1467).

but leaders of states alone are prepared to receive *Virtue* (XCI). *Sovereignty* (LXXVI) stands firmly on the side of virtue, not animal strength. Cosimo de' Medici was foremost among the leaders of states who attempted to learn the precepts of life from written tablets and who worshiped wisdom, combining both the virtue and the wisdom necessary to rule.

Scala uses naturalistic arguments to defend the authority of one man in the army or the state in two official orations he delivered at this time, in both also stressing the need for reform and a return to simple institutional beginnings.[24] There can be no doubt that the paternal rule of a wise man, such as Cosimo, represented for him the best form of government, just as rational deism, stripped of all superstition and dogma, represented for him the best form of religion.

On Laws and Legal Judgments, 1483

This is also the conclusion of Scala's dialogue *On Laws and Legal Judgments*, which he wrote about eighteen months later.[25] The argument is presented as indirectly as in the *Apo-*

---

[24] See Scala's *Oratio* to C. Sforza, 4 October 1481 (ch. 6, n. 51 above), fols. 2v ("Utrum navigatoria tandem gubernatore, domestica patre familias, armentoria pastore, gymnastica magistro regetur, rex autem et disciplina militaris qua omnes totius civitatis fortune continentur, sine rectore erit? Presertim si grues in volatu principem, si apes sibi regem cui paveant, quam seguantur constituunt, atque imaginem ut mihi quidem videntur et similitudinem nobis prebent quandam rei publice gubernande"); 5r ("Multo enim conspicitur maior intra castra rerum omnium licentia, quam bene institute militie conveniat. A qua quidem . . . iam nos habemus pro severitate antiqua castrorum incontinentiam, pro parcitate luxuriam. . . . Mores sunt iam restituendi Constanti Sfortia prisce Sfortiane militie. Ac precepta illius discipline auctore iam te ac duce renovanda"); and his *Oratio* to Innocent VIII on 15 December 1484: "Nomina item pro rerum locorumque diversitate variantur. Et patres quidem familias domum pro arbitrio gubernant. Res vero publicas magistratus et principes. Exercitus Imperatores. Regna Reges"; "Tuque opitulante . . . confirmaris languentem prope ac collapsam religionem nostram" (Rome, Stephan Plannck; cf. Santini, *Firenze e i suoi oratori*, p. 270; cf. ch. 4, n. 134 and ch. 6, n. 49 above). This paternalistic view of authority is Platonic, see *Republic*, 342 D-E, 345 C-E, 488 A-499 E, 590 D-E; *Politicus*, 258 E-259 D.

[25] *De legibus et iudiciis dialogus*, ed. from Siena, Bibl. Communale, MS G VIII 46, fols. 59r-103v, by L. Borghi in *Bibliofilia* 42 (1940): 256-282.

logues, not in the form of fables but as two opposing arguments about the nature of law: is law eternal and unchanging or should it vary according to times and circumstances? The traditional idealistic view of law as the embodiment of reason and justice is upheld by Bernardo Machiavelli, the practicing lawyer, the pragmatic view of law by the empiricist Scala. The argument is given topicality by being influenced not only by the pseudo-Platonic dialogue the *Minos*, recently translated by Ficino and then being revised for publication,[26] but also by the presence in Florence of the ancient codex of Justinian's *Digest*, of whose importance as a basis for law reform Scala was precociously aware.[27] As we shall see, his dialogue represents a vital debate about law in the city with contemporary relevance.

Scala's argument is presented first. He introduces it by referring to the existence of countries living without laws—such as Turkey, where according to Florentine merchants Pashas exercised *ad hoc* justice before only the prosecutor and de-

---

All references will be to this edition. Scala says he wrote it during Lorenzo de' Medici's absence as official envoy with Bernardo Rucellai to the Congress at Cremona in 1483 (preface, p. 257; Lorenzo's instructions are dated 5 February and he left Florence on 11 February 1483, Fabroni, *Laur. Medicis vita* 2: 241, ASF *Dieci di Balìa, Missive, Leg. Comm.* 5, fol. 50v).

[26] See Kristeller, "Marsilio Ficino as a Beginning Student of Plato," p. 43, and on its influence on the dialogue, see below.

[27] On the contemporary movement for law reform and the influence of the *Digest* (referred to by Scala on pp. 260-261, predating Poliziano's interest in it), see Maffei, *Gli inizi*, esp. pp. 84-94. On Marsuppini's interest in law reform, see ch. 1, n. 31 above. The traditional idealist view of law is illustrated by Salutati's *De nobilitate legum et medicinae*, ed. E. Garin, Florence, 1947, and a more critical view (making the point that laws impede territorial expansion) by Poggio Bracciolini's "2a. convivalis disceptatio utra artium, medicinae an iuris civilis praestet," ed. E. Garin, *La disputa delle arti nel quattrocento*, Florence, 1947, pp. 15-33 (esp. 17, that Roman law is not universal, and 29; Scala's criticism of law is in the mouth of a lawyer, not a doctor, however). In general, W. Ullman, *The Medieval Idea of Law as represented by Lucas de Penna*, London, 1946; C. Calisse, *A History of Italian Law*, in *Continental Legal History Series*, 8, London, 1928; Cairns, *Legal Philosophy*. On Bernardo Machiavelli, Scala's interlocutor, Gilbert, *Machiavelli and Guicciardini*, pp. 318-319. On law and contemporary politics in Florence, see ch. 14 below.

fendant but were subject to the death penalty if their verdict was later reversed by the Sultan (the subject of one of his apologues),[28] or the islands discovered by John of Portugal where people lived without laws like savages. Since Roman law was evidently not universal it would be better to be governed by the law of nature: "the only certain model and example for a good life, from which good conduct and just laws can be deduced. . . . It is altered neither by time, place, nor by any other reason; it is most constant, unchangeable, uniform, inviolable, everlasting; whoever neglects it, wanting to divest himself of his human nature, must fear God, the author of this law."[29]

So far Scala's praise of natural law is entirely traditional, following Cicero, Gratian and Aquinas.[30] It serves as a basis for criticizing the glossators and their parasites, the contemporary lawyers, who made their living from the obscurity of law, cynically able to win whatever verdict they wanted according to the amount of money they were paid.[31] Before Justinian, there were said to be two thousand books of Roman law and many people wasted their lives and patrimonies in litigation. The Florentines prudently established a variety of law courts and allowed each of the twenty-one guilds, possessing its own college and consuls, to hear its own lawsuits. By ancient statute there was wisely (since it prevented what was clear becoming obscured by a multiplicity of interpretations) no appeal from the decisions of their courts, although by a recent law appeal in important cases could be made to the Court of the Mercanzia in Florence.[32] The Merchants'

[28] P. 262, the subject of his apologue *Dolus malus* (LXII).

[29] Pp. 262-263. Cf. Cicero, *De legibus*, 1. 6. 18-19; *De republica*, 3. 22. 33.

[30] P. 263: "Nonne idem et Salvator precipit? [quoting from Matth. 22, 37-40, on the first two commandments] . . . Quod apertissime significat ista nature incommutabili lege omnes omnium gentium et nationum contineri leges"; cf. Gratian, 1, dist. 5, *P.L.* 187, col. 37; Aquinas, *Summa theologica*, 1a-2a, qu. 94, 4; Salutati, *De nobilitate legum*, p. 18 (but cf. Hobbes, *Leviathan*, pt. 1, ch. 14, ed. M. Oakeshott, Oxford, 1946, p. 85, where it constitutes the second of his rationally based laws of nature).

[31] Pp. 265-266, 267.

[32] P. 265, referring to the law passed on 14 June 1477, see ch. 14, n. 26 below.

Court consisted of six laymen, "chosen not as experts in law but because they are naturally shrewd and good men"; it heard mercantile disputes and there was no appeal from its decisions. Above the door of the court was written: "the home of equity and truth," and it enjoyed great fame abroad, difficult cases being brought to it from all over the world, as people once used to consult the oracles at Dodona, Delphi and Delos.[33] Such skill in making judgments was lost when civil formulae were introduced for settling disputes, for once laws are passed, not a syllable can be changed for any reason however good—hence his apologue on *Laws* (which he quotes).[34] For this reason Brutus' severity in punishing his sons with death according to the laws should be criticized, for, even if done to defend liberty against tyranny, it was contrary to nature and the people would surely have been more lenient.[35] It is almost impossible to envisage everything that will result from one decree: "For we see many things happening every day, so many chance events affecting human affairs and so many different situations arising every day that need to be dealt with by freer powers and more discretionary sentences."[36]

Here Scala reaches the climax of his argument, that just as our minds innately disapprove of badly designed buildings, so they abhor cruel judgments and whatever seems to disagree with reason and nature:

> How much better therefore . . . one could live according to the direction of a good man and a good judge under the guidance of nature (which is always free and immune to

[33] P. 268. On the Court of the Mercanzia in Florence, Bonolis, *Giurisdizione della Mercanzia*, and ch. 14 below.

[34] P. 268, ed. Müllner, XXVI. Cf. Filelfo's "Oration on Justice," Laur. MS Redi 130, fol. 123v; Poggio Bracciolini's "2a. Disceptatio" (n. 27 above), p. 28; L. Brandolini, "De comparatione reipublicae et regni," *Magyar Tudományos Akadémia* 2 (Budapest, 1890): 138.

[35] P. 269. Scala refers to Livy (2.5): "quo poenam meriti fuissent."

[36] *Ibid.*: "Multa enim evenire quotidie videmus, tot versantur res humane casibus, tot sunt que quotidie emergunt earum diversitates, in quibus merito solutiorem facultatem liberiusque iudicium desideres."

any outside ordinances, fully attending to what has to be decided in every eventuality according to the time and circumstances of each), than according to that necessity which men imposed on themselves.[37] ... For just as sailors without their captain are borne hither and thither at random and often perish, smashed against the rocks, engulfed by waves, or, driven by gusts of wind, are borne where they cannot later be recovered by human means; or as a flock of sheep is dispersed if it loses its shepherd; or as soldiers are thrown into confusion and suffer death and other dangers without their commander: so, if you neglect, scorn and reject the ruler, custodian and leader of all human affairs and actions, you must expect and suffer the worst.[38]

Bernardo Machiavelli's defense of an idealistic law is more traditional, although it uses arguments drawn from Ficino's recently translated Platonic and pseudo-Platonic dialogues, adopting Socrates' defense of an eternal and immutable law to counter Scala's empiricism. He begins by defining the six kinds of law in Justinian's *Institutes*, which were distinguished according to the authority that sanctioned them, whereas in Florence only the people could pass laws (unless they delegated their authority for a particular reason and a limited period), and the laws were called *provisiones* or *reformationes* whoever sanctioned them. Cosimo de' Medici defined law as "the fortress of justice"—as Scala should know better than Bernardo, having lived with him as part of his household—and did so with such a mixture of charm, prudence and seriousness that he reminded one of Socrates, honeyed by Plato's style.[39]

[37] *Ibid.*: "Quanto igitur . . . vivi potuit melius ad boni viri, bonique iudicis arbitrium duce natura . . . quam eam sibi imposuisse homines necessitatem." On the "good man" who will make a "wise judge": Plato, *Republic*, 409 C. On buildings, *De legibus*, p. 269: "Nam ut in edificiis dictante natura inconcinna non probant, sic in iudiciis abhorrent . . ." etc.; cf. n. 49 below.

[38] P. 270.

[39] P. 273: "Arcem iustitie leges appellare Cosmus consuevit." On laws in Rome (quoting from the *Institutes*, 1. 2. 1 and 4-8) and Florence, pp. 270-272.

According to the ancients, law had divine origins which legislators confirmed either to make people more obedient by interposing the authority of the gods, or to reveal its natural origins by means of fables.[40] If law is "the invention of truth," as Socrates defines it in the *Minos*, and only those decrees that are just and honorable are properly speaking laws, they should be eternally valid: "for truth is an unchangeable and divine force which, although intermingled with human affairs, is itself nevertheless immortal and eternal."[41] For this reason, although the law restricting women's adornment was passed when Hannibal was threatening Rome and was repealed twenty years later, who can doubt that the same law would be passed and repealed again by anyone experiencing the same situation and argument?

In fact Bernardo Machiavelli's definition of law as "the true reason of government, which directs those whom it governs to the best end by appropriate means" and his description of four kinds of law—divine, celestial, "moving" and human—which Plato is said to have identified in the *Timaeus*, *Phaedrus* and the *Gorgias*, are taken straight from Ficino's introduction to the *Minos*, as is his list of ancient lawgivers who claimed to have spoken through the mediation of the gods.[42]

Bernardo Machiavelli disagrees with Scala that humans are capable of making free judgments. Law is necessary to curb our passions and keep the peace—assisted in Florence by the

[40] P. 275: "Non modo quia sic putaverunt posse populos reddere preceptis suis obsequientiores auctoritate interposita deorum, verum etiam ut . . . de vera legum origine his accomodatissime confictis fabulis significarent"; cf. Machiavelli, *Discorsi*, I, II: "E veramente mai fu alcuno ordinatore di leggi straordinarie in uno popolo che non ricorresse a Dio, perchè altrimenti non sarebbero accettate."

[41] P. 274. On time and truth, cf. n. 19 above.

[42] P. 276: "Lex igitur est, inquiunt, vera gubernandi ratio, que ad finem optimum per commoda media que gubernantur dirigit," see Ficino, *Opera*, I: 1134, *In Minoem, vel de lege, Epitomae*; his four species of law and list of lawgivers (in Scala on p. 275) is on p. 1135. However, Ficino's definition is not so different from that of Aquinas ("quaedam rationis ordinatio ad bonum commune et ab eo qui curam communitatis habet promulgata," *Summa theologica*, I. 2a., 90, 4) and his four species of law, divine, eternal, natural and human (*ibid.*, I. 2a. 91, 1-4).

bimonthly oration on justice.[43] Our nature is such that, having obtained power, we would act in our own interests and soon become tyrants. Moreover, if there were any people so stupid as not to understand the language of letters—which Scala seemed to think, but he doubted, in view of the fact that animals and birds can communicate by sounds—surely we should not take them as our model of how to live?[44] The word for law is closely associated with justice, and kingdoms without justice are—as St. Augustine says—nothing more than organized robber bands.[45] The art is not to blame if the craftsman is bad, nor medicine if the doctor is bad: what is needed is a new Justinian to prevent the great work of emending and clarifying Roman law from being wasted by the ambition of those who claim to be lawyers.

Still interested in the origin and use of words, the dialogue ends with a discussion of the meaning of the word "religion" as it began by discussing the meaning of "carnival" and "Saturnalia." It is Bernardo Machiavelli who concludes that because of "the different kinds of races and their different opinions about the gods," rites of worship and sacrifice to the gods were from the beginning very different, but that since the advent of Christ we cannot err from his holy religion contained in pontifical laws.[46]

[43] P. 277: "Ex quo inter maiorum recte instituta illud quoque vehementer probare sum solitus atque admirari, quod bimestribus singulis in senatu pretoribus magistratibusque atque aliis dicundo iuri prepositis assidentibus de iustitia accuratissima habetur oratio." On the "Oration on Justice," cf. ch. 10, n. 5 above. On laws, "natura et ratione duce," taking up arms against violators of our peace and "ipse pulcherrimum regnum tenent"; cf. *ibid.*, p. 269: "quicquid rationi natureque, que regnum obtinere in mentibus nostris debent, non vident convenire," and Scala's apologue *Sovereignty (Regnum LXXVI)*, above.

[44] Pp. 277-278.

[45] Pp. 278-279, quoting from the *City of God*, 4.4 (cf. Scala's "Oration on Justice," ch. 10, n. 6).

[46] Pp. 280-281, quoting from Cicero, *De natura deorum* 2.28.72; Lactantius, *Divine Institutes*, 4.28.2 (*P.L.* 6, 535-536); Lucretius, *De rerum natura*, 1.931-932; 4.7; Macrobius, *Saturnalia*, 3.3.8-9 (quoting Virgil, *Aeneid*, 6.598-599); and *New Testament*, James 1:26-27. On carnival time in Florence and the Saturnalia, pp. 258-259.

Stated in dialogue form Scala's conclusion is again ambiguous. He gives the last word to Machiavelli, the idealist and traditionalist who values unchanging laws, chivalry and noble ancestry,[47] the orthodox Christian whose confession of faith forms the conclusion of the work, while he himself as a new man[48] adopts a relativist position favoring a natural law adjustable to changing situations and circumstances. His position is appropriate, of course, but more than that, his argument in favor of a flexible law administered by a good man and judge corresponds so closely to the argument of the *Apologues* as to leave us in no doubt that it represents his own opinion. As in the *Apologues* Cosimo de' Medici is portrayed as the wise man who would be naturally fitted for such a role— "Socrates, honeyed by Plato's style," "the Father of our Country and a most wise citizen" who detested carnival time and thought (like Plato) that children should be instructed in the liberal arts and taught civic gravity at an early age instead of being overstimulated in this way: for what inheres in our minds from the beginning, we are told, is like the firm foundation walls of a building, and if correctly laid prepares the way for a good and happy life.[49]

But although the central argument about law is presented as two opposing points of view—as indeed it was at the time —the two protagonists nevertheless share much common ground. Stoicism was based on Platonic foundations and its

[47] P. 266.

[48] P. 266: "Magis certe multo est arduum suo, ut aiunt, Marte sine maiorum adminiculis fieri nobilem. Quod tibi ingenti cum laude tua evenisse pro nostra amicitia vehementer gratulor" (B. Machiavelli to Scala).

[49] Pp. 273: "ut referre sic facile Cosmum dixerim excultam illam, que in Socrate fuit olim, ornatamque Platonis mellita deinde elocutione sapientiam"; and 258: "Sed ea mihi carnispriviorum licentia sepe videri nimia solet, et detestari etiam et pernitiosam putare Cosmus Medices pater patrie noster sapientissimus civis consuevit . . . bonis artibus et discere prima aetate prudentiam gravitatemque civilem Cosmus malebat. . . . Sunt enim universarum actionum nostrarum que principio inherescunt nostris animis, ut in edificiis, quasi firmissima pedamenta." According to Alberti (*De re aedificatoria*, 3, 5, ed. Orlandi and Portoghesi, 1: 189), "Pedamentis extruendis, hoc est fundamentis ad aream usque complendis." On Plato and "the good man and judge," see n. 37 above.

eternal natural law, exercised as Scala would have it by a good man and judge, is not so different from the eternal law administered by Plato's philosopher ruler. For both the free play of individual reason was preferable to rigid and immutable laws: freedom for the sovereign or judge, but not for the people. The contrast with Bruni's defense of "laws and legal judgments" as the guardians of popular liberty earlier in the century is striking.[50] Significantly, this is not an argument used by Bernardo Machiavelli to defend law for, as we know from Scala's parrot, liberty is too expensive a luxury to enjoy at the cost of one's life. Both apologue and dialogue point clearly to the direction in which Scala's political thought was tending.[51]

[50] *Historiarum florentini populi libri XII*, ed. Santini and di Pierro, p. 82, discussed by Rubinstein, "Florentine Constitutionalism and Medici Ascendancy in the 15th Century" in *Florentine Studies*, p. 445.

[51] See pp. 287-288 and ch. 14 below.

CHAPTER XII

The Last Decade

HISTORY OF THE FLORENTINE PEOPLE

But it is true you are writing a history, a long and arduous undertaking, I think. *Poliziano to Scala, 1493*[1]

Scala's *History of the Florentine People* was, indeed, "a long and arduous undertaking."[2] He began work on the project in the early or mid-1480s, and by the time of his death only four books had been completely transcribed, the fifth ending in the middle of a sentence relating to the year 1268. Although more was written than was copied, it seems unlikely he achieved as much as he had hoped.[3] It was in a sense an official undertaking, for two of Scala's predecessors had written similar histories of the

[1] *Opera*, p. 131: "Sed historiam certe componis, longum opinor opus et arduum," 25 December 1493; cf. St. Augustine, *City of God*, 1, preface: "Magnum opus et arduum sed Deus adiutor noster sit."

[2] *Historia Florentinorum*, ed. J. Oligero, Rome, 1677, to which all subsequent references will be made. This edition, based on the sole Laur. MS 68, 26 (see n. 3 below) was reprinted in the *Thesaurus antiquitatum Italiae*, ed. J. G. Graevius, Leyden, 1723, 8. 1. cols. 1-78. The only two serious studies of the history are by N. Rubinstein, "B. Scala's *Historia Florentinorum*" ("Scala"), valuable for placing it in the context of earlier and contemporary Florentine scholarship, and D. J. Wilcox, *The Development of Florentine Humanist Historiography in the 15th Century*, ch. 7, "B. Scala and the *Historia Florentinorum*," pp. 177-202, containing a detailed analysis of Scala's "techniques"; cf. E. Fueter, *Geschichte der Neueren Historiographie*, Munich and Berlin 1936 (repr. 1968), pp. 24-25. It would benefit from a still more exhaustive analysis of its sources, particularly Villani, Bruni and Flavio Biondo, but here I simply attempt to place it in the context of Scala's thought and writings.

[3] The last folio of Laur. MS 68, 26 (80v) contains the catchwords "illic operiretur" as evidence that more was written than survives. It appears to be in the hand of Luca di Fabiano Ficini, Scala's chancery assistant in 1492 (see ch. 7, n. 66 above) and a scribe of Marsilio Ficino's (Kristeller, *Supplementum*, 2: 333, and "Some Original Letters and Autograph Manuscripts of M.F.," *Studi in onore di T. de Marinis*, Verona, 1964, 3: 12, pl. III/8). According to Zeno (*Dissertazioni Vossiane*, 2: 260, quoting Vossius, *De historicis latinis*, Lyons, 1627, 3: 556) Scala "scrisse in XX libri la Storia Fiorentina dall'origine della città fino al 1450, ma prevenuto dalla morte diede solamente a cinque libri l'ultima mano"; cf. Manni, *Vita*, p. 47. It is dated in the 1490s by Rubinstein, see n. 11 below.

city as chancellors, and Scala must have felt he had to follow in their footsteps.[4] At about the time he began to work on the history he made a member of the chancery responsible for writing "annals, describing the daily events of the Florentine people" and at the same time he reorganized the keeping of chancery documents so that "the writings relating to the Florentine Commune may be more easily found." Although we have no evidence that he ever used this material himself for his history, Scala may, directly or indirectly, have encouraged his assistant Filippo Redditi to achieve what he was unable to achieve himself; for it was Redditi, the very man whom Scala made responsible for copying laws and treaties in 1484, who later wrote a history of his own times, moved by the fact that he possessed knowledge of events in which he had himself participated or learned "from the reliable evidence of others."[5]

The surviving books of the *History* give us only a limited idea of what sort of a work he intended it to be, factual or epideiktic. His early *Life of Vitaliano Borromeo* had clearly belonged to the second category, although in it Scala took pains to explain that it was based on the first-hand evidence of people who knew Vitaliano personally, reporting what he had heard "from some people who were intimate friends of Vitaliano."[6] In June 1484 he was granted permission to borrow the third part of Sozomen's *Universal Chronicle* from Pistoia, to assist with "the history or whatever he says he is writing,"[7]

---

[4] Rubinstein, "Scala," p. 50; Wilcox, *Development*, pp. 3-6. Bruni was rewarded by the Commune with tax reductions and the Italian translation of his *History of Florence* was paid for by it.

[5] Redditi to Bernardo Rucellai, ed. Bandini, *Collectio*, p. 98: "nec prorsus sum expers agnitionis rerum nostrarum nostrorumque temporum, quibus aut ipse interfui aut ea ab aliis constanti fide percepi." His work was the "gesta temporum nostrorum . . . acta Populi Florentini ab initio Volaterrani belli [1472] usque ad praesentis temporis curriculum," and in addition "Commentariolos," etc. (pp. 98-99). On Redditi and Scala's chancery reforms in 1483-1484, see ch. 7 above.

[6] *Vita*, pp. 6, 21: "Ego certe audivi ex nonnullis qui Vitaliani familiares erant . . ."

[7] S. Ciampi, *Notizie del Canonico Sozomeno*, Pisa, 1810, p. 23, n. (a): "si dice componere o historia o altro" (22 June 1484); cf. Rubinstein, "Scala,"

and two years later he made it clear in a letter to Giovanni
Lorenzo Buoninsegni in Siena that he intended his *History of
the Florentine People* to be based on new factual evidence:
"Our history is under way. If we had the chance of talking
together more often, I would profit from our friendship to
ask your advice about many things. The history of Siena is
so repeatedly bound up with our own that I would like you
to let me know if you ever discover any more precise record
of your origins and history. Nothing would give me greater
pleasure at this time than your help in making the books of
my history more informed."[8] His chancery reforms must have
had this intention, too. And the evocative description, in the
preface to his *History*, of the difficulties of historical research
suggests it is based on his own experience. What could be
more laborsome, he asks, than in addition to the task of actually writing the history having first to discover the material
on which to base it—which either does not survive, "or if you
do happen to discover any is virtually useless due to its state
of neglect, or because it is disorganized or badly composed,
without any indication of time, place, events or persons."[9] It
echoes his despair on entering the chancery in 1465 and finding incoming letters "put into some bundle" and "getting lost
within a short time," suggesting that he was always very con-
scious of the problems of conservation and recording the past
—and perhaps overdeterred by them.

Archaeology, too, serves as historical evidence, and Scala's
History makes full use of it. Aqueducts and baths provide
early evidence of Roman Florence, contemporary archeologi-
cal discoveries reveal that the level of the Roman city was

---

pp. 49, 58; and G. Zaccagnini, preface to his edition of the *Chronicon universale (1411-1455)*, *RIS* n.s. 1908, 16, 1. p. xxxix.

[8] Venice, Bibl. Marciana, MS lat. XI, 83 (4360), fol. 114r, dated "1486":
"Nostra modo historia in manibus est. . . . Nihil hoc tempore facere potes
gratius quam si tua opera effeceris ut mei istoriarum libri instructiores fiant."
Cf. also Scala's letter to Carlo Barbavaro in Milan, 7 August 1482 (Modena
MS, fol. 32v): "non vere modo, quod in historia primum est . . ."

[9] *Historia*, pp. 1-2; cf. Wilcox, *Development*, p. 179.

lower than in the fifteenth century.[10] Scala refers to the recent discovery of a spurious decree of Desiderius at Viterbo.[11] He illustrates stories in vivid detail, with first-hand evidence where available, and he introduces new situations and people by physical or psychological descriptions to make them readily accessible to his readers by association.[12] For nature sees to it, he explains in his preface, that everyone prefers his own or what is similar to it to what is alien, and because we are also born with a natural desire to learn and will learn more from the things we love, the Florentines (he implies) will learn most from the history of Florence.[13]

[10] *Historia*, pp. 6-7, 36-37; cf. Rubinstein, "Scala," pp. 55-56, and Wilcox, *Development*, pp. 183-190.

[11] *Historia*, p. 75; Rubinstein, "Scala," pp. 49-50. This spurious decree is published and discussed by R. Weiss, "An Unknown Epigraphic Tract by Annius of Viterbo," in *Italian Studies Presented to E. R. Vincent*, Cambridge, 1962, pp. 102-103, 113-114. This and the reference in bk. 1 to Poliziano's theory about the origin of the name Florence from Flora (which he proposed in 1492-1494) are used by Rubinstein (above) to suggest a date between 1492 and 1494 for bk. 1, and post-1494 for the remainder. However, this overlooks two pieces of important internal evidence relating to Venice and Pisa which suggest an earlier date (fully discussed by Wilcox in append. B, "Dating of Scala's *Historia Florentinorum*," pp. 209-210), while the references to Barbarian invasions in bk. 2 which Rubinstein thinks relate to the French invasion of Italy in 1494 ("Scala," pp. 49, 58-59) are in fact identical with ideas expressed in his 1481 *Oratio* (a year after the Turkish invasion of Otranto: discussed more fully below), and do not therefore necessarily support a 1490s date for the *History*. Bk. 1 contains an allusion to one of Scala's apologues transcribed in 1481, and the preface to bk. 4 praising Florence as a "bonarum artium gymnasium" (pp. 114-115) is perhaps echoed in M. Verino's eulogy of Scala's history in the 1480s (see ch. 8, n. 49 above): "Quis secula nostra priscis non preferat, cum vel una nostra civitas sit tanquam officino omnium artium liberalium ex qua innumeri oratores, poetas, historici, mathematici, philosophici, medici, iurisconsulti tanquam ex equo troiano egrediantur?" If the two references to recent scholarship referred to by Rubinstein were interpolated and added to bks. 1 and 2, the surviving work could have been written in the course of the 1480s and early 1490s and transcribed between 1492 and 1494, with perhaps more drafted than was copied. Since the third part of Sozomen's *Chronicle*, which he borrowed in 1484 (n. 7 above), covers the period from the end of the thirteenth to the beginning of the fifteenth centuries, it would suggest Scala was then embarking on research for this period.

[12] *Historia*, pp. 7, 19, 23-24, 34-36, 113 (cf. Wilcox, *Development*, p. 181, n. 19); *ibid.*, pp. 183-190, and on psychological considerations, 190-193.

[13] *Historia*, p. 2; Wilcox, *Development*, p. 179, n. 11.

Here Scala refers to the popular view of history as "the teacher of life," which was widely accepted in the Middle Ages as well as the Renaissance: "The first thing in history is that it will offer examples of every kind of conduct, both public and private, and it will show you what is the best thing to do."[14] But can history both establish the truth about the past and tell us what to do? Far from seeing history as a storehouse of certain moral truths like earlier medieval writers, Scala saw it as a reflection of the moral and political uncertainties of the present. The problem of how to behave he admitted he found "most difficult." History can offer examples of behavior that are relevant in identical situations: as he says in the dialogue *On Laws and Legal Judgments*, the law restricting women's adornment passed when Hannibal was threatening Rome would be passed and repealed again in the same situation.[15] The arguments remain the same, but the solution they offer is not an absolute one, simply a choice between different points of view. This is the reason why history and rhetoric are more closely associated with each other than they appear at first sight to be, for the historian needs the forensic skill of a rhetorician to argue the opposing claims of self-interest and morality that underlie the political debate.

Like Thucydides, and Leonardo Bruni, Scala illustrates these conflicting arguments in a series of orations inserted into his narrative, using them to illustrate his—by now—familiar ideas about human nature and politics.[16] The theme that agreement is essential if both sides are not to destroy themselves in conflict is the subject of an oration by the Florentine commander

[14] *Ibid.*: "Atque illud in historia primum est, quidquid agas, sive id [sit] publicum, sive sit privatum, rerum omnium suppeditabit exempla, quidque melius factu sit . . . percommode ostendet" (and in Wilcox, above). Cf. Livy, *Ab urbe condita*, preface, 10; Sallust, *Jugurthine War*, 4, 1-9; and Scala's preface to the *Collectiones Cosmianae*, Laur. MS 54, 10, fols. Iv, 2r-v.

[15] Ed. Borghi, p. 274 (although the argument is in the mouth of Bernardo Machiavelli).

[16] See J. de Romilly, *Histoire et raison chez Thucydide*, Paris, 1967, esp. pp. 180-239; C. N. Cochrane, *Thucydides and the Science of History*, Oxford, 1929; and on Bruni, N. Struever, *The Language of History in the Renaissance*, Princeton, N.J., 1970, pp. 127-134. On Scala's use of orations, see his preface to bk. 3, p. 76 (Wilcox, *Development*, p. 198).

advising the Fiesolans to unite with Florence after their supposed defeat in 1010.[17] Livy, as well as Dionysius of Halicarnassus and Plutarch, must have provided him with a model to follow,[18] and it can be no coincidence that it is in this speech that he refers to "Aesop's fable about *imperium*" as a means of making a non-anachronistic allusion to the same theme in his own apologue, *Imperatoria* (Generalship).[19] Other orations, delivered both in direct and indirect speech, illustrate the moving power of oratory, man's inability to anticipate all future events and do more than to "notice present events with acumen and manage them usefully"; patriotism; and the helplessness of alliances in the struggle for power.[20] He illustrates Florence's decision to send troops to evict the tyrant of Siena, Provinciano di Silvano, with two orations, one putting the "reckless" and idealistic popular argument (which won the day with its cry of liberty against tyranny), the other Teggaio's statesmanlike and realistic counter-argument (taken from the *Somnium Scipionis*), which advises the Florentines to await the advantage of time and not risk war and ridicules the idea that the nature of the Florentines and Sienese will ever change.[21] Here Scala argues both sides of the question where Bruni in his *History of Florence* puts only the second;[22] but

[17] *Historia*, pp. 14-16; cf. Rubinstein, "Scala," p. 54; Wilcox, *Development*, pp. 200-201.

[18] Livy, *Ab urbe condita*, 1:23.7-9. Scala himself refers to Dionysius of Halicarnassus and Plutarch as his sources (p. 18), but he later compares the Romans and Albans with Florentines and Fiesolans (pp. 133-134), suggesting this was always in his mind.

[19] P. 15: "Imperium profecto, de quo tota pugna extitit, ut utrique amitteremus, aliquando fuit necesse. Quod et Aesopi quoque ille milvii bellus apologus admonere facile, si sana mente simus, potest"; cf. Scala's apologue *Imperatoria* (XXX): "Duces eventum pugnae formidabant. Ergo in colloquium tandem cum venissent pepigerunt indutias."

[20] Pp. 32-34 (cf. Wilcox, *Development*, p. 188 and n. 63), 44-48, 86-88 (cf. the apologue *Amicitia*, XXXIX).

[21] Pp. 120-125 (120-122: "orationem . . . audacem magis quam fortem," 122-125, Teggaio's speech: "qui reipublicae praesunt, venerationis debeatur, quippe qui secundum Deos immortales primos in civitate magistratus excolendos putem" (cf. pp. 258-259 above), quoting also from Hesiod, *Works and Days*, p. 25). Relevant apologues are *Libertas* (XLII), *Tempus* (XLI) and *Fides* (XX).

[22] *Historiarum florentini populi libri XII*, eds. Santini and di Pierro, p. 36,

later Scala presents the argument of the Ghibelline communes who wanted Florence to be destroyed in 1261 (arguing that true love of one's country expresses itself, not in surrounding the city with walls nor in glorying in its name, but in "events and deeds"), where Bruni presents the opposing argument of Farinata degli Uberti, who according to Scala replied only with "a grave and simple oration," which saved his native city from ruin.[23]

In these orations Scala contrasts the realities of power and politics with idealistic arguments in favor of liberty and patriotism, just as he had done in the *Apologues* or the dialogue of 1483. His *History* also reflects their doubt and uncertainty, finding it "most difficult" to know what to do, and equally difficult to discover the truth about Florence's past. Just as he puts forward conflicting political arguments, so he decides to present all conflicting theories about Florence's early history. Like Livy, whose scepticism he shares about "achieving accuracy when describing the remote past," he draws no hard and fast line between myths and history[24] and presents differing accounts of Florence's origin and her name. It is true his approach is neither as severely critical nor as brilliantly scholarly as those of Bruni or Poliziano,[25] but when he has empirical evidence he uses it and without it he quotes all sources impartially.[26] Like Bruni, but less dogmatically, he uses rhetoric to describe the political arguments that history serves to illustrate.

---

using the functional argument that no one is farseeing enough to fight wars as successfully as carpenters and architects build buildings or captains sail boats.

[23] *Historia*, pp. 131-134; *Historiarum*, pp. 41-42. Rubinstein's comment that Scala is trying to rival Bruni "by substituting a speech of his own invention" (p. 58) misses the point that he is stating the opposite argument to that offered by Bruni or giving both.

[24] *Historia*, pp. 3, 6, 17, etc.; cf. Livy, *Ab urbe condita*, 2.21.4. and preface, 6: "nec adfirmare nec refellere in animo est."

[25] *Historia*, pp. 3-6. His "non-committal approach" is compared unfavorably with those of Bruni and Poliziano by Rubinstein, "Scala," p. 52.

[26] On Scala's debt to Bruni and his reevaluation of Villani, anticipating sixteenth-century trends, see E. Santini, "La fortuna della Storia Florentina di L. Bruni nel Rinascimento," *Studi storici* 20 (1911): 117-195, esp. 181-182,

The *History* is rhetorical in another way, however. It glorifies Florence as blatantly as his *Life of Vitaliano Borromeo* glorified his patron's father. As he told Poliziano, it was "the Florentine people [who] elevated me to the Priorate, then to the Gonfaloniership, and finally voted me a member of the Senate and the Equestrian Order"[27] and in a sense his *History* was intended to repay this debt, as those of Bruni and Poggio repaid theirs. Chancellors were paid servants of the commune and it was as much a part of their duties to praise and defend their employers as it was of any courtly secretary.[28] The praise, in the preface to Book IV, of Bruni and the humanists of his generation—who did so much to rescue Latin eloquence from barbarian darkness and make Florence a "gymnasium of the liberal arts"—is a *locus classicus* of humanist rhetoric, largely irrelevant to the argument of the *History* except as praise of Florence, like the eulogy, inserted into Book I, of Ghiberti's doors and Brunelleschi's dome, exceptionally detailed and accurate though this is.[29]

Humanistic, too, is the grief Scala expresses in Book I and in the preface to Book II over the state of Italy. This has been used as evidence for a post-1494 date for these books.[30] But the context of his despair is the barbarian invasions of Italy in the early Middle Ages, which cause him to reflect upon the equally unhappy contemporary state of Italy, then threatened by the infidel Turks as much as by the French. In fact the passages almost exactly repeat one in his 1481 *Oration* praising Costanzo Sforza, in which tears are brought to his eyes by the sight of internal strife in Italy and by foreign aggression, sug-

---

187-188. On his sources, Rubinstein, "Scala," pp. 53-54, 57-58, and on his consistency in "acknowledging his use of other writers," Wilcox, *Development*, p. 181. On his merits, cf. nn. 35-37 below.

[27] See p. 217 above.

[28] See Scala's two apologetic writings in defense of Florence, the *Excusatio Florentinorum* of 1478 and the *Apologia contra vituperatores civitatis Florentiae* of 1496 (ch. 6, above).

[29] *Historia*, pp. 114-115, 8-9, 23-24 (referring also to the epigram on Brunelleschi's tomb by the "clarus poeta," Carlo Marsuppini).

[30] Rubinstein, "Scala," pp. 49, 58-59.

gesting his grief was a literary topos, inspired by the barbarian destruction of Roman "letters, arts and monuments" as much as by contemporary history.[31]

Scala's interpretation of the role of Charlemagne in Florentine history is also more rhetorical than historical. In contrast to Bruni, who (in a period of tepid Franco-Florentine relations) thought Florence had never been entirely destroyed and was merely restored by Charlemagne, Scala (in a period in which the French alliance was all-important to Florence) thought that Charlemagne completely rebuilt Florence after its destruction by Totila. Since no pre-Carolingian buildings survived (contrary to what both Bruni and Scala—who excluded only the baptistry from Totila's assault—thought), the matter was one of conjecture and political convenience.[32]

[31] Cf. 1481 *Oratio*, fol. 2r: "Atque aut nos inter nos quis potissimum imperet obstinatissime decernimus," *Historia*, p. 20: "Namque ita divisae vires non iam cum hoste et barbaris, sed ipse plerumque inter se crudelius etiam quam cum illis hostibus"; *Oratio*, *ibid*: "Aut . . . experiri vires in solo patrio in italici celi amenitate contra externos impetus iniuriasque compellimur," *Historia*, pp. 39, 40: "a nostris iam iam timendum potius qui . . . novis continuo et inusitatis perturbationibus hanc pulcherrimam patriam involutando contendere mihi cum barbaris de dedecorando hoc patrio solo . . . videantur"; *Oratio*, fols. 1v-2r: "Ac fuit quondam tempus, cum in Affrica, in Hispania, in Gallia, in Grecia, in Asia ad Thaurum etiam et Caucasum arma nostra conspicerentur. Nunc sorte mala Italie quod sine lacrimis vix possum commemorare . . ."; *Historia*, p. 20: "Nam quis etiam lachrimas continere queat miserabilesque singultus, cui sit ante oculos Italia Regina quondam et domina provinciarum exterarumque omnium regionum"; *Oratio*, fol. 1v: "Conditio gravis est profecto et plena discriminis totius Italie . . . que fato quodam suo, ut mihi videri solet, quieta esse unquam non didicerit"; *Historia*, p. 40: "quanquam in vestra forsitan non est manu, ut mitius iam agatis cum Italia. . . . Sed erratorum fortasse veterum fato quodam inevitabili." On the humanistic theme of the destruction of Roman civilization, *Historia*, p. 21: "Atque adeo late ruina patuit rerum cunctarum, ut ad literas quoque et bonas artes pervenerit calamitas, atque ingenia cum monimentis omnia pariter deperiere." Cf. also the apologue Scala describes to Poliziano, *Opera*, pp. 146-147. An obvious source for Scala is Flavio Biondo, see D. Hay, "F.B. and the Middle Ages," *Proceedings of the British Academy*, 45 (1959): 107-108.

[32] *Historia*, pp. 31, 42-43; Bruni, *Historiarum*, p. 146; cf. E. Santini, "L.B.A. e i suoi Historiarum . . . libri XII," *Annali d. Scuola Normale Superiore di Pisa* 22 (1910): 36-38; and on the legend, Rubinstein, "The Beginnings of Political Thought in Florence," *Journal of the Warburg and Courtauld*

Scala—like Livy—also allowed more power to fate and destiny than Bruni. Italy's chronic internal discords he attributes to the influence of fate, and he often alludes to "the play of fortune" and its power, apparently to explain events for which no other explanation is available.[33] He also accepted the value of oracles and portents, reporting the oracle that according to legend encouraged Atlas to found Fiesole, quoting Dante's account in the *Convivium* of the fiery cross seen in the sky as a harbinger of the destruction of Florence, and Villani's account of the utterance of a cardinal astrologer after the Ghibelline victory of 1260: "vincent victi iam neque ipsi vincentur," which Bruni omits.[34]

Scala summarized his attitude to the historical discipline in his apologue on *History* (XXXVIII). The historian is approached by a steward who, because he knew Scala wrote history and thought he was also an orator, wanted him to plead his cause when his fruits were stolen from his garden. But the historian replies that both have the same cause: history is his garden, past events and the laborious acquisition of various disciplines his fruits; his god is glory, and instead of walls he has a study: since his fruits are often carried off by daily

---

Institutes 5 (1942): 215-216. On Scala and this legend, Rubinstein, "Scala," pp. 53, 57; Wilcox, *Development*, pp. 11-14. It is true that Scala apparently passes over or ignores Bruni's opinion that Florence was never entirely deserted, but not that he did not realize he disagreed with him over the question of whether Charlemagne rebuilt or merely restored the city (pp. 38 and 43). On Scala's use of the legend in state letters, see ASF *Missive* 49, fol. 29v (31 May 1477, ed. Canestrini-Desjardins, *Négotiations*, 1: 167-168). On Roman Florence, G. Maetzke, *Florentia* (*Istituto di Studi Romani*, ser. 1, 5), Rome, 1941; M. Lopez Pegna, *Firenze dalle origini al Medio Evo*, Florence, 1962; C. Hardie, "The Origin and Plan of Roman Florence," *The Journal of Roman Studies* 55 (1965): 122-140.

[33] Pp. 40, 108; 86, 103, 116 (play of fortune); 30, 33, 121, 131; cf. Livy, *Ab urbe condita*, 1. 3. 56. Cf. Wilcox, *Development*, pp. 194-195: "there is a suggestion that man has a responsibility to use to his own advantage what fortune has given him" (on fortune, cf. ch. 13 below).

[34] Pp. 4, 30-31 (quoting from Dante, *Il convivio*, 2. 14. 174-180; Scala's reference to Seneca also comes from Dante, *ibid.*), 130 (cf. G. Villani, *Cronica*, 6. 81, ed. Dragomanni, 1: 304), 132; cf. Wilcox, *Development*, pp. 192 (and n. 88), 193.

distractions, he, too, needs a patron and he urges the steward to go and find himself another advocate. Here Scala alludes to the apparent connection between history and oratory, and although he attempts to deny it by saying that he, too, needs an advocate, we have seen how in fact his history combined the search for truth with rhetoric. His free admission of the difficulties of the subject, both here and in his preface to his *History*, explains perhaps why so little of his projected work was written. He was used by Bartolomeo Cerretani[35] and admired by Piero Parenti,[36] and had his *History* been completed and more widely known at the time of his death, its influence might have been greater than it was.[37]

DEFENSE AGAINST THE CRITICS OF FLORENCE, 1496

Scala's last dated work, his *Defense Against the Critics of Florence* of 1496, was even more of an official duty than his *History*.[38] Like his *History*, it combines rhetoric with political philosophy. Scala's situation had changed and his optimistic naturalism is replaced by a more pessimistic view of man's fallen state: if we followed nature as our guide, we would be

[35] "Historia fiorentina," BNF MS II, III, 74, fol. 17r ("pensando che la gloria delli hystorici sia la nuda et apertta verita"). He lists Scala as one of the historians he used to "farci far la via et appog[i]arssi" (fol. 19r) and he quotes him on fols. 23v, 25r and 28r. Cerretani was related to Scala by marriage, see above, ch. 9.

[36] Tommasini, *Vita*, 1:95, n. 1, Scala's letters were "approvatissime."

[37] In a letter to A. Michiele (30 June 1533, the reference to which I owe to Prof. Rubinstein) Donato Giannotti refers to Scala's *History*, which "non fu mai data fuori et io per opera che ne facessi non la poteti mai vedere" ("Lettere inedite di D. Giannotti," ed. L. Ferrai, *Atti d. R. Istituto Veneto*, ser. 6, 3 (1884-1885): 1582). From his references to the *History*, it seems likely he learnt what he knew about it from Cerretani's "History" which Cerretani himself showed him (*ibid.*, p. 1583). Wilcox (*Development*, pp. 9-10) seems to underestimate the extent to which Scala was admired as a historian during his lifetime (see also ch. 8, n. 49 above). His reputation got overtaken by political events and new criteria for historical writing, and Francesco Guicciardini, for one, would scarcely have admired him. However, by reevaluating Villani, Scala may have encouraged a return to vernacular histories like those of Guicciardini himself.

[38] Cf. ch. 5 above and, on the MS draft and printed edition, ch. 5, n. 37.

governed by the paternalistic rule of one man, but having sinned we live in a civil republic in which there are many kinds of people and states and as many kinds of law. Now his definition of the different forms of government is Aristotelian in deference to the Dominican Savonarola, in defense of whose government Scala wrote his work,[39] but in other respects his basic philosophy has changed remarkably little. He opens, for instance, with a striking reference (in this context) to Democritus, the Epicureans and Lucretius, quoted by "the king of the Latins, Virgil himself";[40] and although he has modified his attitude to fortune after the sudden changes of the preceding years, he still exhibits the rationalism of a Christian stoic, believing that we invent fortune as a god only because of our ignorance in situations over which we have no control, but that it does not exist in nature, because nothing is done except by the most famous "cause" of nature, God.[41]

In other respects his view of society is as realistic and secular as in his earlier writings: "A republic is a large number of people gathered together for their own advantage, achieved better with the help of several than in solitude. For I think that whenever men formed themselves into groups, they did so for no other reason than for their own interest, serving the common interest in order to achieve in the end their personal

[39] *Defense*, fol. a6r-v. On Savonarola's *Trattato circa il reggimento e governo della città di Firenze* of 1498 (ed. L. Firpo, Turin, 1963) and its Thomist republicanism, see D. Weinstein, *Savonarola and Florence*, pp. 295-309; Rubinstein, "Politics and Constitution," pp. 160-161. Scala follows Hippodamus in Aristotle's *Politics* (1267b) in defining three classes in the state—soldiers, farmers and artisans (fol. b1v)—but disagrees with Aristotle's low estimate of the number of good men in any state (fol. b2v, cf. *Politics*, 1302a).

[40] *Defense*, fol. a3r, referring to the *Georgics*, 2: 490-492.

[41] *Ibid.*, fol. a3v, quoting from Juvenal, *Satires*, 5: 365-366: "causa notissima naturae, quae et Deus est." Here and in his *History* (fol. a4r and p. 134) he uses the verb *desaevire* to describe fortune, in the *History* suggesting that we should prudently use the opportunities it offers and in the *Defense* saying that human prudence can do little against fortune "quandocunque desaeviat" unless God is kind. Scala had strongly criticized the idea of fortune's power in an oration and letter to Federigo of Urbino in 1472; cf. ch. 13, n. 22 below.

advantage."[42] Religion contributes to the good and happy life, "without which men are not only not men, but are not even civilized"; there are no people so wild and barbarous as to have no form of religion: after the Romans had evicted their kings they kept the name and used it for those who presided over sacred rites, so highly was religion esteemed, and although the Israelites were divided into twelve tribes, they had only one leader, Moses (quoted by Machiavelli as an example of a successful armed prophet and statesman).[43] Scala did not with Machiavelli's hindsight say prophets must be armed to succeed, but he quotes a long series of pagan, Jewish and Christian soothsayers, diviners and prophets to show that practically no nations lack some knowledge of future events: for God, because of our frailty, fills our minds with "a certain apprehension of future events" so that through visions and dreams we might foresee and provide against future misfortunes.[44] Prophecy, like religion, is thus explained in psychological terms as in his *History*, as a phenomenon shared by all cultures.

The writing is particularly interesting as one of the earliest defenses of a religious regime by a secular rationalist. Although its view of human nature is more pessimistic than that of his earlier writings, it retains their realistic and pragmatic attitude to religion as a natural phenomenon shared by all people. This was not the attitude of the Protestant reformers, but it returned to form the basis of a more tolerant attitude in a later period.

[42] *Defense*, fol. a6r: "in unum aggregata multitudo comodorum gratia propriorum . . . non aliena causa, sed sua in cetum convenisse quandoque homines et communi utilitati inservisse, ut ex publica tandem facilius consequerentur suam." Lucretius' and Machiavelli's accounts of the origin of society are similarly utilitarian (*De rerum natura*, 5, 925ff, 1013ff; *Discorsi*, 1.2).

[43] *Defense*, fol. b3r; cf. Machiavelli, *Il principe*, ch. 6.

[44] *Ibid.*, fol. b4r-v: "praesensionem quandam mentibus rerum futurarum immisit, ut per visa, per somnia, per nos ipsi aliquid provideremus."

CHAPTER XIII

System and Eclecticism in Scala's Thought

Nature and customs, the changing world, time and chance: you ingeniously record them all. Fortunate Scala! though you speak with ancient tongue, you give new life to antiquity through your devotion.
Antonio Geraldini, poem to Scala[1]

As an enthusiastic reader and admirer of Scala's writings, Geraldini was well qualified to judge his achievement.[2] The problem is one of distinguishing originality from plagiarism, as he well understood. Nearly all Scala's writings were based on ancient models or used ancient ingredients, and they are consistently allusive. But far from detracting from his achievement, Geraldini thought Scala's success lay precisely in making the ancient discussion of philosophy and the problems of the changing world relevant to the present. If he is right, Scala's apparent eclecticism should reveal a coherent system of ideas and his allusiveness should reveal novelty, not conventionality. Some common themes and ideas have emerged from the preceding chapters and must now be evaluated as a whole.

Aristotelianism was still the predominant influence in Florence when Scala was a student, not only in the university and the monastic *studia* where scholastic logic was still taught but more widely among the merchants, who welcomed Aristotle's newly translated ethical and political doctrines.[3] Unlike his

---

[1] Laur. MS 54, 3, fol. 45r, ed. Müllner, pp. 5-6: "Tetrastycon ad Bartholomeum Scalam Vexilliferum Iustitie rei publicae Florentiae": "Naturam et mores, seriem, res, tempora, casus / Et demum artifici schemate cuncta notas: / Felix, qui prisco cum sis sermone locutus, / Scala, tamen cultu saecla vetusta novas." Scala was Gonfalonier of Justice in June-July 1486.

[2] See ch. 8, nn. 5, and 49.

[3] Bec, *Les Marchands écrivains*; the treatises of Bruni (*De studiis et litteris* and *Isagogicon, Schriften*, pp. 5-41); Matteo Palmieri (*Della vita civile*, ed. F. Battaglia, Bologna, 1944; Donato Acciaiuoli ("Se sia più difficile o bene o male operare" in Rucellai, *Zibaldone*, pp. 91-102); and Ficino (early treatises in Kristeller, *Studies*, pp. 55-97). Logic was taught by Angelo da Lecco at San Marco, by Niccolò Tignosi in the Studio and by Argyropoulos privately, della Torre, *Storia*, pp. 334-343; Kristeller, *Studies*, p. 42; Thorndike, *Science and Thought in the 15th Century*, New York, 1929, pp. 161-

friends Donato Acciaiuoli and Marsilio Ficino, however, Scala apparently learned no scholastic logic as a student and he showed no knowledge of Aristotle's *Ethics* until reading notes on Argyropoulos' lectures to Cosimo in the 1460s, and no knowledge of the *Politics* until still later.[4] He seems to have felt little sympathy for Aristotle's philosophy as a whole, and when he finally adopted Aristotle's definition of government to describe the republican state under Savonarola, he made it clear it was for him a second-best state.[5] The reasons for this were political and personal, as well as reflecting his early "humanist" prejudice against scholasticism. His own personal austerity and youthful poverty must have made him less susceptible to Aristotle's materialism than his more affluent companions, while as an admirer of Medicean paternalism he did not share Aristotle's preference for rule by a fairly broadly based class of propertied citizens. His dialogue *On Laws and Legal Judgments* of 1483 discusses the very question of whether the state should be ruled, like a family, by the unlimited authority of one man over which Aristotle disagreed most firmly with Plato.[6] And Scala's unambiguous answer was that he, like Plato, favored the rule of a paternal guardian free to take account of day-to-day exigencies.

This dialogue is the most Platonic of Scala's writings, based on Ficino's translation of and commentary on the pseudo-*Minos* and referring to the *Hipparchus*, the *Gorgias* and the *Republic*. In it Scala's interlocutor says to him: "I know you have often admired the wisdom of Plato, that outstanding man and philosopher of clearly divine intelligence, and were delighted that thanks to the efforts of Cosimo, our distinguished *pater*

179, 308ff; Gherardi, *Statuti*, pp. 462, 444 (and see now ASF *Monte* 2275, fol. 35v; 1121, fol. 25r; and 1652, fols. 462v, 463r, for Tignosi's medical teaching in the Studio in 1445 and back payments in 1451); Vespasiano da Bisticci, *Vite*, 1: 246; Cammelli, *I dotti bizantini*, 2: 102-103; della Torre, *Storia*, pp. 394-395.

[4] In his *Oratio* to Costanzo Sforza of 1481.

[5] In his *Defense*, see ch. 5 above.

[6] Aristotle, *Politics*, 1252a; cf. 1286a.

patriae, . . . they began to become better known,"[7] and we can probably accept this as a fair statement of his attitude to Plato —admiration but not total dedication. He had been intimately involved with the revival of Platonism in Florence in the late 1450s before Ficino embarked on his work of translation, and the fact that Ficino later thanked him as well as Landino and Poliziano for helping him with his work suggests mutual interest in Plato, perhaps under the instruction of Landino, to whom Ficino dedicated his lost *Institutiones Platonicae* of 1456.[8] Both Scala and Ficino wrote treatises on ancient philosophical sects at this time, possibly also as a result of Landino's teaching, in which they both returned to the tripartite definition of philosophy associated with Plato and the Stoics in preference to Aristotle's bipartite division previously in vogue.[9] Scala was subsequently close to Cosimo de' Medici at the time when Ficino was beginning to translate the first ten Platonic dialogues and some Hermetic writings for Cosimo, and the influence of this more mystical aspect of Platonism can be seen in Scala's *Dialogue of Consolation* with its description of life as the preparation for death and quotations from Hermetic and Orphic writings.[10] Although the dialogue *On Laws and Legal Judgments* was not written until the early 1480s, it uses commentaries and translations made by Ficino before Cosimo's death, reflecting, perhaps, the revival of Scala's early interest in Plato that came about when Ficino prepared his work for publication.[11]

---

[7] Ed. Borghi, p. 276: "Platonis ego, summi viri et ingenii plane divini philosophi, novi te sepe solere admirari sapientiam, et letari plurimum quod illius scripta, Cosmi precipue patris patrie nostre opera . . . magis venire in hominum notitiam occeperint." On neoplatonism in Florence, ch. 11, n. 17 above.

[8] See ch. 8, n. 43 above. According to Ficino's letter to Filippo Valori of 5 November 1491 (our only evidence that he dedicated the lost *Institutiones* to Landino), he was advised to lay it on one side until he had studied Greek more deeply (*Opera*, 1: 929; della Torre, *Storia*, p. 514).

[9] See ch. 10, n. 26 above.

[10] Laur. MS 54, 10, fols. 119v: "ea tandem vera philosophia est, ut Platoni quoque placet, quae mortis habet commentationem," and 107v-108r.

[11] See ch. 11 above.

There is no doubt that Scala was a skilled practitioner in the currently fashionable language of neoplatonism. The dialogue *On Laws and Legal Judgments* and the *Apologues* discuss neoplatonic theories about the body and soul, the contrast between reason and pleasure and the nature of wisdom and knowledge, which Scala uses like Ficino to convey sober moral advice about life, while in poems and letters to friends he plays on the theme of Platonic love.[12] But in his dialogue he personally rejects Socrates' argument for eternal law in favor of a more flexible law founded on reason and adjustable to changing circumstances—supporting the political implications of Plato's *Republic* but rejecting its rigid transcendentalism. Nor did he share Ficino's mysticism or attribute Ficino's importance to the motive power of love and desire, which he viewed with consistent mistrust.

Scala's attitude to Platonism explains his attitude to the two other most important philosophies to be revived in the fifteenth century, Epicureanism and Stoicism. It may have been Ficino who introduced Scala to Lucretius in the later 1450s and early 1460s, beginning Scala's lifelong love-hate relationship with this Epicurean poet whose rationalism attracted him as powerfully as his doctrine of pleasure as the highest good repelled him: "For if pleasure is the only criterion, who will cultivate friendship and practice faith and justice, obey the dictates of fortitude and follow continence? Virtue must either be nothing or it must be sought for its own sake and not for pleasure."[13] He followed the lead of earlier humanists in suggesting that Epicurus was not as bad as he was thought to

[12] See ch. 11 above; poems referred to in ch. 10, n. 60 above; and letters to Agostino Dati, Buonaccorso Massari, Jacopo Ghivizano and Niccolò Borghesi referred to in ch. 8, n. 12 above.

[13] *On Philosophical Sects*, ed. Stein, p. 547; cf. *Dialogue of Consolation*, Laur. MS 54, 10, fol. 113v: "Nam et Epicurei, qui etsi mihi penitus improbandi videntur, tamen audio a quibusdam non omnino contemni. . . . Utrum tandem, Epicure, ut dolorem fugias, incendes patriam, sacrasque edes et templa Dei profanabis?" On Lucretius in the Renaissance, M. Lehnerdt, *Lucretius in der Renaissance*, Konigsberg, 1904; G. D. Hadzsits, *Lucretius and his Influence*, London, 1935, pp. 248ff., and on Epicureanism in general, see n. 14 below.

be, but he still could not bring himself to share the enthusiasm of Valla, Ficino or Landino for his theory of love and pleasure. He viewed the physical doctrines of the Epicureans with as much uneasiness as their moral doctrines, and he criticized the "random behavior of atoms" in as many unlikely contexts as he criticized their sleeping gods and theory of pleasure—in a poem praising a pope or in an official *Defense* of Savonarolan Florence.[14]

Despite this, Epicureanism held great fascination for him. He transcribed in his autograph notebook the opening lines of Lucretius' *De rerum natura*, he quoted extracts from it several times in his *Dialogue of Consolation*, and he even wrote his own poem in imitation of it, "De rerum [natur]alibus," which was admired by his contemporaries but has since apparently disappeared.[15] We know that Scala interpreted Greek myths as historical accounts of man's evolution and he must have valued Lucretius for his primitivist theory of mankind as well as for his sceptical rationalism.[16] When he quotes Lucretius in his

[14] See ch. 10, n. 48 above and the *Defense*, fol. a3r: "Sunt igitur qui existiment regi a fortuna omnia quae etiam produxerit. Utputa qui principia quoque creatarum rerum fortuitae cuidam concursioni indivisibilium minutorum tradiderint." Petrarch and Boccaccio were the first humanists to revise their opinions of Epicurus, G. Radetti, "L'Epicureismo nel pensiero umanistico del Quattrocento," *Il pensiero della rinascenza e della riforma*, 6 (Milan, 1964): 840-841 ff; Allen, "The Rehabilitation of Epicurus," pp. 1-15; in general, also Garin, "Ricerche sull' Epicureismo"; Long, *Hellenistic Philosophy*, pp. 241-243.

[15] Modena MS, fol. 20v, transcribing lines 1-5 in bk. 1, "Aenedum genitrix"—"lumina solis"; for his extracts in the *Dialogue*, see n. 17 below, and in his poem to Pius II, ch. 10, n. 48 above. On the poem, ch. 8, n. 49 above.

[16] See his "Oration on Justice," Laur. MS 90 sup., 52, fol. 130r: "Nam fabulosa non movent sed aliud pro alio significantes intelligo. Quid enim humeris coelum substulisse Athlas et Hercules nisi primi astrorum speculatores fuisse putetis? Eoque ipso Prometheum" [similarly Aesculapius and the Muses]; cf. ch. 10 above; and his *Dialogue of Consolation*, Laur. MS 54, 10, fol. 106r: "Illud etiam multo absurdius mihi videri solet de Pirrhae nos Deucalionisque lapidibus esse generatos. Nam robora quidem et truncos procreasse homines minime putarim poetas quoque ipsos id existimasse, sed incultam olim eorum vitam sine lare, sine domo, per silvas passim significare voluisse. Ita cum e truncis, quos pro tectis contra vim et intemperiem uterentur, aeris nudi aliquando et horridi egrederentur, causam dedisse Graecis scriptoribus confingendi fabulas." On Lucretius' theory, A. O. Love-

Dialogue of Consolation, it is for Lucretius' vivid account of the miseries of life, which reflects the same realism as his own *Apologues*: "O wretched, o wretched minds of men! O hearts in darkness! Under what shadows and among what dangers your lives are spent, such as they are. . . . Fever's heat departs no sooner if your bodies toss on crimson sheets, or under figured covers, than if you have to lie on a poor blanket. . . . If man's fears, anxieties, pursuing horrors, move, indifferent to any clash of arms, untroubled among lords and monarchs, bow before no gleam of gold, no crimson robe, why do you hesitate, why doubt that reason alone has absolute power?"[17] Scala's ambivalence remains in his last dated writing, the *Defense*, in which he ascribes the origin of society to the utilitarian motives described by Lucretius, yet still remains unconvinced by Lucretius' theory of creation by "the fortuitous meeting of indivisible atoms."[18]

Certainly Scala did not want to "doubt that reason alone has absolute power" and this is why in his poem to Pius II he prefers "the masculine sect of Zeno" to the "random behavior" of Epicurean atoms: "for it must be that the world is governed by supreme reason."[19] Stoicism must be regarded as the most important influence on Scala and the philosophy approximating most closely to his own position, not simply as a creed of self-reliance appealing to him as a self-made man, but because it combined Platonic idealism with materialism, preaching the importance of reason as an eternal standard of right and wrong that was empirically discoverable through nature and individual reason. Thanks to the popularity of Cicero's *De officiis* in the early fifteenth century, Stoicism was no

---

joy and George Boas, *Primitivism and Related Ideas in Antiquity*, Baltimore, 1935, especially pp. 22ff., 222-242; Panofsky, "The Early History of Man in Two Cycles of Paintings by Piero di Cosimo," *Studies in Iconology*, pp. 33-67, especially 40-43.

[17] *De rerum natura*, 2, lines 14-16, 34-36, 48-52, transl. R. Humphries, *The Way Things Are*, Bloomington, Indiana, 1969, in Scala's *Dialogue*, Laur. MS 54, 10, fols. 116v, 119r.

[18] *Defense*, fols. a3r-v; cf. n. 14 above and ch. 12, n. 42 above.

[19] See ch. 10, n. 48 above.

longer interpreted as the doctrine of withdrawal it had been in the Middle Ages but as a practical doctrine of political involvement, discussing duty and moral dilemmas in public life in a way adapted to the taste of fifteenth-century statesmen. A wider interest in Stoicism was also encouraged by the translation of Cicero's *Academics* and his praise of natural law in *De legibus*.[20] Scala shows the influence of all these writings: he was one of the first of his generation to be interested in the *Academics* and he quickly read and criticized the *Manual* of Epictetus. Despite his criticism, and although he renounced his "Stoicity" in his *Dialogue of Consolation* in deference to Cosimo de' Medici, he was deeply attracted by many aspects of this philosophy, as Poliziano himself recognized.[21]

In his writings he consistently contrasts Stoic providence with Epicurean fortune and Stoic *honestas* with Epicurean *voluptas*. His criticism of the element of chance in Epicurean atomism is reflected in the "difficult and most unpopular opinion" he expressed in an *Oration* and letter to Federigo of Urbino in 1472, that fortune does not exercise the power generally attributed to her, calling it elsewhere the name people

[20] On Stoicism in general, J. von Arnim, *Stoicorum veterum fragmenta*, Leipzig, 1905-1924, extracts transl. in *Greek and Roman Philosophy after Aristotle*, ed. J. L. Saunders, Toronto, 1966, pp. 59-150; L. Edelstein, *The Meaning of Stoicism*, Cambridge, Mass., 1966; and recently, Long, *Hellenistic Philosophy*, pp. 107-209 (and bibliography on pp. 254-255); F. H. Sandbach, *The Stoics*, London, 1975. So far it lacks its historian in the early Renaissance, but cf. Long, pp. 238-241; and now Bouwsma, "The Two Faces of Humanism" (see ch. 14, n. 42 below) and, in the sixteenth century, L. Zanta, *La Renaissance du stoicisme au 16e siècle*, Paris, 1914; J. L. Saunders, *Justus Lipsius, The Philosophy of Renaissance Stoicism*, New York, 1955.

[21] On "illam . . . Stoicitatem, quam tu nunc primum fecisti ut non probem, etsi antea sum sectatus," see Laur. MS 54, 10, fols. 114v-115r. On 1 August 1479, Poliziano, in reply to Scala's criticism of Epictetus' *Manual* which he had translated, said: "non enim vel ego tanto me dignor honore, vel Epicteto tam faveo quam te illi favere certo scio," "Pro Epicteto Stoico," ed. Garin, *Prosatori latini*, p. 912; and G. Rensi, *Epicteti Stoici Enchiridion ab A. Politiano e Graeco versum*, Milan, 1926, p. 131. On Poliziano's translation, Maier, *Politien*, pp. 374-380; R. Oliver, "Politian's Translation of the *Enchiridion*," *Transactions of the American Philological Association* 89 (1958): 185-217, with a scathing note on Scala on p. 198, n. 38.

give to events whose cause they do not know.[22] He preferred to believe with the Stoics that "man and God are ruled by supreme reason" and that happiness lies in the exercise of virtue, not in the enjoyment of Epicurean pleasure. Having climbed the ladder to success (mainly) by his own efforts, Scala must have felt personal sympathy for a creed that preached the virtues of austerity and self-reliance, and it is no coincidence that the panels of the frieze decorating his own house illustrate principally Stoic themes.

The clue to the panel *Tempestas*, for instance, in which a farmer, a sailor, a gardener and a shepherd complain to the gods about the weather, seems to be provided by a sentence in the *Manual* of Epictetus, in which Epictetus says that no one who is harmed can like what he thinks is the cause of his harm: thus "the farmer reviles the gods, so does the sailor, the merchant, and those who lose their wives and children."[23] At the beginning of the *Manual* Epictetus warns that we will be upset if we believe that the things which by nature are servile are free and vice versa, for happiness and freedom lie in recognizing what is in our power and what is not,[24] and this provides the theme of the frieze in his courtyard.[25] Its general arrangement may be explained by Aristotle's dictum (which Scala quoted in a speech in 1481): "the whole of life is divided into leisure and business, war and peace: business we undertake for the sake of leisure and war for the sake of peace."[26] Business could be the theme of the panels on the

---

[22] See n. 41 below. On Scala's *Oration*, see ch. 6, n. 50 above: "La fortuna non tanto potere nel Capitano quanto alcuni stimano," p. 242. His letter is in Rome, Bibl. Vat. MS Urb. lat. 1193, fols. 87r-90v, ed. A. Cinquini in *Classici e Neolatini*, 1 (1905): 17-19: "Difficilis equidem res et minime popularis, ut dematur fortuna de rebus nostris, praesertim bellicis." He concludes in Stoic vein: "Nos virtute sola contenti erimus." Federigo's reply to this letter is edited by P. Alatri, *Lettere di stato e d'arte*, Rome, 1949, pp. 94-95.

[23] *Enchiridion*, ed. Rensi, p. 98 (ch. 36).

[24] *Ibid.*, p. 64 (ch. 2).

[25] On the frieze, ch. 9, n. 48 above.

[26] Aristotle, *Politics* 1333a, cf. *Ethics*, 1177b (cf. Chastel's neoplatonic interpretation of this contrast, in the tradition of Landino's *Camaldulensian*

south wall, *Imperatoria, Gloria Militaris* and *Negligentia*, illustrating the public virtues of compromise, counsel and industry; leisure the theme of the panels facing them on the north side, *Amor, Magnanimitas* and *Iurgium*. War is clearly the theme of the west wall, representing the conflict of brutish animal passions and virtue in *Ebrietas, Praelium* and *Regnum*, faced by the "peaceful" panels of *Tempestas, Victoria* and *Quies*. But the virtues of peace are as illusory as those of leisure: the weather is capricious and unpredictable, there can be no victory until envy is cured, quiet is practically unattainable and is always accompanied by penitence; it is impossible to combine love and work, marriage is always accompanied by strife. Nature has a double aspect as the supreme voice of reason and the source of our most irrational passions, and the tension this creates can be seen in the reliefs as well as in Scala's writings, particularly on the west wall, illustrating the theme of his letter to Paul II in 1467: "Mars upsets everything, men obey force not reason." But although we may spend our life working to obtain leisure and fighting to obtain peace, Scala ironically reminds himself at home in the courtyard that the apparent merits of leisure and peace are illusory, human nature being what it is, and that hard work and virtue alone are worth pursuing for their own sake.

The two themes that run through Scala's thought and writings—the importance of reason and the importance of nature[27]

---

disputations, *Arte et humanisme*, p. 277). Scala quotes from Aristotle in his *Oratio* to Costanzo Sforza, fol. 5r: "Dividitur omnis vita Aristotele teste in Otium et Negotium, Bellumque et Pacem. Et Negotium quidem suscipimus propter otium, Bellumque gerimus propter pacem," cf. his *Oration* to Federigo of Urbino, p. 240. For his letter to Paul II, see ch. 11, n. 23 above.

[27] On reason and nature, cf. pp. 269, 286, 291, 309 and 315 above; cf. *On Laws and Legal Judgments*, ed. Borghi, pp. 267: "cum ratione et natura (quid est enim Iuppiter aliud?)"; 269: "ac quicquid rationi naturaeque, quae regnum obtinere in mentibus nostris debent, non vident convenire"; 272: "Utrum huiusmodi aliquid a ratione naturaque esse alienum potest?"; 277: "et precipue natura et ratione duce." They are contrasted only in the *Defense*, describing a fallen state: "Et duci non arbitrio tuo et ratione, sed naturae necessitate" (fol. a3v).

—accord well with Zeno's doctrine that knowledge is based on sense perception confirmed by reason, which in its turn participates in the rational law of nature governing the universe. Such a law played a vital role in providing a principle of uniformity and universality for the individual in a period of change. It had originally helped to prepare the way for Christianity by stressing man's equality and universal brotherhood in a period of political change, and now in another period of transition it provided a basis for a more flexible religion and legal code. Scala's dialogue *On Laws and Legal Judgments* shows how aware he was of the need for such a reform, in view of the multiplicity of religions and laws revealed by foreign travel and exploration,[28] and his suggestion that Stoic natural law should provide the foundation of jurisprudence and rational deism the basis of religious belief anticipates developments of the sixteenth and seventeenth centuries.

But Stoicism had Platonic foundations, and by equating nature with God it was also entirely compatible with Christianity.[29] Did Scala's "ancient tongue" conceal only conventional Christian thought or does it mark a move toward a more natural religion? The question is a vital one for understanding his importance and novelty and yet it is impossible to speak with certainty about his inner beliefs, not least because of his own allusiveness. He was certainly a practicing Christian; he built a chapel in his house (and perhaps another opposite), he was a member of a lay confraternity practicing flagellation, he was patron of a chapel in the country and when he died he was buried in the monastery opposite his house. Moreover, on at least three or four occasions he made specific statements of his Christian beliefs in his writings.[30] Externally there was

[28] Ed. Borghi, esp. pp. 262-263, 281. On the influence of the Stoic law of nature, A. P. d' Entrèves, *Natural Law*, rev. ed., London, 1970; Cairns, *Legal Philosophy*, pp. 133-143, etc.; Long, *Hellenistic Philosophy*, pp. 107, 235-240; Edelstein, *The Meaning of Stoicism*, pp. 82-85, 90-91.

[29] Cf. ch. 10, n. 40, and ch. 11, n. 29 above.

[30] In *On Philosophical Sects*, ed. Stein, p. 551; *Dialogue of Consolation*, Laur. MS 54, 10, fols. 121r-122v; *On Laws and Legal Judgments*, ed. Borghi, p. 281; and, by implication, in the *Defense*, esp. fol. b4r-v; cf. chs. 10 and

nothing to suggest he was not devout. Yet perhaps he was not as unquestioning as his outward behavior suggests.

In the first place it is surprising that he apparently made no religious bequests in his will, leaving it to his son to institute an annual mass for his soul. Moreover, that arbiter of fifteenth-century architectural taste, Alberti, had recommended that all houses of distinction should contain a chapel "easily visible at a first glance from the entrance hall" (as Scala's was), where the *pater familias* could receive his guests and seek peace of mind.[31] Membership of a religious confraternity was a social as much as a religious activity,[32] and the sermons on penitence Scala delivered to his company conform closely to ideas expressed in his other writings: the need to eradicate sensual appetite or *voluptas* in order to return to the path of true reason and to free the soul from the contagion of the body in order to escape from the foggy prison of life into the brilliance of the promised land.[33] There is no mention in them of the love

---

11, above. See also his letter to Piero de' Medici (Turin, Bibl. Civica, *cit.*): "Si ita loqui hominem Christianum decet."

[31] Alberti, *De re aedificatoria*, ed. Orlandi and Portughesi, 1: 419.

[32] The confraternities also practiced charitable activities and sometimes provided schools for children, see in general, G. M. Monti, *Le confraternite*, 1: 197-202, 253-265 (in Florence), 2: 31-54 (organization); Kristeller, "Lay Religious Traditions and Florentine Platonism," *Studies*, pp. 99-122; del Lungo, *Florentia*, pp. 191-205; Trexler, "Ritual in Florence," in *The Pursuit of Holiness*, ed. C. Trinkaus and H. A. Oberman, Leiden, 1974, pp. 205-218. On "The Company of the Magi" in Florence, R. Hatfield, *Journal of the Warburg and Courtauld Institutes* 33 (1970): 107-161.

[33] See BNF MS Magl. Strozz. XXXV, 211 (on which, Bandini, *Specimen*, 2: 161; Kristeller, "Lay Religious Traditions," *Studies*, p. 105, n. 17), fols. 140v-142r, 146r-147r, esp. 141v: "colle discipline in mano al tutto humiliati battendo e percotendo questi nostri corpi," 142r: "se vogliamo pervenire alla terra della promissione, illuminiamo le nostre menti co' razi de questo fulgentissimo sole, se vogliamo uscire dalle obscura[ti]ssime tenebre e caliginoso carcere del peccato . . . stirpando la radice e lle branche d'ogni terrena voluptà et colla disciplina in mano vendichiam le 'ngiurie che questo misero corpo . . . ha inverso la Somma Maestà commesse"; 146v: "E conoscendo noi l'anima nostra essere immaculata e dalla contagione del corpo deturpata . . . piglieremo la disciplina volontaria, daremo a questo corpo dalla sensualità vinto qualche battitura . . . e allo imperio della vera

of God, but only of the virtues of obedience and penitence, suggesting that his religious beliefs added no new dimension to his private and political philosophy of life. The fact that he felt it necessary to make an overt statement of his Christianity in at least three of his treatises suggests, perhaps, that his writings on ancient philosophy and law were not without suspicion of unorthodoxy at the time. It is revealing that Scala was considered by his contemporaries to be free to publish whatever he could, unlike Poliziano, Ficino and Bartolomeo Fonzio, who were priests. Describing in 1501 the scruples he felt about writing on pagan subjects, Bartolomeo Fonzio says: "things were very different for Scala, Landino, Pico, Nesi and Crinito: it was positively right that they should publish whatever they could, since no religious restraints stood in their way. We ministers of God, however, certainly *can* publish whatever we composed when we were as yet only laymen, but whether we *should* with a clear conscience I know not."[34] However "free" Scala may have been, Bartolomeo Fonzio makes it clear that humanists did feel that their writings conflicted with orthodox dogma, despite often declaiming the opposite.

Scala had been marked by the rational scepticism of Cicero and Lucretius as a young man and it left its mark on his religious thinking for the rest of his life.[35] He was scornful of all the superstitious trappings of religion, which he said had their

---

ragione si sottopongha." The manuscript does not state which company Scala belonged to. On the basis of companies listed in Magl. Strozz. XXXV, 211, he could have belonged to the company of San Vincenzio, or the Magi, after it amalgamated with the flagellant company of Zampillo (Hatfield, above, pp. 126-127). On other humanist sermons on penitence, Trinkaus, "In Our Image," 2: 616-633.

[34] *Epistolarum libri III*, ed. L. Juhasz, Budapest, 1931, p. 49 (to Gianfrancesco Zeffio, 11 September 1510, Marchesi, *Bartolomeo della Fonte*, p. 94; and Picotti, *Ricerche umanistiche*, p. 135): "Nam Politiano Ficinoque exceptis . . . longe alia fuit ratio Schalae, Landini, Pici, Nesii et Criniti, qui dare in lucem quae poterant etiam debebant, nulla religione impediente. Nos vero ministri Dei possumus quidem, sed nescio quae saeculares adhuc lusimus an salva conscientia debeamus."

[35] On Scepticism in the Renaissance, Schmitt, *Cicero scepticus.*

origin in fear.[36] He was apparently unmoved by any form of mysticism or by the idea that the love and contemplation of God was man's highest experience, obeying the precepts of Christianity insofar as they conformed to a natural law of reason.[37] He used the word Fate to describe the apparently inevitable facts of history or our situation, which it is not in our power to control.[38] Providence he described as forethought or looking ahead in time, man's reason giving him access to the providential law of nature governing the universe.[39] Astrologers he normally disagreed with, he said, and he ridiculed their art, "which has already reduced some to such insanity in their prediction of future events that they think no bat, butterfly or glowworm can make the least movement without the hand of fate."[40] Fortune was the name given by people to events whose cause is not known and it was not fortune but ourselves who should be called blind.[41] Oracles and portents were valuable as utterances of truths apprehended only by the wise and experienced or by psychological intuition.[42] His attitude is strikingly consistent, whether he is writing for fellow hu-

[36] See his apologues *Religio* (XXII), ed. Müllner; *Inferorum regnum* and *Vivi mortui*, Turin, Bibl. Civica.

[37] *On Laws and Legal Judgments*, ed. Borghi, pp. 262-263.

[38] He uses the word to describe Italy's "fated" history of invasions and discord (ch. 12, n. 31 above), to say that "the fate" of his apologues is outside his control, and that the cave and the nightingale cannot change places (*Apologi centum*, nos. XXXIV, XXXV and XIII).

[39] See his apologue *Providentia* (XXVIII), ed. Müllner; and the *Defense*, fol. a3v: "Natura certe fortunam non habet, apud quam nihil fit nisi a causa notissima naturae, quae et Deus est."

[40] *On Laws and Legal Judgments*, ed. Borghi, p. 278: "astrologis, a quorum ego opinionibus saepe soleo discrepare, presertim cum rerum futurarum tenere se scientiam profitentur," and his letter to Poliziano, *Opera*, p. 136; cf. also his *Historia*, p. 132.

[41] *Defense*, fol. a3v: "ubi rem committere fortunae necesse est, idest eventum expectare earum causarum quas ignoraveris," quoting from Juvenal, see also ch. 11, n. 16, and n. 39 above. Cf. Giovanni Rucellai, "Cos' è fortuna," and Ficino's letter on fortune, both in Rucellai, *Zibaldone*, pp. 103-116. On fortune in general, A. Doren, *Fortuna in Mittelalter und in der Renaissance*, Leipzig-Berlin, 1924, from *Vorträge der Bibliothek Warburg*, 1922-1923, I: 71-144; H. R. Patch, *The Goddess Fortuna in Medieval Literature*, Cambridge, Mass., 1927.

[42] See pp. 306 and 309 above.

manists or declaiming to his confraternity, and it must reflect his own personal conviction.

Scala was not the first rationalizing chancellor in Florence, nor the last. He follows Leonardo Bruni, a reformer and political realist like himself,[43] and he anticipates Niccolò Machiavelli.[44] In other ways he was strongly influenced by Leon Battista Alberti.[45] For Alberti and Scala the deterministic element in life is provided by the providential law of nature, which offers a universal law for artists, scientists, politicians and moralists to follow. Change lies in the natural cycle of development and decay. Free will is expressed by the individual's use of his reason to anticipate and adjust to change—by jumping from top to top of endless wheels of fortune, in Machiavelli's evocative image. Machiavelli attributed more importance than Scala to the element of sheer chance or fortune in life, but both men describe the same natural cycle of institu-

[43] See Marzi, *Cancelleria*, pp. 188-198; ch. 12, n. 16 above.

[44] On Machiavelli's rationalism and empiricism, see, *inter alia*, F. Gilbert, *Machiavelli and Guicciardini*, pp. 153-200; R. von Albertini, *Firenze dalla repubblica al principato*, Turin, 1970, pp. 44-67; L. Olschki, *Machiavelli the Scientist*, Berkeley, California, 1945; and the recent reappraisal of S. Anglo, *Machiavelli: a Dissection*, London, 1969, with references to bibliographies on pp. 266-267. On the influence of Livy and Polybius on M., see F. Gilbert, "The Composition and Structure of M's *Discorsi*," *Journal of the History of Ideas* 14 (1953): 136-156; of Lucretius, S. Bertelli, "Noterelle Machiavelliane: ancora su Lucrezio e M.," *Rivista storica italiana* 76 (1964): 774-790 (but cf. Gilbert, *Machiavelli and Guicciardini*, pp. 319-320, n. 1); and of Seneca, N. Wood, "Some Common Aspects of the Thought of Seneca and M.," *Renaissance Quarterly* 21 (1968): 11-23.

[45] There are references in *On Laws and Legal Judgments*, ed. Borghi, pp. 258, 269, suggesting his influence on Scala, see ch. 11, nn. 37 and 49 above. Common themes in their writings include the choice between *honestas* and *voluptas*, Alberti, *Opere volgari*, 2: 110-111; the Epicureans, *ibid.*, pp. 126, 240; the origin of cities "per loro necessità e utilità," *ibid.*, p. 266; the law of nature, "summa e divina legge de' mortali . . . a ciascuno li sta imposto e innato da chi governa l'universa natura," *ibid.*, p. 195. On his thought in general, P. H. Michel, *Un Ideal humain au XV siècle, la pensée di L.B.A.*, Paris, 1930, and J. Gadol, *L.B.A. Universal Man of the Early Renaissance*, Chicago, 1969. On his life, C. Grayson, in *Dizionario biografico*, *s.v.*; G. Mancini, *Vita di L.B.A.*, 2nd edn., Florence, 1911, and his *intercenale*, "Pupillus" (ed. Grayson, in "The Humanism of L.B.A.," *Italian Studies* 12 (1957): 37-56, describing his childhood).

tional growth and decay and share the same realistic view of human nature, of the role of religion in the state, of the need for reform and the relevance of classical antiquity to the present.[46] Scala never wrote a political treatise, but his dialogue *On Laws and Legal Judgments* shows he was as aware as Machiavelli of the implications of such a philosophy in the field of politics, for in the state it is "the good man and judge" who must be as free as the individual in private life to adjust to "the many different situations arising every day."[47]

Scala's system of ideas is eclectic but coherent: like St. Basil he visits every flower to make his honey. As we have seen, Stoicism was probably the most important ingredient, itself an eclectic philosophy. But Plato made his own independent contribution, as did Lucretius. Nor was Stoicism the withdrawn and deterministic doctrine it had been in the Middle Ages, for it was leavened by his doubting, sceptical attitude to life and his sense of change and uncertainty, which marks him as a man of his times, fully aware of the changing, widening universe. In this respect he had much in common with the humanists of the Greek enlightenment, who were the forerunners and models of their Italian counterparts.[48] Not only did Scala stress, as they had, the importance of education and of rhetoric to express an open dialogue about life but he shared their rationalistic and sceptical attitude to religion and their concern

[46] Scala, *On Laws and Legal Judgments*, ed. Borghi, p. 259: "Deinde more humane nature ruentibus semper in deteriora rebus," M., *Discorsi*, 1, 2, *Istorie Fiorentine*, 5, 1; on the role of religion: Scala, *Defense*, fol. b3r-v; M., *Discorsi*, 1, 11 and 12 (cf. ch. 11, n. 40 above); and on portents, Scala, *History*, pp. 4, 30-31, 130, 132; M., *Discorsi*, 1, 56; on the need for reform, Scala, *Orations* (ch. 11, n. 24 above); *On Laws*, p. 279 and *passim*; M., *Discorsi*, 3, 1 (and on the role of a single man in introducing reform, cf. Scala, *On Laws*, p. 269, M., *Discorsi*, 1, 9); on the relevance of classical antiquity (that the same laws are relevant when circumstances are the same), Scala, *On Laws*, p. 274; M., *Discorsi*, preface to bk. 1; cf. also on the utilitarian origin of society, Scala, *Defense*, fol. a6r, M., *Discorsi*, 1, 2.

[47] *On Laws and Legal Judgments*, p. 269.

[48] See esp. W.K.C. Guthrie, *The Sophists*, Cambridge, 1971 (*A History of Greek Philosophy*, 3, pt. 1, Cambridge 1969); M. Untersteiner, *The Sophists* (English transl.), Oxford, 1954.

for correctly naming things in a changing world.[49] He thought it important to "invent names with great care, so that they agree with the things they variously describe," fully aware that "names vary on account of the differences of things and places"—as did laws and the characters of people.[50]

This sense of relativism, however, did not lead Scala into complete scepticism and pessimistic retreat from the world, nor (by reaction) into Platonic dogmatism. He adopts a midway position, Socratic in systematically doubting everything, Platonic in finding a political solution in the sovereignty of the philosopher ruler. He finds the common factor underlying the apparent confusion of laws and religious beliefs in man's rationality, interpreting myths as man's attempt to explain his own history and the religious origin of law as his attempt to create his own code of moral behavior. Not all men, however, are equally endowed with reason and, as they are as changeable as a flock of birds in flight, it is far better, he thought, to be ruled by one wise man who can apply his reason freely to changing circumstances for the benefit of everyone else. So instead of being a sterile doctrine of political inactivism, as it was in the hands of the Stoics, Scala's rationalism contains the seeds of a dynamic argument for political absolutism.

For the political implications of Scala's thought are obvious, despite the allusiveness of many of its arguments. Politics was almost as dangerous a field for free expression in republican Florence as religion, yet there can have been few Florentines

[49] Guthrie, *Sophists*, pp. 204-219, and on rationalist theories of religion, *ibid.*, pp. 226-249.

[50] See ch. 10, n. 20, and his *Oration* to Innocent VIII, ch. 11, n. 24 above; *On Laws and Legal Judgments*, pp. 261-262; cf. p. 281 (on religions: "Colendi . . . deos et sacrificandi ritus admodum varius . . . fuit. . . . Quod et nostra tempestate pro varietatibus gentium, proque opinionum que de diis habentur diversitatibus, accidere videmus"); *Defense*, fol. a6v: "Ex diversitate nanque regionum diversitas fit vivendi. Unde fiunt leges consuetudinesque non diversae modo sed plerunque contrariae inter se"; letter and poem to M. Giannerini, Modena MS, fols. 3r-4r: "homines quoque diversis in regionibus diversa ingenia moresque afferre," quoting Theophrastus and Virgil.

[325]

who would have failed to understand the direction of Scala's argument about politics and law, reflecting as closely as it did contemporary debate on this subject. The question of whether laws were immutable or not was not simply of academic interest in fifteenth-century Florence but was intimately concerned with the question of the validity of the Medici regime. Scala in arguing for the unfettered rule of "the good man or judge" revealed himself to be an advocate of Medicean sovereignty.

PART FIVE
Conclusion

CHAPTER XIV

Scala and the State

I could not restrain myself from doing what I believe to be my duty toward the state and toward you, which to me has always seemed—and seems—to be one and the same thing. *Scala to Lorenzo de' Medici, 1480*[1]

Scala's principal mandate as chancellor was to reform and modernize the state bureaucracy. He was favored by the Medici not simply because of his poverty (*pace* Guicciardini), but because he was shrewd, intelligent and as a lawyer by training well adapted to their purposes. These talents were needed to modernize the chancery and make it capable of serving an increasingly centralized and powerful state. The chancery was still medieval in structure when he was appointed to office, and as government itself became exercised by new, longer-term magistracies it became imperative for the chancery to adapt itself to the new situation. It was the aim of Scala's reforms to give it the flexibility it needed to serve these new magistracies, and to give its officers authority to act as their fully responsible representatives: civil servants, not professional notaries acting as imperial nominees.[2]

These changes were the inevitable consequence of the increasing power of the state in the fifteenth century, not only in Florence but elsewhere, and some measure of reform would have been needed whatever regime was in power—hence the broad basis of Scala's support in Florence.[3] Nevertheless, it is clear that the Medici had a strong political interest in developing a centralized state served by an efficient administrative

---

[1] 12 February 1480, ASF *MAP* 34, 418: "non mi potrei contenere che non facessi quello mi pare mio obligo inverso la patria et in ve[r]so di voi, che a me è paruto sempre et pare una cosa medesima" (on *patria* as "state," cf. Scala to G. M. Sforza, 18 August 1470, ASMi SPE Fir. 279: "che è coniuncta con quella della mia città et patria").

[2] See ch. 7, above.

[3] By the "academicians" of Argyropoulos as well as by the Mediceans in 1465, by the Council of the People as well as by the Medicean Council of Seventy in the 1480s, see above.

machine. For this reason it was possible for Scala to claim that his duty to the state and his duty to Lorenzo de' Medici were identical, for in implementing his reforms and in collaborating with the Medici in his official duties he was, as he saw it, contributing toward greater efficiency and more effective government.

Yet his position, like that of the Medici themselves, involved an essential paradox. One of the distinguishing features of the Medici regime was its respect for the laws of the city, and Scala knew as well as anyone how meticulously all the constitutional changes the Medici introduced were sanctioned by laws, which Cosimo used to delight in calling "the fortress of justice."[4] Similarly, Scala's career was entirely constitutional, every step up the ladder was authorized by laws which granted him citizenship, approved him in office and awarded him the highest honors the state had to offer. Nor was his respect for law any less than Cosimo's—either theoretically, in his writings and orations, or in practice, in his criticism of laws broken in the Guelf Party for want of a quorum as "not at all a fitting thing" or his concern that Lorenzo de' Medici's mission to Naples in 1479 should be entirely "honorable" and legalized by the state.[5]

Despite such scrupulousness, however, it was clear to everyone that behind the facade of legality changes were taking place and appointments were being made that were counter to the spirit if not the letter of the law. All major changes to the constitution were approved not by the ordinary legislative councils, but by special Balìe, which were supposedly created only in times of political crisis. This was the method used to promote Scala's career: he was reappointed in office for ten years (instead of the statutory one year) by the 1466 Balìa, given Florentine citizenship by the 1471 Balìa (instead of the Councils, who normally approved exceptional grants of citi-

---

[4] See ch. 11, n. 39 above. The legality of the Medici regime is convincingly demonstrated by Rubinstein, *Government* (e.g. p. 188, describing the "almost pedantic concern with legality and technical efficiency" shown by the accoppiatori in 1471-1472).

[5] See ch. 7, n. 14; and ASF *MAP* 34, 408, 420 and 414 (ch. 4 above).

zenship), and by authority delegated by this Balìa he was given exemptions and privileges concerning the offices he could hold as chancellor, and his reappointment.[6]

Legislation was also passed retrospectively to legitimize existing procedure. As chancellor of the Guelf Party Scala had himself heard Otto Niccolini (one of the leading legal experts of the regime) state in a meeting that there were no laws preventing a decision on the *borsellino* when in fact the relevant laws were not rescinded until two weeks later, and he had also seen Giovanni de' Medici absolved by the Colleges from paying the fine of 500 florins he had incurred as surety for someone who had broken the Guelf Party's laws.[7] Later as chancellor of the republic he had seen the government break the law by not holding a scrutiny at the appointed time, knowing that it would later be absolved from paying the fine.[8] He himself had been responsible for transmitting messages to Lorenzo de' Medici from the Signoria in anticipation of "measures being taken to legalize whatever is in excess of the regulations" (though scrupulously reporting that he was authorized to transmit this message).[9] Everything was legal that was subsequently authorized by the councils—and many things, like Lorenzo de' Medici's widely recognized influence on elections,[10] were not even culpably illegal.

[6] See ch. 3 above. On *Balìe* and their effect of "drastically" interfering "with the normal channels of legislation," Rubinstein, *Government*, pp. 68-69.

[7] ASF *Cons. Prat.* 56, fol. 142v, and *Capt. P. G.* 9 rosso, fol. 59v; and ch. 2, n. 34 above.

[8] In 1468, Rubinstein, *Government*, p. 172; and ASMi SPE Fir. 275 (S. Sacramori to G. M. Sforza, 1 December 1468: "Nel fatto de quisti beneditti scrottini . . . pigliaranno questo partito che non se vencha et chaderanno in pena et poy per consigli se li remetta et fazasene gratia, et questo me pare sia el parere de Piero [de' Medici] per non alterare hora più la ciptà").

[9] See ch. 4, n. 35 above.

[10] Revealed in letters to Lorenzo de' Medici, e.g. Antonio Pucci, 6 December 1479 (ASF *MAP* 61, 65: "Tu sai come si rimase di fare nuovi priori") and 5 February 1480 (*MAP* 61, 73: "Voi sapete che ene viene il tempo di fare e nuovi priori. . . . Ma sapete et havete provato voi e segreti delli huomini") and A. Rinuccini's *Dialogus de libertate*, p. 285.

Two examples will serve to illustrate this contrast between theory and practice. A Dieci di Balìa had been created in June 1478 with absolute powers to conduct the impending war against the pope and Ferrante of Naples. At the end of their first six-month term of office in December 1478, when their books were presented for inspection, "a few small difficulties" were discovered which prevented them from being approved by "the normal procedure":[11] many horse and foot soldiers had been dispatched before their contracts had been approved by the Dieci and the Signoria (although their salaries were subsequently approved) and some "ministers" employed by the Dieci had not been approved by the Cento, as a result of "making many provisions too quickly."[12] Although it was by then too late to approve these appointments, on 29 December 1478 the Cento agreed to confirm all the contracts and payments made by the Dieci in the first six months of their office as well as the appointments of staff serving the Dieci.[13]

The incident illustrates the scrupulous legality of the regime as well as its perhaps less scrupulous use of retrospective legislation to validate its actions. It also illustrates how narrow the dividing line was between the public interest of speed and efficiency and the private benefit of a restricted minority. According to Francesco Guicciardini, the appointment and payment of *condottieri* during the Pazzi war was arranged by

[11] ASF *Dieci Delib.* 25, fol. IIIr-v (29 December 1478, reporting the decree of the Cento): "volendo asseptare tutte le scripture del detto primo uficio . . . truovono alchune piccole difficultà, le quali impedischono potersi fare a pieno per la via ordinaria tale effecto."

[12] *Ibid.*, fol. IIIv: "di che n'è suto in buona parte cagione lo havere havuto a fare molti provedimenti con troppa celerità."

[13] *Ibid.*: "Che per vigore della presente provisione le condocte facte . . . vaglino et habbino pieno effecto, etiam che si potessi dire essere manchato in quelle qualche solennità, et debbino i presenti Dieci farne acconciare le scripture . . . et di così fare habbino piena auctorità, et le electioni facte de' loro ministri . . . s'intendino senza fare altra deliberatione al tutto confermate et vaglino le scripture et roghi et altre cose per loro facte come se fussino di loro seguite le debite approvationi et solennità a' debiti tempi e ne' modi convenienti." On the employment of Poliziano, Medici tutor, and others as scribes of the Dieci in June 1478, see Lorenzo de' Medici's *Letters*, vol. 3.

Lorenzo de' Medici to bring profit to himself at the expense of the city (by making the Bartolini bank, in which he held shares, withhold about 8 percent of the payment due to the *condottieri*, thereby forcing them to reduce their companies and obliging the city to conclude more *condotte* than should have been necessary). Although it was not unusual for soldiers to be paid through the city's bankers, the incident recalls Cosimo and Averardo de' Medici's reputed dictum, "that the only time when one could become great in the city was during war, by providing for the military needs of the city, lending money to the commune."[14] Significantly, the war years were the only occasion during his lifetime when Lorenzo was openly called a tyrant for sacrificing the public interest to his private interest.[15]

The second example illustrates even more strikingly the way in which the public interest was becoming identified with the interest of the Medici family, for the sake of which normal laws could be overridden. In 1482 Lorenzo de' Medici was granted tax concessions, not by appeal to the councils, as was normal, but by the discretionary decision of a special financial commission of Seventeen Reformers; for, they said, if he were to publicize the true condition of his finances by appealing to the councils, the state itself would lose credit: "since the health of the present regime depends largely on the preservation of the said Lorenzo both in fact and in appearance, and the good state of the Monte depends on the preservation of the regime." Like Scala, who described his duty to Lorenzo and to the state as "one and the same thing," the Seventeen

---

[14] Guicciardini, *Storie fiorentine*, pp. 76-77. Cosimo and Averardo's dictum, reported by Niccolò Tinucci, is quoted with due reserve by Molho, *Florentine Public Finances*, pp. 188-189. Examples of Florentine difficulties in paying troops are given by M. Mallett, *Mercenaries and their Masters*, London, 1974, pp. 100-101, 130-131.

[15] By A. Rinuccini in his *Dialogus de libertate*, pp. 288-289, 301, referring to the pope's letter to the Florentine people of 7 July 1478 asking them to expel Lorenzo as a tyrant (see ch. 4, n. 68 above); cf. Rubinstein, *Government*, p. 197. Cf. his description of Lorenzo written after his death: "come Julio Cesare insignorirsi della repubblica" by enjoying all honors, power and public authority, *Ricordi storici*, p. cxlvii.

Reformers identified "the public need" with "the preservation of the said Lorenzo," "since the one cannot stand without the other."[16] The adage *Salus publica suprema lex* was thus converted in practice as well as in theory into *salus Medicea suprema lex*, anticipating the argument of Scala's dialogue *On Laws and Legal Judgments* written six months later.

The problem of defining the role of the Medici in Florence is not a simple one of deciding between two starkly conflicting views of government, between tyranny and freedom. Lorenzo de' Medici was not a tyrant in the sense of ruling without laws or even blatantly against the public interest, for as we have seen legality was the keynote of his regime and (with the exception of the war years 1478-1480) the public order and peace he helped to secure for Florence did contribute to the public interest. He was perhaps a tyrant in the sense of "managing all [the city's] affairs so that everything goes according to his will,"[17] in "pressing on men" and "being understood by signs."[18] But as Bartolus of Sassoferrato emphasized, few governments are "wholly devoted to the common good without any admixture of tyranny." The issues involved are better represented in Scala's dialogue than in such dichotomous terms as liberty and tyranny.

[16] "pendendo la salute del presente stato in gran parte dalla preservatione di detto Lorenzo et in facti et in dimostratione et dalla conservatione dello stato pendendo el buon essere del Monte . . . per fare el bisogno publico con la preservatione di detto Lorenzo, che l'uno sanza l'altro stare non può," edited from the register of the Seventeen Riformatori by L. F. Marks (in his thesis, "The Development of the Institutions of Public Finance at Florence during the Last Sixty Years of the Republic, c.1470-1530," Oxford, D. Phil. 1954, append. 2, p. 284), who has generously allowed me to quote from it here.

[17] Bartolus of Sassoferrato, *De tyrannia*, ch. 12, sec. 45 (transl. E. Emerton, *Humanism and Tyranny: Studies in the Italian Trecento*, Cambridge, Mass., 1925, p. 153). Aristotle's definition of a tyrant is in the *Politics*, 1279b and 1295a. Lorenzo de' Medici defined himself as "non . . . Signore di Firenze ma Cittadino con qualche autorità" (to Pierfilippo Pandolfini, 26 November 1481, BNF MS Autogr. Palat., 6, 25).

[18] Guicciardini, *Dialogo*, p. 35: "E che misera condizione è . . . avere a interpretare la volontà di chi vuole essere inteso a' cenni! In che, come ognuno sa, Lorenzo preme sopra tutti gli uomini."

As we have seen, the dialogue discusses the precise question raised by Scala's own position and the position of the Medici regime in Florence: was traditional law eternally valid or should laws be altered according to changing times and circumstances? In arguing for pragmatism and flexibility against the sanctity of law Scala was reflecting his own position in the state as Medicean chancellor. He was all too used to discussing laws in his official letters according to circumstances, sometimes arguing that it was impossible to depart from the laws of the city, at others that it was the prerogative of free people to pass new laws since no human being was wise enough to achieve perfection or to foresee everything.[19]

The contrast between these two points of view was also reflected in political debate in Florence at this time. In the debate over the fate of the Guelf Party in 1459-1461, for instance, Matteo Palmieri declared in a consultative meeting: "there is no need of new laws . . . since many laws have been passed which provide successfully for every aspect. The fault lies not with the laws, but with the corrupt use made of them by men . . . it should therefore be decreed that the laws must be observed."[20] Two years later, however, Luigi Guicciardini adopted the opposite position in arguing: "it should not be

[19] See Scala's letters to Lorenzo de' Medici (4 January 1480), ASF *MAP* 34, 410: "salvis legibus" and to Niccolò Borghesi, Venice, Bibl. Marciana, MS lat. XI, 83, fol. 87r: "Non vero nosti mores Florentinorum: quin servemus sancta foedera, non possumus"; cf. ASF *Missive* 45, fol. 221v (to Battista de Amelia, "futuro Potestati"): "Non possiamo per le leggi nostre proroghare per uno dì la vostra entrata"; *ibid.*, fol. 33v (to the Podestà and Captain, "duobus praetoribus urbanis," 8 October 1465): "Ut res sunt hominum non debet reputari alienum a rerum publicarum rectoribus si quotidie abrogantur instituta civitatum et quotidie novas instituuntur leges. Nulla enim humana sapientia tanta esse potest, quae et perfectionem rerum penitus cognoscat, aut quae praevidere cuncta possit, quae tempus omnia commutans affert"; cf. Del Serra, "Delle azioni di Don Biagio Milanesi," BNF MS Magl. XXXVII, 325 (describing the Passignano affair; cf. ch. 4 above), fol. 64v: "Ma la Signoria, excusandosi per certi loro statuti . . ."

[20] ASF *Cons. Prat.* 55, fol. 126r (9 June 1459): "nec opus esse pro ea recte ordinanda novis legibus, quoniam plurime leges condite sunt que super omnibus partibus oportune providerunt. Verum non a legibus defectum esse, sed a mala consuetudine hominum . . . et ita statuendum ut leges ipsi observentur."

thought that the same laws are always useful in the city; they should be changed when necessary as the condition of the times changes."[21] "As the condition of the times changes": that was exactly Scala's reason for wanting "freer powers and more discretionary sentences" to deal with the "many different situations arising every day." Nothing is eternal and laws must be changed or retained according to their usefulness. As Medicean reformers, both he and Luigi Guicciardini adopt the same argument for flexibility instead of the more conservative argument of Matteo Palmieri, represented by Bernardo Machiavelli in Scala's dialogue.[22]

Fifteenth-century Florence faced an erosion of traditional law not dissimilar to that in Athens at the time the *Minos* was written,[23] also caused by expanding horizons and by loss of confidence in the previously revered authority of Roman canon and civil law. On one hand the old authority of the Councils of the People and the Commune, the supreme legislature, was being increasingly curtailed, their most important work being transferred first to the select Council of Cento and after 1480 to the still more select "senate" of Seventy.[24] On the other hand the fifteenth century saw the rapid growth of administrative law exercised by magistracies like the Otto di

[21] *Ibid.* 56, fol. 151v (6 March 1461): "nec existimari semper easdem leges utiles esse in civitate, quas variari quandoque oportet, prout conditiones temporum variantur."

[22] It was in fact one of Alamanno Rinuccini's criticisms of the Miceans in his dialogue *De libertate* that "eas ipsas leges ita ab omnibus contemni . . . paucorum improborum civium libido ipsarum legum vicem obtineat" (p. 283); cf. Machiavelli, *Discorsi*, I, 49. The opinions of Luigi Guiccardini and Scala anticipate "the remarkable words" of Domenico Bonsi in 1510: "che si debbi prestare fede alla Signoria et che il volere certezza di ogni cosa è impossibile et che bisogna governarsi secondo li accidenti et non volere la città ruini per volere stare in sulla observanza delle leggi" (Martines, *Lawyers*, p. 426, n. 62).

[23] See G. C. Field, *Plato and his Contemporaries*, London, 1967, esp. pp. 87-96; G. R. Morrow, *Plato's Cretan City*, Princeton, N.J., 1960, esp. pp. 3-13, and (on the *Minos*) 35-39. On fifteenth-century movements for legal reform, cf. ch. 11, n. 27 above.

[24] Rubinstein, *Government*, pp. 113-116, 199-203. On the Seventy as "the Florentine senate," see ch. 6, n. 38 above.

Guardia, which increasingly extended its competence in crimes against the state and other categories of offenses.[25] In 1415 the function of the independent Appellate Judge was transferred to the Captain of the People. In 1435 the old office of Executor of the Ordinances of Justice was abolished. In 1463 the staff and salary of the Podestà were reduced. In 1477 the office of the Captain of the People was abolished, part of his authority passing to the Six of Mercanzia, the Court Mercantile praised by Scala in his dialogue for its *ad hoc* justice, the remainder to the executive magistracies of the Signoria and the Otto di Guardia.[26] Since both these judicial offices had previously been held by foreign lawyers who were considered impartial, the effect of these changes could be seen as a serious encroachment by the executive on traditional law. As the 1477 reform of the Mercanzia stated and Scala reiterated, the judgments of the Mercanzia were founded on will, not reason, and there was no appeal from its decisions, which were made by laymen "chosen not as experts in law but because they are naturally shrewd and good men."[27] The same was true of the Signoria[28] and the Otto di Guardia, which had with *balìa* absolute power "to judge and sentence those accused of crimes against the state of the city and its good government."[29]

Lorenzo de' Medici, as we have seen, was closely implicated in these reforms.[30] According to Guicciardini he was particu-

[25] Antonelli, "La magistratura," pp. 11-23, esp. 20-23.

[26] ASF *Cento Delib.* 2, fol. 10r (7 June 1477, "Remotio Capitanei Populi"), 12r-14r (14 June 1477, "Curie mercantie reformatio"), 24v-27v (23 July 1477, "De appellationibus" and "Collaterales potestatis"); cf. ch. 4, n. 54 above; and in general, Martines, *Lawyers*, pp. 132-138.

[27] See ASF *Cento Delib.* 2, fol. 12v: "perchè il giudicio non in ragione bisogna si fondi, ma puossi dare volontario et nessuno rimedio rimane"; cf. Scala's dialogue *On Laws and Legal Judgments*, p. 268: "Sex viros non iuris expertos illos quidem, sed natura scitos et bonos deligunt."

[28] On the authority of the Signoria, see Guicciardini, *Dialogo*, p. 234; cf. n. 22 above.

[29] Antonelli, "La magistratura," p. 26, quoting from the Lex Gismondina of 1478, that when the Otto has *balìa* it can "giudicare e condannare a loro pienissimo arbitrio chiunque avesse tentato o compiuto reato alcuno 'contro lo stato della città o buon governo di quella o in vergogna o vilipendio d'essa.' "

[30] See ch. 4, n. 24 above.

larly interested in the affairs of the Mercanzia and endeavored to ensure that the inner ruling group got favorable judgments.[31] He was a member of the Otto di Guardia in April 1478 when it was granted supreme powers to reform itself and codify its laws, and when the successive Otto destroyed their work, he insisted that it was replaced.[32] His political interest in these all-powerful bodies is obvious. But we would be mistaken to think that his intention was simply to increase their *ad hoc* authority. On the contrary, it seems to have been primarily to define and delimit their authority, achieving the work of reforming the Mercanzia and "limiting the authority of the Otto di Balìa," which had apparently won him great favor when he had first attempted it in 1471.[33] Although the scope of the Mercanzia's authority was increased in some directions in 1477, it was limited in others in which it had been ambitiously expanding,[34] similarly the Otto di Guardia, whose authority was restricted to crimes against the state, all civil cases being excluded from its competence except those concerning the Jews.[35] A genuine desire for simplification and clarification seems to have been a powerful motive for reform, as with so many of Scala's reforms in the chancery. Nevertheless, just as in the chancery this process transformed the medieval notarial chancery into a secular organ executing the commands of the centralized state, so the 1477-1478 reforms took authority from the medieval professionally qualified judiciary and put it in the hands of unqualified laymen dependent on the state for their powers. As effective rulers of the state, the Medici of course benefited from this process.

This was no palace revolution destroying democracy and

[31] *Dialogo*, pp. 26-27, cf. 57.

[32] Guicciardini, *Storie fiorentine*, pp. 41-42; cf. ch. 4, n. 43 above.

[33] According to the Milanese ambassador, S. Sacramori, ch. 4, n. 24 above.

[34] See ASF *Cento Delib.* 2, fol. 12v-13r; cf. Bonolis, *La giurisdizione della Mercanzia*. They were not allowed to concern themselves with litigation concerning dowries, testaments, division of property, etc. Most important, perhaps, were the clauses revoking all statutes passed by the Mercanzia in contravention of communal statutes and declaring that they would in future be invalid unless authorized by the communal councils (fol. 13r).

[35] Antonelli, "La magistratura," p. 26.

establishing autocracy overnight, but a gradual, legal transformation of the constitution by a small group of citizens
vitally interested in law and its formative influence in the
state. These were the men who asked Ficino to translate
Plato's *Laws* for them (but before he was yet capable of doing
so, translating for them instead the *Minos* used by Scala),[36]
and these were the men who quoted from Plato's *Republic* in
the preface to their partisan legislation depriving the Pazzi of
the Borromei inheritance, claiming on his authority to be acting
in the interest of the whole state.[37] Such prefaces are pre-
scribed in the *Laws* as a means of encouraging the citizens to
obey the laws "in a more cooperative frame of mind" or, as
Ficino later explained, as freely as if the laws were their fathers rather than tyrants compelling obedience by force and
fraud.[38] This is exactly the type of filial obedience the Medici

[36] Ficino, *Opera*, 1 : 611-612 (to Otto Niccolini, Benedetto Accolti, Piero
Pazzi and Bernardo Giugni: "Persuasistis mihi, ut Graecas Platonis *Leges*
latinas efficerem; ad idem cohortatus est me etiam magnus Cosmus"; cf.
Kristeller, *Supplementum*, 1: cxlix; "Marsilio Ficino as a Beginning Student
of Plato," p. 45 (correcting della Torre, *Storia*, pp. 545-546 and myself, *Studi
medievali*, 3rd ser., 11 (1970): 309, that Ficino translated the *Laws* for them,
rather than the *Minos*). On Venetian interest in the *Laws* for its theory
of "mixed government" stimulated by George of Trebizond's translation
of this work for the city, see F. Gilbert, "The Venetian Constitution in
Florentine Political Thought," *Florentine Studies*, ed. Rubinstein, pp. 468-
469; cf. E. Garin, "Ricerche sulle traduzioni di Platone nella prima metà
del sec. XV," *Medievo e rinascimento, studi in onore di B. Nardi*, Florence,
1955, 1 : 372-373 and n. 48. There is a short extract from the *Laws* in Latin
(4. 716 A-B) in ASF *MAP* 21, 149. On the *Laws*, see Morrow, *Plato's Cretan
City* (n. 23 above), esp. pp. 544-572, and on the *Minos*, *ibid*.

[37] ASF *Statuti* 29, fol. 416v (18-20 March 1477), beginning: "Inter Platonis
philosophorum principis praecepta ad eos qui republice presunt, hoc habetur
ut totum corpus reipublice curent, ne dum aliquam partem tuteantur, re-
liqua deserant" (quoting from the *Republic* 519 E). On this law concerning
intestate inheritances (introduced according to Guicciardini by Lorenzo
de' Medici in order to deprive the Pazzi of the Borromeo patrimony and
hence an important contributing factor to the Pazzi conspiracy), see *Storie
fiorentine*, pp. 31-32; "Memorie di Famiglia," p. 35; *Dialogo*, p. 31; and
Perosa's edition of Poliziano's *Commentarium*, p. 14, n. 1.

[38] *Laws*, 4. 723 A; cf. Ficino, *Opera*, 2: 1488 [488]: "prooemia quadam
exhortatoria, quibus humanissime cives adducti, libenter parere velint, ac
sponte, velut filii legum illis obtemperent, quibus alii solent, quasi tyrannis
inviti parere, ac pro viribus, vel fraude, vel violentia earum imperium sub-

hoped to win from the Florentines by means of their scrupulous legalism.

Plato exercised a powerful influence on late fifteenth-century Florence thanks to Ficino's translation of the whole Platonic corpus, completed by about 1469 and printed in 1484.[39] By teaching that "his Plato" discouraged good men from involving themselves in public life as long as the city was well governed, and that of the three traditional forms government by one was the best, Ficino must have helped to prepare the soil for Medicean autocracy.[40] So, too, did Scala. As a lawyer and politician Scala—like the Medici themselves—saw the problem of their role in Florence in terms of law: which was sovereign, the ruler ("the good man or judge") or the laws? This was the question that subsequently exercised theorists of the sovereign state, and if Scala's answer is more equivocal than theirs, placed as it is in dialogue form, his argument favoring the free and flexible play of reason by the good man or judge above the law offers as powerful an argument for sovereignty as later theories based on the will.[41] Scala's sovereign

---

terfugere." On Ficino and the *Laws*, cf. E. Wind, "Platonic Tyranny and the Renaissance Fortuna. On Ficino's Reading of *Laws* IV, 709 A-712 A," in *De Artibus Opuscula XL, Essays in Honor of E. Panofsky*, ed. M. Meiss, New York University Press, 1961, 1: 491-496. However, he produces the naturalistic argument for sovereign rule (see n. 42 below) only in the dedication to Federigo of Urbino of the *Politicus*, urging Lorenzo de' Medici in his dedication to him of the *Republic* to rule with the counsel of older men, *Opera*, 2: 1294-1295, 1396-1397 [290-291, 392-393]. On Plato's concept of law, see Cairns, *Legal Philosophy*, pp. 29-76, esp. 50-52.

[39] Kristeller, "Marsilio Ficino as a Beginning Student of Plato," p. 43.

[40] Guicciardini, *Dialogo*, pp. 11-12, 53.

[41] The Medicean protagonist in Guicciardini's *Dialogo* similarly justifies Lorenzo de' Medici's intervention in legal matters as that of an arbiter or mediator: "el rimedio presente: quivi era el ricorso, quivi la appellazione," *ibid.*, p. 56. On the legal origins of the theory of sovereignty, see F. Calasso, *I glossatori e la teoria della sovranità*, Milan, 1951; C.N.S. Woolf, *Bartolus of Sassoferrato: his Position in the History of Medieval Political Thought*, Cambridge, 1913. On humanist legal discussion of the concept of "merum imperium," M. P. Gilmore, *Argument from Roman Law in Political Thought*, Cambridge, Mass., 1941. Aspects of sovereignty, including the right to give mandates and delegate powers, are discussed by Gaines Post, *Studies in Medieval Legal Thought*, esp. pp. 91-162, 281, etc.; cf. Martines, *Lawyers*, pp. 119-129, 405-448.

may in theory have been restricted by the universal law of nature, but in implication he is as powerful as the emperor in the propaganda of Byzantine imperialists, who used similar Platonic arguments to suggest the emperor was above the law.[42] The concept of the emperor as the living law had of course been familiar to the Middle Ages from Justinian,[43] but it was given new vitality in the fifteenth century by the revival of Platonism, which first took place in Florence. How appropriate that it should first be applied to Medicean rule. We do not know how Gemistus Pletho fired Cosimo de' Medici's interest in Plato when he came to Florence in 1439, but as court philosopher to the Paleologues and author himself of a treatise on *Laws* he and subsequently his pupil Argyropoulos may well have helped to promote Byzantine imperialist ideas in Florence.[44] Shrewd politician that he was, Cosimo would certainly have been interested in the practical as well

[42] On the role of kings and philanthropic rulers as good shepherds, fathers, pilots and commanders of their people on the model of Zeus, softening harsh laws by acting as "the animate and living law," see the orations of Themistios in praise of Constantius and Theodosius, F. Dvornik, *Early Christian and Byzantine Political Philosophy*, 2 (Dumbarton Oaks, Washington, D.C., 1966):622-624, the reference to which I owe to Professor Peter R. L. Brown. Although in many ways Scala's thought conforms to the more rigidly deterministic pattern of Stoic idealism, which W. J. Bouwsma has recently convincingly contrasted with "the pragmatic secularism" of Augustinian humanism in the fifteenth century ("The Two Faces of Humanism: Stoicism and Augustinianism in Renaissance Thought," *Itinerarium italicum*, dedicated to Kristeller, ed. H. A. Oberman with T. A. Brady, Leiden, 1975, pp. 3-60, esp. 46), his argument for the free play of reason enables him to achieve the flexibility of Augustinian voluntarism, in this way bridging the two traditions.

[43] W. L. Ullman, *Law and Politics in the Middle Ages*, London, 1975; E. Kantorowicz, *The King's Two Bodies*, Princeton, N.J., 1957.

[44] See Pletho's *Mémoire* to Prince Theodore Paleologus, *P.G.* 160, cols. 841-866: "Et in navi gubernator omnia pro quo solet arbitrio dirigere, quae ad vectorum salutem pertinent, et in exercitu dux, quae ad militum victoriam (alioqui nec vectoribus nec militibus vel tantillo tempore res recte procederent, nisi ab uno utraeque viro regerentur; et apertissime maximis in periculis monarchiam simul tutissimam et utilissimam deprehendimus)." On his *Laws*, interpreted philosophically as cosmic principles of reason upon which the value of states rests, see ch. 10, n. 11 above. For Argyropoulos' prefaces to Cosimo of his translation of Aristotle in which he refers to Cosimo as Plato's philosopher ruler, see the appendix to my article, "The Humanist Portrait," pp. 214-221, esp. 215 (cf. p. 196).

as the speculative implications of Platonism. He and his friend the lawyer-chancellor Carlo Marsuppini shared a wide interest in the nature of law, and Cosimo was of course one of the men who specifically asked Ficino to translate Plato's *Laws* for him.[45] In this book the laws are supreme but are interpreted and emended by a small group of wise elder statesmen, the Guardians of the Laws, who also contribute members to the supreme Nocturnal Council, an arrangement that must have appealed to Cosimo and his friends since it described so aptly their ambition to interpret and emend the Florentine constitution by means of a similar élite of lawyers and wise citizens. It offered a useful bridgehead, too, to more autocratic ideas. Plato's argument in the *Republic* in favor of the unlimited sovereignty of the philosopher ruler was developed only by a later generation—by Pletho's pupil Argyropoulos,[46] by Ficino, commissioned by Cosimo to translate all Plato's writings,[47] by Scala, Marsuppini's successor in Cosimo's confidence, and not least by Cosimo's grandson, Lorenzo de' Medici. In his play, the *Rappresentazione di San Giovanni e Paolo*, in which he could have intended to portray himself as the Emperor Constantine,[48] Lorenzo reproduces the same Platonic argument as Scala's dialogue for the naturalistic authority of the emperor over his people like a shepherd over his flock, free from the control of laws.[49] He is allusive, like Scala, but the direction of his thought is clear.

Scala stands at the threshold of a new era. Unlike Machiavelli he did not live to see the Medici exercising sovereign au-

---

[45] See n. 36 above.   [46] See n. 44 above.

[47] Although he did not apply it to Lorenzo de' Medici himself (see n. 38 above).

[48] Cf. P. Burke, *Culture and Society in Renaissance Italy, 1420-1540*, London, 1972, pp. 164-165.

[49] Lorenzo de' Medici, *Opere*, ed. A. Simioni, 2 (Bari, 1914): 114: "Il re e 'l savio son sopra le stelle / ond' io son fuor di questa vana legge. . . . Io seguirò, pastor di questa gregge." The law is the deterministic law of the stars and the speaker is not Constantine himself but his nephew and successor, but the allusions to the naturalistic theory of sovereignty are clear. The play is dated 1489 in A. d'Ancona, *Sacre rappresentazioni*, 2 (Florence, 1872):237.

thority in Florence,[50] but he did put into effect a series of reforms in the chancery that were all subsequently described as marks of sovereignty: letters patent, "sealed or testified with the seals or other permanent signs of the authority sovereign," public ministers who "have authority from the sovereign to procure the execution of judgments given; to publish the sovereign's commands . . . ," serving an authority that should not be "subject to the civil laws" but free to change them as the circumstances demanded.[51] By identifying Lorenzo de' Medici with the state as closely as he did, he must in practice as well as theory have been prepared to execute the will of either master. Changing circumstances demand flexibility. Nothing is universally valid: names, laws and people change at different times and in different parts of the world. Scala was well cast for the role of secretary of the secular state, which like himself was ready to adapt itself to "the many different things happening every day . . . and many different situations."

[50] Machiavelli refers to the authority of Pope Leo X and Cardinal Giulio de' Medici in Florence as "una monarchia; perchè voi comandate all' armi, comandate a' giudici criminali, avete le leggi in petto," *Discursus florentinarum rerum post mortem iunioris Laurentii Medices*, ed. S. Bertelli, *Arte della guerra e scritti politici minori*, Milan, 1961, p. 275.

[51] By Hobbes, *Leviathan*, Blackwell ed., Oxford, 1946, chs. 22, 23, 29, pp. 147, 159, 212 ("A fourth opinion, repugnant to the nature of a commonwealth, is this: that he that hath the sovereign power is subject to the civil laws"; cf. Bodin, "Concerning sovereignty" in *Six Books of the Commonwealth*, Blackwell edn, Oxford, 1967, p. 28). Bodin also suggests that civilians should read Plato to learn how to establish law by comparative methods, *ibid.*, introduction, p. x.

Select Bibliography

(*Note*: the bibliography includes only works cited more than once and in abbreviated form in footnotes to the text.)

Alberti, L. B. *De re aedificatoria*, ed. G. Orlandi and P. Portoghesi. Milan, 1966.
———. *Opere volgari*, ed. C. Grayson. Bari, 1960, 1966.
Allen, D. C. "The Rehabilitation of Epicurus and his Theory of Pleasure in the Early Renaissance." *Studies in Philology* 41 (1944): 1-15.
Ammannati, J. *Epistolae et commentarii*. Milan, 1506.
Andreucci, O. *Il fiorentino istruito nella chiesa della Nunziata*. Florence, 1857.
Antonelli, G. "La magistratura degli Otto di Guardia a Firenze." *ASI* 112 (1954):3-39.
Bandini, A. M. *Catalogus codicum latinorum bibliothecae Mediceae Laurentianae*. Florence, 1774-1778.
———. *Collectio veterum aliquot monumentorum*. Arezzo, 1752.
———. *Specimen literaturae florentinae sec. XV*. Florence, 1747-1751.
Bec, C. *Les Marchands écrivains: affaires et humanisme à Florence, 1375-1434*. Paris, 1967.
Benvenuti, G. B. *Quadri storici fiorentini*. Florence, 1887.
Bertelli, S. "Machiavelli e la politica estera fiorentina." *Studies on Machiavelli*, ed. Gilmore. Florence, 1972, pp. 31-72.
Biadi, L. *Storia della città di Colle in Val d'Elsa*. Florence, 1859, repr. Multigrafica, Rome, 1971.
Bigi, E. *La cultura del Poliziano e altri studi umanistici*. Pisa, 1967.
Biscaro, G. "Note di storia dell' arte e della coltura a Milano dai libri mastri Borromeo (1427-1478)." *ASLomb.*, ser. 5, 41 (1914):71-108.
Bologna, C., ed. *Inventario de' mobili di Francesco di Angelo Gaddi*. Per Nozze Bümuller-Stiller, Florence, 1883.
Bonolis, G. *La giurisdizione della mercanzia in Firenze nel secolo XIV*. Florence, 1901.
Bottiglioni, G. *La lirica latina in Firenze nella 2a. metà del secolo XV*. Pisa, 1913.
Bracciolini, P. *Opera omnia*, ed. R. Fubini, 4 vols. Turin, 1964-1969.
Bresslau, H. *Handbuch der Urkundenlehre für Deutschland und Italien*, 3rd edn. Berlin, 1960.

Brown, A. M. "The Humanist Portrait of Cosimo de' Medici, Pater Patriae." *Journal of the Warburg and Courtauld Institutes* 24 (1961):186-221.

Brown, A. M. and de la Mare, A. C. "Bartolomeo Scala's Dealings with Booksellers, Scribes and Illuminators, 1459-63." *Journal of the Warburg and Courtauld Institutes* 39 (1976):237-45.

Bruni, L. *Epistolarum libri VIII*, ed. L. Mehus. Florence, 1741.

———. *Historiarum florentini populi libri XII*, ed. E. Santini and C. di Pierro. *RIS*, 19, pt. 3, 1914.

———. *Humanistisch-Philosophische Schriften*, ed. H. Baron. Leipzig and Berlin, 1928.

Bueno de Mesquita, D. M. "Lodovico Sforza and His Vassals." *Italian Renaissance Studies*, ed. Jacob. London, 1960, pp. 184-216.

Cairns, H. *Legal Philosophy from Plato to Hegel*. Baltimore, 1967.

Calderini, A. "Ricerche intorno alla biblioteca e alla cultura greca di Francesco Filelfo." *Studi italiani della filologia classica*, 20 (1913): 204-424.

Cambi, G. *Istorie* in *Delizie degli eruditi toscani*, ed. I. di San Luigi, vols. 20-23. Florence, 1785-1786.

Cammelli, G. *I dotti bizantini e le origini dell' umanesimo*, vol. 1 (*Manuele Crisolora*) and vol. 2 (*Giovanni Argiropulo*). Florence, 1941.

Canestrini, G. *La scienza e l'arte di stato*. Florence, 1862.

Canestrini, G. and Desjardins, A. *Négotiations diplomatiques de la France avec la Toscane*, vol. 1. Paris, 1859.

Cardini, R. *La critica del Landino*. Florence, 1973.

Carmina illustrium poetarum italorum. Florence, 1719-1726.

Cerioni, L. *La diplomazia sforzesca nella seconda metà del quattrocento e i suoi cifrari segreti* (Fonti e studi del corpus membranarum italicarum, vol. 7). Rome, 1970.

Chastel, A. *Art et humanisme à Florence au temps de Laurent le Magnifique*. Paris, 1959.

Crinito, P. *De honesta disciplina*, ed. C. Angeleri. Rome, 1955.

Curtius, E. R. *European Literature and the Latin Middle Ages*. New York, 1953.

Dati, A. *Opera*. Siena, 1503.

de la Mare, A. C. *v.* Brown, A. M. and de la Mare, A. C.

Delizie degli eruditi toscani, ed. I. di San Luigi. Florence, 1770-1789.

della Torre, A. *Storia dell' Accademia Platonica di Firenze*. Florence, 1902.

del Lungo, I. *Florentia: uomini e cose del '400*. Florence, 1897.

———. "Tra lo Scala e il Poliziano." *Misc. Stor. Vald.* 4 (1896):179-180.

del Piazzo, M., ed. *Protocolli del carteggio di Lorenzo il Magnifico per gli anni 1473-4, 1477-92* (Deputazione di storia patria per la Toscana: documenti di storia italiana, ser. 2, ii). Florence, 1956.

—————. *Il protocollo del carteggio della Signoria di Firenze, 1459-1468* (Quaderni della Rassegna degli Archivi di Stato, 39). Rome, 1969.

de Maio, R. *Savonarola e la Curia Romana*. Rome, 1969.

de Roover, R. *Il banco Medici dalle origini al declino (1397-1494)*, Florence, 1970, rev. edn in Italian of *The Rise and Decline of the Medici Bank*. Cambridge, Mass., 1963.

de Rosmini, C. *Vita di Francesco Filelfo*. Milan, 1808.

Dini, L. "Bartolommeo Scala," *Misc. Stor. Vald.* 4 (1896):60-63.

Dizionario biografico degli Italiani (Istituto della Enciclopedia Italiana). Rome, 1960 (in progress).

Dobelli, A. "Alcune rime di Bartolomeo Scala." *Giornale Dantesco* 6 (1897):118-123.

Dumont, J. *Corps diplomatique*, 3, pt. 1. Amsterdam, 1726.

Eubel, C. *Hierarchia catholica medii aevi*, vol. 2. Münster, 1901.

Fabroni, A. *Laurentii Medicis Magnifici vita*. Pisa, 1784.

—————. *Magni Cosmi Medicei vita*. Pisa, 1789.

Ficino, M. *Opera omnia*. Basle, 1576, repr. Turin, 1959.

Filelfo, F. *Epistolarum familiarium libri XXXVII*. Venice, 1502.

Flamini, F. *La lirica toscana del rinascimento*. Pisa, 1891.

Fubini, R. "Note Machiavelliane." *Studies on Machiavelli*, ed. Gilmore. Florence, 1972, pp. 373-393.

Gabotto, F. and Badini Confalonieri, A. *Vita di Giorgio Merula*. Alessandria, 1893.

Gaddi, family. Priorista, extracts ed. G. Aiazzi. *ASI*, ser. 1, 4 (2) (1853):41-49. British Library, MS Egerton 3764.

Garin, E. "I cancellieri umanisti della repubblica fiorentina da Coluccio Salutati a Bartolomeo Scala." *Cultura filosofica*, pp. 3-37.

—————. *La cultura filosofica del rinascimento italiano*. Florence, 1961.

—————. *Medievo e rinascimento*. Bari, 1954.

—————. "Ricerche sull' epicureismo del quattrocento." *Cultura filosofica*, pp. 72-86.

Gentile, M. L. "Bartolommeo Scala e i Medici." *Misc. Stor. Vald.* 11 (1903):129-138.

Gherardi, A. *Statuti dell' Università e Studio fiorentino* (Documenti di storia italiana, vol. 7). Florence, 1881.

Giannotti, D. "Discorso intorno alla forma della repubblica di Firenze." *Opere*. Florence, 1850, 1:17-42.

Gilbert, F. *Machiavelli and Guicciardini*. Princeton, N.J., 1965.

Gilmore, M. P., ed. *Studies on Machiavelli*. Florence, 1972.

Giustiniani, V. R. *Alamanno Rinuccini, 1426-99*. Cologne, 1965.

Gombrich, E. H. *Norm and Form: Studies in the Art of the Renaissance*, vol. 1, 2nd edn. London, 1971.

———. *Symbolic Images: Studies in the Art of the Renaissance*, vol. 2. 2nd edn. London, 1972.

Guasti, A., ed. *I capitoli del Comune di Firenze. Inventario e regesto.* Florence, 1866-1893.

Guicciardini, F. *Dialogo e discorsi del reggimento di Firenze*, ed. R. Palmarocchi. Bari, 1932.

———. "Memorie di famiglia." *Scritti autobiografici*, pp. 3-50.

———. "Ricordanze." *Scritti autobiografici*, pp. 53-98.

———. *Scritti autobiografici e rari, Opere*, vol. 9, ed. R. Palmarocchi. Bari, 1936.

———. *Storie fiorentine*, ed. R. Palmarocchi. Bari, 1931.

Gutkind, C. *Cosimo de' Medici, Pater Patriae, 1389-1464.* Oxford, 1938.

Holmes, G. *The Florentine Enlightenment, 1400-50.* London, 1969.

Indice generale degli incunaboli delle biblioteche d'Italia (Ministero della pubblica istruzione, Indici e Cataloghi, n.s. 1). Rome, 1953-1972.

Jacob, E. F., ed. *Italian Renaissance Studies.* London, 1960.

Kristeller, P. O. "Marsilio Ficino as a Beginning Student of Plato," *Scriptorium* 20, pt. 1 (1966):41-54.

———. *Renaissance Thought [I]* and *II.* New York (Harper Torchbooks), 1961, 1965.

———. *Studies in Renaissance Thought and Letters.* Rome (Edizioni di storia e letteratura, 54), 1969.

———. *Supplementum Ficinianum.* Florence, 1937.

———. "An Unknown Correspondence of Alessandro Braccesi." *Classical, Mediaeval and Renaissance Studies in honor of B. L. Ullman.* Rome (Edizioni di storia e letteratura, 94), 1964, pp. 311-359.

Landino, C. *Carmina omnia*, ed. A. Perosa. Florence, 1939.

———. *De vera nobilitate*, ed. M. T. Liaci. Florence, 1970.

Landucci, L. *Diario fiorentino*, ed. I. del Badia. Florence, 1883.

Lazzari, A. *Ugolino e Michele Verino: studi biografici e critici.* Turin, 1897.

Long, A. A. *Hellenistic Philosophy.* London, 1974.

Luiso, F. P. "Riforma della cancelleria fiorentina nel 1437," *ASI*, ser. 5, 21 (1898):132-42.

Machiavelli, N. *Discorsi sopra la prima deca di Tito Livio.*

Maffei, D. *Gli inizi dell' umanesimo giuridico.* Milan, 1956.

Magnani, R. *Relazioni private tra la Corte Sforzesca di Milano e Casa Medici, 1450-1500.* Milan, 1910.

Maier, B. A. *Politien. La formation d'un poète humaniste (1469-80).* Geneva, 1966.

Mallett, M. *The Florentine Galleys in the 15th Century.* Oxford, 1967.
———. "The Sea Consuls of Florence in the 15th Century." *Papers of the British School at Rome* 27 (1959):156-169.
Manni, D. M. *Bartholomaei Scalae vita.* Florence, 1768.
Marchesi, C. *Bartolomeo della Fonte.* Catania, 1899.
Marchini, G. *Giuliano da San Gallo.* Florence, 1942.
Martines, L. *Lawyers and Statecraft in Renaissance Florence.* Princeton, N.J., 1968.
———. *The Social World of the Florentine Humanists, 1390-1460.* London, 1963.
Marzi, D. *La cancelleria della repubblica fiorentina.* Rocca San Casciano, 1910.
Marzini, R. "Bartolommeo Scala da Colle di Val d'Elsa." *Misc. Stor. Vald.* 32 (1924):56-62.
Masai, F. *Pléthon et le Platonisme de Mistra.* Paris, 1956.
Medici, L. de'. *Lettere,* ed. R. Fubini and N. Rubinstein. Florence, 1977- (in progress).
Molho, A. *Florentine Public Finances in the Early Renaissance, 1400-1433.* Cambridge, Mass., 1971.
Monti, G. M. *Le confraternite medievali dell' Alta e Media Italia.* Venice, 1927.
Moreni, D. *Notizie istoriche dei contorni di Firenze,* vol. 3. Florence, 1792.
Naldi, N. *Epigrammaton liber,* ed. A. Perosa. Budapest, 1943.
Nardi, J. *Istorie della città di Firenze.* Florence, 1858.
Nogara, B., ed. *Scritti inediti e rari di Biondo Flavio.* Rome (Studi e Testi, 48), 1927.
Omont, H. "La Bibliothèque grecque di F. Filelfe." *Bibliofilia* 2 (1900):138-140.
Paatz, W. and E. *Die Kirchen von Florenz,* 6 vols. Frankfurt am Main, 1940-1954.
Palmarocchi, R. *La politica italiana di Lorenzo de' Medici. Firenze nella guerra contro Innocenzio VIII.* Florence, 1933.
———. "Lorenzo de' Medici e la nomina cardinalizia di Giovanni," *ASI* 110 (1952):38-52.
Pampaloni, G. "Il giuramento pubblico in Palazzo Vecchio a Firenze e un patto giurato degli antiMedicei, Maggio 1466." *Miscellanea di studi in memoria di G. Cecchini: bulletino senese di storia patria* 71 (2) (1964):212-238.
———. "Gli organi della Repubblica fiorentina per le relazioni con l'estero." *Rivista di studi politici internazionali* 20 (1953):261-296.
Panofsky, E. *Studies in Iconology: Humanistic Themes in the Art of the Renaissance.* New York (Harper Torchbooks), 1962.

Parronchi, A. "The Language of Humanism and the Language of Sculpture." *Journal of the Warburg and Courtauld Institutes* 27 (1964):108-136.

Pastor, L. *Storia dei papi*, ed. A. Mercati. Rome, 1958-1964.

Patetta, F. "La *Nencia da Barbarino*, ecc." *Rendiconti d. R.Accademia dei Lincei* (cl. scienze mor. stor. e filol.), ser. 6, 12 (1936):159-189.

Pauly-Wissova. *Real-Encyclopaedie der classischen Altertumswissenschaft*. Stuttgart, 1931.

Pellegrini, F. C. *Sulla repubblica fiorentina a tempo di Cosimo il Vecchio*. Pisa, 1880.

Perini, D. A. *Un emulo di Fr. Girolamo Savonarola: Fra Mariano da Genazzano*. Rome, 1917.

Pesenti, G. "Alessandra Scala: una figurina della rinascenza fiorentina." *GSLI* 85 (1925):241-267.

Picotti, G. B. *La giovinezza di Leone X*. Milan, 1927.

——. *Ricerche umanistiche*. Florence, 1955.

Pieraccini, G. *La stirpe de' Medici di Cafaggiolo*. Florence, 1924-1925.

Poliziano, A. *Coniurationis Pactianae anni MCCCCLXXVIII commentarium*, ed. A. Perosa. Padua, 1958.

——. *Opera omnia*, rev. edn with pagination. Lyons, 1533.

——. *Prose volgari inedite, e poesie latine e greche edite e inedite*, ed. I. del Lungo. Florence, 1867.

Prosatori latini del quattrocento, ed. E. Garin (La letteratura italiana, storia e testi, 13). Milan and Naples, 1952.

Prosatori volgari del quattrocento, ed. C. Varese (La letteratura italiana, storia e testi, 14). Milan and Naples, 1955.

Pulci, Luigi. *Il Morgante e lettere*, ed. D. De Robertis. Florence, 1961.

Repetti, E. *Dizionario geografico, fisico, storico della Toscana*. Florence, 1833-1845, repr. Multigrafica, Rome, 1969.

Richa, G. *Notizie istoriche delle chiese fiorentine*. Florence, 1754-1762.

Rinuccini, A. *Dialogus de libertate*, ed. F. Adorno. *Atti e memorie dell' accademia toscana di scienze e lettere La Colombaria* 22 (1957): 270-303.

——. *Lettere ed orazioni*, ed. V. R. Giustiniani. Florence, 1953.

—— family. *Ricordi storici di Filippo di Cino Rinuccini dal 1282-1460, con la continuazione di Alamanno e Neri suoi figli fino ad 1506*, ed. G. Aiazzi. Florence, 1840.

Rochon, A. *La Jeunesse de Laurent de Medicis, 1449-78*. Paris, 1963.

Roscoe, W. *The Life of Lorenzo de' Medici*. London, 1796.

Ross, J. *The Lives of the Early Medici*. London, 1910.

Rubinstein, N. "Bartolomeo Scala's *Historia Florentinorum*." *Studi di bibliografia e di storia in onore di T. de Marinis*. Verona, 1964, pp. 49-59.

————. "The Beginnings of Niccolò Machiavelli's Career in the Florentine Chancery." *Italian Studies* 11 (1956):72-91.

————. *The Government of Florence under the Medici (1434 to 1494).* Oxford, 1966.

————. "Politics and Constitution in Florence at the end of the 15th Century." *Italian Renaissance Studies,* ed. Jacob. London, 1960, pp. 148-183.

————. "I primi anni del Consiglio Maggiore di Firenze (1494-99)." *ASI* 112 (1954):151-194, 321-347.

Rubinstein, N., ed. *Florentine Studies.* London, 1968.

Rucellai, G. *Giovanni Rucellai ed il suo Zibaldone,* ed. A. Perosa. London, 1960.

Sabbadini, R. *Le scoperte dei codici latini e greci ne' secoli XIV e XV.* Florence, 1905, 1914, repr. 1967.

————. *Storia del Ciceronianismo.* Turin, 1885.

Salvemini, G. *La dignità cavalleresca nel comune di Firenze.* Florence, 1896.

Sanpaolesi, P. "La casa fiorentina di B. Scala." *Studien zur toskanischen Kunst. Festschrift für L. H. Heydenreich.* Munich, 1964, pp. 275-288.

Santini, E. *Firenze e i suoi "Oratori" nel Quattrocento.* Milan-Palermo, 1922.

Santoro, C. *Gli uffizi del dominio Sforzesco, 1450-1500.* Milan, 1948.

Sanuto, M. *I diarii,* ed. R. Fulin. Repr. Bologna, 1969-1970.

Scala, B. *Apologi centum,* ed. C. Müllner. Vienna, 1896.

————. *Apologia contra vituperatores civitatis Florentiae.* Florence, 1496.

————. *Defense: v. Apologia* above.

————. *De legibus et iudiciis dialogus,* ed. L. Borghi. *Bibliofilia* 42 (1940):256-282.

————. *De sectis philosophorum,* ed. L. Stein. *Archiv für Geschichte der Philosophie* 1 (1888):540-551.

————. *Excusatio Florentinorum.* Florence, 1478.

————. *Historia Florentinorum,* ed. L. Oligero. Rome, 1677.

————. *Hundred Apologues: v. Apologi centum* above.

————. *On Laws and Legal Judgments: v. De legibus* above.

————. *On Philosophical Sects: v. De sectis philosophorum* above.

————. *Oratio ad summum pontificem Innocentium Octavum* [Rome, 1484- ?].

————. *Oratio pro imperatoriis militaribus signis dandis Constantio Sfortie Imperatori.* Florence, 1481-.

————. "Oratione facta per Messer B. Scala al magnifico Capitano de' Fiorentini et Conte d'Urbino quando ricievè le bandiere in sulla ringhiera in 1472," ed. G. Zannoni. *Rendiconti della R. Accademia dei Lincei* 5 (1894):239-244.

———. *Vita Vitaliani Borrhomaei*, ed. C. Bartolini. Rome, 1677.

Schmitt, C. B. *Cicero Scepticus: a Study of the Influence of the Academica in the Renaissance.* The Hague, 1972.

Schmitz-Kallenburg, L. *Practica Cancellariae Apostolicae saeculi XV exeuntis.* Münster, 1904.

Schnitzer, J. *Quellen und Forschungen zur Geschichte Savonarolas.* Munich, 1902, and Leipzig, 1910.

Soranzo, G. "Lorenzo il Magnifico alla morte del padre e il suo primo balzo verso la Signoria." *ASI* 111 (1953):42-77.

Statuta Populi et Communis Florentiae. "Friburgi," 1778-1783.

Storia di Milano, ed. Fondazione Treccani degli Alfieri. Milan, 1953-1966.

Targioni Tozzetti, G. *Relazioni d'alcuni viaggi fatti in diverse parti della Toscana*, 2nd edn, vol. 7. Florence, 1774.

Tommaseo, N. and Bellini, B. *Dizionario della lingua italiana.* Turin, 1865-1879.

Tommasini, O. *La vita e gli scritti di N. Machiavelli.* Rome-Turin-Florence, 1883.

Trinkaus, C. *"In our Image and Likeness": Humanity and Divinity in Italian Humanist Thought.* London, 1970.

Ullman, B. L. *The Humanism of Coluccio Salutati.* Padua, 1963.

Vasari, G. *Le vite de' più eccellenti pittori, scultori ed architetti italiani*, ed. G. Milanesi. Florence, 1878-1885.

Vedovato, G. *Note sul diritto diplomatico della repubblica fiorentina.* Florence, 1946.

Venice. *I libri commemoriali della repubblica di Venezia (Regesti)*, 5 (Monumenti storici della R. deputazione veneta di storia patria, ser. 1, vol. 10). Venice, 1901.

Verino, U. *De illustratione urbis Florentiae.* Paris, 1790.

Vespasiano da Bisticci. *Vite di uomini illustri del secolo XV*, ed. L. Frati, 3 vols. Bologna, 1892-1893.

Voigt, G. *Die Wiederbelebung des classischen Alterthums.* 1893, repr. Berlin, 1960.

Walker, D. P. *The Ancient Theology: Studies in Christian Platonism from the 15th to the 18th century.* London, 1972.

Weinstein, D. *Savonarola and Florence.* Princeton, N.J., 1970.

Wilcox, D. J. *The Development of Florentine Humanist Historiography in the 15th Century.* Cambridge, Mass., 1969.

Zeno, A. *Dissertazioni Vossiane.* Venice, 1752-1753.

Index

Library of Congress Cataloging in Publication Data

Brown, Alison, 1934-
    Bartolomeo Scala, 1430-1497, Chancellor of Florence.

    Bibliography: p.
    Includes index.
    1. Scala, Bartolomeo, 1430-1497.   2. Florence—
History—1421-1737.   3. Statesmen—Italy—Florence—
Biography.   4. Florence—Biography.
DG737.58.S28B76   945'.51'050924 [B]   78-70280
ISBN 0-691-05270-0